Soft Power in Central Asia

Contemporary Central Asia: Societies, Politics, and Cultures

Series Editor: Marlene Laruelle, George Washington University

At the crossroads of Russia, China, and the Islamic world, Central Asia remains one of the world's least understood regions, despite being a significant theater for muscle-flexing by the great powers and regional players. This series, in conjunction with George Washington University's Central Asia Program, offers insight into Central Asia by providing readers unique access to state-of-the-art knowledge on the region. Going beyond the media clichés, the series inscribes the study of Central Asia into the social sciences and hopes to fill the dearth of works on the region for both scholarly knowledge and undergraduate and graduate student education.

Recent Titles in Series

Central Asia in the Era of Sovereignty: The Return of Tamerlane?, edited by Daniel L. Burghart and Theresa Sabonis-Helf

State-Building in Kazakhstan: Continuity and Transformation of Informal Institutions, by Dina Sharipova

Tajikistan on the Move: Statebuilding and Societal Transformations, edited by Marlene Laruelle

Visions of Development in Central Asia: Revitalizing the Culture Concept, by Noor O'Neill Borbieva

The Nazarbayev Generation: Studies on Youth in Kazakhstan, edited by Marlene Laruelle

Modern Central Asia: A Primary Source Reader, edited by Yuriy Malikov

The Cinema of Soviet Kazakhstan 1925–1991: An Uneasy Legacy

The Central Asia–Afghanistan Relationship, edited by Marlene Laruelle

The Cinema of Soviet Kazakhstan 1925–1991: An Uneasy Legacy, by Peter Rollberg

Soft Power in Central Asia: The Politics of Influence and Seduction, edited by Kirill Nourzhanov and Sebastien Peyrouse

Soft Power in Central Asia

The Politics of Influence and Seduction

Edited by
Kirill Nourzhanov and Sebastien Peyrouse

LEXINGTON BOOKS
Lanham • Boulder • New York • London

Published by Lexington Books
An imprint of The Rowman & Littlefield Publishing Group, Inc.
4501 Forbes Boulevard, Suite 200, Lanham, Maryland 20706
www.rowman.com

Copyright © 2021 The Rowman & Littlefield Publishing Group, Inc.

All rights reserved. No part of this book may be reproduced in any form or by any electronic or mechanical means, including information storage and retrieval systems, without written permission from the publisher, except by a reviewer who may quote passages in a review.

British Library Cataloguing in Publication Information Available

Library of Congress Cataloging-in-Publication Data

Library of Congress Control Number: 2021933762

ISBN 978-1-7936-5077-1 (cloth)
ISBN 978-1-7936-5079-5 (pbk)
ISBN 978-1-7936-5078-8 (electronic)

Contents

Preface   vii

Introduction: Framing Soft Power in Multiple Societal and (Geo-)
Political Contexts in Central Asia   1
Kirill Nourzhanov and Sebastien Peyrouse

PART I   25

1. U.S. Soft Power in Central Asia   27
   Alexander Diener and Vincent Artman

2. Russian Soft Power in Central Asia: Government Policy
   Helped by Resurgent Russophilia   57
   Kirill Nourzhanov

3. An Increasingly Hard Chinese Soft Power in Central Asia?
   Reshaping Joseph Nye's Concept under Authoritarianism   85
   Sebastien Peyrouse

4. The European Union and Central Asia: Absent Soft Power
   in a Far Neighborhood   117
   Emilian Kavalski

5. Trajectory of Turkish Soft Power in Central Asia after the
   Collapse of the Soviet Union   135
   M. Murat Yurtbilir

6. Israel in Southern Eurasia: The Legitimacy Quest of
   a Contested Entity   167
   Bruno De Cordier

PART II **197**

7 Russian and Chinese Hard/Soft Power Projection
　in Kazakhstan: Challenge and Response　　　　　　　199
　Reuel R. Hanks

8 Less Attraction, More Fear: The Future of China's
　and Russia's Soft Power in Kyrgyzstan　　　　　　　　215
　Aminat Chokobaeva and Drew Ninnis

9 The Soft Power of Neoliberal Civil Society:
　The Case of Post-Communist Tajikistan　　　　　　　　249
　Karolina Kluczewska and Payam Foroughi

Index　　　　　　　　　　　　　　　　　　　　　　　271

About the Contributors　　　　　　　　　　　　　　　279

Preface

The American political scientist Joseph Nye coined the term "soft power" thirty years ago. Its underlying idea, which is that foreign policy actors can produce outcomes through attraction and persuasion instead of coercion and monetary incentives, has featured prominently in the international relations literature and gained much currency among government officials, public intellectuals, and expert commentators worldwide.

The idea of this book was triggered by our feeling that in the case of Central Asia soft power has not received sufficient and systematic attention. The existing scholarship on the region's international affairs tends to privilege the geopolitical approach (often coded as the "New Great Game") with a heavy focus on the military and economic balance of power pursued by a handful of dominant external actors. In such narratives, soft power, if mentioned at all, is relegated to a postscript in the story of superpower rivalry, containment, and counter-containment.

We first mulled the volume on the sides of a workshop held in 2017 at the Australian National University, which discussed the multivector foreign policies of the Central Asian republics. The event was well-informed and provided insights into a difficult juggling act being performed vis-à-vis Moscow, Beijing, and Washington. Yet, we thought that an emphasis on the traditional themes of Russian security presence, Chinese investment, and the U.S. efforts to retain global hegemony no longer sufficed in explaining the complexity of policy choices on the ground. The time was ripe for soft power to be brought into the equation due to three interlocking developments in the 2010s.

First, all major players started to bolster their public and cultural diplomacy targeting Central Asia (e.g., Russia and China) or at least engaged in the revision and recalibration of the existing programs (e.g., the United States and the European Union). That nothing succeeds quite like the soft power of attraction began to be accepted even by the hard-core aficionados of the Great Game.

Second, the number of state and non-state actors projecting influence into the region grew substantially lifting the matter of multivectorism in the region beyond the trilateral Russia, China, and the West mold. Most of them did not possess the conventional hard power capability and had to tap into normative and cultural resources in order to shape local preferences.

Finally and perhaps most significantly, Central Asians themselves embraced the concept of soft power with alacrity, both as its objects and subjects. By now the region's politicians, experts, and general public had become aware of the objectives, techniques, and societal impacts of soft power. Some countries started modest programs of outward projection of their own, primarily in the form of advancing the national brand globally. All of them, without exception, began to take stock of external charm offensives and try to moderate and regulate them whenever possible.

When we approached colleagues with the proposal of a volume on Central Asia that would depart from a standard geopolitical analysis and portray the region as a marketplace of intangible influences and ideas, where might is not always right and a zero-sum outcome is not preordained, we were surprised by a swift and positive reaction—the idea of such a book was clearly in the air. To be sure, the topic of soft power in Central Asia had been investigated before but mainly through think tank papers or articles based on policy-oriented or journalistic approaches that addressed questions related to current events, such as specific soft power initiatives or the short-term impact of soft power on a targeted country. We hope that this volume, containing as it does contributions from some of the leading and rising experts in the field of Central Asian studies, will provide a more in-depth and holistic treatment of the phenomenon that is increasingly important to our understanding of how the region's international relations work.

The volume does not offer full or final answers to the questions about soft power we raise in the introductory chapter, nor do we claim to have provided an exhaustive account of the politics of attraction and seduction in the region. We do believe that its selection of articles with a focus on great powers, smaller countries, non-state actors, and local perspectives is a good starting point for further discussion on how competition for the hearts and minds of the peoples of Central Asia has been unfolding.

We would like to mention that preparation of this book has been very stimulating yet challenging for us. We wish to express our deepest gratitude to all our esteemed colleagues who have contributed chapters to this book from around the world and showed remarkable resilience and infinite patience in the face of a few unwelcome surprises thrown in by the COVID-19 pandemic.

Our special thanks are reserved for Dr Elisabeth Yarbakhsh whose superb editing services, sound advice, and good humor have been indispensable to the project.

We are grateful to Eric Kuntzman from Lexington Books and his professional team for their support.

Kirill Nourzhanov and Sebastien Peyrouse

Introduction
Framing Soft Power in Multiple Societal and (Geo-) Political Contexts in Central Asia

Kirill Nourzhanov and Sebastien Peyrouse

Since its inception by the American political scientist Joseph Nye, the notion of soft power has captured the attention of leading decision makers. It has been discussed in expert, academic, and journalistic circles around the globe and has made its way into international journals, newspapers, and academic publications.[1] These have debated the pertinence and challenges of the concept and have explored how some of the most influential states, such as Russia, China, the United States, and Turkey, as well as the European Union, have conceptualized their own soft power policies and implemented them in many regions of the world, including in Asia, Africa, and Latin America, and how this has impacted the targeted regions. However, beyond a handful of academic chapters,[2] the issues and implications of soft power in Central Asia and in each of its five states—Kazakhstan, Kyrgyzstan, Tajikistan, Turkmenistan, and Uzbekistan—have remained significantly understudied. The topic has been investigated mainly through think tank papers or newspaper articles based on policy-oriented or journalistic approaches that address questions related to current events, such as select soft power initiatives or the short-term impact of soft power on a targeted country. Despite the undeniable contribution of these publications, most have missed the complexity of the concept and its implementation; failing to recognize the multitude of actors involved in soft power processes and its multiple societal impacts on the region and its populations. This book aims to contribute toward filling this gap.

Since the breakup of the Eastern bloc, Central Asia has been analyzed primarily through the prism of hard power and the great powers' geopolitical and geostrategic games in the region. These "games" are materialized in alliance and counter-alliance agreements with the states of the region, and in economic rivalries over access to local resources, in particular hydrocarbons. This approach has given rise to a plethora of work devoted to the geopolitical and geoeconomic place of Central Asia both internationally and on the Eurasian continent after more than a century and a half of Russo-Soviet domination, as well as the possible orientations, whether through rapprochement or distancing, between the five Central Asian states and foreign actors. Such works look to the role of the Russian former "Big Brother" and raise questions related to the severing of its economic ties and subsidies which had hitherto provided essential support to the security and economy of the Central Asian republics. They consider the possible rapprochement of the Central Asian republics with Turkey or Iran, on the basis of their common Turkish-Persian linguistic and cultural heritage, or with other Muslim countries such as Pakistan or the Gulf countries by virtue of their shared religious background. Some of the publications explore the interest of these prospective new partners in gaining political, economic, or religious influence in a region from which they had hitherto been isolated.

Moreover, from the 2000s, the relationship between China, which in less than ten years has become the region's main economic partner, and the Central Asian states has seen a growing number of publications addressing the benefits or the potential imbalance of China's massive economic investments and their political and social impact on the region. Discussions have also emerged around the role of other players, for example, from Asia (including Japan, South Korea, and Malaysia), from the Middle East (including Israel), and from the West (especially in respect of the role of the European Union and of the United States) which sought to gain economic and political influence in a geographical space opened by the collapse of the USSR.

Yet, this approach has consisted less of studying the impact of soft power policy fed by cultural and religious commonalities or by common political and societal ideals which arose from the collapse of the Soviet bloc and more of studying the components of hard power, that is, the military-economic-security games of alliance, and the agreements and rivalries involving external powers and Central Asian states. This focus on hard power has been stimulated by geopolitical narratives, including the writings of the British geographer Sir Halford MacKinder (1861–1947) or by more recent works such as Zbigniew Brzezinski's influential *The Grand Chessboard*.[3] This has also led many experts and analysts to frame the region as the heart of the "Heartland" and a scene of a new "Great Game" among the great powers. Such imagery is inspired by the international politics of the nineteenth century when the two main world powers, the British and Russian Empires, vied for influence in this part of the world, ending with what is now contemporary Central Asia under the influence of the latter, in accordance with the 1895 agreement between London and St. Petersburg.

However, the notion of the Great Game, and the analysis of the region it inspired, has sparked debate. It has been challenged on the one hand by the end of domination of the region by two or three great powers. This is not to say that the region does not spur rivalries, as exemplified by competition among Russia, China, and the United States to get access to local resources and keep or gain political influence.[4] Multiple actors, whether individual states, unions (such as the European Union), or international organizations (the UN, the OSCE, the IMF, etc.), interact with each of the states of the region through a multitude of bilateral and multilateral political, economic, and social commitments, and international conventions, and hence contribute to balancing the influence of the parties involved. The new context at the end of the twentieth century—and into the beginning of the twenty-first century—undermines the overly simplified perception of a reiteration of the nineteenth-century Great Game. Central Asian states are by no means mere pawns in the regional or global political games of a handful of powerful states, as was the case in the nineteenth century. The region is no longer made up of khanates significantly weakened by mutual rivalries and conflicts which enabled the Russian Empire to conquer the region without encountering strong resistance. Central Asia today is made up of five independent states all of which have built their own policies and skillfully play on rivalries among foreign actors, either individually or through alliances with other Central Asian states.[5]

This contemporary paradigm implies that influence and domination of the region based mostly on hard power is unlikely to be sustainable. Forging long-term relationships with each of the Central Asian states may require less the stick of military or economic coercion than the carrot of convincing political circles of the win-win dimension of proposed or materialized bilateral relations and engagement. Softening hard power policy related to the military and the economy is all the more necessary to ensure the longevity of alliances and agreements forged with key political figures. Central Asian states are, to varying degrees, ruled by authoritarian regimes which have almost systematically prevented the rise of alternatives to political elites through rigged elections and repression of the media and the opposition, and have significantly weakened the rule of law, despite their engagement in several international organizations (notably the UN and the OSCE). The first president of independent Kazakhstan, Nursultan Nazarbayev, presided over the country from independence to 2019. Late President Karimov ruled Uzbekistan from 1991 until his death in 2016. President Rahmon has ruled Tajikistan since 1992, and President Berdymukhammedov has presided over Turkmenistan since his predecessor's death in 2006. These long-standing regimes have followed multivector foreign policies, motivated by imperatives of regime security. This has entailed complex patterns of formal alliance-making and opportunistic alignments. One case of multivectorism is furnished by Uzbekistan which distanced itself from Russia after independence and then significantly reduced its relations with the United States after the latter harshly criticized late President Karimov for the massacre in Andijan in 2005. Another example is Turkmenistan which, having declared permanent neutrality status that was recognized by the UN in 1995, eluded bilateral and international constraints that the late President Niyazov and the current President Berdymukhammedov deemed contrary to their interests.

Moreover, and importantly, it would be presumptuous to consider that a foreign actor, however powerful, could impose its influence only through military and economic strength as was the case at the time of the Great Game and Russo-Soviet domination. Actors cannot afford to ignore the hearts and minds of the local population, nor assume the sustainability of relations with Central Asian countries based on the alleged ability of authoritarian regimes to control their populations and forcefully impose their foreign policies. This has been exemplified by Central Asian perceptions of Beijing's growing influence in the region since 2010. From the 2000s, the relations between China and Central Asia have been endorsed and stimulated by Central Asian political authorities and elites, motivated among other things by political and personal financial interest gains that could be garnered from the economic involvement of China in their countries. Although the Central Asian political authorities have used the tools of the state apparatus and the media to propagate the rationale of developing extensive relations with Beijing, the growing Chinese influence in Central Asia has raised increasing concern among the populations, manifested through a growing Sinophobic sentiment, and even protests and violence, which are now viewed as a potential threat to Chinese interests in the region. For their part, the European Union and the United States have hoped to forge solid relations and bring their own societal paradigm to the region, but, for various reasons, they are struggling, as revealed by several studies[6] and argued in chapter 9 of this book. Such findings contrast with the rhetoric according to which the West, and in particular America, is now Eurasia's arbiter, with no major Eurasian issue soluble without America's participation and certainly not if it is contrary to American interests.[7] Finally, the rise of nationalism and the activism and even violence that emanates from nationalist movements and which targets the West, China, or Russia, demonstrate that popular forces are capable of opposing the designs of foreign states and domestic governments.

Hence, the time of coercion through the exercise of exclusively military or economic hard power is over. Any state, geographically close or distant, powerful or more modest, that aspires to influence, has engaged in soft power policy to entice the hearts and minds of local people, including the elites. Soft power policy is essential to supporting or guaranteeing the sustainability of any foreign state's political relations, economic investments, and even, in the case of Russia and China, security and stability at their borders. Understanding the substrate of geopolitical games and the fabric of relations between the states of Central Asia and their partners therefore requires an in-depth analysis of the framing and interpretation of soft power by states, of the initiatives to set it up and to implement it, of the local reception to soft power, and of its past and potential future successes, failures, and reshaping.

The analysis and interpretation of soft power devised by a given state and implemented in another state or region is all the more complex in that the very notion of soft power continues to be debated. *Soft power* as defined by Nye remains a variable-geometry concept which can be both "difficult to detect and easy to exaggerate, which makes the exercise of soft power sometimes difficult to identify."[8]

SOFT POWER: BROAD CONTOURS OF A POPULAR CONCEPT

The concept of soft power occupies a place of honor in the vocabulary of international affairs. First articulated by Nye in 1990, it referred to co-optive strategies with which "you make others want what you want," as opposed to the coercive thrust of hard power, with which "you get other states to do what you want."[9]

Having gone through numerous iterations, Nye's original idea continues to inform and enthuse academics and politicians alike. The concept has traveled far beyond the Anglosphere having become a standard reference point across the globe for any discussion on non-coercive projection of influence by state and non-state actors in international politics. A 2014 survey of U.S. senior government officials involved in national security decision-making in the 1990s and 2000s placed Nye as number one on the list of public intellectuals who influenced them; he was also ranked as the sixth most influential theorist in the discipline of Political Science and International Relations by his academic peers.[10] Nye's works are on the compulsory reading list for students at the Diplomatic Academy of the Russian Foreign Ministry where many accord him greater stature than Henry Kissinger and Zbigniew Brzezinski.[11] Since 1997, references to soft power have increased exponentially in China; the concept now "peppers academic and policy discussions about world politics, Chinese foreign policy, domestic politics, and even corporate governance."[12]

Nye's many critics have commented on his sometimes contradictory definitions of soft power's essence, sources, and instruments; its relationship with hard power; its inherent Western liberal bias; and the problem of measuring it.[13] This volume's chapters echo such criticisms. Nonetheless, even to the opponents of soft power "the idea is useful because it captures something about international politics that other languages miss."[14] Whether rationally or intuitively, the concept appeals to governments across the world that assign their own idiosyncratic meaning to it. The concept's elasticity and intellectual suppleness are its assets; soft power is socially constructed, contextual, and flows in both directions between the projector and the target.[15]

This volume's case studies illustrate the complex nature of soft power projection in Central Asia. They all share in Nye's generalization:

> Soft power rests on the ability to shape the preferences of others. At the personal level, we are all familiar with the power of attraction and seduction. In a relationship or a marriage, power does not necessarily reside with the larger partner, but in the mysterious chemistry of attraction. . . . Soft power is not merely the same as influence. After all, influence can also rest on the hard power of threats or payments. And soft power is more than just persuasion or the ability to move people by argument, though that is an important part of it. It is also the ability to attract, and attraction often leads to acquiescence. Simply put, in behavioral terms soft power is attractive power.[16]

Each chapter provides insights into the mysterious chemistry of attraction in the region using varied perspectives, both geographic and disciplinary. They show how different state and non-state actors define and indigenize the notion of soft power, articulate its objectives, and implement it. Naren Chitty's idea about the fungibility of soft power between the realm of immediate foreign policy gains and long-term national brand construction[17] finds ample corroboration in the volume, with Russia being at the instrumentalist end of the spectrum and the European Union at the opposite end.

One of the recurring themes in the volume is the universal applicability of what Nye identifies as the three "basic resources" of soft power—culture, political and social values, and moral foreign policy.[18] Central Asia provides several examples where a weakness in the middle component—values—is compensated by relative strength in other areas, especially culture. Conversely, non-state actors boast considerable success on the ground promoting certain ethical causes without access to cultural heritage and national diplomatic support—or hard power assets. The region appears to buck Nye's assumption—widely shared in the West—that democracy, liberty, and a free-wheeling market are irresistibly seductive; a sentiment expressed in the comment that, "America's civil society . . . radiates soft power and helps the United States attract foreign partners. By contrast, China and Russia's stodgy state-directed charm offensives lack genuine appeal."[19] In fact, experts from the latter two countries claim that Moscow and Beijing are on track to achieving "a universally positive reception" precisely because they do not engage in liberal normative suasion.[20]

According to Nye, "the development of soft power need not be a zero sum game."[21] In recent years the opposite has been happening: a growing geopolitical rift between the West on the one hand and Russia and China on the other has led to a situation where they regard efforts at promoting influence and attraction by the "other" in an increasingly Manichean way. The U.S. National Endowment for Democracy (NED) has advanced the notion of "sharp power"—a "malign and aggressive" form of soft power practiced by Beijing and Moscow as opposed to the "benign" unobtrusive variant espoused by the West.[22] Conversely, the Russian Foreign Minister, Sergey Lavrov, has characterized U.S. soft power as "crude brainwashing" designed "not so much to propagate its culture and language but to change the mood of the political class, aiming at the subsequent regime change."[23] The volume acknowledges the polarization of the debate but does not pass value judgment on who the good and the bad guys might be in Central Asia; it merely conveys the picture of Central Asia as a marketplace of different ideas and projects

The question of demarcating soft power and hard power is intellectually challenging but ultimately not critical for the purposes of the volume. Over time, Nye's thinking oscillated between positing the former's relative autonomy to including it as an enabler of military and economic might in the integrated "smart power" strategy.[24] So far no external actor has elaborated an official and comprehensive "smart power" approach to Central Asia choosing instead to deploy soft and hard power depending on the specific issue. Chapters in Part II reveal that as far as domestic perception is concerned, local audiences often do not make a clear distinction between military, economic, and cultural dimensions of co-optation anyway, thus making the issue quite academic.

CENTRAL ASIANS AS SUBJECTS AND ACTORS OF SOFT POWER PROJECTION

The volume's overall position is that governments and people in Central Asia are not passive objects of the politics of seduction. Part II, in particular, provides ample illustration of the bidirectional flow of soft power. It might be useful to summarize at the outset, three basic ways in which the local actors' agency manifests itself.

First, Central Asians, especially in the younger and more educated cohort, are aware of the phenomenon of soft power, discuss and reflect upon it, and practice selectivity when consuming exogenous meta-narratives of attraction. They readily internalize messages that resonate with their sensibilities and preferences. The rest they can ignore, subvert, or resist. A survey of Kazakhstani students' attitudes to the European Union highlighted their impression of Western Europe as a great place for holidaying and shopping alongside their indifference to the European success story in the areas of democratic politics and human rights. While relative paucity of information and language barriers may have played a role, ultimately it was up to the "informants' inner disposition to choose just a consumerist image of Europe at the expense of its other possible images."[25] Savvy projectors monitoring the perception and response by their target audiences leverage a feedback loop and adjust their strategies accordingly; as Nye advised, "wielding soft power often requires learning and adapting to followers' needs."[26]

Second, the region's governments act as moderators and gatekeepers. They graft external actors' storylines onto national narratives casting them as "benign others" or "spoilers."[27] Most significantly, they regulate means of communication without which soft power resources may not be efficiently disseminated and converted. All Central Asian republics have adopted legislation empowering authorities to police information space in the name of national security. Since 1999, Kazakhstan alone has passed more than a dozen normative acts to prevent "the dilution of the spiritual base of Kazakhstani society by expansion on the part of other countries in the realm of culture."[28] Tajikistan's 2008 Concept of State Information Politics talked about the danger of "information-cultural aggression and expansion" and the need to "liberate and protect the domestic information market" from excessive foreign presence that promoted "feelings uncharacteristic of the mentality of the Republic of Tajikistan's population."[29] One example of this discourse of menace is a recent publication by Tajikistan's main government think tank which brooded darkly about the scourge of "smart power" which had apparently been responsible not only for the rise of the Islamic State but also the Arab Spring and a raft of "colored revolutions" in the former Soviet Union.[30] While normally it is the international Islamist networks that officials in Central Asia securitize as the prime cultural threat, other foreign actors have experienced increased control, licensing restrictions, and petty oversight with regard to their soft power activities. This trend is likely to continue.

Finally, the statement that "Central Asian countries are in very rudimentary stages in respect of developing soft power"[31] is too harsh and is liable for reconsideration. They may not be as affluent as many of the external projectors discussed in the volume but their track record against opportunity is quite impressive. This particularly relates to nation branding campaigns.[32] Efforts to develop international tourism have been especially successful, with Lonely Planet proclaiming Central Asia as the top travel destination in 2020, just before the COVID-19 pandemic struck. Public diplomacy has moved up the ladder of foreign policy activities across the region. The president of Uzbekistan decreed in 2018 that the country's Foreign Ministry prioritizes "systemic and targeted information interaction with national and foreign expert communities, mass media, social and academic circles."[33] Cultural and humanitarian diplomacy has followed suit. For example, Tajikistan's 2015 Foreign Policy Concept dedicated a separate section to this particular area of soft power for the first time and stressed the utility of migrant workers and diaspora to the advancement of the country's attractive image abroad.[34] Kazakhstan is the only country in the region that offers official development assistance, primarily to Afghanistan and to Central Asian neighbors.[35]

It is reasonable to assume that in a dyadic relationship the flow of soft power from a Central Asian state would be much weaker compared to a bigger and richer partner such as the United States or China. It doesn't have to be negligible though. The presence of hundreds of thousands of Kyrgyz, Tajik, and Uzbek temporary and permanent migrants in Russia is universally interpreted as a sign of that country's attractiveness—but might they not be regarded as the soft power multipliers for home countries as well? Sell-out performances by Central Asian artists at giant venues in Moscow and Saint Petersburg first organized by diasporic communities but eventually enjoyed by the locals, and the ubiquitousness of the region's cuisine across Russia, testify to the value of this resource that is now being officially harnessed by Bishkek, Dushanbe, and Tashkent. A steady rise in the number of Central Asians living in China, Europe, Turkey, and the United States will surely create further opportunities for the region's cultural diplomacy.

A recent study has documented the substantial progress attained by Kazakhstan and to a lesser extent Kyrgyzstan and Uzbekistan in the area of strategic communication via online media platforms. Its central claim is that international audiences increasingly form opinions about Central Asia based on indigenous sources—both government and nongovernment—that are becoming not only more professional and sophisticated but also more accessible thanks to translation into major foreign languages.[36]

However, there are not many qualitative and especially quantitative studies assessing the impact of Central Asian soft power projection abroad holistically. The matter is further complicated by the general methodological problem of measuring soft power.

THE QUESTION OF MEASURING SOFT POWER

The evaluation of soft power effectiveness entails a two-directional focus: projectors' resources, capabilities, and transmission mechanisms; and projectees' affections and acquiescence. The former is relatively less problematic, and most chapters follow a standard script outlining different agents' specific intangible assets (e.g., culture, values, and credible policies); government and nongovernment institutions involved in their conveyance and conversion; and their framing and packaging for the target audience. Gauging the outcomes of attraction is more difficult. Changed policy behavior is a good indicator but as Nye observed, unlike military might or economic action, soft power often works indirectly and in the background, and takes a long time to bring effect.[37] Under such circumstances, opinion surveys help parse the power to attract.

What is the best single indicator of a nation's soft power? In 2005, RAND Corporation came up with a tentative answer: poll responses to the question, "Where would you like to live other than your own country?"[38] The ability to attract people to work, live, or study has indeed become one of the core metrics in the regularly updated global soft power ratings such as the Portland Soft Power 30 Index (SP 30) and the Anholt Ipsos Nation Brands Index (NBI). The relevance of these instruments to Central Asia is limited though, because the region is normally omitted in the process of data collection. Just because Germany sits on top of the worldwide indices of soft power does not necessarily mean it is the most seductive country as far as Turkmenistan is concerned.

StrategEast Westernization Index (SEWI) covers all five Central Asian states alongside nine other former Soviet republics (bar Russia) and assesses "the adoption and implementation of the Western model by looking at five key areas" in the region: political, economic, legal, language and cultural, and lifestyle.[39] SEWI is a useful tool but it suffers from its own set of limitations. It is not based on sociological surveys but relies instead on expert opinion (one per country) and qualitative appraisals supplied by Western institutions such as Freedom House. The notion of "Westernization" is a monolithic construct lumping together influences from the United States, the United Kingdom, and the European Union.[40] Some of its indicators border on Orientalism (e.g., the use of smartphones being presented as an element of Western lifestyle).

The Eurasian Development Bank Integration Barometer (EDBIB) is an excellent resource for studying Russian soft power in Central Asia (with the exception of Turkmenistan). It assesses mutual attraction across three broad categories (political, economic, and sociocultural) which are further disaggregated into indicators of friendly reputation, consumer inclinations, preferences in immigration, cognitive interest, attractiveness of education, tourism-related orientation, interest in cultural products, and so on.[41] The methodology is based on opinion polls taken in the years between 2012 and 2017. Unfortunately, EDBIB appears to have gone into occultation after 2018.

In sum, comprehensive approaches and datasets that would enable researchers to measure soft power in Central Asia reliably and comparatively haven't yet been developed. Chapters use different surveys, variables, and indicators that are not easily reconciled for the purpose of illustrating and corroborating the dynamics of attractiveness in the region. There is scope for further research here.[42]

THE BOOK'S STRUCTURE

This book has been structured to reflect the multiple dimensions that have shaped the conception, the implementation, and the reception of soft power in Central Asia over the three decades since independence of the Central Asian states. The first part presents six case studies on how foreign states have conceived and reformatted their approach to soft power in order to meet their own goals in target states. It addresses the implications that the reshaping of soft power has raised about the very concept as originally developed by Nye.

It begins with what has been called the "big three":[43] the United States, Russia, and China, which are seen as the main players in the geopolitical and geoeconomic rivalries in Central Asia. Alexander Diener and Vincent Artman examine the rugged course, over time, of U.S. soft power in Central Asia and how it has been redesigned to meet Washington's priorities in a changing global political context and its (dis-)interests in the region. While the United States has drawn on the purported popularity in the 1990s of the concepts of democracy, freedom, and human rights among Central Asian populations in search of a new political model after the fall of the Soviet bloc in order to push Central Asian authorities to adopt a system of political and economic liberalism, the post-9/11 context and the "war on terror" have led Washington to considerably revise its soft power policy in the region. Since the military operations in Afghanistan in 2002, Washington has progressively muted pressure and criticism of Central Asian regimes' abuses of human rights, including freedom of expression and other pillars of democracy. This is true even in the most authoritarian states, such as Karimov's Uzbekistan, and has been done in order to secure Central Asian support from political elites for its military operations and logistical components, such as access to military bases in Uzbekistan and Kyrgyzstan. The contingency and what has been analyzed locally as the inconsistency of Washington's "charm offensive" in the region has been exacerbated by U.S. disengagement in Afghanistan, initiated under Obama in 2011 and continued under the presidency of Donald Trump, which led to decreased U.S. engagement in the region. Yet, as the authors demonstrate, this has not prevented the United States from pursuing soft power initiatives, such as the establishment of the American University of Central Asia, outreach programs like "American Corners," or the many development programs initiated by USAID which, although sometimes modest, have sought to support Central Asian populations, including in the poorest states of the region such as Kyrgyzstan and Tajikistan. The components of soft power are also reflected in the U.S. Strategy for Central Asia 2019–2025, which includes the promotion of development of Central Asia. However, Washington's declarations of intent have contrasted with a perceived disengagement or lack of engagement, and with the local perception of Washington's double narrative. This has fed Central Asian populations' disillusionment with U.S. regional and global policy and a feeling that Central Asia had been a mere pawn in the U.S. operations in Afghanistan or a geopolitical laboratory to keep a symbolic presence, with the goal of containing the influence of China and Russia in this part of the world.

Kirill Nourzhanov highlights the Russian case to show both the malleability of the soft power concept and the weakness of its implementation, which has resulted from Moscow's difficulty in giving its policy concrete and systematic substance. Soon after independence, Russia abandoned references to democratic ideals in its effort to attract Central Asian governments and local populations. Yet it did not offer alternative political values aimed at sustaining its overall foreign policy but instead has relied on a wide range of political themes and metaphors intended to thwart Western soft power practices in the region. In addition, it has promoted cultural and educational initiatives, developed and implemented by the state apparatus of cultural and humanitarian diplomacy and multiple government agencies, regional authorities, parliamentary bodies, media organizations, GONGOs, and corporate entities. Nourzhanov highlights several of the weak links in the policy of soft power as conceived and implemented by Moscow, and its reception in Central Asia. This includes the lack of Russian involvement in the NGO sector, either as a soft power operator or an object of partnership in Central Asia. Russian soft power has been less a matter of constructed policy than of ad hoc support initiatives, as exemplified by the Russian response to the COVID-19 crisis where it dispatched medical support to several countries in the region. Importantly, Russian failure to utilize the full potential of humanitarian aid diplomacy and, more generally, the inconsistent substance and implementation of its soft power in Central Asia has disturbed its balance with hard power and instead made of it "a poor cousin to conventional ways of securing Russia's influence in the former Soviet space."

Having become a key partner of the region in less than ten years, China has substantially reshaped Nye's concept to make it suit its own domestic and foreign political and economic interests. Besides cultural tools, Beijing has put economics at the forefront of its soft power offensive in order to mitigate increasing concerns about its economic influence in Central Asia. In other words, China has sought to soften the hard power dimension of its foreign investments and instead demonstrate its contribution to local economic development and well-being of the local population. Moreover, China has aimed to set itself up as a new model of economic development, different from and purportedly more reliable than the ones hitherto driven by Western states and international organizations such as the IMF or the World Bank. To do so, the Chinese government has markedly reshaped the concept of soft power to make it consistent with its single-party rule by countering the Western model with the portrayal of the alleged success of its own model of democracy with Chinese characteristics, that is, a development model which secures the stability of the political regime and, in return, guarantees the sustainability of social development.

Importantly, as Sebastien Peyrouse's chapter shows, China's choice of actors and tools has blurred the very concept of soft power and led to its intermixing or even confusion with other concepts. Beijing's authoritarian approach, which has driven its state apparatus to monopolize the mode, tools, and implementation of its foreign policy, has consisted more of public diplomacy than of traditional soft power. As argued by David Shambaugh, soft power is "largely about the capacity of a society to attract others, rather than a government to persuade others."[44] Public diplomacy may contribute to the promotion of soft power, however, its impact is likely to be significantly weakened if it is not supported and relayed by private and independent actors. Overall, this confusion is likely to have led to a distorted perception of soft power and to some counterproductive impacts: the consubstantial authoritarianism of Beijing's regime, combined with what is viewed locally as China's excessive and unbalanced economic influence, has contributed to feeding the fear that China inspires across borders, including in Central Asia.

Beyond the "Big Three," many other actors have embarked on soft power policies in Central Asia which have been little studied. In order to continue the discussion on the inherent complexity of soft power mentioned in the previous cases, but, in addition go beyond the frame of geopolitical competition and containment between the great powers, this book also addresses three case studies which have been selected for their diverse geographical origin, their constitution (individual state vs. entity of states like the European Union), and their goals.

The first case is that of the European Union, the foreign policy of which has been subjected to a range of domestic questions, including concerning the economic crisis, Euroscepticism, and EU enlargement. In this challenging context, Emilian Kavalski addresses the question of whether the EU's soft power "has been catalyzed (i.e., given impetus and direction) or constrained (i.e., subject to a process of external- or self-limitation)." The EU's soft power has been all the more difficult to implement since it emanates from a group of states whose diversity of policies has resulted in divergent or even contradictory foreign strategies. This lack of unity in the EU has added to the difficulty of going beyond the main EU domestic priorities such as enlargement and the European Neighborhood policy (ENP), in which Central Asian states are not included, and hence to develop a soft power policy in regions which are remote from its priorities. Moreover, soft power has been only one component of the EU's normative power policy, defined as "the ability to shape the conception of 'normal',"[45] and which the European Union has used in the post-Soviet space to position itself as a viable model for reference. This ambivalence has hindered the shaping of a soft power foreign policy in "far neighborhoods" like Central Asia. Overall, Brussels has failed to initiate regular interactions and implement initiatives with the Central Asian states. As the author concludes, "the process-tracing of the EU's external outreach reveals reactive, inconsistent, and disconnected interactions with this region. Instead of a soft power, the EU emerges as a 'bit player'—an actor with a very limited impact and leverage on regional affairs."

In Turkey, as presented by M. Murat Yurtbilir, the Justice and Development Party (Adalet ve Kalkınma Partisi—AKP), which came to power in 2002, significantly developed the country's soft power policy by increasing its foreign engagement in the sector of environment, culture, and education, implemented by Diyanet Foundation, the Ministry of National Education, the Gülen movement, the Turkish Cooperation and Development Agency (TIKA), and the Presidency for Turks Abroad and Related Communities, among others. However, despite Turkey's assets in Central Asia embodying its linguistic and cultural proximity, Ankara's policy has illustrated the contingent nature and hence the fragility of soft power. First, despite many initiatives, the materialization of Turkish soft power in Central Asia came under an evolving international context and was subject to Ankara's foreign policy prioritization. Since 2013, Turkish soft power has been largely Middle East–oriented, illustrating the contraction of the multidimensional nature of Turkey's foreign policy since the AKP came to power.[46] Second, the contingency of soft power also has ensued from the contingent nature of the tools used to implement it, as exemplified by the banning of Gülen schools after the 2016 coup attempt allegedly initiated by Fethullah Gülen. This led the Turkish government to call on authorities to shut down these schools in Kazakhstan and Kyrgyzstan, where they had been perceived by local populations as one of the rare alternates to a deficient and corrupt local education system. Although Nursi teaching had been banned in Uzbekistan in 1997 and in Tajikistan in 2015, Ankara's offensive against Gülen schools, which had been an essential emblem of Turkish commitment in the region since the 1990s, has considerably weakened Turkey's visibility in the region despite its efforts to compensate through cultural and humanitarian cooperation.[47] Finally, the change in the very nature of Turkish soft power policy risks hindering its expected impact on the region. The author argues that the major objectives of Turkish soft power have switched from filling the political and social vacuum in the 1990s based on the linguistic and cultural ties lost during the Russian-Soviet rule of the 1990s, toward an emphasis on Islam since the AKP came to power. Such a policy is likely to spark reservations in a region attached to secularism and where political regimes are very reluctant to allow any foreign interference that might call this principle into question.

We made a point of including in this book less visible yet still quite active actors in Central Asian countries. One such case is Israel, which has looked to the large Jewish minority, which had been settled in Central Asia since the fifth century, to implement strong relations with the region. Although most Central Asian Jewish minorities migrated to Israel or Western countries after the fall of the Soviet regime, most have retained active social and economic connections in the region, and it is those connections that Israel took advantage of to implement its soft power policy. Tel Aviv has used a plethora of tools, including social media, promotion of training for agricultural development, technology, health care, tourism, investment, and, to some extent, the promotion of Jewish-Judaist culture. However, as the author Bruno de Cordier argues, the case of Israel has differed from Western, Russian, or Chinese cases in that it has not sought to propagate or win converts among non-Jews, nor promote a specific societal-developmental model among society overall. Rather, Israel's soft power policy in Central Asia has essentially aimed at sustaining cooperation, boosting trade and opportunities for the Israeli private sector in these predominantly Muslim countries, and preventing the spread of anti-Semitic clichés that could challenge Israeli interests in the region. The Israeli case is perhaps an example of a more pragmatic and possibly even more effective soft power policy, particularly as it is one less marked by political and geopolitical designs and rivalries.

As noted above, this book challenges the notion of the Great Game, which would make the states and populations of the region into mere passive actors, receptacles for a policy of rival foreign states. All are independent countries which act and respond, use foreign states' policies to their advantage, or put up resistance to external initiatives which they deem contrary to their interests, including those from large powers such as China and Russia. We have included in this volume three case studies, namely Kazakhstan, Kyrgyzstan, and Tajikistan, to assess how these countries receive, perceive, and respond to foreign states soft power, including through resistance.

In the case of Kazakhstan, Reuel Hanks addresses the local reception to Russian and Chinese soft power and argues that despite their use of soft power, both have failed to enhance their influence on Kazakhstani policy making. By relying essentially on strong economic investments and on support for Central Asian elites, China has, intentionally or unintentionally, mingled and confused hard power with soft power, which must be earned through the support of local populations, who however have interpreted

Beijing's engagement through resource extraction, economic hegemony, and exportation of surplus labor, rather than as cooperation rooted in mutual respect and the shared goals of development and joint benefit. In the case of Russia, the Kremlin's foreign policy has materialized as an exercise in soft coercion, through which the concept of soft power has been viewed as a "kind of hybrid concept somewhat similar to the Soviet 'agitprop,' wherein image management and public diplomacy are simply an extension of more direct measures." Although Moscow remains strongly influential in the region, thanks to its historical and cultural legacy, as well as the Russian language, which is still widely practiced throughout the region, and to the millions of Central Asian labor migrants who work in Russia every year and see it as an economic engine in Eurasia, Hanks argues that soft power is not definitively established and that its accomplishments might erode away. This trend might be accentuated with increasing nationalist or xenophobic trends throughout the region, directed, among others, against Russian language, culture, or against the Eurasian Economic Union, which is criticized in Kazakhstan as an essential pipeline for Moscow's outsized influence and benefits. Moreover, the Kazakhstani government, although it denies having any anti-Russian domestic policy, has endeavored to limit the influence of Russian-produced media and control its Russian language content. This therefore raises a question about Moscow's ability to effectively revise its policy, and further erodes the assertion that local populations take at face value the soft power policy of any state, whatever its assets.

Analyzing the local reception to the use of soft power also requires disaggregating its impact by target states, whose responses fall under multiple criteria including their geographical position, economic strength or weakness, and political stability, and hence is likely to vary significantly from one state to another. Aminat Chokobaeva and Drew Ninnis argue that the security and economic weaknesses of Kyrgyzstan, and its reliance on support from foreign states, especially Russia and China, including military cooperation, trade, and economic investment, have weakened the distinction between soft power and hard power, and revealed the potentially coercive nature consubstantial with each of them. The authors argue that Russia's use of media has been intended to influence the electoral behavior of the Kyrgyzstani electorate, making a soft power tool into a coercive one. Conversely, hard power can have soft power effects: Russian military cooperation and influence, an instrument par excellence of hard power, has been perceived as a security guarantee for countries that have had significant difficulties in maintaining reliable defense systems since their independence. This raises two types of questions. First, whether Central Asian leaders are acting out of genuine attraction or out of a fear of possible drastic consequences that could come with challenging, and therefore weakening, Russia's or China's engagement in the country. Second, whether such constrained dependence resulting from close links, often legitimized by local political authorities, is likely to cause a growing gap between the welcome that authorities give to these countries' engagement and the reluctance of the populations, which remain unconvinced by the charm offensive materialized through the use of soft power. Conducting in-depth studies about the reception from local populations to soft power is therefore essential to analyze the impact that the failure of a foreign country's charm offensive may have on the relations between a government and its population, including social disturbances or unrest, as illustrated by some popular responses to the influence and presence of China in Kyrgyzstan.

In chapter 9, which is dedicated to Tajikistan, Karolina Kluczewska and Payam Foroughi do not address soft power developed by an individual country but by multiple Western development organizations, including international organizations (IOs), international non-governmental organizations (INGOs), and domestic nongovernmental organizations (NGOs). These agencies have strived to seduce the local populations by using the foreign aid they have provided to local civil society and its activists entrepreneurs. This chapter here again demonstrates that soft power and how it is received is not a stable phenomenon, but rather relies on the credibility of actors who frame and implement it and fluctuates over time. Since the early 1990s, development actors in Tajikistan have relied on multiple tools of persuasion to attractively portray the concept of neoliberal civil society to local actors. This included project funding and humanitarian aid; funding of NGO projects; and proposing new ideas to compensate for the post-Soviet vacuum. Nearly three decades after the arrival of neoliberal civil society to Central Asia, the authors argue that the alleged impact of Western organizations' soft power has been eroded by foreign development actors targeting mostly one social group, that is, local activists who formed NGOs and were expected to promote liberal ideas domestically. However, in the context of current economic decline in Tajikistan, the attraction of local activists to neoliberal civil society has been shaped mainly by material incentives and to gain economic support to secure the financial survival of their organization and therefore their personal living. This approach in reality has verged more on hard power through the coercive dimension that conditionality of foreign funding implies, than on spreading values and developing competence through soft power. This neoliberal society approach has been made all the more fragile by the decrease of support from Western development actors, which has led to a decline in local interest in participating in neoliberal civil society.

This book does not claim to be exhaustive. Many topics pertaining to the issue of soft power in Central Asia remain to be studied, including about the use of soft power source in countries such as Iran, the Gulf countries, or Asian states such as India, Japan, or South Korea, which have interacted with the states of the region since independence, as well as the local reception of such soft power, for example in Turkmenistan, where it has been difficult to conduct research since the country's independence due to the extremely authoritarian nature of the political regime. This book, however, aims to provide avenues of reflection about the complexity of the global phenomenon of soft power in the Central Asian region. As suggested by Kavalski in chapter 4, soft power appears to have become one of those concepts open to contestation; its meaning and practices are anything but clear cut and universally accepted. The point is that soft power is inherently context-dependent; the constitution of attractive values is invariably "a subjective matter in the eye of the beholder, and not dependent on supposed inherent traits or predispositions." This book therefore hopes to contribute to a more general debate on the concept of soft power, its multiple forms, and its strengths and fragilities; thereby bringing new elements of comparison and reflection to the ongoing debate the concept of soft power generates on a global scale.

NOTES

1. A great many of these are discussed through this volume.

2. Notably, Kerry Longhurst, Agnieszka Nitza-Makowska, and Katarzyna Skiert-Andrzejuk, "Re-thinking Soft Power: China, Russia and the European Union in Central Asia," *Sprawy Międzynarodowe* 72, no. 3 (2019): 151–69; Soledad Jiménez-Tovar and Martin Lavička, "Folklorized Politics: How Chinese Soft Power Works in Central Asia," *Asian Ethnicity* 21, no. 2 (2020): 244–68; Marlene Laruelle (ed.), *China's Belt and Road Initiative and Its Impact in Central Asia* (Washington, DC: The George Washington University, Central Asia Program, 2018).

3. Zbigniew Brzezinski, *The Grand Chessboard: American Primacy and Its Geostrategic Imperatives* (New York: Basic Books, 1997).

4. As demonstrated in the second chapter of this volume.

5. For a comprehensive critical account of the Geopolitical and "Great Game" approaches to the study of Central Asia, see Matthew Edwards, "The New Great Game and the New Great Gamers: Disciples of Kipling and Mackinder," *Central Asian Survey* 22, no. 1 (2003): 83–102.

6. Sebastien Peyrouse (ed.), "How does Central Asia View the EU?," *Eucam Working Paper*, no. 18 (2014), http://www.eucentralasia.eu/uploads/tx_icticontent/EUCAM-WP18-How-does-Central-Asia-view-the-EU-1.pdf

7. Brzezinski, *The Grand Chessboard*, 194 (quoted in the second chapter of this volume).

8. See chapter 2 of this volume.

9. Joseph S. Nye Jr., *Bound to Lead: The Changing Nature of American Power* (New York: Basic Books, 1990), 31.

10. Paul C. Avey and Michael C. Desch, "What Do Policymakers Want From Us? Results of a Survey of Current and Former Senior National Security Decision Makers," *International Studies Quarterly* 58, no. 2 (2014): 236.

11. M.A. Neimark, *'Miagkaia sila' v mirovoi politike* (Moscow: Dashkov & Co., 2018), 15.

12. Hongying Wang and Yeh-Chung Lu, "The Conception of Soft Power and Its Policy Implications: a Comparative Study of China and Taiwan," *Journal of Contemporary China* 17, no. 56 (2008): 426.

13. For a concise summary of such criticisms, see Ying Fan, "Soft power: Power of attraction or confusion?," *Place Branding and Public Diplomacy* 4, no. 2 (2008): 147–58.

14. Robin Brown, "Alternatives to Soft Power: Influence in French and German External Cultural Action," in *Routledge Handbook of Soft Power*, ed. Naren Chitty, et al. (Abingdon: Routledge, 2017), 37.

15. Joseph S. Nye Jr., *The Future of Power* (New York: Public Affairs, 2011), 84.

16. Joseph S. Nye Jr., *Soft Power: The Means to Success in World Politics* (New York: Public Affairs, 2004), 5–6.

17. Naren Chitty, "Soft power, Civic virtue and World Politics (section overview)," in *Routledge Handbook of Soft Power*, ed. Naren Chitty, et al. (Abingdon: Routledge, 2017), 25–26.

18. Nye, *The Future of Power*, 90.

19. Michael Beckley, *Unrivaled: Why America Will Remain the World's Sole Superpower* (Ithaca: Cornell University Press, 2018), 112.

20. N. N. Emel'ianova, "'Miagkaia sila' kak kontsept: kriticheskii analiz," *Mezhdunarodnaia analitika* 3, no. 25 (2018): 16.

21. Joseph S. Nye Jr., "The Information Revolution and Soft Power," *Current History* 113, no. 759 (2014): 21.

22. Christopher Walker and Jessica Ludwig, "From 'Soft Power' to 'Sharp Power': Rising Authoritarian Influence in the Democratic World," in *Sharp Power: Rising Authoritarian Influence* (report, The National Endowment for Democracy, Washington DC, 2017), 8–25.

23. Lavrov quoted in "Lavrov rasskazal, chem slavitsia amerikanskaia 'miagkaia sila'," *RIA Novosti*, 17 September 2020, https://ria.ru/20200917/lavrov-1577408994.html.

24. Joseph S. Nye Jr., "Get Smart: Combining Hard and Soft Power," *Foreign Affairs* 88, no. 4 (2009): 163. Curiously, Nye's inconsistency drew criticism from an official from the Russian government agency tasked with soft power promotion who wrote an article entitled, somewhat pretentiously, *How to Apply Soft Power Correctly*. In it, he argued that Nye "was compelled to make concessions to the military component" of power in deference to the hawks in the U.S. policy establishment. (Aleksandr Ganoshchenko, "Kak pravilno primenit' kontseptsiiu 'miagkoi sily'," *Mezhdunarodnaia zhizn'* 9 [2019]: 109).

25. A. B. Yessimova and S. A. Panarin, "Western Europe through the Eyes of Students of Kazakhstan Universities: Countries' Images and Driving Force for their Formation," *Vestnik RUDN: International Relations* 19, no. 1 (2019): 116.

26. Joseph S. Nye Jr., *The Powers to Lead* (New York: Oxford University Press, 2008), 141.

27. Yu-Wen Chen and Olaf Günther, "Back to Normalization or Conflict with China in Greater Central Asia?," *Problems of Post-Communism* 67, no. 3 (2020): 236.

28. E. Nechaeva and A. Shchegortsova, "Obespechenie informatsionnoi bezopasnosti kak kliuchevaia zadacha mediamanadzhmenta Respubliki Kazakhstan," *Bulletin d'Eurotalent-FIDJIP*, no. 1 (2019): 115.

29. "Kontseptsiia gosudarstvennoi informatsionnoi politiki Respubliki Tadzhikistan," *Approved by the Decree of the President of Tajikistan No. 451*, April 30, 2008, http://www.cawater-info.net/pdf/tj-451-2008.pdf.

30. Parviz Muhammadzoda and Khujamurod Safaralizoda, "Nerui hushmand va durnamoi himoyai manfiathoi milli," *Tojikiston va jahoni imruz* 70, no. 2 (2020): 11–23.

31. Dabir Ahlawat, "Central and South Asia: An Overview of Soft Power Prospective (section overview)," in *Routledge Handbook of Soft Power*, ed. Naren Chitty, et al. (Abingdon: Routledge, 2017), 342.

32. See Erica Marat, "Nation Branding in Central Asia: A New Campaign to Present Ideas about the State and the Nation," *Europe-Asia Studies* 61, no. 7 (2009): 1123–36; Aigerim Zhak'ianova, "Resursy 'miagkoi sily' vo vneshnei politike Kazakhstana," *Diskurs-Pi* 26, no. 1 (2017): 101–10.

33. "O merakh po korennomu sovershenstvovaniiu sistemy Ministerstva inostrannykh del Respubliki Uzbekistan i usileniiu ego otvetstvennosti za realizatsiiu prioritetnykh napravlenii vneshnepoliticheskoi i vneshneekonomicheskoi deiatelnosti," *Decree of the President of the Republic of Uzbekistan No. 5400*, April 5, 2018, https://lex.uz/docs/3611113.

34. "Concept of the Foreign Policy of the Republic of Tajikistan," *Ministry of Foreign Affairs of the Republic of Tajikistan*, March 1, 2015, https://mfa.tj/en/main/view/988/concept-of-the-foreign-policy-of-the-republic-of-tajikistan.

35. Aidana Yergalieva, "Kazakh Foreign Ministry to Create Agency to Systematize KazAID," *Astana Times*, August 20, 2020, https://astanatimes.com/2020/08/kazakh-foreign-ministry-to-create-agency-to-systematize-kazaid/.

36. A.V. Grozin, "Internet-kommunikatsii v Tsentralnoi Azii," in *Tsentralnaia Evraziia: Territoriia mezhkulturnykh kommunikatsii*, ed. A.K. Alikberov (Moscow: IVRAN, 2020), 188–219.

37. Nye, *Soft Power: The Means to Success in World Politics*, 99.

38. Gregory F. Treverton and Seth G. Jones, *Measuring National Power* (Santa Monica: RAND Corporation, 2005), 17.

39. *StrategEast Westernization Index 2018*. Washington, DC: StrategEast, 2018, 10.

40. SEWI is upfront about its normative preferences and bias whereas critics of SP30 accuse it of "legitimising Anglo-American political values, economic models and even cultural tastes" surreptitiously. (Chang Zhang and Ruiqin Wu, "Battlefield of Global Ranking: How do Power Rivalries Shape Soft Power Index Building?," *Global Media and China* 4, no. 2 [2019]: 187).

41. Igor Zadorin et al., *EDB Integration Barometer-2017* (Saint Petersburg: EDB Centre for Integration Studies, 2017).

42. A recent comparative study of the U.S., Russian, and Chinese soft power projection in Kazakhstan used a system of "soft power points" across four components: foreign policy principles; successful economic model; cultural-civilizational values; and successful social model. This undoubtedly productive idea was let down by an arbitrary equivalence scale where one soft power point could be generated by 1 high-level state visit; 10 new film releases or national food restaurants; 1,000 joint commercial ventures; 1,000 students; 100,000 tourists (both inbound and outbound), or 100 million USD in official aid. (G.V. Kozlov, "Prikladnoi analiz vliianiia na Kazakhstan politiki 'miagkoi sily' SShA, RF i KNR," *Postsovetskii materik* 25, no. 1 [2020]: 32–73.)

43. Alexander Cooley, *Great Games, Local Rules* (Oxford: Oxford University Press, 2012), 162.

44. David Shambaugh, *China Goes Global: The Partial Power* (New York: Oxford University Press, 2013), 167.

45. Ian Manners. "Normative Power Europe: A Contradiction in Terms?," *Journal of Common Market Studies* 40, no. 2 (2002): 252.

46. Muharrem Ekşi and Mehmet Seyfettin Erol, "The Rise and Fall of Turkish Soft Power and Public Diplomacy," *Gazi Akademik Bakis Dergisi* 11, no. 23 (2018): 40–42.

47. See for example: "V chem zakliuchetsia 'miagkaia sila' Turcii v Kyrgyzstane I zachem ona nuzhna?," *Radio Azattyk*, October 22, 2019, https://rus.azattyk.org/a/kyrgyzstan-turkey-ambassador-fyrat-aitmatov/30016346.html.

REFERENCES

Avey, Paul C., and Michael C. Desch. "What Do Policymakers Want From Us? Results of a Survey of Current and Former Senior National Security Decision Makers." *International Studies Quarterly* 58, no. 2 (2014): 227–46.

Ahlawat, Dabir. "Central and South Asia: An Overview of Soft Power Prospective (section overview)." In *Routledge Handbook of Soft Power*, edited by Naren Chitty, Li Ji, Gary D. Rawnsley, and Craig Hayden, 341–45. Abingdon: Routledge, 2017.

Beckley, Michael. *Unrivaled: Why America Will Remain the World's Sole Superpower.* Ithaca: Cornell University Press, 2018.

Brown, Robin. "Alternatives to Soft Power: Influence in French and German External Cultural Action." In *Routledge Handbook of Soft Power*, edited by Naren Chitty, Li Ji, Gary D. Rawnsley, and Craig Hayden, 37–47. Abingdon: Routledge, 2017.

Brzezinski, Zbigniew. *The Grand Chessboard: American Primacy and Its Geostrategic Imperatives.* New York: Basic Books, 1997.

Chen, Yu-Wen, and Olaf Günther. "Back to Normalization or Conflict with China in Greater Central Asia?" *Problems of Post-Communism* 67, no. 3 (2020): 228–40.

Chitty, Naren. 2016. "Soft Power, Civic Virtue and World Politics (Section Overview)." In *The Routledge Handbook of Soft Power*, edited by Naren Chitty, Li Ji, Gary D. Rawnsley, and Craig Hayden, 9–36. London and New York: Routledge.

Cooley, Alexander. *Great Games, Local Rules: The New Great Power Contest in Central Asia*. New York: Oxford University Press, 2012.

Edwards, Matthew. "The New Great Game and the New Great Gamers: Disciples of Kipling and Mackinder." *Central Asian Survey* 22, no. 1 (2003): 83–102.

Ekşi, Muharrem, and Mehmet Seyfettin Erol. "The Rise and Fall of Turkish Soft Power and Public Diplomacy." *Gazi Akademik Bakis Dergisi* 11, no. 23 (2018): 15–45.

Emel'ianova, N. N. "'Miagkaia sila' kak kontsept: kriticheskii analiz." *Mezhdunarodnaia analitika* 3, no. 25 (2018): 7–24.

Fan, Ying. "Soft Power: Power of Attraction or Confusion?" *Place Branding and Public Diplomacy* 4, no. 2 (2008): 147–58.

Ganoshchenko, Aleksandr. "Kak pravilno primenit' kontseptsiiu 'miagkoi sily'." *Mezhdunarodnaia zhizn'* 9 (2019): 102–11.

Grozin, A. V. "Internet-kommunikatsii v Tsentralnoi Azii." In *Tsentralnaia Evraziia: Territoriia mezhkulturnykh kommunikatsii*, edited by A. K. Alikberov, 188–219. Moscow: IVRAN, 2020.

Jiménez-Tovar, Soledad, and Martin Lavička. "Folklorized Politics: How Chinese Soft Power Works in Central Asia." *Asian Ethnicity* 21, no. 2 (2020): 244–68.

Kozlov, G. V. "Prikladnoi analiz vliianiia na Kazakhstan politiki 'miagkoi sily' SShA, RF i KNR." *Postsovetskii materik* 25, no. 1 (2020): 32–73.

Laruelle, Marlene, ed. *China's Belt and Road Initiative and Its Impact in Central Asia*. Washington, DC: The George Washington University, Central Asia Program, 2018.

Longhurst, Kerry, Agnieszka Nitza-Makowska, and Katarzyna Skiert-Andrzejuk. "Re-thinking Soft Power: China, Russia and the European Union in Central Asia." *Sprawy Międzynarodowe* 72, no. 3 (2019): 151–69.

Manners, Ian. "Normative Power Europe: A Contradiction in Terms?" *Journal of Common Market Studies* 40, no. 2 (2002): 235–58.

Marat, Erica. "Nation Branding in Central Asia: A New Campaign to Present Ideas about the State and the Nation." *Europe-Asia Studies* 61, no. 7 (2009): 1123–36.

Muhammadzoda, Parviz, and Khujamurod Safaralizoda. "Nerui hushmand va durnamoi himoyai manfiathoi milli." *Tojikiston va jahoni imruz* 70, no. 2 (2020): 11–23.

Nechaeva, E., and A. Shchegortsova. "Obespechenie informatsionnoi bezopasnosti kak kliuchevaia zadacha mediamanadzhmenta Respubliki Kazakhstan." *Bulletin d'Eurotalent-FIDJIP*, no. 1 (2019): 113–17.

Neimark, M. A. *'Miagkaia sila' v mirovoi politike*. Moscow: Dashkov & Co., 2018.

Nye, Joseph S. Jr. *Bound to Lead: The Changing Nature of American Power*. New York: Basic Books, 1990.

Nye, Joseph S. Jr. *The Future of Power*. New York: Public Affairs, 2011.

Nye, Joseph S., Jr. "Get Smart: Combining Hard and Soft Power." *Foreign Affairs* 88, no. 4 (2009): 160–163.

Nye, Joseph S. Jr. "The Information Revolution and Soft Power." *Current History* 113, no. 759 (2014): 19–22.
Nye, Joseph S., Jr. *The Powers to Lead.* New York: Oxford University Press, 2008.
Nye, Joseph S. Jr. *Soft Power. The Means to Success in World Politics.* New York: Public Affairs, 2004.
Peyrouse, Sebastien. "How does Central Asia View the EU?" *Eucam Working Paper*, no. 18 (2014), http://www.eucentralasia.eu/uploads/tx_icticontent/EUCAM-WP18-How-does-Central-Asia-view-the-EU-1.pdf.
Radio Azattyk. "V chem zakliuchetsia 'miagkaia sila' Turcii v Kyrgyzstane I zachem ona nuzhna?" *Radio Azattyk*, October 22, 2019. https://rus.azattyk.org/a/kyrgyzstan-turkey-ambassador-fyrat-aitmatov/30016346.html.
RIA Novosti. "Lavrov rasskazal, chem slavitsia amerikanskaia 'miagkaia sila'," 17 September 2020. https://ria.ru/20200917/lavrov-1577408994.html.
Shambaugh, David. *China Goes Global: The Partial Power.* New York: Oxford University Press, 2013.
Strategeast. *StrategEast Westernization Index 2018.* Washington, DC: StrategEast, 2018.
Tajikistan, Ministry of Foreign Affairs of. "Concept of the Foreign Policy of the Republic of Tajikistan." *Ministry of Foreign Affairs of the Republic of Tajikistan*, March 1, 2015. https://mfa.tj/en/main/view/988/concept-of-the-foreign-policy-of-the-republic-of-tajikistan.
Tajikistan, President of. "Kontseptsiia gosudarstvennoi informatsionnoi politiki Respubliki Tadzhikistan." *Approved by the Decree of the President of Tajikistan No. 451*, April 30, 2008. http://www.cawater-info.net/pdf/tj-451.
Toleukhanova, Aigerim. "Kazakhstan and China: Fear, Loathing and Money." *Eurasianet.org*, June 21, 2016. https://eurasianet.org/kazakhstan-china-fear-loathing-and-money.
Treverton, Gregory F., and Seth G. Jones. *Measuring National Power.* Santa Monica: RAND Corporation, 2005.
Uzbekistan, President of. "O merakh po korennomu sovershenstvovaniiu sistemy Ministerstva inostrannykh del Respubliki Uzbekistan i usileniiu ego otvetstvennosti za realizatsiiu prioritetnykh napravlenii vneshnepoliticheskoi i vneshneekonomicheskoi deiatelnosti." *Decree of the President of the Republic of Uzbekistan No. 5400*, April 5, 2018. https://lex.uz/docs/3611113.
Walker, Christopher, and Jessica Ludwig. "From 'Soft Power' to 'Sharp Power': Rising Authoritarian Influence in the Democratic World." In *Sharp Power: Rising Authoritarian Influence*, 8–25. Report, The National Endowment for Democracy, Washington DC, 2017.
Wang, Hongying, and Yeh-Chung Lu. "The Conception of Soft Power and Its Policy Implications: a Comparative Study of China and Taiwan." *Journal of Contemporary China* 17, no. 56 (2008): 425–47.
Yergalieva, Aidana. "Kazakh Foreign Ministry to Create Agency to Systematize KazAID." *Astana Times*, August 20, 2020. https://astanatimes.com/2020/08/kazakh-foreign-ministry-to-create-agency-to-systematize-kazaid/.

Yessimova, A. B., and S. A. Panarin. "Western Europe through the Eyes of Students of Kazakhstan Universities: Countries' Images and Driving Force for their Formation." *Vestnik RUDN: International Relations* 19, no. 1 (2019): 100–18.

Zadorin, Igor, Ivan Karpov, Alexey Kunakhov, Roman Kuznetsov, Arteom Rykov, Lyudmila Shubina, and Vladimir Pereboev. *EDB Integration Barometer-2017*. Saint Petersburg: EDB Centre for Integration Studies, 2017.

Zhang, Chang, and Ruiqin Wu. "Battlefield of Global Ranking: How do Power Rivalries Shape Soft Power Index Building?" *Global Media and China* 4, no. 2 (2019): 179–202.

Part I

Chapter 1

U.S. Soft Power in Central Asia

Alexander Diener and Vincent Artman

"The Great Game." "The Grand Chessboard." "The Geographical Pivot of History." "The New Silk Road." "The Near Abroad." "The Non-Integrating Gap." It is through the images, clichés, and mythologies evoked by such romantic phrases that the history of imperial contestation in Central Asia has often been known. A place marked by remoteness, obscurity, exoticism, and danger, Central Asia as a geopolitical subject has seldom been understood on its own terms. Rather, the region's very centrality has ironically reinforced its geopolitical peripherality as a zone of competition among regional powers and global hegemons.

For example, Zbigniew Brzezinski, in *The Grand Chessboard*, reinforces a sense of Central Asia's marginality and historical determinism in the post-Soviet era, by arguing that the Caspian basin would become a site of contestation between important regional players such as Russia, Turkey, China, and Iran. He suggests that each is "driven not only by the prospect of future geopolitical and economic benefits but also by *strong historical impulses*."[1] Brzezinski further adds:

> Although distant, the United States, with its stake in the maintenance of geopolitical pluralism in post-Soviet Eurasia, looms in the background as an increasingly important if indirect player, clearly interested not only in developing the region's resources but also in preventing Russia from exclusively dominating the region's geopolitical space. In so doing, America is not only pursuing its larger Eurasian geostrategic goals but is also representing its own growing economic interest, as well as that of Europe and the Far East, in gaining unlimited access to this hitherto closed area.[2]

Ultimately, he concludes that "America is now Eurasia's arbiter, with no major Eurasian issue soluble without America's participation or contrary to America's interests."[3] He also warns that in the absence of "sustained and directed American involvement," the forces of chaos and fragmentation threaten not only Eurasia, but the world as a whole.[4]

For Brzezinski, American "geostrategy for Eurasia" must therefore emphasize "geopolitical pluralism," the fostering of "strategically compatible partners," and the eventual emergence of "a global core of genuinely shared political responsibility."[5]

Such assessments were rooted in dominant interpretations of the demise of the Soviet Union and the end of the Cold War, which appeared to usher in an era of uncontested American hegemony in world affairs. At the same time, it also produced "a condition of geopolitical vertigo, a state of confusion where the old nostrums of the Cold War were redundant and new ones had not yet been invented, issued and approved."[6] If the world's sole remaining superpower, flush with the self-assuredness that it had ushered in the "end of history,"[7] had little interest in dominating the globe militarily, it nevertheless perceived an opportunity to reconfigure the geopolitical landscape on its own terms.

However, even at the time it was considered "unlikely that democratic America will wish to be permanently engaged in the difficult, absorbing, and costly task of managing Eurasia by constant manipulation and maneuver, backed by American military resources."[8] Rather, from the "geostrategic" perspective favored in realist foreign policy circles, the application of "soft" or "co-optive"[9] forms of power in remote (from the American point of view) places like Central Asia would be preferable to the prospect of having to employ military force to maintain hegemony, or even to achieve lesser political objectives, as amply demonstrated by the logistical challenges encountered by the United States in trying to prosecute the war in Afghanistan.[10]

Soft power can be "'high,' targeted at elites, or 'low,' targeted at the broader public," and it "stems from both governments and nongovernmental actors," giving it a multifaceted, decentered character.[11] Soft power can thus appear in the guise of formal academic exchange programs, language training, membership in international organizations, or international aid and investment. But, just as importantly, it is also transmitted through more informal channels such as movies, music, and popular culture. Ultimately, the aim of soft power is to win "hearts and minds" by leveraging the "universalism of a country's culture and its ability to establish a set of favorable rules and institutions that govern areas of international activity."[12]

Soft power levers, moreover, are subject to interpretation. Efforts to "do good" can be interpreted and portrayed, rightly or wrongly, as attempts to undermine rivals or co-opt regional partners. Any deployment of soft power must therefore be considered in terms of its potential for blowback, both within a given state and in relation to the interests of those states also vying for influence. It is for this reason that strategically selecting issues through which to deploy soft power is essential—and fraught with ethical and political pitfalls. The Obama administration, for example, made LGBT rights a central tenet of U.S. foreign policy in 2011. This contrasted to Russia's denial of LGBT rights as a tenet of its foreign policy, which involved everything from blocking benefits for families of gay UN employees to pressuring countries in its sphere to outlaw "homosexual propaganda." Ultimately, Russian attitudes toward LGBT rights carried more resonance in Central Asia than American ones, and countries like Kyrgyzstan passed strict "anti-gay propaganda" laws modeled on Russian templates.[13] On this issue and others like it, the United States has been forced to define its priorities in moral, geopolitical, and economic terms as it decides where and how to deploy soft power.

Similarly, many of the methods and channels for mobilizing soft power can be double-edged swords. Film, music, television programs, and even popular forms of literature are commonly imported from the United States and either translated or subtitled for mass consumption in Central Asia. But the presence of substantial Russophone populations in all of the Central Asian states means that there is a preexisting consumer base for Russian media, which often conform to the ideologies and narratives promoted by the Russian government. While newspapers, especially government-sponsored outlets like *Kazakhstanskaya Pravda,* are among the main ideological and informational outlets for local authorities, in an ironic mimicry of Cold War airwave intrusion (i.e., Voice of America and Radio Free Europe), both U.S. and Russian television, radio, and increasingly, social media, transmit information to and construct meanings for the populations of the Central Asian states in ways that often bypass or subvert official gatekeepers.

But both the Russian and Chinese governments, and indeed the governments of the Central Asian states themselves, are keenly aware of the power of social media, which is monitored and controlled with an eye to its potential weaponization. Social media, and indeed the internet more broadly, are viewed with a mixture of skepticism—as a potential site for agitation—and ambition. While the local regimes have been less adept on this front, Russia and China have adroitly wielded social media for their own purposes (e.g., Russian influence on U.S. elections, the massive disinformation campaign against Ukraine, and efforts to shape narratives surrounding Uyghur separatism).

It is crucial, however, to remember that soft power is ultimately employed in order to further the geopolitical ambition of those wielding it. Soft power, in other words, is still power. So if "geography is about power,"[14] then the mobilization of soft power in places like Central Asia should be understood as an alternative means of playing out an otherwise traditional geopolitical contest between "Great Powers." After all, the United States is not the only, nor arguably even the most important, contender for influence in Central Asia today: both Russia and China, for their own reasons, seek to extend their influence in the region, and both enjoy advantages, not the least of which is proximity, that the United States does not. Turkey, Iran, the European Union, and India, among others also have interests in Central Asia. American policy toward Central Asia, meanwhile, has largely been characterized by disinterest punctuated primarily by the need to respond to the exigencies of the "War on Terror" and the ongoing war in Afghanistan.

This does not mean that American soft power in Central Asia is insignificant or unimportant. Quite to the contrary, certain initiatives, such as the establishment of the American University of Central Asia, outreach programs like "American Corners," which in Bishkek serve upward of 80,000 people per year,[15] and the various development programs under the aegis of USAID, are notable for their successes, even if they have sometimes been modest. But taken as a whole, the uses of American soft power in the region both demonstrate its limitations and highlight the ways in which it enables the United States to constitute Central Asia as an object of geopolitical contestation.[16]

The purpose of this chapter is to examine the evolution of American soft power in Central Asia, from early hopes of fostering democracy and development, through the War on Terror and the abortive attempts to secure the Northern Distribution Network, and, ultimately, to the present-day state of confusion and disengagement that characterizes American policy toward the region.

EARLY OPTIMISM

When the former Soviet Republics of Central Asia became independent, the region suddenly transformed into "a new frontier for the policy of the United States."[17] According to Marlene Laruelle and Sebastien Peyrouse,

> Washington's long-term objectives in Central Asia were established at the beginning of the 1990s and have not changed significantly since then: avert the return of Russian domination, prevent the emergence of a new hegemonic power in the region (Iran or China), promote energy and strategic partnerships that turn the region toward South Asia or the West, and contribute to political and economic reforms.[18]

To this end, in 1992 Congress passed the Freedom for Russia and Emerging Eurasian Democracies and Markets (FREEDOM) Support Act.

The legislation highlighted a number of different areas in which the United States was prepared to offer assistance. Among them were humanitarian needs, democracy promotion, developing market institutions and free trade, food security, and education. In return, Central Asian governments would adopt democracy and the rule of law, implement free market systems, guarantee human rights, respect international law, and, tellingly, terminate all support for the Communist regime in Cuba.

Inducements, particularly in the sphere of sorely needed economic assistance, were thus offered to Central Asian regimes with the intent to co-opt and, ultimately, integrate them into the ideological and economic infrastructure of post–Cold War American hegemony. In short, soft power was the centerpiece of U.S. attempts to develop the sorts of "strategically compatible partners" in Central Asia that it was believed would underpin an era of American preeminence in world affairs. As Stephen Blank notes,

> [The] imbrication of today's liberal ideology of globalization, democratization and reform with the use of America's formidable instruments of power applies particularly to Central Asia. Strategic interests, energy access, the denial of a resurgent Russian empire and a value-laden international policy to promote democracy as the main goal appear in both the rhetoric and actuality of the USA's regional presence, *making it difficult to distinguish between the motives of policies towards and programs to aid Central Asian institutions.*[19]

And yet, in spite of these ambitions, and excepting the successful efforts to denuclearize Kazakhstan, the application of American soft power in Central Asia produced only modest results during the immediate post-Soviet period. Economic reforms were sluggish; political liberalization was almost nonexistent (outside of Kyrgyzstan); and the gulf between what the United States hoped to derive from its engagement in the region and how much local elites were willing to actually accommodate, was simply too great. Consequently, and perhaps unsurprisingly, American engagement in Central Asia remained relatively muted:

> There was far more show than substance in . . . early bilateral relationships. US foreign assistance to all five countries from FY1992 to FY2002 was less than $3 billion. . . . Spread thinly across more than a dozen categories, the United States offered the Central Asian states little more than symbolic help in meeting the tasks of economic, political and social restructuring.[20]

Ultimately, during this period Central Asia served chiefly as a symbol of American altruism, "important to the narrative of American foreign policy in Eurasia, but marginal in terms of the financial support and diplomatic energy that Washington . . . [actually] committed."[21]

AFGHANISTAN AND THE GLOBAL WAR ON TERROR

The destruction of the World Trade Center in 2001 was a pivotal moment in American policy toward Central Asia. Suddenly, the region was transformed in the minds of policymakers from an impoverished, peripheral post-Soviet backwater into a front line in the "Global War on Terror." Soon, this formerly "remote" corner of the map would become a crucial node in the "Northern Distribution Network" (NDN) that funneled supplies into Afghanistan. Deteriorating relations with Pakistan meant that the NDN increasingly became the preferred route for transporting material into Afghanistan:

> At the end of 2009, just 10 percent of cargos for US and ISAF forces in Afghanistan were moving through NDN. By the end of 2010, the NDN accounted for 30 percent of cargos; the United States was shipping 1,000 containers a week, with 98 percent of these shipments passing through Uzbekistan. By the end of 2011, US officials hope that the NDN percentage will have increased to 75 percent.[22]

In addition, the U.S. military began operating out of the Karshi-Khanabad ("K2") and Manas air bases, in Uzbekistan and Kyrgyzstan, respectively, and reached similar deals with Turkmenistan, Kazakhstan, and Tajikistan as well.[23] As the war in Afghanistan wore on and the situation in Pakistan became more parlous, "Afghanistan's northern neighbors . . . regained their forgotten place in the American security architecture for Afghanistan."[24]

Maintaining relationships with local governments, who were acutely aware of their sudden importance to the United States, however, was not always a straightforward proposition. More often than not, the exigencies of prosecuting the war in Afghanistan conflicted with broader goals related to fostering democratic institutions or promoting human rights. During this period, the U.S. government "tried to pursue a dual policy that promoted the strategic aims of the [Department of Defense] (access to the theater of conflict and 'stability' in Uzbekistan) while emphasizing that the cooperation would only be sustainable if Uzbekistan undertook political and economic reforms."[25] For the most part though, these expectations were not met. American-Uzbek relations cooled significantly in the wake of the May 2005 massacre of unarmed protesters by government troops in Andijan. Eventually, the Uzbek government ordered American troops to leave Karshi-Khanabad in response to U.S. criticism of the violence. The limits of American co-optive power were revealed when then president, Islam Karimov, appeared nonplussed in the face of threats that tens of millions of dollars of aid would be withheld if Uzbekistan did not consent to a full investigation of the Andijan massacre. Indeed, WikiLeaks cables reporting on U.S. negotiations with Karimov in the years following Andijan, revealed a president unconcerned about U.S. regard for his government, and harboring a strong distaste for "what he called American 'pressure and diktats' to reform."[26]

Meanwhile, the Manas airbase in Kyrgyzstan, which handled 98 percent of coalition forces destined for Afghanistan,[27] remained in operation until 2014. While President Askar Akaev was effusive in his praise for the U.S.-led "War on Terror,"[28] relations between the countries subsequently declined. Although the base was an important source of jobs for many Kyrgyzstani workers, it was also the subject of controversy. In part, this discontent was due to recurring allegations of corruption, but concerns about safety, complaints about noise and the jettisoning of fuel by American aircraft, and the killing of a contractor by an American serviceman also soured Kyrgyzstani attitudes toward the American presence. Neither offers by the United States to pay more for access to the base nor occasional charitable and goodwill measures like training Kyrgyzstani firefighters or donating money to programs providing heart surgery to Kyrgyzstani children were enough to prevent the base from being shuttered in 2014. Subsequently, operations were transferred to a base in Romania.

If courting local governments was an important, although ultimately doomed, part of American efforts in Afghanistan, then attempts to enhance American economic influence in Central Asia by linking Afghanistan's fortunes with that of the rest of the region were not met with much greater success. The "New Silk Road" initiative inaugurated by Secretary of State Hillary Clinton in 2011,[29] was envisioned as "a suite of joint investment projects and regional trade blocs that [would] have the potential to bring economic growth and stability to Central Asia."[30] According to Clinton, "Turkmen gas fields could help meet both Pakistan's and India's growing energy needs and provide significant transit revenues for both Afghanistan and Pakistan. Tajik cotton could be turned into Indian linens. Furniture and fruit from Afghanistan could find its way to the markets of Astana or Mumbai and beyond."[31] From the start, however, there were questions about the feasibility of the New Silk Road project. The relatively modest sums promised by the United States were not only insufficient considering the scope of the project's stated ambitions, but declined relative to the amount earmarked for military purposes. Moreover, the total amount of aid delivered to the Central Asian republics was less than 3 percent of what was spent in Afghanistan alone.[32] As early as 2013, the "centerpiece" of the New Silk Road initiative, the Turkmenistan-Afghanistan-Pakistan-India (TAPI) pipeline was "languish[ing] for lack of any financing," with the initiative itself derided as "merely a bureaucratic contrivance" on the part of the State Department.[33] Furthermore, as we will see, the attempt by the United States to usurp the legacy of the "Silk Road" alarmed policymakers in China, who viewed that mantle as their own.

DRAWDOWN AND NEGLECT

The closure of the Manas Transit Center coincided with a drawdown in the number of American troops committed to the Afghanistan theater, from a high of roughly 100,000 in 2010–2011 to about 8,400 in 2017.[34] The shuttering of the Manas air base also signaled a general disengagement by the United States from Central Asia.

> In contrast to both Russia and China, no senior US policymaker . . . during President Obama's second term even mentioned Central Asia, let alone traveled there to engage local governments on issues of mutual concern. This absence of high-level activity speaks volumes about the importance assigned to Central Asia and the Caucasus.[35]

The failure of the abortive "New Silk Road" initiative to gain traction, either within the region or among the U.S. policymakers ostensibly committed to implementing it, was a reflection both of Central Asia's diminishing importance in the U.S. security calculus and of a general sense that the region was simply not worth the effort. Indeed, there were by this time increasing signs of "fatigue with Central Asia—a remote region that was not willing to follow the model of economic and political transformation prescribed by Western advisers . . . hopes of transforming Central Asia into a zone of stability, democracy, and market-based prosperity were not taking root."[36] In other words, the idealistic pretensions of soft power were not bearing much fruit in Central Asia, where free markets, human rights, and democracy remained parlous indeed. Moreover, by 2010, trade with the United States comprised an insignificant proportion of the total trade of any of the Central Asian states,[37] well behind Russia, China, the European Union, Turkey, Iran, South Korea, and Ukraine, a sign of "minimal long-term US commitment in the region."[38]

Although the COVID-19 pandemic provided an opportunity for USAID to showcase its activities in Central Asia,[39] there are few signs that this policy of general disinterest and neglect is likely to shift in the near future. While the 2016 Republican Party platform called on the United States to "work toward the integration of the Central Asian republics into the global economy through foreign investment, which can bring with it market and political reforms and a firmer establishment of the rule of law,"[40] such refrains largely echoed America's position on the region since the early 1990s and have not been matched by much in the way of concrete action.

Indeed, the Trump administration's interest in Central Asia somewhat predictably focused on questions of terrorism and security.[41] Meanwhile, some conservative commentators[42] have curiously begun to view engagement with the Central Asian states, and Kazakhstan in particular, as a panacea for the seemingly intractable problem of Afghanistan:

> Regional players know the Afghan actors well, and have worked with some of them for decades. The Trump administration obviously recognizes this, and has been busy rebuilding and strengthening relationships with countries in the region. The countries of Central Asia, namely its largest and most developed ones, Kazakhstan and Uzbekistan, should be counted on to be engaged the most. They have the potential, the wherewithal, and the political will to engage, with some results to show for their involvement already.... In the tumultuous world, a long-lasting partnership with Kazakhstan and Uzbekistan in Central Asia will certainly help American security in Eurasia and Afghanistan.[43]

While such prescriptions are fanciful at best and evince little understanding of the region or its history, they are notable insofar as they represent a reiteration of the idea that co-optive power could be used to foster "strategically compatible partners" to shore up American interests in the world. Tellingly, however, instead of trying to base such partnerships on the appeal of democratic institutions and the lure of access to markets, the 2017 National Security Strategy (NSS) declares that the United States will "seek Central Asian states that are resilient against domination by rival powers, are resistant to becoming jihadist safe havens, and prioritize reforms."[44]

RUSSIA, CHINA, AND "SOFT" GEOPOLITICS

The United States, of course, is not alone in viewing Central Asia as a linchpin of its security strategy and governments there as potential partners in ensuring regional stability, developing energy resources, and upholding a particular geopolitical order. There is no space to describe all of the different players with a stake in Central Asian affairs, and Turkey, Iran, and India all deserve more consideration than can be devoted here. Instead, we will provide brief overviews of what are indisputably the two most important external actors in Central Asia, Russia and China, each of whom, for its own reasons, perceives the region as fundamental to its geopolitical ambitions and who both, like the United States, see themselves as engaged in competition for influence in the region.

Russia

For understandable reasons, Russia has in many respects the greatest capacity for employing soft power in Central Asia. Centuries of tsarist and Soviet domination mean that historical, political, and cultural ties between the region and the former imperial center persist. Moreover, Russia "understands very well the importance of Central Asia for itself and for the world as a whole,"[45] with its primary concerns being the development of energy resources and the perceived threat posed by terrorism and religious extremism to regional stability. In this respect, then, Russia's interests in Central Asia do not diverge significantly from those of the United States.[46]

Russia enjoys certain advantages, however, that the United States does not. "People-to-people relation is a key component of Russia's influence" in Central Asia,[47] and various Soviet cultural and institutional legacies persist. As Andrei Tsygankov points, "Russian mass media, a large and efficient economy, familiar language and religion, aspects of historical legacy, family ties, and electronic products" all form elements of Russian soft power in Central Asia.[48] First and foremost, however, is the continued widespread use of the Russian language. The status of Russian has declined dramatically since independence, an effect both of the out-migration of ethnic Russians and of official efforts to promote titular languages (and, in some cases, to abandon the Cyrillic alphabet altogether).[49] But Russian remains the most commonly spoken second language in Central Asia, and continues its previous function as a *lingua franca*, both within the region and with citizens of other states that were formerly part of the Soviet Union.[50] These advantages have not been lost on Russian policymakers, who argue that "the Russian language, Russian culture, and the Russian information space should be viewed as being of comparable importance to economic or political-military instruments for the realization of Russian interests."[51]

At the same time, however, the geopolitics of the Russian language can be a double-edged sword. In May 2020 Uzbekistan's Ministry of Justice proposed a draft law mandating the use of Uzbek, rather than Russian, by all state bureaus, a move that elicited criticism from Russia. As Farkhod Tolipov has argued:

> Political experts often use terms such as "soft power" and "hard power" to describe political tools at the disposal of great powers in order to promote their interests in and exert influence on other countries. However, there are situations when soft power is utilized for hard goals, blurring the separation line between the two terms. [Russian Ministry of Foreign Affairs spokesperson Maria] Zakharova's statement discredits Russia's genuine soft power by substituting it with an artificial surrogate. Whereas she mentioned the "spirit of history, time and quality of bilateral relations," her statement rather echoed the spirit of neo-Imperialism.[52]

Moscow's sensitivity toward what it perceives as anti-Russian resentment in former Soviet Republics has manifested in alarm over the "color revolutions" in Georgia, Ukraine, and Kyrgyzstan, as well as by the "Arab Spring," all of which the Russian government views as "the result of a deliberate policy to use democracy promotion to expand the US sphere of influence," with the ultimate goal being to foment regime change in Moscow.[53] Such beliefs spurred the development of a variety of soft power instruments, not the least of which are news networks such as RT (formerly Russia Today) and Sputnik. These networks, and others like them, promote a Russian viewpoint on world affairs. Their task is made easier by the fact that, for Central Asian audiences, their programming is often more appealing than local television, "a welcome antidote to bland home-produced offerings."[54]

Peter Rutland and Andrei Kazantsev have argued that Russian military interventions in Georgia and Ukraine reveal the limits of Russian soft power, which they declare to be little more than a "handmaiden to Russia's hard power."[55] Joseph Nye, meanwhile, has declared that neither Russia nor China truly "get" soft power.[56] Such assessments, however, appear somewhat off the mark, and Russian soft power has played an important role in shaping the geopolitical landscape in Central Asia, especially vis-à-vis the United States.

For example, in the aftermath of the Soviet collapse, U.S. Peace Corps operations were opened across Eastern Europe, Central Asia, and even Russia itself. The Peace Corps, of course, "has been one of the most effective forms of American soft power since it was created by John F. Kennedy almost 50 years ago."[57] This fact was undoubtedly considered by President George H. W. Bush, who remarked in 1990, to the first group of volunteers bound for Hungary and Poland: "It is as if the Peace Corps has been in training for this historical moment. It shows our mission, our desire for peace, knows no political or geographical bounds."[58] By 1993, Peace Corps volunteers were teaching English, developing communities, assisting in health programs, and, implicitly, embodying and spreading American values, in four of the five Central Asian countries. The sole exception was Tajikistan, which was at the time embroiled in civil war.

The activities of Peace Corps volunteers in Central Asia continued until 2005, when Uzbekistan banned the program; Turkmenistan followed suit with a capricious drawdown from 2009 to 2012. And after an eighteen-year tenure in Kazakhstan, Peace Corps ceased operations there in 2011. Echoing Russia, which had banned the Peace Corps some ten years prior, the Kazakhstani government contended that the state had reached a level of development where such a program was no longer necessary. Rumors nevertheless abound that Kazakhstan's security services harbored fear that Peace Corps volunteers were engaged in espionage. Today only the Kyrgyz Republic retains a Peace Corps presence.

The belief that Peace Corps might serve as a smokescreen for spying has been actively fomented by Russia and Russian-language media; on the whole,

"Russia promotes a skeptical view of NGOs and civil society organization. Russia considers Peace Corps volunteers to be spies. . . . These views are repeated in Russian media, frequently consumed in Central Asia."[59] Moreover, both Kazakhstan and Kyrgyzstan have either implemented or considered legislation that mimics Russia's 'Foreign Agents' law, which make it more difficult for NGOs receiving foreign funding to operate."[60]

Ironically, Russia itself launched a program in 2018 to send teachers to Tajikistan. Although the program is modest at this point—only twenty-eight teachers are involved thus far—it is nevertheless envisioned as the first step in providing a Russian alternative to the American-backed Peace Corps: "Authorities in Russia make no secret that assistance exercises like these are potentially valuable tools in the country's soft power armory, similar in some ways to the US-funded Peace Corps volunteer program."[61] The strategy seems to be bearing fruit: in January 2020 the Tajik Parliament approved a plan to construct five new Russian-language schools in the country, funded by the Russian government, a decision that reflects "the Tajik authorities' willingness to maintain close ties with Moscow and reflects a growing demand among Tajiks for Russian language education."[62]

Beyond their role in raising suspicions about Peace Corps and other NGOs, Russian-language media have produced real dividends in other arenas as well. As James Nixey points out, by 2010, "although Russia played no direct role in Kyrgyzstan's violence in April and June of that year, the Kremlin was disenchanted enough with President Kurmanbek Bakiyev and his government's policies to do something about it. . . . Russian TV broadcasts in Kyrgyzstan and online news sites produced hard-hitting pieces about top-level corruption. These often truthful (if selective) exposés helped prepare the ground for Bakiyev's end."[63]

Russian media also "whipped up anti-American sentiment to push for the closure of the US airbase at Manas,"[64] and public opinion surrounding the base, already sharply divided, became even more polarized. The increasingly negative mood on the part of the public, as well as Russian promises to write off hundreds of millions of dollars of Kyrgyz debt, its delivery of a large military aid package, and a further pledge to finance crucial hydropower projects, spelled the end for the American Transit Center at Manas, which closed in July 2014.[65] At the same time, Russia's lease on its airbase at Kant, just 35 kilometers (about 20 miles) from the American base at Manas, will remain in operation until at least 2027.

The closure of the Manas base also points to another important aspect of Russian soft power in Central Asia: namely, its economic ties with the region. While the Russian economy cannot compare in size with that of China, its importance to Central Asia is nevertheless substantial. Russia cannot compete with China as a trading partner, but as the Manas Transit Center controversy illustrates, promises (not always kept) to provide various forms of economic and military aid have can be effective levers for achieving foreign policy goals.

It is also worth noting the importance of labor migration and remittances as tools of Russian soft power in Central Asia. Around two million migrants from Central Asia, most from Tajikistan, Uzbekistan, and Kyrgyzstan, live and work in Russia.[66] Remittances from these workers, most of whom are unskilled and working in sectors like construction, are substantial: in 2011 the figures amounted to 2.7 billion USD to Tajikistan, 1.4 billion USD to Kyrgyzstan, 4.9 billion USD to Uzbekistan, with rather less going to Kazakhstan and Turkmenistan.[67] While conditions for these migrants are frequently deplorable, and their existence often parlous at best, the personal and economic networks facilitated by migrant labor to Russia nevertheless ensure that the Central Asian states remain in Moscow's orbit, at least to a certain extent. Bilateral agreements between Russia and countries such as Kyrgyzstan and Tajikistan have attempted (arguably with limited success) to regularize migration and employment procedures and to provide labor migrants with at least some protections and guarantees.[68]

Compared to the United States, Russia's relationship with Central Asia has a number of added complexities, not the least of which is a history of imperial domination and exploitation. At the same time, however, this history means that there is a certain degree of cultural familiarity, enabled by pervasive knowledge of the Russian language, as well as abiding political and economic relationships from the tsarist and Soviet periods, that continue to structure the geopolitical landscape in Central Asia in Russia's favor. Ultimately, "Central Asian societies continue to view the world through the Russian prism, regarded as a more familiar 'West' than the more foreign Western Europe or the United States."[69] From Moscow's perspective, on the other hand, Central Asia remains an unequal partner, one that it does not seek to control outright, but rather to keep firmly within its orbit: "Russia cannot be denied its own political, military, and economic interests in the post-Soviet world, and Moscow's policies can be interpreted as an effort to preserve existing influence in the region for the purpose of greater stabilization, rather than imperial control."[70]

China

In recent years, China has emerged as a key player in Central Asia. According to Niklas Swanström, "It is evident that Central Asia is a key concern of Chinese foreign policy, following closely behind other fundamental issues such as Taiwan and the 'one-China' principle."[71] Indeed, "Beijing has developed a prioritized policy orientation towards Central Asia, in contrast to the

American policy, which seems to have a much more reluctant *ad hoc* presence based on the war against terrorism."[72]

Much as in the cases of the United States and Russia, China's interest in Central Asia is partly motivated by security concerns. In particular, Beijing is preoccupied with ongoing discontent among its sizable Uyghur minority, which shares a myriad of cultural, linguistic, and historical ties with Central Asia and is clustered in Xinjiang, which borders on Kazakhstan, Kyrgyzstan, and Tajikistan. But much of Beijing's new influence in Central Asia has been driven by economic development. Between 1992 and 2007, trade between the Central Asian states and China increased from 531 million USD to more than 6 billion USD.[73] By 2011 these figures had risen to nearly 29 billion USD, with China being the second largest trading partner for all of the Central Asian republics save Kyrgyzstan, for whom it was the largest.[74] By contrast, American trade with Central Asia as a whole has witnessed steep declines and is likely to remain mired in the "doldrums" for the foreseeable future; distance, lack of access, and diminishing interest hamper Washington's ability to compete economically with China in the region.[75]

One reason for this, of course, has been the ongoing implementation of China's Belt and Road Initiative (BRI), which, symbolically, was unveiled by Xi Jinping during a visit to Kazakhstan in 2013.[76] BRI seeks to foster greater integration between China, Eurasia, East and Southeast Asia, and Africa. Despite the fact that the trade routes are net losers,[77] trade competition with the United States at the global level has induced China to "minimize possible risks of American pressure on China. The country can hardly challenge American sea dominance in the foreseeable future, so it needs to develop alternative routes for natural resource imports and commercial goods exports that can't be controlled by the United States."[78] As a result, "it is China, not the USA or Russia, that has begun to fill the dearth of consumption goods and provisions in Central Asia."[79] China has invested heavily in infrastructure in the region as well, a powerful inducement for cash-strapped Central Asian economies.

The BRI thus stands as a direct competitor both to Russia's ambitions to foster a subtle neocolonial relationship with Central Asia, as well as to the United States' faltering "New Silk Road" initiative. In fact, BRI was articulated as a response to the "New Silk Road": "Chinese policymakers felt historic ownership of the Silk Road . . . [and were] flummoxed to find that Hillary Clinton used the term Silk Road to describe a US policy." According to one Chinese diplomat, "when [the] US initiated this we were devastated. We had long sleepless nights. And after two years, President Xi proposed [a] strategic vision of our new concept of Silk Road."[80] Central Asia, in this way, has been drawn, somewhat indirectly, into a global contest for economic and political primacy between China and the United States.

Some observers have interpreted China's growing involvement in Central Asia in terms of "a new version of classical vassal relations";[81] however this seems unlikely. Rather, Chinese influence in Central Asia, like that of Russia and the United States, can best be understood through the lens of soft power. That is, it is not so much that China seeks to dominate Central Asia, but rather, as in the cases of the United States and Russia, seeks to co-opt regional players, through economic, cultural, and other inducements, into accepting its own geopolitical *Weltanschauung*. This, then, is entirely consistent with China's strategic realignment under Xi Jinping, which has been characterized by the "purposeful and even assertive pursuit of China's national interests whilst vigorously seeking to maintain a peaceful external environment."[82]

Jian Zhang argues that "Chinese foreign policy has been so far largely dependent on economic diplomacy; using economic ties to enhance political and strategic relations. The country neither possesses the much-needed soft power that can shape and influence norms of international politics, nor does it have sufficient strategic capabilities to be a credible security provider in the region."[83] Arguably, however, this misses the point, since China's no-strings-attached economic inducements are often more attractive than those proffered by the United States, which often come freighted with cumbersome stipulations. "U.S. and European soft-power efforts are focused on democracy promotion and encouraging good governance abroad, while China's engagement involves lucrative trade and energy deals and produces tangible results like newly-built roads, hospitals, and schools."[84]

While China has a long way to go before the majority of Central Asians "view the world through a Chinese prism" (an objective, perhaps, of the numerous Confucius Institutes now operating throughout Central Asia), it is clear that Beijing is attempting to articulate a new narrative for itself in the region. By claiming the mantle of the Silk Road—and thereby preempting the United States' attempt to do the same—this narrative seems to emphasize a shared history of commerce and interconnection and a future characterized by mutually beneficial interconnectedness, albeit with China as the senior partner.

SOFT POWER AND THE PERPETUAL "GREAT GAME"

Both Russia and China, then, have intervened in their own ways in Central Asia. The former has leveraged its vestigial cultural, linguistic, economic, and political ties to the region, while the latter presents itself as a wealthier, more dynamic, and potentially more fruitful partner than Moscow. Both, meanwhile, seek to undermine American influence in Central Asia. However, as Alexander Cooley notes that:

Though it will disappoint some, the record suggests that there have been no real "losers" in the new "Great Game." In part, this has been the result of Washington, Moscow, and Beijing pursuing strategic goals that were mostly non-exclusive; but it has also been a function of these powers adjusting their strategies to more successfully play by the region's local rules. In this sense, the "Big Three" have also converged into supporting the Central Asian regimes and their local practices in order to secure cooperation and access.[85]

This analysis is undoubtedly correct, and despite occasional dramatic moments like the closure of the U.S. Transit Center at Manas Airport, the tenor of the putative "new Great Game" in Central Asia has for the most part been characterized by understated maneuvering for influence—political, economic, ideological, and cultural. Such maneuvering, furthermore, may be intended to undermine the sway of rival powers, but is not necessarily meant to expel them outright.

And so, despite the more genteel pretensions of the idea of soft power, in the final analysis we must admit that, to a significant degree, it represents a muted restatement of a rather traditional sort of "Great Power politics" in the heart of Eurasia. According to a recent report by the Carnegie Foundation, "the United States explicitly rejected the geopolitical approach to Central Asia, and instead embarked upon a long-term effort to support the creation of democratic governance, free-market economies, and regional economic integration."[86] But as we have seen, these objectives have been approached haphazardly and inconsistently at best. More importantly, they are largely indistinguishable from a "geopolitical approach" driven by the mobilization of co-optive, rather than coercive, power.

This should not be surprising, since the ghosts of the old "Great Game" have haunted American visions of Central Asia almost since the collapse of the Soviet Union. Former Deputy Secretary of State Strobe Talbott bid his symbolic "farewell to Flashman"[87] while musing that "it has been fashionable to proclaim, or at least to predict, a replay of the 'Great Game' in the Caucasus and Central Asia. The implication, of course, is that the driving dynamic of the region, fueled and lubricated by oil, will be the competition of the great powers to the disadvantage of the people who live there."[88]

At the same time, Talbott essentially outlined the contours of a new kind of struggle in Central Asia, one in which the world's sole superpower would vouchsafe from afar the independence of the region's newly sovereign states. If "integration" was to be "[o]ne of the watchwords of our dialogue with Russia," then it nevertheless must be integration of the right sort: "as long as Russia stays on a path of reform, *including in the way it conducts its relations with its neighbors*, and that means the way it defines integration in the context of the CIS," then the "doors and benefits" of international institutions would be open to it.[89] But he also noted that "Russia's leaders in the past seemed capable of feeling secure, strong, and proud only if others felt weak, insecure and humiliated," and warned that if "the largest member [of the Commonwealth of Independent States] tries to make 'commonwealth' into a euphemism for domination of its neighbors—then the CIS will deserve to join that other set of initials, USSR on the ash heap of history." Thus, it would be necessary for American "presence and influence" in Central Asia to constitute a force for the "right" kind of integration.[90]

The strategic priorities that have driven American involvement in Central Asia have evolved over the past two decades, but certain patterns can be detected. Early dreams of fostering liberal democracy and free markets, the rule of law, and human rights, were in part motivated by the hope that the disintegration of the Soviet Union would provide an opportunity to integrate Central Asia into the American-led neoliberal global economy. These hopes began to fade by the end of the 1990s, but were replaced by growing fears of Russian revanchism.[91] The onset of the "War on Terror" gave pretext for further engagement, though of a different sort, as the region's proximity to Afghanistan made it an attractive logistical alternative to Pakistan. But as the war in Afghanistan has entered a new, and perhaps more static, phase, and as relationships with partners such as Uzbekistan and Kyrgyzstan have soured, the objectives of American soft power in Central Asia have shifted once again. Today, while free markets, human rights, and democracy are paid lip service, what limited attention is devoted to Central Asia is largely focused on matters of counterterrorism, security, and, to a lesser extent, economic development.

Nevertheless, through all of the changes in American policy toward Central Asia, one theme that has remained constant has been the emphasis on preserving the sovereignty and independence of the Central Asian states, which is envisioned as a means of checking Russian and Chinese ambitions in the region.[92] It is no accident that American aid to Central Asia increased dramatically after the 1993 shelling of Russia's parliament, which convinced many in U.S. foreign policy circles that there was a real danger nascent of Russian democracy giving way to authoritarian habits. Prefiguring Talbott's abortive farewell to Flashman, one study by the Hudson Institute warned that "Central Asia and the Transcaucasus were coming under a new Russian hegemony, if not yet imperial control, by late 1994."[93] From this perspective, the mobilization of American soft power in Central Asia implicates the United States in a sort of twilight struggle to achieve not dominance, but rather to produce a kind of geopolitical lacuna in which the states of the region will function as a bulwark against both Islamic extremism and the anticipated expansionism of their Chinese and Russian neighbors.

Thus, reports of the May 2018 meeting between U.S. President Donald Trump and Uzbek President Shavkat Mirziyoyev in Washington noted that the event was "a chance to shore up relations with a strategically located country that is courted by China and Russia and was once a key staging area for US operations in neighboring Afghanistan."[94] While human rights groups pressed the White House to insist that Uzbekistan address long-standing abuses,[95] it was ultimately the "sizable delegation of officials and business leaders, who reportedly intend[ed] to sign around 4 billion USD of contracts and business deals with US companies," as well as the reputed purchase of American weapons for "combatting terrorism," that occupied center stage during the visit.[96]

This move comes at a time when, "after being dismissed as a phenomenon of an earlier century, great power competition [has] returned. China and Russia [have begun] to reassert their influence regionally and globally . . . . In short, they are contesting our geopolitical advantages and trying to change the international order in their favor."[97] Decrying the "mercantilism" of its rivals, the United States seeks to "encourage aspiring partners" with traditional soft power inducements like free trade, coupled with "a development model that partners with countries that want progress, consistent with their culture, based on free market principles, fair and reciprocal trade, private sector activity, and rule of law."[98] In short, then, the 2017 NSS envisions American economic and cultural soft power as a way of checking Chinese influence, which comes "at the expense of the sovereignty of others," and Russian ambition, which "creates an unstable frontier in Eurasia."[99]

CONCLUSION

Of course, much more could be written of Central Asia's subjection to soft power in the form of economic leverage, media exposure, and cultural connections. For example, the United States, like Russia and China, has exercised both the provision and withholding of government-to-government aid, as well as the facilitation or impediment of foreign direct investment from the private sector. More abstract has been the demonstration of respect or disrespect that attends membership—or its refusal—in various international organizations. While some Central Asian regimes are relatively unconcerned with their international reputations (e.g., Turkmenistan), others aspire to liberal-democratic, "green," and "McDonald's-worthy" status.

Today, of course, the American presence in Central Asia continues to be presented in altruistic terms, with emphasis put on the medical, educational, disability, and environmental efforts channeled through governmental and nongovernmental entities. But the notion that the United States will be the "arbiter" of Eurasia's future, as Brzezinski imagined, or that "sustained and directed American involvement" in Central Asia is a prerequisite for stability, seems fanciful. This is especially clear in light of a 2020 survey of Kazakhs that reveals that far greater numbers desire increased ties with Russia and China than with the United States. Indeed, almost 65 percent of Kazakhs surveyed indicated that they want *less* American presence in their country.[100]

The problem with soft power is that it is, in the end, soft; unlike tanks, bombers, and infantry divisions, soft power is sometimes both hard to detect and easy to exaggerate. It is difficult to even begin to assess the degree to which the putative universalism of American culture, the attractiveness of which is often taken for granted, actually affords a measure of influence that can reliably circumvent governments and speak directly to the masses—or the extent to which that even matters. As the example of China suggests, the availability of American consumer products and popular culture does not necessarily mean that countries will automatically gravitate toward the American worldview.

Indeed, as Kathleen Collins argues, "Central Asian regimes and their populations are increasingly convinced that the US presence is the region was short-term and self-serving, while Russia and China remain for the long haul."[101] In all likelihood, they are not wrong. American involvement in Central Asia since the end of the Cold War has evolved in fits and starts, and, apart from the desire to check Russian and Chinese ambitions, has largely been guided by contingency. The United States is not likely to abandon the region entirely, since the perceived necessity of shoring up the Central Asian states against the constant specter of terrorism is reason enough to keep at least a modicum of attention among American policymakers. However, cost, distance, and persistent lack of expertise on the region mean that American thinking on Central Asia will be distorted by Afghanistan for the foreseeable future.[102]

Consequently, what often recedes from the foreground is any sense of geopolitical subjectivity on the part of the Central Asian states themselves: from a policy standpoint the region continues to be understood as a marginal place where outside powers vie among one another for influence with regional clients. But as Paul Goble has noted, tentative steps toward increasing cooperation between regional powers is indicative of the reality that Central Asia is no longer—and never was—merely a zone of contestation between "Great Powers." While Goble concedes that it is "unlikely that any of the five Central Asian regimes can break away cleanly from [Russia, China, or the United States] anytime soon: geography, history and culture work against that," he also notes that cooperation between them nevertheless "means that there will increasingly be a new player on the board in this region, one Moscow, Beijing and Washington will all have to take into consideration."[103] Similarly,

S. Frederick Starr and Svante Cornell argue that there is "little doubt that the current reforms [in Uzbekistan] are all organized around solid commitment to the rule of law, the rights of citizens, elective governance, an open market economy, religious tolerance, cordial relations with the great powers without sacrificing sovereignty, and a new embrace of the Central Asian region itself as an actor on the world state."[104]

Ultimately, the perception that a "new Great Game" is indeed playing out in Central Asia between Russia, China, and the United States is predicated on the idea that soft power initiatives like BRI or the American "New Silk Road" actually constitute deliberate moves on a "Grand Chessboard." Correct or not, such perceptions have an agency of their own, and the widespread view that there is indeed a "new Great Game" has unfortunately coalesced into something more palpable. The 2017 National Security Strategy, with its tough language on Russia and China, its pledges to help the Central Asian states defend their sovereignty against their more powerful neighbors, and its bromides about spreading American values, is an example of how soft power, far from merely co-opting new partners, recapitulates the very geopolitical contestation that it supposedly repudiates.

NOTES

1. Zbigniew Brzezinski, *The Grand Chessboard: American Primacy and Its Geostrategic Imperatives* (New York: Basic Books, 1997), 135–36, emphasis added.
2. Ibid., 139.
3. Ibid., 194.
4. Ibid., 195.
5. Ibid., 198.
6. Gerard Toal [Gearóid Ó Tuathail], "New World Order Geopolitics: Introduction," in *The Geopolitics Reader*, ed. Gearóid Ó Tuathail, Simon Dalby, and Paul Routledge (London: Routledge, 1998), 103.
7. Francis Fukuyama, *The End of History and the Last Man* (New York: Free Press, 1992).
8. Brzezinski, *The Grand Chessboard*, 198.
9. Joseph S. Nye Jr., *Bound to Lead: The Changing Nature of American Power* (New York: Basic Books, 1990).
10. Reed Livergood, "Afghanistan Conundrum: Logistical Support Options after the Manas Air Base Closing," *American Diplomacy*, May 2009, http://www.unc.edu/depts/diplomat/item/2009/0406/comm/livergood_afghanistan.html; Jim Nichol, "Uzbekistan's Closure of the Airbase at Karshi-Khanabad: Context and Implications," (report, CRS Report for Congress, Washington DC, January 11, 2006).
11. Joshua Kurlantzick, "China's Charm: Implications of Chinese Soft Power," (report, Carnegie Endowment for International Peace, June 5, 2006), 47.
12. Nye, *Bound to Lead,* 31–32.

13. Andrew North, "'We'll Cut Off Your Head': Open Season for LGBT Attacks in Kyrgyzstan," *The Guardian*, May 4, 2016, https://www.theguardian.com/world/2016/may/04/kyrgyzstan-lgbt-community-fear-attacks-russia.

14. Gerard Toal [Gearóid Ó Tuathail], *Critical Geopolitics: The Politics of Writing Global Space* (Minneapolis: University of Minnesota Press, 1996), 1.

15. See "American Corners," *U.S. Embassy in the Kyrgyz Republic*, https://kg.usembassy.gov/education-culture/american-corners/ (accessed May 27, 2018); Paul Rockower, "This American Corner," (Blog) *USC Center on Public Diplomacy*, April 15, 2013, https://www.uscpublicdiplomacy.org/blog/american-corner.

16. Alexander Diener, and Nick Megoran, "Central Asia as Place," in *Central Asia: Contests for Understanding*, ed. David Montgomery (Pittsburgh: University of Pittsburgh Press, forthcoming).

17. Stephen Blank, "The United States and Central Asia," in *Central Asian Security: The New International Context*, ed. Roy Allison and Lena Jonson (Washington, DC: Brookings Institution Press, 2001), 151.

18. Marlene Laruelle, and Sebastien Peyrouse, *Globalizing Central Asia: Geopolitics and the Challenges of Economic Development* (Armonk: M. E. Sharpe, 2013), 43.

19. Blank, "The United States and Central Asia," 128, emphasis added.

20. Martha Brill Olcott, *Central Asia's Second Chance* (Washington, DC: Carnegie Endowment for International Peace, 2005), 67.

21. Laruelle and Peyrouse, *Globalizing Central Asia*, 43.

22. Alexander Cooley, *Great Games, Local Rules: The New Great Power Contest in Central Asia* (New York: Oxford University Press, 2012), 45.

23. Ibid., 32.

24. Laruelle and Peyrouse, *Globalizing Central Asia*, 49.

25. Lora Lumpe, "A Timeline of U.S. Military Aid Cooperation with Uzbekistan," (occasional paper series, Open Society Foundations, Central Eurasia Project, October 2010), https://www.opensocietyfoundations.org/publications/timeline-us-military-aid-cooperation-uzbekistan#publications_download, 4.

26. Joshua Kucera, "America's Uzbekistan Problem," *The New York Times*, December 28, 2011, https://www.nytimes.com/2011/12/29/opinion/americas-uzbekistan-problem.html.

27. Olga Dzyubenko, "U.S. Vacates Base in Central Asia as Russia's Clout Rises," *Reuters*, June 4, 2014, https://www.reuters.com/article/us-kyrgyzstan-usa-manas/u-s-vacates-base-in-central-asia-as-russias-clout-rises-idUSKBN0EE1LH20140603.

28. Askar Akaev, *Kyrgyz Statehood and the National Epos "Manas,"* (New York: Global Scholarly Publications, 2003).

29. Joshua Kucera, "Clinton's Dubious Plan to Save Afghanistan with a 'New Silk Road'," *The Atlantic*, November 2, 2011, https://www.theatlantic.com/international/archive/2011/11/clintons-dubious-plan-to-save-afghanistan-with-a-new-silk-road/247760/.

30. James McBride, "Building the New Silk Road," *Council on Foreign Relations*, May 22, 2015, https://www.cfr.org/backgrounder/building-new-silk-road.

31. Hillary Clinton, "Remarks at New Silk Road Ministerial Meeeting," *U.S. State Department Archived Content*, September 22, 2011, https://2009-2017.state.gov/secretary/20092013clinton/rm/2011/09/173807.htm.

32. Stephen Blank, "Whither the New Silk Road and US Central Asia Policy?" *The Central Asia and Caucasus Analyst*, March 8, 2013, http://www.css.ethz.ch/en/services/digital-library/articles/article.html/161006.

33. Stephen Blank, "AWOL: U.S. Policy in Central Asia," *The Central Asia and Caucasus Analyst*, October 30, 2013, https://www.cacianalyst.org/publications/analytical-articles/item/12848-awol-us-policy-in-central-asia.html.

34. Andrew Rafferty, "The War in Afghanistan: By the Numbers," *NBC News*, August 22, 2017, https://www.nbcnews.com/politics/politics-news/war-afghanistan-numbers-n794626.

35. Blank, "AWOL."

36. Eugene Rumer, Richard Sokolsky, and Paul Stronski, *U.S. Policy Toward Central Asia 3.0* (Washington DC: Carnegie Endowment for International Peace, 2016), 15.

37. The highest number was for Kazakhstan, at 3.3 percent. Trade with the U.S. made up 2.5 percent of Tajikistan's trade total, while the numbers for Kyrgyzstan, Turkmenistan, and Uzbekistan were 1.1 percent, 1 percent, and 1.2 percent respectively. See Laruelle and Peyrouse, *Globalizing Central Asia*, 53.

38. Ibid.

39. See for example "The United States Supports Uzbekistan's Efforts to Combat COVID-19," *USAID*, June 7, 2020, https://www.usaid.gov/uzbekistan/press-releases/jun-7-2020-united-states-supports-uzbekistan-efforts-covid-19

40. See Republican Platform 2016, available at https://prod-static-ngop-pbl.s3.amazonaws.com/media/documents/DRAFT_12_FINAL%5B1%5D-ben_1468872234.pdf (accessed May 20, 2018).

41. Paul Stronski, "Uncertain Continuity: Central Asia and the Trump Administration," *Carnegie Endowment for International Peace*, July 27, 2017, https://carnegieendowment.org/2017/07/27/uncertain-continuity-central-asia-and-trump-administration-pub-72677.

42. For example, Luke Coffey, "Why Trump's Meeting with Kazakhstan's President was so Important," *The Heritage Foundation*, January 17, 2018, https://www.heritage.org/asia/commentary/why-trumps-meeting-kazakhstan-president-was-so-important; L. Todd Wood, "Central Asia can Aid U.S. National Security," *The Washington Times*, October 18, 2017, https://www.washingtontimes.com/news/2017/oct/18/central-asian-global-security-forefront/.

43. Wood, "Central Asia Can Aid U.S. National Security."

44. "National Security Strategy of the United States of America," *The White House*, December 18, 2017, https://www.whitehouse.gov/wp-content/uploads/2017/12/NSS-Final-12-18-2017-0905-2.pdf.

45. Marina Lebedeva, "'Soft Power' in Central Asia: Participants and their Actions," *Vestnik MGIMO-University* 35, no. 2 (2014): 49.

46. Fiona Hill, "The United States and Russia in Central Asia: Uzbekistan, Tajikistan, Afghanistan, Pakistan, and Iran," *Brookings*, August 15, 2002, https://

www.brookings.edu/on-the-record/the-united-states-and-russia-in-central-asia-uzbekistan-tajikistan-afghanistan-pakistan-and-iran/.

47. Laruelle and Peyrouse, *Globalizing Central Asia*, 20.

48. Andrei P. Tsygankov, "If Not by Tanks, Then by Banks? The Role of Soft Power in Putin's Foreign Policy," *Europe-Asia Studies* 58, no. 7 (2006): 1079.

49. Aneta Pavlenko, "Multilingualism in Post-Soviet Countries: Language Revival, Language Removal, and Sociolinguistic Theory," *The International Journal of Bilingual Education and Bilingualism* 11, no. 3 and 4 (2008): 275–314.

50. Aneta Pavlenko, "Russian as a Lingua Franca," *Annual Review of Applied Linguistics* 26 (2008): 77–99.

51. Lebedeva, "'Soft Power' in Central Asia," 49.

52. Farkhod Tolipov, "Hard or Soft Power? Russia Reacts to Uzbekistan's Draft Language Policy," *CACI Analyst*, June 08, 2020, http://cacianalyst.org/publications/analytical-articles/item/13623-soft-or-hard-power?-russia-reacts-to-uzbekistans-draft-language-policy.html.

53. Peter Rutland and Andrei Kazantsev, "The Limits of Russia's 'Soft Power'," *Journal of Political Power* 9, no. 3 (2016): 396.

54. James Nixey, "The Long Goodbye: Waning Russian Influence in the South Caucasus and Central Asia," (briefing paper, Chatham House, London, June 1, 2012) https://www.chathamhouse.org/publications/papers/view/184065, 14.

55. Rutland and Kazantsev, "The Limits of Russia's 'Soft Power'," 396.

56. Joseph S. Nye Jr., "What China and Russia don't get about Soft Power," *Foreign Policy*, April 29, 2013, https://foreignpolicy.com/2013/04/29/what-china-and-russia-dont-get-about-soft-power/.

57. Kevin F. F. Quigley, and Lex Rieffel, "Ten Times the Peace Corps: A Smart Investment in Soft Power," *Brookings*, September 5, 2008, https://www.brookings.edu/research/ten-times-the-peace-corps-a-smart-investment-in-soft-power/.

58. "Remarks at a White House Ceremony Marking the Entry of the Peace Corps into Central Europe," *The American Presidency Project*, June 15, 1990, http://www.presidency.ucsb.edu/ws/index.php?pid=18600.

59. Ryan P. McCarthy, "The Peace Corps' Declining Role in Central Asia," *The Diplomat*, October 29, 2015, https://thediplomat.com/2015/10/the-peace-corps-declining-role-in-central-asia.

60. Anna Lelik, "Kyrgyzstan: Foreign Agents Bill Nixed, NGOs Rejoice," *Eurasianet*, May 12, 2016, https://eurasianet.org/kyrgyzstan-foreign-agent-bill-nixed-ngos-rejoice; Joanna Lillis, "Kazakhstan: NGO Law Approved Amid Civil Society Resistance," *Eurasianet*, December 2, 2015, https://eurasianet.org/kazakhstan-ngo-law-approved-amid-civil-society-resistance.

61. "Russia Deploys Teachers to Tajikistan on Goodwill Mission," *Eurasianet*, April 27, 2018, https://eurasianet.org/russia-deploys-teachers-to-tajikistan-on-goodwill-mission.

62. Farangis Najibullah, "No Shortage of Students as Tajikistan Builds New Russian Schools," *Radio Free Europe/Radio Liberty*, January 18, 2020, https://www.rferl.org/a/tajikistan-new-russian-schools/30384557.html

63. Nixey, "The Long Goodbye," 9.

64. Ibid., 14.

65. Erica Marat, "Kyrgyzstan's Decision to Renounce Manas Transit Center Favors Russia," *The Central Asia-Caucasus Analyst*, June 26, 2013, https://www.cacianalyst.org/publications/analytical-articles/item/12764-kyrgyzstans-decision-to-renounce-manas-transit-center-favors-russia.html.

66. Marlene Laruelle, "Central Asian Labor Migrants in Russia: The 'Diasporization' of the Central Asian States?" *China and Eurasia Forum Quarterly* 5, no. 3 (2007): 105.

67. V. V. Naumkin et al., "Russia's Interests in Central Asia: Contents, Perspectives, Limitations," (report, Russian International Affairs Council, June 25, 2013), 24.

68. Sergei V. Ryazantsev, Norio Horie, and Kazuhiro Kumo, "Migrant Workers from Central Asia into the Russian Federation," in *Sociology, Economics and Politics of Central Asian Migrants in Russia*, ed. Kazuhiro Kumo, S Norio Horie, and Sergei V. Ryazantsev (discussion paper, Institute of Economic Research, Hitotsubashi University, Tokyo, 2011).

69. Laruelle and Peyrouse, *Globalizing Central Asia*, 20.

70. Tsygankov, "If Not by Tanks, Then by Banks?" 1080.

71. Niklas Swanström, "China's Role in Central Asia: Hard and Soft Power," *Global Dialogue* 9, no. 1/2 (2007): 79.

72. Niklas Swanström, "China and Central Asia: A New Great Game or Traditional Vassal Relations?" *The Journal of Contemporary China* 14, no. 45 (2005): 570.

73. Gaël Raballand and Agnés Andrésy, "Why Should Trade between Central Asia and China Continue to Expand?" *Asia Europe Journal* 5, no. 2 (2007): 239.

74. Laruelle and Peyrouse, *Globalizing Central Asia*, 36.

75. Casey Michel, "The Unsurprising Doldrums of US-Central Asia Trade," *The Diplomat*, August 3, 2016, https://thediplomat.com/2016/08/the-unsurprising-doldrums-of-us-central-asia-trade/.

76. Formerly known as "One Belt, One Road."

77. Ivan Zuenko, "Why China Subsidizes Loss-making Rail Transport via Russia and Kazakhstan," *Carnegie Moscow Center*, September 13. 2016, https://carnegie.ru/commentary/64555.

78. Ibid.

79. Swanström, "China and Central Asia," 579.

80. Theresa Fallon, "The New Silk Road: Xi Jinping's Grand Strategy for Eurasia," *American Foreign Policy Interests* 37, no. 3 (2015): 141.

81. Swanström, "China and Central Asia," 581–83.

82. Jian Zhang, "China's New Foreign Policy under Xi Jinping: Towards 'Peaceful Rise 2.0'?" *Global Change, Peace & Security* 27, no. 1 (2015): 7.

83. Ibid., 17.

84. Esther Pan, "China's Soft Power Initiative," *Council on Foreign Relations*, May 18, 2006, https://www.cfr.org/backgrounder/chinas-soft-power-initiative#p2.

85. Cooley, *Great Games, Local Rules*, 162.

86. Rumer et al. *U.S. Policy Toward Central Asia 3.0*, 3.

87. Sir Harry Flashman, of course, was the fictional character in a series of books by George MacDonald Fraser in which the hero plays a part in the Great Game, the "Scramble for Africa," and other imperial adventures between 1839 and 1894.

88. Strobe Talbott, "A Farewell to Flashman: American Policy in the Caucasus and Central Asia," (address, Johns Hopkins School of Advanced International Studies, Baltimore, Maryland, July 21, 1997), https://1997-2001.state.gov/regions/nis/970721talbott.html.

89. Ibid., emphasis added.

90. Ibid.

91. Alexander Diener, "Assessing Potential Russian Irredentism and Separatism in Kazakhstan's Northern Oblasts," *Eurasian Geography and Economics* 56, no. 5 (2015): 469–92.

92. Alexander Diener, "Parsing Mobilities in Central Eurasia: Border Management and New Silk Roads," *Eurasian Geography and Economics* 56, no. 4 (2015): 376–404. To a lesser extent, there has also been a desire to prevent Iran from gaining a foothold in Central Asia.

93. William Odom, and Robert Dujarric, *Commonwealth or Empire?: Russia, Central Asia, and the Transcaucasus* (Indianapolis: Hudson Institute, 1995), 251.

94. "Uzbekistan's Mirziyoev Meets Trump in 'Historic' White House Visit," *Radio Free Europe/Radio Liberty* (RFE/RL), May 14, 2018, https://www.rferl.org/a/mirziyoev-us-visit-uzbek-leader-white-house-2002/29230271.html.

95. "US: Focus on Rights as Uzbek Leader Visits," *Human Rights Watch*, May 16, 2018, https://www.hrw.org/news/2018/05/15/us-focus-rights-uzbek-leader-visits.

96. Uzbekistan's Mirziyoev Meets Trump," *RFE/RL*.

97. "National Security Strategy of the United States of America," 27.

98. Ibid., 39.

99. Ibid., 25–26.

100. Laruelle, Marlene et al., "Kazakhs Are Wary of Neighbors Bearing Gifts." *Open Democracy*, April 30, 2020, https://www.opendemocracy.net/en/odr/kazakhs-are-wary-neighbours-bearing-gifts/

101. Kathleen Collins, "The Limits of Cooperation: Central Asia Afghanistan and the New Silk Road," *Asian Policy* 17, no. 1 (2014): 25.

102. Hill, "The United States and Russia in Central Asia."

103. Paul Goble, "Central Asia Ready to Move on Without Russia," Eurasia Daily Monitor, *The Jamestown Foundation*, March 20, 2018, https://jamestown.org/program/central-asia-ready-move-without-russia/.

104. S. Frederick Starr, and Svante Cornell, "Uzbekistan: A New Model for Reform in the Muslim World?" *CACI Analyst*, May 12, 2018, https://silkroadstudies.org/resources/pdf/publications/1805FT-UZ-3.pdf

REFERENCES

Akaev, Askar. *Kyrgyz Statehood and the National Epos "Manas."* New York: Global Scholarly Publications, 2003.

American Presidency Project, "Remarks at a White House Ceremony Marking the Entry of the Peace Corps into Central Europe," June 15, 1990. http://www.presidency.ucsb.edu/ws/index.php?pid=18600.

Blank, Stephen. "AWOL: U.S. Policy in Central Asia." *The Central Asia and Caucasus Analyst*, October 30, 2013. https://www.cacianalyst.org/publications/analytical-articles/item/12848-awol-us-policy-in-central-asia.html.

Blank, Stephen. "The United States and Central Asia." In *Central Asian Security: The New International Context*, edited by Roy Allison and Lena Jonson, 127–51. Washington, DC: Brookings Institution Press, 2001.

Blank, Stephen. "Whither the New Silk Road and US Central Asia Policy?" *The Central Asia and Caucasus Analyst*, March 8, 2013. http://www.css.ethz.ch/en/services/digital-library/articles/article.html/161006.

Brzezinski, Zbigniew. *The Grand Chessboard: American Primacy and Its Geostrategic Imperatives*. New York: Basic Books, 1997.

Clinton, Hillary. "Remarks at New Silk Road Ministerial Meeeting." *U.S. State Department Archived Content*, September 22, 2011. https://2009-2017.state.gov/secretary/20092013clinton/rm/2011/09/173807.htm.

Coffey, Luke. "Why Trump's Meeting with Kazakhstan's President was so Important." *The Heritage Foundation*, January 17, 2018. https://www.heritage.org/asia/commentary/why-trumps-meeting-kazakhstan-president-was-so-important.

Collins, Kathleen. "The Limits of Cooperation: Central Asia Afghanistan and the New Silk Road." *Asian Policy* 17, no. 1 (2014): 18–26.

Cooley, Alexander. *Great Games, Local Rules: The New Great Power Contest in Central Asia*. New York: Oxford University Press, 2012.

Diener, Alexander. "Assessing Potential Russian Irredentism and Separatism in Kazakhstan's Northern Oblasts." *Eurasian Geography and Economics* 56, no. 5 (2015): 469–92.

Diener, Alexander. "Parsing Mobilities in Central Eurasia: Border Management and New Silk Roads." *Eurasian Geography and Economics* 56, no. 4 (2015): 376–404.

Diener, Alexander, and Nick Megoran. "Central Asia as Place." In *Central Asia: Contests for Understanding*, edited by David Montgomery. Pittsburgh: University of Pittsburgh Press, forthcoming.

Dzyubenko, Olga. "U.S. Vacates Base in Central Asia as Russia's Clout Rises." *Reuters*, June 4, 2014. https://www.reuters.com/article/us-kyrgyzstan-usa-manas/u-s-vacates-base-in-central-asia-as-russias-clout-rises-idUSKBN0EE1LH20140603.

Eurasianet. "Russia Deploys Teachers to Tajikistan on Goodwill Mission," April 27, 2018. https://eurasianet.org/russia-deploys-teachers-to-tajikistan-on-goodwill-mission.

Fallon, Theresa. "The New Silk Road: Xi Jinping's Grand Strategy for Eurasia." *American Foreign Policy Interests* 37, no. 3 (2015): 140–47.

Fukuyama, Francis. *The End of History and the Last Man*. New York: Free Press, 1992.

Goble, Paul. "Central Asia Ready to Move on Without Russia." *Eurasia Daily Monitor*, The Jamestown Foundation, March 20, 2018. https://jamestown.org/program/central-asia-ready-move-without-russia/.

Hill, Fiona. "The United States and Russia in Central Asia: Uzbekistan, Tajikistan, Afghanistan, Pakistan, and Iran." *Brookings*, August 15, 2002. https://www.brookings.edu/on-the-record/the-united-states-and-russia-in-central-asia-uzbekistan-tajikistan-afghanistan-pakistan-and-iran/.

Human Rights Watch. "US: Focus on Rights as Uzbek Leader Visits," May 16, 2018. https://www.hrw.org/news/2018/05/15/us-focus-rights-uzbek-leader-visits.

Kucera, Joshua. "America's Uzbekistan Problem." *The New York Times*, December 28, 2011. https://www.nytimes.com/2011/12/29/opinion/americas-uzbekistan-problem.html.

Kucera, Joshua. "Clinton's Dubious Plan to Save Afghanistan with a 'New Silk Road'." *The Atlantic*, November 2, 2011. https://www.theatlantic.com/international/archive/2011/11/clintons-dubious-plan-to-save-afghanistan-with-a-new-silk-road/247760/.

Kurlantzick, Joshua. "China's Charm: Implications of Chinese Soft Power. Report, Carnegie Endowment for International Peace, June 5, 2006.

Laruelle, Marlene. "Central Asian Labor Migrants in Russia: The 'Diasporization' of the Central Asian States?" *China and Eurasia Forum Quarterly* 5, no. 3 (2007): 101–11.

Laruelle, Marlene, Gerard Toal, John O'Loughlin, and Kristin M. Bakke. "Kazakhs are Wary of Neighbors Bearing Gifts." *OpenDemocracy*, April 30, 2020. https://www.opendemocracy.net/en/odr/kazakhs-are-wary-neighbours-bearing-gifts/.

Laruelle, Marlene, and Sebastien Peyrouse. *Globalizing Central Asia: Geopolitics and the Challenges of Economic Development*. Armonk: M.E. Sharpe, 2013.

Lebedeva, Marina. "'Soft Power' in Central Asia: Participants and their Actions." *Vestnik MGIMO-University* 35, no. 2 (2014): 47–55.

Lelik, Anna. "Kyrgyzstan: Foreign Agents Bill Nixed, NGOs Rejoice." *Eurasianet*, May 12, 2016. https://eurasianet.org/kyrgyzstan-foreign-agent-bill-nixed-ngos-rejoice.

Lillis, Joanna. "Kazakhstan: NGO Law Approved Amid Civil Society Resistance." *Eurasianet*, December 2, 2015 .https://eurasianet.org/kazakhstan-ngo-law-approved-amid-civil-society-resistance.

Livergood, Reed. "Afghanistan Conundrum: Logistical Support Options after the Manas Air Base Closing." *American Diplomacy*, May 2009, http://www.unc.edu/depts/diplomat/item/2009/0406/comm/livergood_afghanistan.html.

Lumpe, Lora "A Timeline of U.S. Military Aid Cooperation with Uzbekistan." Occasional paper series, Open Society Foundations, Central Eurasia Project, October 2010. https://www.opensocietyfoundations.org/publications/timeline-us-military-aid-cooperation-uzbekistan#publications_download.

Marat, Erica. "Kyrgyzstan's Decision to Renounce Manas Transit Center Favors Russia." *The Central Asia-Caucasus Analyst*, June 26, 2013.

McBride, James. "Building the New Silk Road." *Council on Foreign Relations*, May 22, 2015. https://www.cfr.org/backgrounder/building-new-silk-road.

McCarthy, Ryan P. "The Peace Corps' Declining Role in Central Asia." *The Diplomat*, October 29, 2015. https://thediplomat.com/2015/10/the-peace-corps-declining-role-in-central-asia.

Michel, Casey. "The Unsurprising Doldrums of US-Central Asia Trade." *The Diplomat*, August 3, 2016. https://thediplomat.com/2016/08/the-unsurprising-doldrums-of-us-central-asia-trade/.

Najibullah, Farangis. "No Shortage of Students as Tajikistan Builds New Russian Schools." *Radio Free Europe/Radio Liberty,* January 18, 2020. https://www.rferl.org/a/tajikistan-new-russian-schools/30384557.html.

Naumkin, V. V., I. D. Zvyagelskaya, E. V. Voiko, V. G. Korgun, E. M. Kuzmina, D. B. Malysheva, S. A. Pritchin, and B. A. Kheifetz. "Russia's Interests in Central Asia: Contents, Perspectives, Limitations." Report, Russian International Affairs Council, June 25, 2013.

Nichol, Jim. "Uzbekistan's Closure of the Airbase at Karshi-Khanabad: Context and Implications. Report, CRS Report for Congress, Washington DC, January 11, 2006.

Nixey, James. "The Long Goodbye: Waning Russian Influence in the South Caucasus and Central Asia." Briefing paper, Chatham House, London, June 1, 2012. https://www.chathamhouse.org/publications/papers/view/184065, 14.

North, Andrew. "'We'll Cut Off Your Head': Open Season for LGBT Attacks in Kyrgyzstan," *The Guardian*, May 4, 2016. https://www.theguardian.com/world/2016/may/04/kyrgyzstan-lgbt-community-fear-attacks-russia.

Nye, Joseph S. Jr. *Bound to Lead: The Changing Nature of American Power*. New York: Basic Books, 1990.

Nye, Joseph S. Jr. "What China and Russia don't get about Soft Power." *Foreign Policy*, April 29, 2013. https://foreignpolicy.com/2013/04/29/what-china-and-russia-dont-get-about-soft-power/.

Odom, William, and Robert Dujarric. *Commonwealth or Empire?: Russia, Central Asia, and the Transcaucasus*. Indianapolis: Hudson Institute, 1995.

Olcott, Martha Brill. *Central Asia's Second Chance*. Washington, DC: Carnegie Endowment for International Peace, 2005.

Pan, Esther. "China's Soft Power Initiative." *Council on Foreign Relations*, May 18, 2006. https://www.cfr.org/backgrounder/chinas-soft-power-initiative#p2.

Pavlenko, Aneta. "Multilingualism in Post-Soviet Countries: Language Revival, Language Removal, and Sociolinguistic Theory." *The International Journal of Bilingual Education and Bilingualism* 11, no. 3 and 4 (2008): 275–314.

Pavlenko, Aneta. "Russian as a Lingua Franca." *Annual Review of Applied Linguistics* 26 (2008): 77–99.

Quigley, Kevin F. F., and Lex Rieffel. "Ten Times the Peace Corps: A Smart Investment in Soft Power." *Brookings*, September 5, 2008. https://www.brookings.edu/research/ten-times-the-peace-corps-a-smart-investment-in-soft-power/.

Raballand, Gaël, and Agnés Andrésy. "Why Should Trade between Central Asia and China Continue to Expand?" *Asia Europe Journal* 5, no. 2 (2007): 235–52.

Rafferty, Andrew. "The War in Afghanistan: By the Numbers." *NBC News*, August 22, 2017. https://www.nbcnews.com/politics/politics-news/war-afghanistan-numbers-n794626.

Republican Party. "Republican Platform," 2016. https://prod-static-ngop-pbl.s3.amazonaws.com/media/documents/DRAFT_12_FINAL%5B1%5D-ben_1468872234.pdf. Accessed May 20, 2018.
RFE/RL. "Uzbekistan's Mirziyoev Meets Trump in 'Historic' White House Visit," May 14, 2018. https://www.rferl.org/a/mirziyoev-us-visit-uzbek-leader-white-house-2002/29230271.html.
Rockower, Paul. "This American Corner." Blog. *USC Center on Public Diplomacy*, April 15, 2013. https://www.uscpublicdiplomacy.org/blog/american-corner.
Rumer, Eugene, Richard Sokolsky, and Paul Stronski. *U.S. Policy Toward Central Asia 3.0*. Washington DC: Carnegie Endowment for International Peace, 2016.
Rutland, Peter, and Andrei Kazantsev. "The Limits of Russia's 'Soft Power'." *Journal of Political Power* 9, no. 3 (2016): 395–413.
Ryazantsev, Sergei V., Norio Horie, and Kazuhiro Kumo. "Migrant Workers from Central Asia into the Russian Federation." In *Sociology, Economics and Politics of Central Asian Migrants in Russia*, edited by Kazuhiro Kumo, S Norio Horie, and Sergei V. Ryazantsev, 59–85. Discussion paper, Institute of Economic Research, Hitotsubashi University, Tokyo, 2011.
Talbott, Strobe. "A Farewell to Flashman: American Policy in the Caucasus and Central Asia." Address, Johns Hopkins School of Advanced International Studies, Baltimore, Maryland, July 21, 1997. https://1997-2001.state.gov/regions/nis/970721talbott.html.
Starr, S. Frederick, and Svante Cornell. "Uzbekistan: A New Model for Reform in the Muslim World?" *CACI Analyst*, May 12, 2018. https://silkroadstudies.org/resources/pdf/publications/1805FT-UZ-3.pdf
Stronski, Paul. "Uncertain Continuity: Central Asia and the Trump Administration." *Carnegie Endowment for International Peace*, July 27, 2017. https://carnegieendowment.org/2017/07/27/uncertain-continuity-central-asia-and-trump-administration-pub-72677.
Swanström, Niklas. "China and Central Asia: A New Great Game or Traditional Vassal Relations?" *The Journal of Contemporary China* 14, no. 45 (2005): 569–84.
Swanström, Niklas. "China's Role in Central Asia: Hard and Soft Power." *Global Dialogue* 9, no. 1/2 (2007): 79–88.
Toal, Gerard [Ó Tuathail, Gearóid]. *Critical Geopolitics: The Politics of Writing Global Space*. Minneapolis: University of Minnesota Press, 1996.
Toal, Gerard [Ó Tuathail, Gearóid]. "New World Order Geopolitics: Introduction." In *The Geopolitics Reader*, edited by Gearóid Ó Tuathail, Simon Dalby, and Paul Routledge, 103–13. London: Routledge, 1998.
Tolipov, Farkhod. "Hard or Soft Power? Russia Reacts to Uzbekistan's Draft Language Policy." *CACI Analyst*, June 08, 2020. http://cacianalyst.org/publications/analytical-articles/item/13623-soft-or-hard-power?-russia-reacts-to-uzbekistans-draft-language-policy.html.
Tsygankov, Andrei P. "If Not by Tanks, Then by Banks? The Role of Soft Power in Putin's Foreign Policy." *Europe-Asia Studies* 58, no. 7 (2006): 1079–99.
U.S. Embassy in the Kyrgyz Republic. "American Corners." https://kg.usembassy.gov/education-culture/american-corners/. Accessed May 27, 2018. USAID. "The

United States Supports Uzbekistan's Efforts to Combat COVID-19," June 7, 2020. https://www.usaid.gov/uzbekistan/press-releases/jun-7-2020-united-states-supports-uzbekistan-efforts-covid-19.

White House, The. "National Security Strategy of the United States of America," December 18, 2017. https://www.whitehouse.gov/wp-content/uploads/2017/12/NSS-Final-12-18-2017-0905-2.pdf.

Wood, L. Todd. "Central Asia can Aid U.S. National Security." *The Washington Times*, October 18, 2017. https://www.washingtontimes.com/news/2017/oct/18/central-asian-global-security-forefront/.

Zhang, Jian. "China's New Foreign Policy under Xi Jinping: Towards 'Peaceful Rise 2.0'?" *Global Change, Peace & Security* 27, no. 1 (2015): 5–19.

Zuenko, Ivan. "Why China Subsidizes Loss-making Rail Transport via Russia and Kazakhstan." *Carnegie Moscow Center*, September 13, 2016. https://carnegie.ru/commentary/64555.

Chapter 2

Russian Soft Power in Central Asia

Government Policy Helped by Resurgent Russophilia

Kirill Nourzhanov

In December 2013, the upper chamber of the Russian parliament invited the Foreign Minister, Sergey Lavrov, to brief them on the country's international relations. Toward the end of an hour-long session, Lavrov was asked a question about the efficiency and mechanisms of Moscow's soft power projection. He seemed to be momentarily lost for an answer and could only talk about a virtual museums project where anybody, "in Berlin, Bishkek or some other place," can stop by at a local Russian cultural center and enjoy an enlightening 3D show. Lavrov added apologetically: "We began to master instruments of soft power . . . much later than those who invented these instruments—our Western partners."[1]

Indeed, it was only in 2010 that the concept of "soft power" first appeared in an official planning document approved by the Kremlin. Called "Main Directions of the Policy of the Russian Federation in the Area of International Cultural and Humanitarian Cooperation," it equated the term with cultural diplomacy and positioned it as an antidote to "propaganda campaigns under the slogan of containing Russia" and a means to attest the Russian Federation's renaissance "as a free and democratic state."[2] In the decade that followed, soft power has been at the center of a vibrant academic and policy debate in Russia. Taking Joseph Nye's foundational text[3] as a point of departure, scholars and statesmen have searched for the optimal modalities of "promoting one's interests and policies through persuasion and creating a positive perception of one's country, based not just on its material achievements but also its spiritual and intellectual heritage."[4]

Russian scholars, international relations experts, and security intellectuals embraced the concept of "soft power" with alacrity. Hundreds of books, articles, and dissertations have been published; already in 2015 one commentator managed to group them in no less than seven distinct interpretive paradigms.[5] The bulk of this growing corpus of literature is quite derivative, mirrors the twists and turns in the debate on soft power in the West including its recent focus on "sharp power,"[6] and has not had a noticeable impact on actual policy formulation.[7]

The official discourse on soft power in Russia is much more streamlined compared to the intellectual ferment in the expert community. Currently it exhibits three features that align reasonably well with Nye's own Realist turn in 2011.[8]

First, there is pronounced instrumentalism: "Soft power is a descriptive rather than normative concept . . . It is simply a form of power, one way of getting desired outcomes."[9] The current reading of soft power by the Kremlin is devoid of explicit normative content. It has dropped references to democratic ideals of the 2010 vintage, but has not replaced them with any other set of political values underpinning its foreign policy identity. Instead, Moscow has shifted focus to a "civilizational code" which rests on "great culture . . . and inexhaustible creative potential,"[10] whatever that might mean. Reducing Putin's "message to the masses in developing societies" to traditionalism and social conservatism[11] is erroneous. Depending on a specific policy objective and geographic location, the Russian leadership uses a broad array of ideological tropes, themes, and images when it tries to persuade and attract. In her discussion of the "Russian World"—the official "civilizational code" doctrine as applied to the former USSR—Marlene Laruelle eloquently characterized it as a deliberately fuzzy mental atlas open to all kinds of rebranding and re-articulation.[12] The perception of Russia as a progressive, modern, secular, and anti-colonial entity is widespread in the former Soviet republics.[13]

Second, Moscow's official narrative has moved from emulation of Western soft power practices to counteracting them.[14] The shift is conditioned by the Kremlin's belief that the United States and its allies now actively resort to the "negative" type of soft power—the "information-psychological warfare" (Nye's "twisting minds" parable[15])—effectively fomenting Russophobia.[16] The 2013 Foreign Policy Concept warned that "increasing global competition and the growing crisis potential sometimes creates a risk of destructive and unlawful use of soft power."[17]

Finally, its rising importance notwithstanding, soft power still remains a poor cousin to conventional ways of securing Russia's influence in the former Soviet space. Hard power of military, security, and economic resources overshadow the soft power of attraction, and even within the narrow realm of diplomacy, soft power is treated merely as an add-on to its "traditional methods" according to the extant Foreign Policy Concept.[18] During 2015–2019, expenditure on soft power projection did not exceed 3 percent of the aggregate federal budget appropriation for "Foreign Policy Activity."[19]

Russian soft power projection today can thus be summarized as a process of creating and maintaining a sustainable positive image abroad resting on a cultural foundation. Long-term cultural relations that generate an enabling environment for the acceptance of Moscow's "hard power" policies transcend government propaganda and ad hoc PR campaigns and entail public diplomacy, humanitarian cooperation, and strategic communication.[20] The last element is especially important today given the Russian leaders' conviction that the country's "natural aspiration to expand its cultural-civilizational presence in the world is met with pained reaction from the West, which treats it as a sort of malignant challenge to humankind."[21]

RUSSIAN SOFT POWER IN CENTRAL ASIA: OBJECTIVES, ACTORS, AND RESOURCES

In the beginning of the 2010s, Russia's Central Asia policy was heavily criticized at home as chaotic, under-resourced, reliant on Soviet-era stereotypes, and utterly unprepared to deal with the new reality of the region's greater openness and generational change.[22] An influential public consultative body, the Civic Chamber of the Russian Federation, published a report in 2012 which stated that:

> We have to admit that Russia has lost, to a considerable extent, its historical positions in the region and is unlikely to recover them in full, at least in the near-term perspective. In order to retrench ourselves on the lines we still retain we need to correct our foreign policy approaches radically, including through the active use of "soft power" .... A key element of the Russian foreign policy concept in Central Asia should consist of purposeful influence on the formation of public mood and future elites in the region.[23]

A cogent official Central Asian strategy is yet to be articulated by the Kremlin; its absence continues to be a source of frustration for the country's diplomats and experts. The Russian Ministry of Foreign Affairs (MFA) currently sees Central Asia as "an important partner for privileged cooperation in the military-political, trade-economic, and cultural-humanitarian spheres as well as in the matter of ensuring common Eurasian security from the southern direction."[24] This definition illustrates three trends in the evolution of the government's strategic thinking over the past ten years. First, it has moved from the rhetoric of wholesale integration to seeking specific areas of common interest where Russia can exercise leadership. Security—understood both as protection against external threats and maintenance of regime stability—is paramount in this regard. Second, Moscow has acknowledged it has both to compete and cooperate with other external actors to achieve its objectives in Central Asia—Russia is a "privileged" but by no means an exclusive partner. Finally, soft power ("cultural-humanitarian spheres") has been slowly moving up the agenda of Russian policy practitioners.

The MFA divides the region's five countries into "allies" and "strategic partners." The former group comprises Kazakhstan, Kyrgyzstan, and Tajikistan, all of whom have membership in Moscow-led blocs—the Collective Security Treaty Organization (CSTO) and the Eurasian Economic Union (EEU). Turkmenistan and Uzbekistan belong to the latter group. Aleksandr Sternik, the Director of the MFA's Third CIS Department responsible for Central Asia, recently argued that Russia's unique position as a harbinger and guarantor of "evolutionary modernization" in the region underpins these alliances/partnerships. In addition to reiterating Moscow's iron-clad commitment to "blocking transgressions on secular traditions of power in Central Asia and any interference into the region's domestic affairs under whatever guise," Sternik stressed that "similar mentality . . . and the unified language and cultural space" between Russia and Central Asia afforded the latter's residents with splendid economic opportunities and career options.[25] Keeping this mental and cultural continuum intact is the main objective of Russian soft power promotion.

The task is carried out predominantly by government agencies and state-funded organizations. The MFA nominally acts as the chief coordination body. Its structural unit, the Federal Agency for the Commonwealth of Independent States, Compatriots Living Abroad, and International Humanitarian Cooperation—*Rossotrudnichestvo*—is responsible for implementing humanitarian, cultural, and scientific programs internationally. In 2019, the agency worked in eighty countries including four in Central Asia (Kazakhstan, Kyrgyzstan, Tajikistan, and Uzbekistan). Its operational budget doubled between 2013 and 2018, reaching four billion rubles per annum. Despite such rapid growth, it was still only about a third of what the British Council—an organization with similar chartered objectives and global remit—received from the UK government.[26] Rossotrudnichestvo prioritizes the former Soviet republics and identifies the following five areas as instruments of humanitarian cooperation and projection of Russia's positive image:[27]

- international development assistance (IDA);
- the Russian language and culture;
- higher education;
- working with compatriots; and
- working with youth.

Other important actors in the game of Russian soft power projection include government bodies beyond the MFA and the federal education and cultural establishment; the parliament; media organizations; NGOs; and corporate entities.

Notwithstanding an explicit reference to the IDA in Rossotrudnichestvo's mission statement, it has remained the exclusive prerogative of the president. Specialized agencies such as the Ministry for Emergency Situations (MES) and the Ministry of Defense (MoD) have their own autonomous and well-heeled humanitarian cooperation programs.[28] The Ministry for Economic Development (MED) has jumped on the bandwagon too, bypassing the MFA. In 2019, for instance, it undertook projects to expedite cultural contacts with Kazakhstan and skill transfer for public servants in Uzbekistan.[29] It has also contemplated the creation of a special department to advance the humanitarian component of economic cooperation with EEU and CIS countries working primarily with the NGO community, environmentalists, and civil rights advocates, the MFA being particularly hesitant about engaging with the last category of interlocutors.[30]

A special mention must be made of the growing role Russian regional authorities have played in advancing humanitarian ties with Central Asia. A fairly typical agreement signed in 2012, between the Orenburg *oblast* in Russia and the neighboring West Kazakhstan Region included a clause on,

> Developing the cooperation in the field of culture, education, sport . . . [and] humanitarian and information exchange involving performing collectives, teachers, students, art exhibitions, thematic seminars and symposia.[31]

The parties to the agreement also undertook to develop a concrete and detailed annual action plan, lest it remain only a document. The practice received a further boost after the Federal Law "On the foundations of cross-border cooperation," was adopted in Russia in 2017, but it was by no means confined to adjacent territories. In 2019, seventy-six out of eighty-five subjects of the Russian Federation had similar arrangements with partners in Kazakhstan.[32] The density of region-to-region cultural and humanitarian links is understandably lower with the Central Asian countries that do not border Russia, yet all of the partnerships including with Turkmenistan have the appropriate legal and institutional infrastructure underpinning them.

The MFA's activities in Central Asia are thus only the tip of the iceberg of soft power projection by various Russian executive bodies. They often act independently of each other and of Rossotrudnichestvo. The latter's coordinating role is mostly visible in specific campaigns and high-profile initiatives such as the commemoration of the seventy-fifth anniversary of the Soviet victory in WWII: it was put in charge of directing all of Russia's "joint projects of ministries and agencies, public organizations and mass media" across the CIS—a colossal undertaking envisaging 385 activities in 2020 alone.[33]

The Russian parliament may have limited agency in formulating the country's foreign policy, which is the president's turf, but it appropriates money and exercises oversight. The State Duma's Committee on the CIS, Eurasian Integration, and Ties with Compatriots is not exactly the legislature's powerhouse and has been left to the leadership by opposition parties, the Liberal-Democrats (LDPR), and the Communists (CPRF), over the past decade. The Committee welcomed increased use of soft power in 2012 although, according to the Committee's members, it should be confined to "propaganda of the Eurasian Union, resistance to the attempts to falsify history, and support for Russian culture."[34] The Committee's recommendation to secure an extra eight billion rubles in funding for Rossotrudnichestvo came to naught, due in large measure to pushback from the Ministry of Finance. By 2018, MPs had become convinced that the agency could do more by overcoming inefficiencies and tapping into internal resources. According to the Committee's Chair, Leonid Kalashnikov (CPRF), the agency "spent 80 percent of its budget on salaries" and "served nobody but itself"—claims that were stoutly denied by Rossotrudnichestvo's leadership.[35] Kalashnikov's deputy, Konstantin Zatulin, mounted a critique from a different angle, accusing the MFA of excessive political correctness and misplaced reluctance to interfere in other countries' domestic affairs. Zatulin opined that the only successful exercise of Russian soft power projection occurred in Crimea in 2014 and called for the creation of "Soros Foundation- or Carnegie-like" NGOs in the former Soviet republics to keep them friendly to Moscow.[36]

If the relevant Duma committee can be seen as a preserve of radical and rather marginal thinkers, the Chair of the upper chamber of the Russian parliament, Valentina Matviyenko, is a genuine political heavyweight. Matviyenko has often performed the role of the Kremlin's fixer, lobbyist, and spin doctor in Central Asia. She has repeatedly positioned herself as defender of labor migrant rights from the region. An honorary citizen of Ashgabat and a "bleeding heart for Kyrgyzstan,"[37] she has been instrumental in unfreezing relations between Russia and Uzbekistan since 2016. Her visit to Tashkent in 2019 was particularly fascinating: she waxed lyrical about increased bilateral visits by officials at all levels (more than 600 over three years); joint parliamentary work on reduction of domestic violence; Russia's gratitude for Uzbekistan's contribution to WWII victory; and utility of the Russian language for job seekers, before enjoining the hosts to consider joining the EEU.[38] Coming from Putin, such advice would have been seen as dangerous pressure, but a senior Russian Senator proved just right to test the waters and to rekindle public debate in Uzbekistan.

In 2013, the Russian government consolidated the media assets that broadcast to foreign audiences (some were dinosaurs inherited from the Soviet era) into a new brand: Russia Today International News Agency (RT). Under fresh and dynamic leadership comprising professional journalists, and with access to increased funding, RT was charged with the dual task of strategically communicating Russian views and countering or even breaking what Putin described as the Anglo-Saxon media monopoly on the global flow of information; it thus became "an extremely important part of the Russian soft power strategy."[39] The RT's multimedia arm, Sputnik, is particularly active in Central Asia where it carries out FM radio broadcasts in Kazakh, Kyrgyz, Tajik, and Uzbek; runs a network of correspondents and press centers; and manages a plethora of newswires and social media platforms. Sputnik works independently of Rossotrudnichestvo but helps the latter with marketing. Without Sputnik's advertising, hashtags, and keywords, Rossotrudnichestvo would have struggled to lure punters to its events.[40]

Russia has a handful of government-organized non-governmental organizations (GONGOs) that assist the MFA with the conduct of public diplomacy. These include the Alexander Gorchakov Public Diplomacy Fund, the Russkii Mir Foundation, the Fund for the Support and Protection of the Rights of Compatriots, and a few regional entities whose main objective is to expedite Track II activities. Academic institutions and think tanks, such as the Valdai International Discussion Club and the Russian International Affairs Council, conduct joint research projects with experts from the region and host visits, seminars, and conferences on the general subject of "whither Russia in Central Asia." Since 2012, a number of small specialized GONGOs have focused on the dissemination of positive information about the EEU and Eurasianism more broadly. Typical among them is the Samrau Eurasian Centre funded by the regional government of Bashkortostan for the purpose of "strengthening dialogue and integration partnership in the Eurasian space via bolstering contacts in the format of public diplomacy."[41]

The NGO sector has traditionally been the weakest link in Russia's soft power projection in Central Asia. The situation may slowly be changing with the increased activity of the Russian Humanitarian Mission (RHM), the first not-for-profit charitable organization operating abroad. Set up in 2010 by Evgenii Primakov, a TV anchor and now a federal MP, it first focused on relief work in the Middle East but has increasingly reoriented itself to the former Soviet Union, especially Central Asia. Primakov accepts that promotion of the Russian language and culture, concerts, exhibitions, visits, round tables, and similar intellectual (and unnecessarily expensive) pursuits are necessary, yet in a refreshingly blunt manner, he believes that what, for instance, people of Kyrgyzstan want from Russia is real help and not "balalaika, accordion, a bust of Pushkin, and tender love and care for ill-defined 'compatriots'."[42] The RHM working with local authorities and NGOs provides targeted and flexible delivery of services where it is most needed, be it shipments of medicine, repairing schools, or organizing a search for missing children. According to an official audit, in 2018 RHM had a permanent staff of ten, ran projects in Kyrgyzstan, Tajikistan, and Uzbekistan, and generated half of it funds as a sub-contractor for Rossotrudnichestvo (fifty-five million rubles) and the other half from private donations.[43] This is not a huge sum of money, but the RHM seems to be a model for public–private partnership in Russia in the area of soft power promotion that diplomats and officials would rather avoid.

Primakov has said rather unpleasant things about Russia's corporate sector, noting its,

> Reluctance to spend anything, avarice, stupidity, lack of concern for interests of the state . . . . The culture of investing in humanitarian politics is still absent in our business circles, with very rare exceptions. At best they sponsor cocktail parties, jets and basketball teams.[44]

While generally correct, Primakov's observation can be slightly adjusted for the case of Central Asia. Gently prodded by the president's administration, Russian tycoons have invested in soft power promotion in the region. Alisher Usmanov, a Russian billionaire who was born in Uzbekistan, has invested millions of dollars in setting up branches of Russian universities in Uzbekistan, endowing scholarships for Uzbek students in Moscow, and sponsoring community development projects in Uzbekistan and Kazakhstan. In 2018, he was awarded the El Yurt Hizmati Order by the Uzbek government for his "tremendous contribution to the strengthening of economic, societal, and cultural-humanitarian ties between Uzbekistan and the Russian Federation."[45] Another flag-bearer for Russian interests is the country's second-largest petroleum company, Lukoil. The privately owned firm does a lot of business in Uzbekistan and has a robust program of "creating a positive image and socially responsible behavior," which includes student scholarships, supporting orphanages, hospitals, and people with disabilities, and sponsoring Russian classical music and opera performances.[46] Large state-owned conglomerates have been slow in following suit, although Gazprom sponsors Tajikistan's football association and Rosatom set up a regional center in Astana in 2018 to market its brand (and "Brand Russia") across the region.

The foregoing depicts the Russian soft power projection apparatus as a complex and growing organism. It may lack a clear sense of direction and coordination but after decades of passivity and resting on the laurels of a common Soviet past, it seems to have woken up from its slumber and joined the battle for hearts and minds in Central Asia, not as a presumptive hegemon but as one of the many contenders for influence.

GAUGING RUSSIAN SOFT POWER IN CENTRAL ASIA

Assessing the success or failure of the Russian effort since 2012 is perforce a speculative task. In the absence of a universally accepted methodology of determining soft power assets or measuring their policy impact,[47] the chapter will provide comments on Russia's attraction and persuasion capabilities in Central Asia following Rossotrudnichestvo's five-point taxonomy plus strategic communication.

International Development Assistance

Russia was a recipient of international aid from 1992 to 2006 and is still figuring out how to maximize soft power accruing from being a donor. Prior to 2014, it did not bother with attaching the "from Russia with love" label to its generosity which was channeled through the United Nations (UN), the World Bank, and other multilateral institutions more or less anonymously.[48] In 2017, Foreign Minister Lavrov proudly told Russian MPs that 77 percent of Russian aid was to be provided bilaterally that year, as "the most effective way to support our friends and allies, and strengthen Russia's position in these countries."[49]

What Lavrov did not mention was that Russia's IDA stood at a miserly 0.08 percent of its GNI, falling far short of the 0.7 percent recommended by the UN and continuing to decline. Kyrgyzstan and Tajikistan were the only two Central Asian beneficiaries in 2017, receiving 129.8 million USD and 16.1 million respectively, from the 1.2 billion USD spent globally.[50] This made Russia the largest donor to Kyrgyzstan but only the sixth largest to Tajikistan.

Language and Culture

Following the Soviet collapse, Russian lost its unique position as the *only* language that mattered for upward mobility; in fact many pundits in the West predicted its irreversible decline.[51] Ethno-demographic change and government policies prioritizing the development of titular languages dramatically reduced Russian usage in the official and political spheres. However, toward the end of the first decade of the twenty-first century, a rise in demand for acquiring and improving competence in Russian began to be felt across Central Asia, despite the continuing shrinkage of the Russian diaspora.

The main reasons for this phenomenon included Russian's transition from the universal language, to that of the professional and creative elites; its utility for labor migrants; and, in William Fierman's apt phrasing, its ability to offer "access to a broader range of cultural production than is available in local languages."[52] The relative weight of these factors is different for each of the region's states but the overall trend toward Russian carving a niche as the most important non-titular language is hard to ignore.

Globalization has ensured stable functioning and self-reproduction of the Russian cultural-linguistic space even without a sizeable presence of ethnic Russians—or much intercession on behalf of Moscow.[53] A recent study showed that between 2006 and 2017, the number of people who used only Russian at home in Kazakhstan dropped from 51 percent to 32 percent. However, parallel to this the use of Kazakh also fell from 42 percent to 34 percent. The share of bilinguals feeling comfortable with both languages rose from 2 percent to 28 percent. The same study also noted that in Kyrgyzstan the percentage of youth fully competent in Russian (25%) had eclipsed the national average (21%).[54]

Why would ethnic Kazakhs who went to Kazakh schools choose to communicate in Russian? Rustem Kadyrzhanov's analysis pointed to several answers: this is a marker of status (highly educated and successful urbanites vs. rural dwellers); the Kazakh language has functional limitations covering areas such as business and technology; they use it for interlocution with non-Kazakh citizens—not just Russians but Germans, Koreans, and many others living in the country.[55] In Tajikistan, Russian, in however flawed a form, is being adopted as a "new mother tongue" by middle-class Tajik and Uzbek families in small towns.[56] Uzbekistan has exhibited similar dynamics: Russian acts a "social marker" of prestige and is unmatched in the corporate world. What distinguishes the Uzbek case is the retention of a relatively high number of Russian or mixed Russian and Uzbek language schools: 862 in 2019 compared to 1,100 in 1992.[57]

Mass labor migration is another factor driving interest in the Russian language. In 2014, Moscow introduced a language test for laborers seeking a work permit. This understandably incentivized hundreds of thousands of Central Asian workers to pick up the requisite skills before leaving home. Apart from the bureaucratic requirements, good knowledge of Russian brings a competitive advantage. A 2013 study of the job market in Moscow showed that migrants from Kyrgyzstan whose command of the language was generally better than their Tajik and Uzbek colleagues received higher wages, occupied more skilled positions, and were actively sought out by potential employers.[58]

Rossotrudnichestvo's documents create an impression of a gargantuan effort to promote the Russian language. Its reported activities in 2017[59] included preparation of textbooks and film collections; teacher training and curriculum development; delivery of printed materials to cultural centers and schools; establishment of Russian testing centers; culture fairs; and a myriad of other accomplishments that looked great on paper. In actuality, the number of people affected on the ground was negligible. Providing one-day training to sixty-nine teachers from Kazakhstan, Tajikistan, and Turkmenistan, running language courses for 439 pupils in Tashkent, or dispatching the grand total of 27,430 textbooks to nine CIS states hardly constituted a game-changer.

An increase in state funding for language promotion is not likely. Responding to a lobbyist's proposal to use the Goethe Institute budget (fifteen billion rubles) as a benchmark, the Russian president retorted along the lines that this should be a demand-driven process, adding that foreigners take up Russian not so much because they love Pushkin and Tolstoy but because Russia once again is becoming attractive economically and politically.[60] This logic is supported by evidence from Uzbekistan which intends to double the number of university graduates with the "Russian Language and Literature" qualification in the near future, using its own resources.[61]

The government of Tajikistan launched in 2014 a program to improve the teaching of the Russian language (and non-language subjects in Russian) in its schools, and had officially applied to Moscow for help. Despite Kremlin's approbation and the personal patronage of the Tajik President Rahmon and Valentina Matviyenko, progress was slow. By the end of 2019, Russia had sent forty-eight teachers to Tajikistan and earmarked 168 million rubles to build five new Russian language schools in the country, to complement the existing twenty-six overcrowded facilities.[62] The projected enrolment of 24,000 pupils in 2020 in such schools will still be a drop in the ocean of 2.2 million schoolchildren.

In Kyrgyzstan, the main challenge is not so much the absence of schools and teachers as a deficit of Russian schoolbooks. In 2017, the RHM and MES delivered 21,280 books to just one rural district there which covered its pedagogical needs.[63] One complication has been the Russian publishers' reluctance to grant copyright licenses for the printing of textbooks in Central Asia. Rossotrudnichestvo devised a partial solution in 2018 when it set up a cache of 180,000 e-books with the leading Russian commercial e-library for free download by teachers, school librarians, and individuals interested in language studies.

Similar to the language, Russian cultural products do not require state promotion. They are en vogue in Central Asia. A recent public opinion survey[64] posed the following question to residents of the former Soviet republics: "From which countries do you think we should invite to our country more entertainers, writers, artists, and should buy and translate more books, movies, musical works and other cultural products?" Results for the three Central

Table 2.1 Desirable Foreign Providers of Cultural Products in Central Asia (Top Three Countries, 2017)

Kazakhstan		Kyrgyzstan		Tajikistan	
Russia	58%	Russia	42%	Russia	37%
Turkey	23%	Turkey	22%	Uzbekistan	19%
France	21%	Kazakhstan	20%	India	10%

Source: Author, based on data from Igor Zadorin, Ivan Karpov, Alexey Kunakhov, et al. *EDB Integration Barometer—2017* (Saint Petersburg: EDB Centre for Integration Studies, 2017), 73.

Asian states that were covered in the poll are summarized in Table 2.1. Russia emerged as a clear winner, with strong performance by Turkey in Turkic-speaking countries, and a noticeable francophone disposition in Kazakhstan. The Anglosphere and China did not register highly on the cultural radar.

Russian pop culture disseminated via TV, radio, and online platforms enjoys wide popularity in Central Asia. In genres such as comedy shows, documentaries, and soap operas Russian is the preferred language of consumption.[65] It is the market rather than Putin's iron will and Rossotrudnichestvo's clever strategy that compels commercial operators such as Uzbekistan's Uzdigital TV to include Russian channels in the packages they sell.

The Russian language and mass culture appear to have good prospects in Central Asia. Turkmenistan may be an exception but there is simply not enough reliable information available about the situation there. One analytical report published by an anonymous expert recently commented on the revival of Russian language education, media, and cultural consumption, in tough competition with Turkish and English. It cited a hefty bribe for enrollment in a Russian class at school as evidence, however spurious.[66]

Higher Education

Moscow attaches far greater significance to the promotion of university education as part of its soft power agenda in Central Asia compared to supporting schools or teaching Russian to labor migrants. The MFA, Ministry of Education, and Rossotrudnichestvo have worked in unison to draw the best and brightest young talent from the region to the Russian higher education system and met with considerable success. In the decade after 2007, the number of students coming to Russia grew enormously (Table 2.2). Russian tertiary institutions expanded their footprint on the ground as well, with 12,277 enrollments in Kyrgyzstan and 9,357 in Tajikistan in 2017.[67]

Favorable regulatory measures (school leavers from Kazakhstan, Kyrgyzstan, and Tajikistan can apply for admission to Russian universities based on national testing results), sophisticated marketing, stipends, and

Table 2.2 The Number of Central Asian Students Studying at Universities in Russia (2007–2017)

Academic year	Kazakhstan	Kyrgyzstan	Tajikistan	Turkmenistan	Uzbekistan
2006/2007	12,257	1,304	1,399	1,300	3,468
2016/2017	39,757	5,699	13,672	17,264	14,168

Source: A. L. Arefiev, *Eksport rossiiskikh obrazovatelnykh uslug*, Vypusk 8 (Moscow: TsSPiM, 2018), 40.

greater connectivity with potential employers made Russia an attractive destination for outbound student mobility. In 2017, the Russian government adopted an ambitious program to bolster the export of higher education services; further increasing enrollments worldwide 3.5-fold and revenues five-fold by 2025. Introducing the program at the Presidential Council on Strategic Development and Priority Projects, the then Prime Minister Dmitry Medvedev noted that:

> Export of education is not only and so much an opportunity to earn money for our universities. First and foremost this is one of the strongest factors of interpersonal communication, the broadening of cultural contacts . . . and, plainly speaking, an element of constructing the long-term policy of our country.[68]

How well the program will work remains to be seen, but it is noteworthy that barely a year after its launch the Russian Minister of Education reported that the number of tertiary students from Kazakhstan had reached 67,000 including 26.8 thousand covered by the Russian taxpayer and 40,000 who paid tuition fees themselves.[69]

Compatriots Abroad

The Russian government's Integrated Plan on Measures Concerning Compatriots Living Abroad for 2018–2020 main objective is to assist the Russian diaspora in developing its own activities first and foremost.[70] Rossotrudnichestvo's report on this assistance for 2018 was a fairly nondescript list of events "catering to the cultural, scientific, language, and spiritual needs of diaspora communities" including concerts, poetry readings, magazine subscriptions, and the upkeep of cemeteries.[71] This is a far cry from the situation ten or fifteen years ago, when senior government officials talked about the unification of these communities under the Kremlin's guidance and their increased access to power in the former Soviet republics.[72]

Moscow is changing its vision of the diaspora from that of foot soldiers and redoubtable loyalists of the "Russian World" to a more nuanced picture of an enfranchised part of post-Soviet societies in the region, who treat their country of residence as their motherland.[73] Their utility as instruments of soft power promotion lies in acting as intermediaries and expediters of dialogue between Russia and Central Asia. An interesting example here is furnished by the Russian Cultural Center in Uzbekistan (RCCU). It is the RCCU rather than Rossotrudnichestvo's cultural center in Tashkent that operates as the focal point for diasporic life. The RCCU has twenty-three branches, has personal support from President Shavkat Mirziyoyev, enjoys patronage from the Russian Orthodox Church, receives small grants from the Russian government, and maintains an active media presence.[74]

At parliamentary hearings in 2019, the President's Special Envoy for International Cultural Cooperation, Mikhail Shvydkoy, questioned the wisdom of spending money on entertaining and enlightening the shrinking and aging ethnic Russian population in Kyrgyzstan and Tajikistan. He proposed the diversion of resources to local Russophile cultural NGOs, authors, and film and theater directors.[75] Should the existing funding rules be relaxed legislatively, this would certainly improve Rossotrudnichestvo's efficiency.

Working with Central Asian Youth

Russia began purposeful work with Central Asian youth in 2011 under the auspices of a presidential decree endowing short visits of young political, academic, and business leaders to the country. Since 2017, youth cooperation has become the key area among all of Rossotrudnichestvo's operations. Now called the "New Generation" program, it is a departure from the usual over-bureaucratized and formal set of events comprising sports competitions, summer camps for young lawyers and environmentalists, and workshops for stand-up comedians and rap singers.[76] The number of participants from Central Asia is not huge (Kazakhstan had a quota of ninety in 2019) but it is a high-visibility endeavor.

Generation Z in Central Asia does not seem to require a lot of persuasion to see Russia in a positive light. A representative survey of youth commissioned by the Friedrich-Ebert-Stiftung in 2016 captured their strong pro-Russian orientation. One indicator was the question about the desired country for residence for those who contemplated to leave home for work, education, or simply to experience a new and fun life (Table 2.3).

In Tajikistan, despite China's economic investment and the West's robust democracy promotion, 76.7 percent of youngsters believed that Russia offered the best role model for the country's development (the United States scored 4.7 percent of the vote, and China 1 percent).[77] Unsurprisingly, they were also the most ardent supporters of Tajikistan's accession to the EEU.

Table 2.3 Preferred Destination for Central Asian Youth Contemplating Relocation

	Kazakhstan	Kyrgyzstan	Tajikistan	Uzbekistan
Russia	54.7%	41.8%	64.4%	32.3%
China	3.8%	3.5%	-	1.5%
The US	9.4%	22.7%	6.7%	13.8%
Europe	12.3%	10.6%	7.8%	15.4%
Turkey	2.8%	3.5%	2.2%	3.1%

Source: Botagoz Rakisheva, *Molodezh' Tsentralnoi Azii, Sravnitelnyi obzor* (Almaty: Friedrich Ebert Stiftung, 2017), 33.

Strategic Communication

In 2019, Margarita Simonyan, RT's editor-in-chief, boasted before the Duma MPs how Sputnik, in five short years, had managed to create a positive image for Russia which it had previously lacked. According to Simonyan, Sputnik was the number one online broadcaster in Kyrgyzstan, Tajikistan, and Uzbekistan, and among the top five in Kazakhstan. She drew an interesting parallel to impress the MPs: "It's akin to Radio Svoboda [RFE/RL] having a larger audience than the Russian media in Russia itself."[78] The reference to the U.S. Congress–funded mouthpiece RFE/RL was not accidental, as the two media organizations are in direct competition in Central Asia, purveying distinctive storylines in local languages in the national interest of their respective home countries.

Sputnik's programs form the most visible and direct means to communicate official Russian viewpoints to Central Asians. Media content generated inside Russia for domestic use is also consumed in Central Asia because it is aesthetically and commercially attractive. Alarmists in the region and beyond often conflate the two. Assuming that everything originating from Russia is "Putin's propaganda" and a "hybrid warfare" ploy, conspiracy theorists portray a highly coordinated and effective brainwashing campaign.[79] A group of opposition figures in Kazakhstan even published a pamphlet claiming that only 10–15 percent of its citizens were still capable of critical thinking; the rest had been "zombified" by the Russian media with the conniving help of Kremlin stooges including the first President Nursultan Nazarbayev.[80]

Serious studies of the Russian media impact on local public opinion have produced a much more nuanced picture. Laruelle et al. established that, in the case of Kazakhstan, watching does not automatically mean trusting.[81] They persuasively argued that the popularity of Russian programs and official media platforms notwithstanding, the country's information sovereignty was not threatened, noting the national government's efforts to limit the Kremlin's news outreach. It is actually the ferociously independent Russian digital space that creates a headache for Astana when it is enthusiastically emulated in Kazakhstan: "Russian soft power consists of the Russian YouTube: the youth of Kazakhstan are afflicted by the Dud' Syndrome," Kazakhstani state media experts claimed in 2019.[82]

A thorough analysis of Russian media broadcasts as soft power tool in Kyrgyzstan proved that they had only a limited influence on setting the agenda and framing public debate in the country. One of its most interesting findings was that greater exposure to the Russian media did not lead to a more positive disposition toward Russia's sociopolitical institutions and values. A significant exception was a strong correlation between this exposure and negative views on U.S. foreign policy.[83] RT's Simonyan may not have caused Kyrgyzstanis to love Russia more but she did pull her weight in preventing them from wholeheartedly embracing American global leadership.

In order to round up a discussion on measuring soft power, a composite "sociocultural attraction" index developed by Eurasian Development Bank pollsters should be mentioned. It is a survey instrument that comprises five areas: cognitive interest; density of personal communication; personal experience; attractiveness of education; and tourism orientation. The latest available publication from 2017, showed that Russia's sociocultural attraction was high ("phenomenally" so for the density of personal ties) in Kazakhstan, Kyrgyzstan, and Tajikistan, which translated into majority support for EEU membership.[84] Unfortunately, Turkmenistan and Uzbekistan were not included in the survey, and no fresh publication seems to be in the pipeline.

CONCLUSION

Soft power is a relatively new tool in the arsenal of Russian foreign policy in Central Asia. Embraced through necessity as a response to generational change and the expiration of the nostalgic resource of common Soviet past in the region, it has been steadily gaining momentum in the penumbra of the traditional areas of engagement such as political, security, and economic cooperation.

Since 2012, the state apparatus of cultural and humanitarian diplomacy has grown considerably. Operating under the nominal aegis of the MFA, it presently comprises a range of government agencies, regional authorities, parliamentary bodies, media organizations, GONGOs, and corporate entities. Notably missing from the mix is the NGO sector, both as a Russian soft power operator and an object of partnership in Central Asia.

Russia's efforts at creating a positive image for itself in the region today are devoid of imperial hubris and are thin on explicit normative agenda including the conservative bent often ascribed to it in the West. "Brand Russia" at present, rests on the tropes of the land of opportunity, an old friend one can trust amid the uncertainties of the globalized world, and a fun and happening place with rich and accessible culture. It also displays negativity toward Western soft power in Central Asia explained as a defensive reaction to the information warfare unleashed by the United States and its allies.

Russia has been successful in some areas of soft power projection more than others. It has clearly made great strides in the university education sector and appealing to urban youth in Central Asia. Also, it has failed in engaging with opposition groups and NGOs and the full potential of humanitarian aid diplomacy is yet to be realized by the Kremlin. The most significant development that puts wind in the sails of Russia's ability to attract is the unanticipated and not yet fully explained renaissance of Central Asia's Russophile sphere since the late 2000s. An endogenous phenomenon, it has created high demand for the Russian language and Russian cultural products. Moscow has prudently resisted the temptation to convert this boon into pressure on the region's governments.

So far Russia seems to have been successful in meeting modest objectives of its soft power projection in Central Asia: to help keep Kazakhstan, Kyrgyzstan, and Tajikistan as allies, and Uzbekistan as a strategic partner. No one knows for sure what is happening in Turkmenistan. There is no reason to believe that the status quo of Russian soft power in Central Asia may change radically in the mid-term perspective.

NOTES

1. "Vystuplenie i otvety na voprosy Ministra inostrannykh del Rossii S.V. Lavrova v ramkakh 'pravitelstvennogo chasa' v Sovete Federatsii Federalnogo Sobraniia Rossiiskoi Federatsii," *Ministry of Foreign Affairs of the Russian Federation*, December 18, 2013, https://tinyurl.com/yayapngb.

2. "Osnovnye napravleniia politiki Rossiiskoi Federatsii v sfere mezhdunarodnogo kulturno-gumanitarnogo sotrudnichestva," *Russian Federation* (approved by the President of the Russian Federation on December 18, 2010), http://www.consultant.ru/cons/cgi/online.cgi?req=doc&base=LAW&n=130289&fld=134&dst=1000000001,0&rnd=0.9589474497930943#05111835804094804.

3. Joseph S. Nye Jr., *Bound To Lead: The Changing Nature of American Power* (New York: Basic Books, 1990).

4. Vladimir Putin, "Meeting with Russian Ambassadors and Permanent Representatives in International Organisations," *Official Site of the President of the Russian Federation*, July 9, 2012, http://en.kremlin.ru/events/president/news/15902.

5. Olga Leonova, "Interpretatsiia poniatiia 'miagkaia sila' v nauke," *Observer* 301, no. 2 (2015): 80–9.

6. Christopher Walker, "What Is 'Sharp Power'?" *Journal of Democracy* 29, no. 3 (2018): 9–23.

7. Olga Leonova, *"Sharp Power*—novaia tekhnologiia vliianiia v globalnom mire," *Mirovaia ekonomika i mezhdunarodnye otnosheniia* 63, no. 2 (2019): 21–28.

8. Joseph S. Nye Jr., *The Future of Power* (New York: Public Affairs, 2011).

9. Ibid., 81–82.

10. "Ukaz Prezidenta Rossiiskoi Federatsii 'Ob utverzhdenii Osnov gosudarstvennoi kulturnoi politiki", *Official Site of the President of the Russian Federation*, December 24, 2014, http://static.kremlin.ru/media/events/files/41d526bc0d7d43e934f4.pdf.

11. M. Steven Fish, "What is Putinism?" *Journal of Democracy* 28, no. 4 (2019): 64.

12. Marlene Laruelle, *The "Russian World" Russia's Soft Power and Geopolitical Imagination* (Washington DC: Center on Global Interests, 2015).

13. According to a 2015 opinion survey, the youth of Tajikistan clearly identified Russia as a global leader in innovation, science, and technological and industrial development. Muzaffar Olimov and Shavkat Sahibov, *Molodezh' Tsentralnoi Azii. Tadzhikistan* (Almaty: Friedrich Ebert Stiftung, 2017), 292; on mixed ideological tropes in the "Russian world" discourse, see S. M. Aleinikova, *"Russkii Mir": Belorusskii vzgliad* (Minsk: RIVSh, 2017).

14. Yulia Kiseleva, "Russia's Soft Power Discourse: Identity, Status and the Attraction of Power," *Politics* 35, no. 3–4, 2015): 316–29.

15. Nye, *The Future of Power*, 81.

16. A. O. Naumov, *"Miagkaia sila," 'Tsvetnye revoliutsii' i tekhnologii smeny politicheskikh rezhimov v nachale XXI veka* (Moscow: ARGAMAK Media, 2016), 21–22.

17. "The Foreign Policy Concept of the Russian Federation (Approved by President of the Russian Federation V. Putin on 12 February 2013)," *The Embassy of the Russian Federation to the United Kingdom of Great Britain and Northern Ireland*, https://www.rusemb.org.uk/in1/ (accessed June 22, 2020).

18. "Foreign Policy Concept of the Russian Federation (Approved by President of the Russian Federation Vladimir Putin on November 30, 2016)," *Official Site of the Foreign Ministry of the Russian Federation*, December 1, 2016, https://www.mid.ru/en/foreign_policy/official_documents/-/asset_publisher/CptICkB6BZ29/content/id/2542248.

19. Anna Gussarova and Yevgeniy Khon, *Russian Soft Power in Kazakhstan (and Central Asia): Taken for Granted?* (Almaty: Friedrich Ebert Stiftung, 2017), 6.

20. Anna A. Velikaya, "The Russian Approach to Public Diplomacy and Humanitarian Cooperation," *Rising Powers Quarterly* 3, no. 3 (2018): 39–61.

21. M. A. Neimark, *"Miagkaia sila" v mirovoi politike* (Moscow: Dashkov & Co., 2018), 196.

22. For a concise summary of such criticisms, see Alexei Malashenko, "Interesy i shansy Rossii v Tsentralnoi Azii", *Pro et Contra*, no. 58 (2013): 21–34.

23. Civic Chamber of the Russian Federation, *'Miagkaia sila' Rossii v novom tysiacheletii: imeiushiisia potentsial i perspektivy razvitiia* (Moscow: Obshchestvennaia Palata RF, 2012), 40; 47.

24. "Rossiia i Tsentralnaia Aziia," *Foreign Ministry of the Russian Federation*, https://www.mid.ru/rossia-i-problemy-central-noj-azii/, (accessed October 8, 2019).

25. A. V Sternik, "Vystuplenie direktora Tret'ego departamenta stran SNG MID Rossii," in *Rossiia i Tsentralnaia Aziia: novye perspektivy* (Moscow: MGIMO-Universitet, 2018), 11–13.

26. The comparison can be stretched further by noting that the government grant of £168 million constituted just 14.3 percent of the British Council's revenue in 2017–18 fiscal year whereas Rossotrudnichestvo relied almost exclusively on state funding.

27. "About Rossotrudnichestvo," *Federal Agency for the Commonwealth of Independent States, Compatriots Living Abroad and International Humanitarian Cooperation*, http://rs.gov.ru/en/about, (accessed October 5, 2019).

28. For example, the Military University under the Ministry of Defense of Russia has acted as the so-called "base [i.e. preferred] training facility" for military specialists from Central Asia in the "humanitarian, law, financial and linguistic spheres." Petr Kamnev, "Shkola komandirov gumanitarnykh voisk," *Voenno-promyshlennyi kurier* 806, no. 43 (November 5, 2019): 6.

29. *Doklad ob itogakh deiatelnosti Minekonomrazvitiia Rossii za 2018 god i zadachakh na 2019 god* (Moscow: Ministry for Economic Development, 2019), 97.

30. "RBK: Minekonomiki sozdaet strukturu po rabote s grazhdanskim obshchestvom v SNG i EAES", *Kommersant*, September 19, 2019, https://www.kommersant.ru/doc/4096688.

31. Cited in V. S. Leshukov, "Normativno-pravovye osnovy gumanitarnogo sotrudnichestva Orenburgskoi oblasti i Zapadno-Kazakhstanskoi oblasti RK," *Sovremennye evraziiskie issledovaniia*, no. 3 (2015): 22.

32. "Putin pribyl v Omsk na Forum mezhregionalnogo sotrudnichestva s Kazakhstanom," *TASS.ru*, November 8, 2019, https://tass.ru/politika/7089245.

33. "V Gosdume RF predstavleny programmy Rossotrudnichestva k 75-letiiu Pobedy dlia stran SNG", *CIS Executive Committee*, March 18, 2020, http://www.cis.minsk.by/news/13332/v_gosdume_rf_predstavleny_programmy_rossotrudnichestva_k_75-letiju_pobedy_dlja_stran_sng.

34. "Gosduma predlagaet uvelichit' gosudarstvennuiu podderzhku raboty s sootechestvennikami za rubezhom," *State Duma of the Russian Federation*, June 19, 2012, http://duma.gov.ru/news/7017/. The Chair of the Committee at the time, an MP from the LDPR, claimed that it was unacceptable for a great power such as Russia to spend the equivalent of only 5 percent of what the US and 30 percent of what Spain did on maintaining language and cultural centers abroad.

35. "Rossotrudnichestvo oproverglo zaiavlenie deputata GD o tratakh na zarplaty", *RIA Novosti*, October 19, 2018, https://ria.ru/20181019/1531021888.html.

36. Konstantin Zatulin, "Finansirovanie nuzhno napravliat' n ate veshchi, kotorye pozvloiat dostich' tseli," *Committee on the CIS, Eurasian Integration and Ties with Compatriots of the State Duma of the Russian Federation*, April 9, 2019 http://komitet.info/about/membersblogs/konstantin-zatulin-funding-should-be-directed-to-those-things-that-will-allow-you-to-reach-the-goal/.

37. Former Kyrgyz President's characterization of Matviyenko cited in Liubov Borisenko, "Valentina Matvienko pribyla s rabochim vizitom v Kirgiziiu," *Rossiiskaia gazeta*, July 3, 2017, https://rg.ru/2017/07/03/valentina-matvienko-pribyla-s-rabochim-vizitom-v-kirgiziiu.html.

38. Nikita Viatchianin, "Valentina Matvienko pozvala Uzbekistan v Evraziiu," *Parlamentskaia gazeta*, October 2, 2019, https://www.pnp.ru/politics/valentina-matvienko-pozvala-uzbekistan-v-evraziyu.html.

39. Michael O. Slobodchikoff and G. Douglas Davis, "Roots of Russian Soft Power: Rethinking Russian National Identity," *Comparative Politics, Russia* 8, no. 2 (2017): 31.

40. By way of example, Sputnik-Uzbekistan proudly reported that Rossotrudnichestvo held 230 events in the Central Asian republic in 2016 attended by 120,000 people. It highlighted the success of the Days of Russian Culture, master classes for teachers of the Russian language, and ninety tourist trips to Russia won by the winners of diverse contests and quizzes. "Itogi goda Rossotrudnichestva: 120 tys. gostei posetili 230 meropriiatii", *Sputnik-Uzbekistan*, December 24, 2016, https://uz.sputniknews.ru/culture/20161224/4463874/rnck-itogi-120-tysyach.html.

41. "O tsentre," *Samrau Eurasian Centre*, http://ecsamrau.com/o_kompanii, (accessed October 16, 2018).

42. Evgenii Primakov, "Khvatit nam balalaek v gumanitarnoi politike," *Novye izvestiia*, April 8, 2019, https://newizv.ru/article/general/08-04-2019/evgeniy-primakov-hvatit-nam-balalaek-v-gumanitarnoy-politike.

43. T. N. Manuilova, "Otchet o rezultatakh kontrolnogo meropriiatiia," *Bulletin of the Accounts Chamber of Russia* 257, no. 5 (2019): 212–39.

44. Primakov, "Khvatit nam balalaek."

45. Altynai Alieva, "Kakuiu rol' igraet Alisher Usmanov v rossisko-uzbekskikh otnosheniiakh?" *IA Tsentr*, July 30, 2019, https://ia-centr.ru/experts/altynay-alieva/kakuyu-rol-igraet-alisher-usmanov-v-rossiysko-uzbekskikh-otnosheniyakh/.

46. "Blagotvoritelnost," *Lukoil Uzbekistan Operating Company*, https://lukoil-international.uz/ru/Responsibility/Charity?wid=widYApchcNikU2ByYMZBbwRbQ, (accessed September 13, 2018).

47. For a concise discussion on the state of the field, see J. P. Singh and Stuart MacDonald, *Soft Power Today Measuring the Influences and Effects* (Edinburgh: British Council and the University of Edinburgh, 2019).

48. Velikaya, "The Russian Approach to Public Diplomacy," 43.

49. "Foreign Minister Sergey Lavrov's remarks and answers to questions during the Government Hour at the State Duma of the Federal Assembly of the Russian Federation," *Foreign Ministry of the Russian Federation*, January 25, 2017, https://tinyurl.com/y8k73r3s.

50. Anna Kholiavko, "Rossiia sokratila pomoshch drugim stranam," *Vedomosti*, November 26, 2018, https://www.vedomosti.ru/politics/articles/2018/11/27/787556-rossiya-sokratila-pomosch.

51. See Olivier Roy, *The New Central Asia: Geopolitics and the Birth of Nations* (London: I.B. Tauris, 2000), 198.

52. William Fierman, "Russian in Post-Soviet Central Asia: A Comparison with the States of the Baltic and South Caucasus," *Europe-Asia Studies* 64, no. 6 (2012): 1097.

53. For a detailed discussion, see Natalya Kosmarskaya and Artyom Kosmarski, "'Russian Culture' in Central Asia as a Transethnic Phenomenon," in *Global Russian Cultures*, ed. Kevin M. F. Platt (Madison: University of Wisconsin Press, 2019).

54. I. V. Zadorin and I. V. Podobed, "Dinamika rasprostraneniia russkogo iazyka v bytovom obshchenii naselenija stran Severnoi Evrazii," *The Eurasian Monitor*, January 30, 2018, http://eurasiamonitor.org/iazyk_i_miediapotrieblieniie.

55. Rustem Kadyrzhanov, "O vliianii postsovetskoi etnodemograficheskoi dinamiki na kultunuiu integratsiiu etnosov v Kazakhstane," *Kazakhstan-Spektr* 88, no. 2 (2019): 79–91.

56. Noora Khudoikulova, "Zhiteli Tadzhikistana o russkom iazyke v respublike," *Slavica Helsingiensia*, no. 45 (2014): 189–207.

57. "Uzbekistan: A Second Coming for the Russian Language?" *Eurasianet*, June 19, 2019, https://eurasianet.org/uzbekistan-a-second-coming-for-the-russian-language. In 2008, the number of such schools stood at 739.

58. Bakhtiiar Akhmedzhanov, "Luchshe chem doma: kirgizskie migrant nakhodiat sebia v stolitse bystree mnogikh moskvichei," *CA-Portal*, April 9, 2013, http://www.ca-portal.ru/article:6021.

59. A. V. Rad'kov, "Analiticheskaia spravka," *Rossotrudnichestvo*, January 18, 2018, https://tinyurl.com/y7o45m5t.

60. "Zasedanie Soveta po russkomu iazyku," *Official Portal of the President of the Russian Federation*, November 5, 2019, http://kremlin.ru/events/president/news/61986/work.

61. Vadim Shneider, "Osnovnye aspekty sotrudnichestva Rossii i Uzbekistana v sfere obrazovaniia na sovremennom etape," *Postsovetskie issledovaniia* 2, no. 7 (2019): 1472–6.

62. "Rossiia profinansiruet razvitie russkikh shkol v Tadzhikistane," *SNG Today*, October 21, 2019, https://sng.today/dushanbe/11577-rossija-profinansiruet-razvitie-russkih-shkol-v-tadzhikistane.html.

63. Ekaterina Ivashchenko,"Gruzite uchebniki samoletami," *Fergana News*, February 7, 2018. https://www.fergananews.com/articles/9790.

64. Igor Zadorin, Ivan Karpov, Alexey Kunakhov, et al. *EDB Integration Barometer—2017* (Saint Petersburg: EDB Centre for Integration Studies, 2017), 73.

65. M-Vector, "Media Research (8th Wave)," *Soros Foundation—Kyrgyzstan*, 2018, https://soros.kg/srs/wp-content/uploads/2019/08/M-Vector-Report-on-Media-Preferences-8TH-WAVE.pdf; Saifiddin Karaev, "Kto chto predpochitaet v Tadzhikistane," *Asia-Plus*, June 7, 2019, https://asiaplustj.info/ru/news/tajikistan/society/20190607/mediaissledovanie-v-tadzhikistane-televidenie-i-sotsseti-nabirayut-populyarnost-gazeti-i-radio-teryayut-auditoriyu.

66. Anon, "Turkmen Paradox: De Jure—There Is No Russian Language, De Facto—It Is Necessary," *Central Asian Bureau for Analytical Reporting*, February 25, 2019, https://cabar.asia/en/turkmen-paradox-de-jure-there-is-no-russian-language-de-facto-it-is-necessary/.

67. A. L Arefiev, *Eksport rossiiskikh obrazovatelnykh uslug, Eksport rossiiskikh obrazovatelnykh uslug* (Vypusk 8. Moscow: TsSPiM, 2018), 488–89.

68. Dmitry Medvedev, "Vstupitelnoe slovo: Zasedanie prezidiuma Soveta pri Prezidente RF po strategicheskomu razvitiiu i prioritetnym proektam", *Official portal of the Government of the Russian Federation*, May 30, 2017, http://government.ru/projects/selection/653/27862/.

69. Olga Vasilieva quoted in "Ministr obrazovaniia Rossii priglasila kazakhstantsev besplatno uchitsia v vuzakh," *Sputnik-Kazakhstan*, March 5, 2018, https://ru.sputniknews.kz/society/20180305/4815854/russia-kazakhstan-obrazovaniye-olga-vasilyeva.html.

70. "Kompleksnyi plan osnovnykh meropriiatii po realizatsii gosudarstvennoi politiki Rossiiskoi Federatsii v otnoshenii sootechestvennikov, prozhivaiushikh za rubezhom," *Ministry of Foreign Affairs of the Russian Federation*, May 4, 2018, https://www.mid.ru/activity/compatriots/commission/-/asset_publisher/ic6G-4m61ZGUP/content/id/3208269.

71. *Doklad o rezultatakh deiatelnosti Rossotrudnichestva po realizatsii vozlozhennykh na nego polnomochii.za 2018 god* (Moscow: Rossotrudnichestvo, 2019), 17.

72. Aleksandr Chepurin, "Sootechestvenniki kak zarubezhnyi resurs," *Nezavisimaia gazeta*, February 13, 2006, http://www.ng.ru/courier/2006-02-13/12_resurs.html.

73. D. E. Letniakov and N. N. Emelianova, "Strategii 'miagkoi sily' v postsovetskoi Tsentralnoi Azii: Rossiia vs SShA, Kitai, India," *Mir Rossii* 26, no. 4 (2017): 122–3.

74. Sergei Mironov, "Tsel'—sotrudnichestvo i sozidanie," *Zvezda Vostoka*, no. 2 (2019): 14–6.

75. Gosudarstvennaia Duma. *O gumanitarnom vektore gosudarstvennoi politiki na sovremennom etape*. Moscow: Izdanie Gosudarstvennoi Dumy, 2019, 33.

76. "Programma 'Novoe Pokolenie,'", *Rossotrudnichestvo*, 2019, http://www.rs.gov.ru/%20%20/activities/4/projects/23.

77. S. Olimova and M. Olimov, "Geopoliticheskie orientatsii molodezhi Tadzhikistana: izoliatsiia vs integratsiia," *Rossiia i novye gosudarstva Evrazii*, no. 2 (2018): 77.

78. Gosudarstvennaia Duma, *O gumanitarnom vektore gosudarstvennoi politiki*, 26.

79. For a typical report, see Kanat Altynbaev, "Central Asians Grow Numb to the Kremlin's Propaganda, Lies on TV," *Caravanserai*, February 8, 2018, https://central.asia-news.com/en_GB/articles/cnmi_ca/features/2019/02/08/feature-01.

80. Kazakhstan 2.0, "How the Kremlin Zombifies the Russian-Speaking Population of Kazakhstan," *Expert.kz*, 2018, https://propaganda.kz.expert/page2119252.html.

81. Marlene Laruelle, Dylan Royce, and Serik Beyssembayev, "Untangling the Puzzle of "Russia's Influence" in Kazakhstan." *Eurasian Geography and Economics* 60, no. 2 (2019): 211–43.

82. "Rossiia, Kitai i Tsentralnaia Aziia. Nekotorye aspekty geopoliticheskoi revnosti," *Valdai Discussion Club*, May 16, 2019, https://ru.valdaiclub.com/events/posts/articles/aspekty-geopoliticheskoy-revnosti/. Yuri Dud' is an independent

Russian vlogger with over six million subscribers on YouTube and an average of ten million views per video.
  83. Hannah S. Chapman and Theodore P Gerber, "Opinion-Formation and Issue-Framing Effects of Russian News in Kyrgyzstan," *International Studies Quarterly* 63, no. 3 (2019): 756–69.
  84. Zadorin et al., *EDB Integration Barometer-2017,* 15; 58–75.

REFERENCES

Akhmedzhanov, Bakhtiiar. "Luchshe chem doma: kirgizskie migrant nakhodiat sebia v stolitse bystree mnogikh moskvichei." *CA-Portal*, April 9, 2013. http://www.ca-portal.ru/article:6021.

Aleinikova, S. M. *'Russkii Mir': Belorusskii vzgliad*. Minsk: RIVSh, 2017.

Alieva, Altynai. "Kakuiu rol' igraet Alisher Usmanov v rossisko-uzbekskikh otnosheniiakh?" *IA Tsentr*, July 30, 2019. https://ia-centr.ru/experts/altynay-alieva/kakuyu-rol-igraet-alisher-usmanov-v-rossiysko-uzbekskikh-otnosheniyakh/.

Anon. "Turkmen Paradox: De Jure—There Is No Russian Language, De Facto—It Is Necessary." *Central Asian Bureau for Analytical Reporting*, February 25, 2019. https://cabar.asia/en/turkmen-paradox-de-jure-there-is-no-russian-language-de-facto-it-is-necessary/.

Arefiev, A. L. *Eksport rossiiskikh obrazovatelnykh uslug, Eksport rossiiskikh obrazovatelnykh uslug*. Vypusk 8. Moscow: TsSPiM, 2018.

Borisenko, Liubov. "Valentina Matvienko pribyla s rabochim vizitom v Kirgiziiu." *Rossiiskaia gazeta*, July 3, 2017. https://rg.ru/2017/07/03/valentina-matvienko-pribyla-s-rabochim-vizitom-v-kirgiziiu.html.

Chapman, Hannah S., and Theodore P Gerber. "Opinion-Formation and Issue-Framing Effects of Russian News in Kyrgyzstan." *International Studies Quarterly* 63, no. 3 (2019): 756–69.

Chepurin, Aleksandr. "Sootechestvenniki kak zarubezhnyi resurs." *Nezavisimaia gazeta*, February 13, 2006. http://www.ng.ru/courier/2006-02-13/12_resurs.html.

CIS Executive Committee. "V Gosdume RF predstavleny programmy Rossotrudnichestva k 75-letiiu Pobedy dlia stran SNG," March 18, 2020. http://www.cis.minsk.by/news/13332/v_gosdume_rf_predstavleny_programmy_rossotrudnichestva_k_75-letiju_pobedy_dlja_stran_sng.

Eurasianet. "Uzbekistan: A Second Coming for the Russian language?" June 19, 2019. https://eurasianet.org/uzbekistan-a-second-coming-for-the-russian-language.

Fierman, William. "Russian in Post-Soviet Central Asia: A Comparison with the States of the Baltic and South Caucasus." *Europe-Asia Studies* 64, no. 6 (2012): 1077–100.

Fish, M. Steven. "What is Putinism?" *Journal of Democracy* 28, no. 4 (2019): 61–75.

Gosudarstvennaia Duma. *O gumanitarnom vektore gosudarstvennoi politiki na sovremennom etape*. Moscow: Izdanie Gosudarstvennoi Dumy, 2019.

Gussarova, Anna, and Yevgeniy Khon. *Russian Soft Power in Kazakhstan (and Central Asia): Taken for Granted?* Almaty: Friedrich Ebert Stiftung, 2017.
Ivashchenko, Ekaterina. "Gruzite uchebniki samoletami." *Fergana News*, February 7, 2018. https://www.fergananews.com/articles/9790.
Kadyrzhanov, Rustem. "O vliianii postsovetskoi etnodemograficheskoi dinamiki na kultunuiu integratsiiu etnosov v Kazakhstane." *Kazakhstan-Spektr* 88, no. 2 (2019): 79–91.
Kamnev, Petr. "Shkola komandirov gumanitarnykh voisk." *Voenno-promyshlennyi kurier* 806, no. 43 (November 5, 2019): 6.
Karaev, Saifiddin. "Kto chto predpochitaet v Tadzhikistane." *Asia-Plus*, June 7, 2019. https://asiaplustj.info/ru/news/tajikistan/society/20190607/mediaissledo-vanie-v-tadzhikistane-televidenie-i-sotsseti-nabirayut-populyarnost-gazeti-i-radio-teryayut-auditoriyu.
Kazakhstan 2.0. "How the Kremlin Zombifies the Russian-Speaking Population of Kazakhstan." *Expert.kz*, 2018. https://propaganda.kz.expert/page2119252.html.
Kholiavko, Anna. "Rossiia sokratila pomoshch drugim stranam." *Vedomosti*, November 26, 2018. https://www.vedomosti.ru/politics/articles/2018/11/27/787556-rossiya-sokratila-pomosch.
Khudoikulova, Noora. "Zhiteli Tadzhikistana o russkom iazyke v respublike." *Slavica Helsingiensia* 45 (2014): 189–207.
Kiseleva, Yulia. "Russia's Soft Power Discourse: Identity, Status and the Attraction of Power." *Politics* 35, no. 3–4 (2015): 316–29.
Kommersant. "RBK: Minekonomiki sozdaet strukturu po rabote s grazhdanskim obshchestvom v SNG i EAES," September 19, 2019, https://www.kommersant.ru/doc/4096688.
Kosmarskaya, Natalya, and Artyom Kosmarski. "'Russian Culture' in Central Asia as a Transethnic Phenomenon." In *Global Russian Cultures*, edited by Kevin M. F. Platt, 69–93. Madison: University of Wisconsin Press, 2019.
Laruelle, Marlene. *The "Russian World" Russia's Soft Power and Geopolitical Imagination*. Washington DC: Center on Global Interests, 2015.
Laruelle, Marlene, Dylan Royce, and Serik Beyssembayev. "Untangling the Puzzle of "Russia's influence" in Kazakhstan." *Eurasian Geography and Economics* 60, no. 2 (2019): 211–43.
Leonova, Olga. "Interpretatsiia poniatiia 'miagkaia sila' v nauke." *Observer* 301, no. 2 (2015): 80–89.
Leonova, Olga. "Sharp Power—novaia tekhnologiia vliianiia v globalnom mire." *Mirovaia ekonomika i mezhdunarodnye otnosheniia* 63, no. 2 (2019): 21–28.
Leshukov, V. S. "Normativno-pravovye osnovy gumanitarnogo sotrudnichestva Orenburgskoi oblasti i Zapadno-Kazakhstanskoi oblasti RK." *Sovremennye evraziiskie issledovaniia*, no. 3 (2015): 18–26.
Letniakov, D. E., and N. N. Emelianova. "Strategii 'miagkoi sily' v postsovetskoi Tsentralnoi Azii: Rossiia vs SShA, Kitai, India." *Mir Rossii* 26, no 4 (2017): 118–42.
Malashenko, Alexei. "Interesy i shansy Rossii v Tsentralnoi Azii." *Pro et Contra*, no. 58 (2013): 21–34.

Manuilova, T. N. "Otchet o rezultatakh kontrolnogo meropriiatiia." *Bulletin of the Accounts Chamber of Russia* 257, no. 5 (2019): 212–39.
Medvedev, Dmitry. "Vstupitelnoe slovo: Zasedanie prezidiuma Soveta pri Prezidente RF po strategicheskomu razvitiiu i prioritetnym proektam." *Official Portal of the Government of the Russian Federation*, May 30, 2017. http://government.ru/projects/selection/653/27862/.
Mironov, Sergei. "Tsel'—sotrudnichestvo i sozidanie." *Zvezda Vostoka*, no. 2 (2019): 14–16.
M-Vector. "Media Research (8th Wave)." *Soros Foundation—Kyrgyzstan*, 2018. https://soros.kg/srs/wp-content/uploads/2019/08/M-Vector-Report-on-Media-Preferences-8TH-WAVE.pdf.
Neimark, M. A. *'Miagkaia sila' v mirovoi politike*. Moscow: Dashkov & Co., 2018.
Naumov, A. O. *'Miagkaia sila', 'Tsvetnye revoliutsii' i tekhnologii smeny politicheskikh rezhimov v nachale XXI veka*. Moscow: ARGAMAK Media, 2016.
Nye, Joseph S. Jr. *Bound to Lead: The Changing Nature of American Power*. New York: Basic Books, 1990.
Nye, Joseph S. Jr. *The Future of Power*. New York: Public Affairs, 2011.
Olimov, Muzaffar, and Shavkat Sahibov. *Molodezh' Tsentralnoi Azii. Tadzhikistan*. Almaty: Friedrich Ebert Stiftung, 2017.
Olimova, S., and M. Olimov. "Geopoliticheskie orientatsii molodezhi Tadzhikistana: izoliatsiia vs integratsiia." *Rossiia i novye gosudarstva Evrazii*, no. 2 (2018): 64–79.
Primakov, Evgenii. "Khvatit nam balalaek v gumanitarnoi politike." *Novye izvestiia*, April 8, 2019. https://newizv.ru/article/general/08-04-2019/evgeniy-primakov-hvatit-nam-balalaek-v-gumanitarnoy-politike.
Putin, Vladimir. "Meeting with Russian Ambassadors and Permanent Representatives in International Organisations." *Official Site of the President of the Russian Federation*, July 9, 2012. http://en.kremlin.ru/events/president/news/15902.
Rad'kov, A. V. "Analiticheskaia spravka." *Rossotrudnichestvo*, January 18, 2018. https://tinyurl.com/y8k7r3s.
RIA Novosti. "Rossotrudnichestvo oproverglo zaiavlenie deputata GD o tratakh na zarplaty," October 19, 2018. https://ria.ru/20181019/1531021888.html.
Rossotrudnichestvo. *Doklad o rezultatakh deiatelnosti Rossotrudnichestva po realizatsii vozlozhennykh na nego polnomochii.za 2018 god*. Moscow: Rossotrudnichestvo, 2019.
Rossotrudnichestvo. "Programma 'Novoe Pokolenie," 2019. http://www.rs.gov.ru/%20%20/activities/4/projects/23.
Roy, Olivier. *The New Central Asia: Geopolitics and the Birth of Nations*. London: I.B. Tauris, 2000.
Russian Federation. "Osnovnye napravleniia politiki Rossiiskoi Federatsii v sfere mezhdunarodnogo kulturno-gumanitarnogo sotrudnichestva." Approved by the President of the Russian Federation on December 18, 2010. http://www.consultant.ru/cons/cgi/online.cgi?req=doc&base=LAW&n=130289&fld=134&dst=1000000001,0&rnd=0.9589474497930943#05111835804094804.

Russian Federation, Civic Chamber of. *'Miagkaia sila' Rossii v novom tysiacheletii: imeiushiisia potentsial i perspektivy razvitiia*. Moscow: Obshchestvennaia Palata RF, 2012.

Russian Federation, Embassy of to the United Kingdom. The Foreign Policy Concept of the Russian Federation (Approved by President of the Russian Federation V. Putin on 12 February 2013)," https://www.rusemb.org.uk/in1/. Accessed June 22, 2020.

Russian Federation, Federal Agency for the Commonwealth of Independent States, Compatriots Living Abroad and International Humanitarian Cooperation. "About Rossotrudnichestvo." http://rs.gov.ru/en/about. Accessed October 5, 2019.

Russian Federation, Ministry for Economic Development of. *Doklad ob itogakh deiatelnosti Minekonomrazvitiia Rossii za 2018 god i zadachakh na 2019 god*. Moscow: Ministry for Economic Development, 2019.

Russian Federation, Ministry of Foreign Affairs of. "Foreign Minister Sergey Lavrov's remarks and answers to questions during the Government Hour at the State Duma of the Federal Assembly of the Russian Federation," January 25, 2017. https://tinyurl.com/y8k73r3s.

Russian Federation, Ministry of Foreign Affairs of. "Foreign Policy Concept of the Russian Federation (Approved by President of the Russian Federation Vladimir Putin on November 30, 2016)," December 1, 2016. https://www.mid.ru/en/foreign_policy/official_documents/-/asset_publisher/CptICkB6BZ29/content/id/2542248.

Russian Federation, Ministry of Foreign Affairs of. "Kompleksnyi plan osnovnykh meropriiatii po realizatsii gosudarstvennoi politiki Rossiiskoi Federatsii v otnoshenii sootechestvennikov, prozhivaiushikh za rubezhom," May 4, 2018. https://www.mid.ru/activity/compatriots/commission/-/asset_publisher/ic6G4m61ZGUP/content/id/3208269.

Russian Federation, Ministry of Foreign Affairs of. "Rossiia i Tsentralnaia Aziia." https://www.mid.ru/rossia-i-problemy-central-noj-azii/. Accessed October 8, 2019.

Russian Federation, Ministry of Foreign Affairs of. "Vystuplenie i otvety na voprosy Ministra inostrannykh del Rossii S.V. Lavrova v ramkakh 'pravitelstvennogo chasa' v Sovete Federatsii Federalnogo Sobraniia Rossiiskoi Federatsii," December 18, 2013. https://tinyurl.com/yayapngb.

Russian Federation, President of. "Ukaz Prezidenta Rossiiskoi Federatsii 'Ob utverzhdenii Osnov gosudarstvennoi kulturnoi politiki," December 24, 2014.

Russian Federation, State Duma of. "Gosduma predlagaet uvelichit' gosudarstvennuiu podderzhku raboty s sootechestvennikami za rubezhom," June 19, 2012. http://duma.gov.ru/news/7017/.

Shneider, Vadim. "Osnovnye aspekty sotrudnichestva Rossii i Uzbekistana v sfere obrazovaniia na sovremennom etape." *Postsovetskie issledovaniia* 2, no. 7 (2019): 1472–6.

Singh, J. P., and Stuart MacDonald. *Soft Power Today Measuring the Influences and Effects*. Edinburgh: British Council and the University of Edinburgh, 2019.

Slobodchikoff, Michael O., and G. Douglas Davis. "Roots of Russian Soft Power: Rethinking Russian National Identity." *Comparative Politics, Russia* 8, no. 2 (2017): 19–36.

SNG Today. "Rossiia profinansiruet razvitie russkikh shkol v Tadzhikistane," October 21, 2019. https://sng.today/dushanbe/11577-rossija-profinansiruet-razvitie-russkih-shkol-v-tadzhikistane.html.

Sputnik-Kazakhstan. "Ministr obrazovaniia Rossii priglasila kazakhstantsev besplatno uchitsia v vuzakh," March 5, 2018. https://ru.sputniknews.kz/society/20180305/4815854/russia-kazakhstan-obrazovaniye-olga-vasilyeva.html.

Sputnik-Uzbekistan. "Itogi goda Rossotrudnichestva: 120 tys. gostei posetili 230 meropriiatii," December 24, 2016. https://uz.sputniknews.ru/culture/20161224/4463874/rnck-itogi-120-tysyach.html.

Sternik, A. V. "Vystuplenie direktora Tret'ego departamenta stran SNG MID Rossii." In *Rossiia i Tsentralnaia Aziia: novye perspektivy*, 8–14. Moscow: MGIMO-Universitet, 2018.

TASS.ru. "Putin pribyl v Omsk na Forum mezhregionalnogo sotrudnichestva s Kazakhstanom," November 8, 2019. https://tass.ru/politika/7089245.

Valdai Discussion Club. "Rossiia, Kitai i Tsentralnaia Aziia. Nekotorye aspekty geopoliticheskoi revnosti," May 16, 2019. https://ru.valdaiclub.com/events/posts/articles/aspekty-geopoliticheskoy-revnosti/.

Velikaya, Anna A. "The Russian Approach to Public Diplomacy and Humanitarian Cooperation." *Rising Powers Quarterly* 3, no. 3 (2018): 39–61.

Viatchianin, Nikita. "Valentina Matvienko pozvala Uzbekistan v Evraziiu." *Parlamentskaia gazeta*, October 2, 2019. https://www.pnp.ru/politics/valentina-matvienko-pozvala-uzbekistan-v-evraziyu.html.

Walker, Christopher. "What Is 'Sharp Power'?" *Journal of Democracy* 29, no.3 (2018): 9–23.

Zadorin, Igor, Ivan Karpov, Alexey Kunakhov, Roman Kuznetsov, Arteom Rykov, Lyudmila Shubina, and Vladimir Pereboev. *EDB Integration Barometer-2017*. Saint Petersburg: EDB Centre for Integration Studies, 2017.

Zadorin, I. V., and I. V. Podobed. "Dinamika rasprostraneniia russkogo iazyka v bytovom obshchenii naseleniia stran Severnoi Evrazii." *The Eurasian Monitor*, January 30, 2018.

Zatulin, Konstantin. "Finansirovanie nuzhno napravliat' n ate veshchi, kotorye pozvloiat dostich' tseli." *Committee on the CIS, Eurasian Integration and Ties with Compatriots of the State Duma of the Russian Federation*, April 9, 2019. http://komitet.info/about/membersblogs/konstantin-zatulin-funding-should-be-directed-to-those-things-that-will-allow-you-to-reach-the-goal/.

Chapter 3

An Increasingly Hard Chinese Soft Power in Central Asia? Reshaping Joseph Nye's Concept under Authoritarianism

Sebastien Peyrouse

In less than three decades since the collapse of the Soviet Union, China has emerged as a key player throughout all Central Asia. With between 26 and 45 billion USD in annual trade, it is either the first or second trading partner of all states in the region, far ahead of Russia which had largely dominated until 2008. Beijing is also the main investor in several key sectors such as oil, gas, mineral ore extraction, infrastructure, and the banking sector, and has gained increasing visibility with the multitude of consumer goods it exports to the region.[1] In addition, the Chinese and Central Asian governments have developed a common narrative on security and signed a set of cooperation agreements to address their version of how Islamism and violent extremism can pose regional threats. In 2013, President Xi Jinping's announcement of the hundreds of billions of dollars' Belt and Road Initiative (BRI) to connect, by trade and infrastructure, Asia with Europe and other continents along ancient trade routes, substantiated China's ambitions in the region.[2]

Yet, despite twenty years of increasingly prominent political, economic, and security relations, China for most Central Asians remains a little known, poorly understood, and even feared country. Despite its success in emerging as the world's third global power in less than three decades, its development model, which combines state capitalism and an export-oriented economy with authoritarian one-party constitutionalism, remains unpopular as compared to other models, in particular the Russian one, which between one-half and three-quarters of Central Asian youth view as a benchmark.[3] More strikingly, since the 2000s, articles critical of China have proliferated in Central Asian media. Although regularly praised for its commitment to the local and global economy, China's presence and investments are also disparaged as self-beneficial, overly invasive, and even challenging to the development and independence of the region.⁴ These dreads are further fed by clichés and phobias inherited from the Soviet regime,⁵ which after the Sino–Soviet rupture had made China an enemy of Islam and of Turkic peoples.

Such apprehensions about China are not specific to Central Asia. From Asia to Africa and Latin America, Beijing's ambitions to become the world's leading power and its fast growing presence abroad have triggered debates, resistance, and even Sinophobic sentiment.⁶ To counter this trend and, subsequently, to mitigate potential or existing tension with local governments and populations abroad, which down the road could threaten China's investments and ambition to achieve great power standing, Beijing has embarked on a "Go Out" (*zouchuqu*) PR policy or, to use Joshua Kurlantzick's formula, a "charm offensive." In the beginning of the 2000s, a Chinese government adviser, Zheng Bijian, elaborated the concept of the "peaceful rise" (*heping jueqi*) to promote China's goals globally.⁷ The inherent threatening undertone of the term "rise" was soon replaced by more neutral "peaceful development," thereby presenting China as an emerging global power that would not threaten any other nation. In 2004, President Hu Jintao (2003–2013) stated China's aspiration to build a "harmonious society," in a "harmonious world," supposedly characterized by multilateral relations, win–win cooperation, and peaceful coexistence between different civilizations.⁸ Concomitantly, in response to the first translations in Chinese of Joseph Nye's publications, Chinese academic circles started publishing analyses on soft power (*ruan shili*). The concept and its stakes were instantly echoed at the highest state level and reflected in the report to the seventeenth CCP Congress in 2007, which identified Chinese soft power as an important feature of national policy.⁹ In the wake of the Congress, Hu Jintao expressly required the government to "increase China's soft power, give a good Chinese narrative, and better communicate China's messages to the world."¹⁰ In other words, China set itself the goal of "winning the hearts and minds of people beyond its borders," as formulated by Nye.¹¹

Nye's concept has given rise to a surge of comments and debates in China. The purported consensus on soft power's significant role in Chinese foreign policy has collided with how it should be constructed and implemented or, put differently, to what extent this originally Western concept could fit into Chinese culture and approach. Nye identified three broad categories of soft power: "culture (in places where it is attractive to others), political values (when it lives up to them at home and abroad), and foreign policies (when they are seen as legitimate and having moral authority)."¹² Chinese scholars' common view has been the paramount significance of soft power's cultural component, that is, how to make Chinese culture attractive in order to gain trust abroad. Yet, other dimensions of soft power, and how they should be adapted to Chinese goals, have continued to be debated within Chinese academic and expert forums. David Shambaugh identified three main schools.[13] The first one is "values as culture" according to which values such as peace and harmony, morality, or volunteering should constitute the main contributions of China to global culture. However, within this approach, lively debates are going on, with some criticizing it as too exclusively cultural, and advocating that it be combined with other elements of the Chinese system, such as economic ones. The second school considers that the Chinese political system, as a model, must be an important element of soft power. Under this approach, China should use soft power to demonstrate its political model as capable and legitimate, so that it becomes appealing to other nations. Finally, the third school focuses on China's approach to economic development as an international model. Although the government claimed in international meetings that every country's "development path" is unique to its national conditions, its policy advocated that the Chinese model of economic development should be used as an essential tool of soft power.

Notwithstanding ongoing debates, Beijing has pursued a multidimensional approach, using cultural tools while at the same time promoting its political and economic model combining a "peaceful development road" with "socialism with Chinese characteristics." In so doing, the Chinese government has markedly reshaped the concept of soft power to accord with its single party rule, the consubstantial authoritarianism of which, combined with China's increasing economic power, distorts the very essence of the concept through the fear China can inspire across borders, including in Central Asia. Second, and subsequently, all dimensions of Chinese soft power, whether cultural, political, or economic, have been elaborated and conducted almost exclusively by its political authorities or by structures strictly controlled by the authorities.

It is in this reshaping of soft power that China's potential success or failure to win the hearts and minds abroad lies. As Shambaugh has demonstrated, "soft power is largely about the capacity of a society to attract others, rather than a government to persuade others."[14] This chapter argues that China's authoritarian approach, which has driven its state organs to monopolize the mode, tools, and implementation of its policy, has consisted more of public diplomacy than of traditional soft power, which is supposed to be drawn from society. For many Central Asian experts, analysts, or citizens, Beijing's approach has significantly blurred the line between hard power, which is usually understood as coercive power through political threats or economic pressure, and soft power; the latter has, for China, mostly consisted of an attempt to lighten the former. This has resulted in a growing gap between the extent of China's financial and material investment in promoting soft power and the approval it has received locally. Beijing's diplomatic offensive is feared as a temporary tool, a concealed hard power designed to impose political and economic influence for the essential benefit of China, and potentially at the expense of development and political, economic, and social autonomy of the Central Asian states.

This chapter studies the politics and impact of Chinese soft power in Central Asia in light of the debates that animate Central Asian political expertise and academic circles, and of the strengths, obstacles, and contradictions of the Chinese political system's authoritarianism and centralism. By demonstrating the multiple dimensions of the impact on and reactions to Chinese politics and presence in Central Asia, and by contrasting that with the unwaveringly positive official discourse that is asserted and with the alleged increasing Sinophobic feeling presented by the media, this article will highlight the specificities of Chinese "home-made" soft power, its underlying ambiguities, and its current and potential future successes and failures in the region in the light of its global experience.

Investigating China's policy in Central Asia would mean contending with the authoritarianism of local governments and with the scarcity of opinion polls. Governments in the region have been reluctant to release publications or surveys that they fear may foster Sinophobic or xenophobic sentiment in their societies and thus threaten their relations with China. As mentioned by the researcher and orientalist Parviz Mullojanov in the case of Tajikistan in particular, the majority of research has focused on studying only the positive aspects of cooperation with China.[15] At the same time, any attempt at more or less critical consideration of various aspects of Chinese expansion in Tajikistan are characterized in the spirit of Soviet times—as "intrigues of external enemies" or "geopolitical competitors" of China.[16] This finding can be generalized throughout Central Asia, despite national variations, including relatively greater freedom of expression in Kazakhstan and Kyrgyzstan which allows researchers, experts, and journalists to express more critical views. In Kazakhstan and Kyrgyzstan, the few studies conducted offer largely favorable opinions, although against a growing debate in the press over the Chinese presence. In Tajikistan, Uzbekistan, and Turkmenistan, no opinion surveys have been published on this topic. This chapter is therefore based on a survey of publications on China's presence in Central Asia by academics and local think tanks, on press articles, and on 120 interviews conducted with academic and think tank experts during regular trips to the region from 2008 to 2018.

The next sections of this chapter will be organized as follows. The first section will elaborate China's motivation to integrate Central Asia into its soft power strategy and narrative. The second part addresses how China has used cultural, political, and economic instruments to try to win the hearts and minds of the Central Asian population. The impact of China's soft power strategy will be analyzed in a third part. This third section will demonstrate how Beijing has been struggling to reverse pervasive phobias in an increasingly globalized Central Asia where, despite the relative authoritarianism of the regimes, a marketplace of foreign ideas and influences (Russian, Turkish, Western, Southeast Asian) compete with one another, where the Soviet legacy remains an important component of political influence, and where the growth of religiosity and of nationalism divert local interest in the Middle Kingdom. In conclusion, the chapter will propose a set of questions that China will need to address if it is to have a more tangible impact on the hearts and minds of Central Asian people.

CENTRAL ASIA IN CHINA'S GLOBAL SOFT POWER STRATEGY

Beijing's use of soft power globally has arisen from the negative consequences of its use of hard power and its ambition to enhance its increasingly tarnished image abroad. In the 1990s, China's confrontational attitude against smaller states, for example, sending warships to disputed areas in the South China Sea, positioned it as a rising power keen to flex its muscles to win territorial disputes. Moreover, China's political pressure on states like the Philippines to limit relations with the United States backfired and instead brought these states closer to Western spheres of influence.[17] For the then newly independent Central Asian states, China's insertion into their domestic and international agendas as well as its hard power policy raised questions. Earning the trust of Central Asian governments and people was all the more sensitive due to the Sino–Soviet rupture in 1963, as Soviet propaganda significantly damaged perceptions of China in the region. Until the collapse of the Soviet Union, although contacts continued on a human level, China was considered at best a nonexistent neighbor and at worst a dangerous one, responsible for the 1969 clashes along the border with Kazakhstan. Numerous clichés, made more relevant by geographic proximity, made China a threatening state and an enemy of Islam.

Beijing's charm offensive strategy in Central Asia has stemmed from several fundamental domestic objectives. First, the sustainability of China's economic growth relies on the success of its foreign economic engagement. It needs to secure a supply of energy and primary resources—including oil, gas, uranium, copper, iron, aluminum and platinum, and timber—which are essential first to its economic development and second to handle its demographic growth and the expected migration of hundreds of millions of people from rural areas to its cities. Yet, China does not control many basic oil shipping lane, and has little influence over key suppliers, such as those in the Arabian Peninsula which China believes strive to slow its development under the influence of Western states. Hence, Beijing needs to diversify its partners and reach geographically closer suppliers. In this context, Kazakhstan, Turkmenistan, and Uzbekistan have gained importance as they have emerged as exporters of oil, gas, and uranium.

Second, for the Chinese Communist Party (CCP), securing China's domestic development has implied reinforcing its economic power abroad through its Go Out policy, that is, by assisting its companies to access new foreign markets. The newly independent Central Asian states, with a population of around 70 million inhabitants on a territory of 4 million square kilometers (over 1.5 million square miles), thus constituted a new market opportunity. This however meant not compelling but persuading Central Asian countries of the benefits of developing trade with a state striving to become the world's strongest economic power, and overcoming perceptions that it may constitute a threat. In other words, China needed to convince governments of the substantial benefits that its companies would supposedly bring, and at the same time counter increasing concern among the public that Beijing might challenge the region's economic autonomy and development.

Beijing's soft power strategy in Central Asia has also aimed at shaping the regional environment, reducing Western influence, and preventing what it claims to be Washington's containment policy through alleged support of the so-called color revolutions and the establishment of Western-friendly regimes. By presenting itself as a reliable and peaceful ally, China has aimed to convey to the states of the region its suspicion about the aim of U.S. power, and to lead them to reject U.S. influence without having to make use of political or military pressure, as it had in Southeast Asia. In addition, for China, Central Asia is not only part of the post-Soviet world but also part of West Asia. China's positive reappraisal of continental routes to the detriment of maritime routes must be understood as part of a long-term historical evolution. Since the nineteenth century and its confrontation with Europe during the Opium Wars, China saw its development built on its maritime façade. For Chinese ruling elites, domestic unity and stability, not to mention great power status, will pass through a rebalancing in favor of the continent.[18] Beijing has therefore increasingly looked toward building a privileged partnership with the Central Asian Muslim world.[19]

Central Asia is also unique to Beijing in terms of its direct connection with some of China's domestic issues. The cultural, linguistic, and religious similarities between the Central Asian and Uyghur populations are not only important, but are also increasingly revived. The Soviet Union was a key political and economic partner of Xinjiang in the 1930s and 1940s, before the founding of the People's Republic of China. The world, as seen from

Urumqi, was turned more toward Moscow than Beijing.[20] In the 1950s and 1960s, tens of thousands of Chinese citizens from Xinjiang immigrated to the Soviet Union; the Uyghur intelligentsia mainly moved to Kazakhstan and to a lesser extent to Kyrgyzstan and Russia.[21] In 1991, the sudden appearance on the international stage of five new states reinforced Chinese concerns about the claims of the Uyghurs, who appear so much like the "sixth people" of Central Asia, still waiting for independence. Central Asia's ethnic contiguity with the Uyghur world is therefore perceived by Beijing more as a danger than as an opportunity, although the Central Asian region is conceived as a key engine for Xinjiang's current economic development and future stabilization. Beijing's "open door policy" and "Far West Development Program" have indeed helped to transform the landlocked Xinjiang region into a place of major subsoil resource exploitation and an outpost for the advancement of Chinese trade in Central Asia, Afghanistan, and Pakistan.

Finally, Beijing's political authorities have made of soft power abroad, including in Central Asia, a tool to revitalize support from the Chinese people and gain domestic legitimacy. In addition, asserting China's power worldwide is meant to materialize the concept of China's dream of an alleged great rejuvenation of the Chinese nation.[22] For the former Chinese president, this meant achieving popular happiness through a combination of tradition with socialist modernity, by making China a wealthy and powerful country, recognized as such abroad.[23] China's soft power policy in Central Asia has therefore stemmed from both its global strategic interests and its specific regional and domestic objectives. It has been primarily driven by the duality of domestic stability, by good neighborly relations with local governments, by the transformation of Xinjiang and Central Asia into areas of transit trade for the conquest of new markets, and as part of a Chinese dream essential to securing the government's legitimacy.[24]

WIELDING CHINA'S SOFT POWER IN CENTRAL ASIA

Despite ongoing debates within Chinese political and academic circles, Beijing launched its soft power offensive in Central Asia by making use of a wide range of components. It has striven to promote Chinese culture which previously had been inaccessible to a majority of the Central Asian population and endeavored to mitigate the perception of risk raised by its economic presence, by demonstrating its purported unequaled contribution to regional development. It has also championed regional political stability by upgrading its relations with Central Asian states to a strategic alliance in the 2000s to push back against what it perceived as a would-be offensive of Western states and values it declared incompatible to the Asian ones.

Promoting Culture through Media, Language, and Education Assistance

In 2003, in a speech delivered at the Australian federal parliament, Hu Jintao stated that Chinese culture did not belong only to the Chinese but to the whole world. For the government, this assertion implied disseminating and popularizing Chinese culture on a global scale, while at the same time customizing it to local contexts. In Central Asia, this meant overcoming local populations' ignorance and fears about China, and promoting its culture alongside other historically strong cultural presences such as Russian and Indian, as well as increasingly influential Turkish and Western ones. Beijing's soft power cultural policy has been materialized through a trinomial approach, combining dissemination of its history, art, and philosophy together with teaching of Mandarin and an increasing commitment to local education.

Beijing has launched a wide range of cultural initiatives, using media, sponsoring exhibitions, conferences, and books on China, and funding research by Central Asian scholars on historical and contemporary China.[25] It has funded Chinese cultural centers in universities and in local Houses of Peoples' Friendship (*dom druzhby narodov*) to spur them to circulate a positive image of China.[26] In addition, Beijing has relied on its overseas media promoted by Xi Jinping as a critical tool for "presenting reliability of China's publicity and ... China's stories, voices and characteristics."[27] The CCP controlled Xinhua News Agency, whose essential task since its inception has been to disseminate state propaganda, has opened several branches in Kazakhstan.[28] Since December 2009, the Chinese international TV channel CCTV, renamed in 2016 as CGTN (China Global Television Network), in Kyrgyzstan has broadcast cultural, geographical, and artistic information about China. China also made its way into local Central Asian media, for example, by broadcasting its own programs through the KTRK or ElTR Kyrgyz channels. In January 2017, the Chinese Embassy funded the Kyrgyz national news agency Kabar to open a special section on China.[29] Beijing also circulates printed copies of the Russian version of its main newspapers *Zhenmin Zhibao* or *Guanmin Zhibao*, or through the free distribution of journals and newspapers, including online access. In Kyrgyzstan, the Chinese magazine *Shelkovyj Put Kulturnoe Razvitie*, publishes articles in Kyrgyz and Russian, and, at 20,000 copies, has become one of the most widely circulated newspapers in the country.[30]

A second major component of China's cultural soft power policy in the region has consisted of the opening of Confucius Institutes.[31] Affiliated with the Chinese Ministry of Education, required to be affiliated with at least one Chinese university, and partly sponsored by China's National Office for Teaching, China has established fifteen such institutes which teach Mandarin and promote Chinese culture in Central Asia. An icon of Chinese global soft power,³² they are expected to fulfill several objectives. First, they participate in China's effort to insert itself into local education. Students who pass the institute's Chinese proficiency test may get admitted to the Chinese university with which the institute is affiliated.³³ In addition, some of the institutes are affiliated with Chinese companies and provide vocational training. In Tajikistan, the Chkalovsk Confucius Institute has been opened on the premises of the local Mining and Technology Institute, and its students can be trained in the metallurgical and petroleum industry with the future possibility of working for Chinese companies operating in the country.³⁴ In Dushanbe, the Confucius Institute was instructed to award stipends to engineers, technicians, and translators destined to work in Sino-Tajik heavy industry companies in order to provide them with further training in China.³⁵

Second, by choosing the name of the philosopher Confucius (551BCE–479BCE), the CCP aims to demonstrate that it has moved away from aggressive communism which under Mao tried to suppress the teachings of Confucianism in China. By promoting the image of a peaceful China, Confucius Institutes are meant to assuage fears in regions increasingly suspicious of the Chinese presence. It is no coincidence that several institutes³⁶ were opened in regions and cities where the presence of Chinese companies or traders has been particularly controversial, such as in Aktobe in 2016 or in Osh in February 2017.

Chinese contribution to local education has gone far beyond the structure of the Confucius Institutes. Since 2007, universities and higher education institutions in China have hosted an increasing number of foreign students. Although a majority come from Southeast Asia, more than 13,000 Kazakh students, around 10,000 Kyrgyz students,³⁷ and nearly 4,000 Tajik and 1,500 Turkmen students study in China every year.³⁸ Central Asian youth's interest in studying in Chinese universities has been fostered by a combination of social, geographic, and economic factors. In a region with high unemployment rates, China is hailed for its ability to provide high-level technical and scientific training and thereby open up promising career prospects. Hosting Central Asian students in Chinese universities also partly compensates for lack of capacity in Central Asian universities, as well as corruption and a generally low level of education. Lastly, China's geographical proximity, especially to Xinjiang which hosts a growing number of Central Asian students, and the relatively low cost of studies in China (which are sometimes even subsidized by Chinese state-owned companies) compared with the West, make Chinese universities increasingly accessible and attractive.

Additionally, since the end of the 2000s, the Chinese government has significantly increased its commitment to Central Asian education. It opened and funded several Chinese departments in local universities and provided Chinese teachers.³⁹ In Kyrgyzstan, China supports eight major universities to teach Mandarin and conduct research on China (*Kitaevedenie*).[40] Beijing has also founded and is planning to found Chinese universities or schools in Central Asia. On September 1, 2017, it inaugurated the first Kyrgyz–Chinese school in Bishkek, built with Chinese funds, to accommodate about 1,300 students.[41] In 2018, Shanghai University announced plans to establish a Shanghai School for International Business.[42]

Softening the Hard Power of Economy

Concomitantly with its broad cultural offensive, Beijing has extended Nye's concept of soft power by including, in Central Asia and globally, components outside the security and military realm. Having chalked up double-digit rates of growth for over three decades, China has put economy at the forefront of its soft power offensive. To counter increasing concerns in Central Asia about its economic influence, Beijing has striven to soften the hard power dimension of its foreign investments and trade by demonstrating its contribution to local economic development and consequently to local populations' well-being. It has thereby aimed to set itself up with its economic partners as a new and sound model of development, different from and more reliable than the ones hitherto driven by Western states and international organizations.

For China, this policy has consisted first of using its status as a developing country to demonstrate engagement and solidarity with countries in transition. It has succeeded in mitigating Western competition by buying local hydrocarbon deposits at higher-than-market prices,[43] by investing in Central Asian countries' unfriendly business climate, and by funding the development of high-cost sectors such as transport infrastructure, where Western companies have been reluctant to invest. The BRI is meant to be the apex of this strategy. By pledging to invest 1.25 trillion USD worldwide by 2025,[44] a significantly higher amount than previously pledged by any other regional or global player, China is presenting this program as something of a Marshall Plan, intended to demonstrate China's contribution to regional and global economic development, and more specifically to its partner states.

China has also skillfully used some unexpected international economic and financial developments to promote its image as a reliable partner by softening its use of economic hard power. Following the 2008 global financial crisis, Chinese economic expansion continued but moved from involvement in the OECD nations' economic cycles to a significant increase of trade and Foreign Direct Investments in developing nations. Through its rapid response to the 2008 Asian financial crisis, it has gained a reputation as a pragmatic actor, able to react and engage more promptly and substantially than the West.[45] Moreover, from the 2000s, China expressly distanced itself from the U.S. foreign policy focus on major powers fighting terrorism, and instead presented itself as a spearhead in the fight against poverty in developing countries and former colonized states.⁴⁶ As it has in other regions such as in Africa,⁴⁷ Beijing has used loans, debt cancelations, and donations to entice Central Asian governments, which were short of financial resources and criticized by Western states for violations of international standards, as well as impacted by Russia's economic crisis related to the drop in world oil prices and Western sanctions over the attempted annexation of Crimea. In Central Asia's neo-patrimonial states, China's unconditional loans have been preferred to those granted by Western states and international organizations, which most often have been conditioned on liberal economic reforms or on improving transparency and reducing corruption.⁴⁸

In so doing, China has sought to emerge as an alternative economic model, advocating a "Beijing Consensus" versus the "Washington Consensus" promoted by Western states. In many developing countries, China has been praised for having successfully resisted pressure from the World Bank and the IMF to privatize its state companies and drastically reduce public spending. Instead, Beijing believes its own policies have demonstrated its ability to initiate substantive but progressive reforms while retaining control over its economy and preserving regime security. This approach has been attractive to authoritarian regimes, which claim their right to conduct economic policy according to their country's own characteristics. It has also persuaded populations that were disappointed or impoverished by the liberal reforms introduced by international organizations in Central Asia and elsewhere. This model has, in fact, significantly resonated in Central Asia. In a study conducted in Kazakhstan by the Friedrich-Ebert-Stiftung, a higher number of Kazakhstanis prefer the Chinese model of development (9.5%) to that of the United States.⁴⁹

A Political "Interfering Non-Interference"?

Political values, identified by Nye as one of the three main resources of soft power,⁵⁰ have been used extensively by Beijing to support the sustainability of its investments in Central Asia, while at the same time promoting its image as a peaceful and non-threatening country. Whereas China's economic weight and some potential concealed political agenda abroad have raised increasing apprehensions on a global scale, Beijing has promoted a principle of non-ideological and non-interfering political relations and inalienable respect for national sovereignty and territorial integrity, in the name of openness to the world, tolerance of others, and civilizational diversity.⁵¹ This approach has been materialized in Central Asia through the development of diplomatic relations, support for local regimes' authoritarianism, and by "building the positive Chinese self through the negative exclusion of otherness,"⁵² in other words, by campaigning to invalidate and delegitimize the so-called Western powers and values.

Since the 1990s, Chinese authorities have, in meetings with Central Asian governments, advocated their concept of "peaceful rise coexistence and development." In so doing, they have sought to demonstrate the definitive end to the Mao and Deng Xiaoping's offensive military policy of the 1970s and 1980s. In the 1990s, China settled most of its border disputes as a gesture of its peaceful intentions. It first set the tone by signing several treaties in Southeast Asia, such as the Friendship and Cooperation Treaty in the framework of the Association of Southeast Asian Nations, under which signatory states committed themselves to mutual respect of their sovereignty. It followed a similar path in Central Asia. While China's Deng Xiaoping claimed 1.5 million square kilometers (almost 600,000 square miles) of the Soviet Union, including 910,000 square kilometers (350,000 square miles) in Central Asia, it signed border agreements in the 1990s and 2000s with the three Central Asian bordering states, gaining merely 34,000 square kilometers (13,000 square miles), but apparently hoping to signal the end of its bellicose intentions.[53]

Both President Hu Jintao and President Xi Jinping distanced themselves from the concept of expanding communist ideology abroad that had prevailed under Mao. Beijing made several strong political gestures to demonstrate China's policy of non-interference, such as in the Philippines where it refused to support a communist rebellion, and in Nepal, where it sent arms to support the monarchy against Maoist groups.[54] For recently independent Central Asian states, this new foreign policy underscored that Beijing would not seek to export a communist political regime, and could even oppose potentially destabilizing groups inspired by the Chinese Communist model. This policy resonated in the region where local governments had raised increasing concerns about relations with some of their Middle Eastern partners, for example, Iran, which they suspected of having hidden political-religious designs. In addition, Beijing, which refused to take action to defend its ethnic minorities threatened, for example, in Indonesia, thereby set itself apart from Russia, which was suspected of instrumentalizing Russian minorities' irredentism to regain some of the political influence it lost with the fall of the Soviet Union.

China's charm offensive has nevertheless been much more than a mere geographical juxtaposition and coexistence with different political regimes. Beijing has promoted a narrative that advocates Asian values as a way of unifying the states of the region and disparaging the so-called Western values such as democracy, universal human rights, or freedom of expression, all allegedly neither desirable nor globally transferable.[55] Conversely, it has preached a principle of a type of democracy merged with national characteristics, that is, democracy with "China characteristics," including the single party system[56] and the so-called Asian concepts such as family-centered stability.

Beijing has carried out this policy through rhetorical support to authoritarian local regimes, both in bilateral and multilateral meetings. The Shanghai Cooperation Organization (SCO), which four Central Asian states have joined, has passed several decisions asserting the right of member states to define their own concept of *human rights*.[57] Beijing, alongside Moscow, has repeatedly denounced the concept of the so-called color revolutions, considered as a type of U.S. or European warfare to destabilize independently minded regimes and bring them under their influence. China was the first country to receive and support former Uzbek President Karimov after the crackdown in Andijan in 2005 that led to the death of more than 1,000 people. Since then, China has openly supported the authoritarianism of Central Asian regimes.[58]

Beijing's countering of Western narratives has gone well beyond rhetorical support, to include concrete support for local political systems, and has striven to undermine the legitimacy of democratic institutions through obstruction of practices designed to support democratic principles.[59] China manifested this strategy in Central Asia through what Alexander Cooley has named the "league of authoritarian gentlemen," that is, by co-organizing with Russia alternate election monitoring missions consisting of SCO and other observation missions aimed at countering and thereby thwarting OSCE and other Western election monitoring reports which have systematically documented their non-free and fraudulent character. The SCO, which never adopted a code of conduct used by most other international observers, instead has systematically declared elections in Central Asia (and elsewhere in the former Soviet space) free and fair, including even in Turkmenistan.[60] In 2018, the SCO stated that Turkmenistan's parliamentary election took place in accordance with the requirements of the electoral legislation of Turkmenistan and the international commitments undertaken by the state. The SCO mission did not report any violations that would have put under question the election's legitimacy.[61] China's political narrative and support, both in bilateral and multilateral venues, have been appreciated by Central Asian regimes, whose policies have been increasingly criticized, both domestically and internationally.

IS CHINA WINNING THE HEARTS AND MINDS OF CENTRAL ASIAN POPULATION?

China's soft power policy appears to have borne fruit. According to a survey conducted by the Kazakh Institute for Sociology, young people in

Kazakhstan and Kyrgyzstan consider the Chinese model of development superior to that of the United States, Kazakhstan, or Turkey.[62] China is credited for its significant investments,[63] for attenuating Central Asia's landlocked character, and for building infrastructure (roads, railways, tunnels, electricity lines, etc.). For thousands of Central Asians, the proximity of China offers a unique opportunity to make a living through small businesses and trade, a situation that most Western, Japanese, Turkish, or Iranian companies cannot match.

Yet, although preferred to the American model, China's economic model of development remains much less popular than those of several other countries. A study conducted by the Friedrich-Ebert-Stiftung among young people shows that while support for the U.S. model remains very low (between 3 and 8%), the Chinese model fares little better, with only 1 percent of votes in Tajikistan, a high of 9.5 percent in Kazakhstan, with 3.6 percent in Kyrgyzstan and 5.2 percent in Uzbekistan. In all these states, both the U.S. and Chinese models remain far behind the Russian model, which is favored by almost half in Kazakhstan (46.7 %) and Uzbekistan (45.3%), and about three quarters in Kyrgyzstan (71.8%) and Tajikistan (76.7%). Other models, such as that of the European Union, or the Turkish model in the Kyrgyz and Tajik case, receive a favorable opinion rate higher than the Chinese model.[64]

This apparent but fragile success of Chinese soft power policy in Central Asia should be put into the context of the short-term objectives and interests of local populations. Young people's positive views of China often stem from pragmatic benefit, such as increased job and business opportunities, rather than from a sincere admiration for a Chinese economic, political, or cultural model. In general, interest among the Central Asian population in learning Mandarin or studying in China, results from job perspectives and does not necessarily correspond with real interest in Chinese culture.

Since the end of the 2000s, Beijing's charm offensive has been hindered by local populations' growing concerns about the impact of Chinese economic involvement in Central Asia as well as about a wide range of societal issues. Beijing's commercial and economic offensives have inspired mixed feelings.[65] Many Central Asian specialists or journalists consider that China is transforming the economies of Central Asian states to suit its own interests,[66] to weaken their potential for autonomy, and to further establish their status as Chinese economic protectorates.[67] The key accusation concerns the limiting of Central Asian economies to the role of producers and exporters of primary resources. As experts explain,[68] Chinese investments are not aimed at the development of local production but at the creation of conditions to aid the export of Chinese products and the import of primary resources.[69] The sectors that are most affected by Chinese competition are light industry, construction (e.g., cement production), and processing and agri-food. Losing these sectors could jeopardize a country's security since it would then be dependent on China for its basic foodstuffs.

The alleged contribution of Chinese companies to regional and local development has become an increasingly sensitive topic in Central Asia. As argued by Bhavna Dave, local people fault China for promised investments that do not materialize and the potential negative effects resulting from the opacity of contract negotiation and signing. Chinese companies are criticized for their unclear objectives and practices, for violating local legislation and instead enforcing Chinese laws, for underpaying local employees or not hiring local staff, and therefore not contributing to reducing the growing unemployment in the region.[70]

Despite being sometimes fed by rumors or false assumptions, such criticisms undermine China's goal of being recognized as a driver of local development and are at odds with the Chinese attempt to demonstrate solidarity with developing countries by assisting their economic and social development. In Central Asia, China's quick economic progress over the last twenty years is seen as a model of domestic development from which to draw inspiration, but also as a threat to its partners due to the economic dependency Beijing's policy generates for its own interests, and by an ensuing risk of political influence over its partners' domestic affairs.[71] Such grievances are not specific to just Central Asia. China's economic system opacity and its inability to hire local staff and help reduce unemployment have been denounced in other countries and continents, such as in Africa.[72]

Moreover, companies from Turkey or Western countries have faced similar criticism. However, China's ostentatious economic presence in Central Asia, combined with its geographic proximity, has fed growing phobias, especially since the cultural tool of soft power, specifically designed to mitigate such fears, clichés, and rumors, has not borne, so far, the expected fruit.

Central Asian populations have remained only moderately receptive to Chinese culture. First, China pays the price of starting late to promote its culture in the region. In the 1990s and 2000s, Beijing focused on the development of its political and economic relations and made little use of its cultural tool in the region, thus unintentionally maintaining the many clichés about itself. In the second half of the 2000s, when the Chinese government embarked on a real policy of cultural promotion, Central Asia was already imbued with rhetoric and suspicion about China's threat to the region.[73]

Since then, Chinese culture has been struggling to gain a significant foothold in the region. The expansion of the Confucius Institutes, considered as the spearhead of China's soft power, has been slowed down by the complex and strictly state-controlled Chinese bureaucracy. First, to open an institute, hosting universities must demonstrate local demand for learning Chinese, have the necessary premises, equipment, funds, and staff, and provide a projection of market demand and a detailed account of project funds.[74] In Central Asian states where administrative bureaucracy remains cumbersome, these mandatory procedures have repeatedly discouraged initiatives. In addition, Confucius Institutes have been insufficiently supported by China's central administration and lack staff. Local teachers' level of instruction is often weak, while Chinese teachers do not speak sufficient Russian, Kazakh, or Uzbek to teach local students and overcome cross-cultural barriers. Moreover, the promotion of Chinese culture has come up against local governments, which are increasingly concerned that the obvious Chinese presence could raise tensions locally. Further, the presence and activities of the Confucius Institutes are neither well advertised on nor outside university campuses, and instead are circulated mainly by word-of-mouth.[75]

The impact of China's cultural promotion abroad has remained modest. Despite a growing number of Central Asian students willing to study in Chinese universities, China appears to be chosen by default, motivated more by financial criteria, and because access to universities in other—especially Western—countries is difficult. In Kazakhstan, only about 14 percent of students wanting to study abroad choose China, which is far behind Russia (29.6%), and Europe and the United States (40%).[76] In addition, a survey conducted in 2017 among young Kazakh students studying in China, showed that only a quarter of them mention a cultural interest in China. Moreover, those who mention their interest in Chinese culture consider this criterion as secondary: 95 percent of respondents chose China owing first to the ease of obtaining visas and logistical support from the Chinese administration to study in China, and second to the low cost of living and studying there.[77]

Beyond the undeniable success of promoting the learning of Mandarin, Hu Jintao's stated ambitions to make Chinese culture universal fall short in Central Asia. Many Central Asians' interest in learning Chinese emanates more from pragmatic objectives than from a real interest in the country's culture. In Confucius Institutes, most only attend language classes and leave the institute once they get the Chinese Proficiency Test (HSK).[78] Moreover, dissemination of Chinese history, literature, and culture has remained limited in scope. Unlike in Southeast Asia—for example, Vietnam, where translations of Chinese novels account for half of all translations of foreign novels—very few Chinese novels and works have been translated into Russian or into any Central Asian language. Beyond the popularity of films such as those featuring Jackie Chan, Chinese cinema has received a cold reception in Central Asia, and has remained in the shadow of Russian and Indian cinemas, which enjoy a comfortable heritage in the region, as well as of American cinema and of South American soap operas.

Finally, China's limited progress in demonstrating its contribution to economic and social development in Central Asia, or in arousing a genuine interest in its culture, has consequently done little to address the local population's clichés and fears about its potential political interference. Phobias linked to Beijing's growing presence remain quite strong in Central Asia. Views of China are still stamped by the old clichés of Soviet propaganda casting China as the historical enemy. Discourses on the "Chinese expansion" (*tikhaia ekspansiia*) into Central Asia have become frequent in Kazakh, Kyrgyz, and Tajik newspapers.[79] The idea that China does not evolve historically, that it pursues a-temporal objectives which stretch across several centuries, or even millennia, and that Chinese authorities in principle conceal their imperialist objectives, are widespread.[80] Beijing is accused of having developed policies prejudicial to nomadic and Turkic peoples, and having a culture that is ethnocentric and aims to assimilate the Turkic/Muslim one. The writings of some Chinese historians and political scientists about the so-called historical affiliation to China and therefore vassal status of certain territories have also raised concerns in Central Asia and beyond.[81] Some Chinese history books have even challenged the delineation of the borders between China and the Central Asian states, despite the existence of border treaties, raising serious concerns in Central Asia. The development program for the "Far West," in the framework of which Beijing has established hundreds of agricultural hamlets along the Chinese side of the Kazakh border for the settlement of millions of Han farmers, is also viewed as a significant threat. These highly militarized colonization brigades (*Xinjiang shengchan jianshe bingtuan*) would be under the direct control of Beijing and not of Urumqi, and, among others functions, act to break the Turkic population continuum between the Central Asians and the Uyghurs.

Many interviewed Central Asian specialists shared the feeling that there exists a so-called civilizational difference between China and Central Asia. Diverse arguments are used to justify the existence of this apparently impassable "culture barrier": some conceive it in terms of Islam, others in terms of Russo-Soviet acculturation, and still others as involving a difference in national essences. Interviewed experts dismissed the notion that a Sinicization of Central Asian societies could take place by any means other than force. Many believed that it is important to maintain the "civilizational barrier" between Central Asia and China on the grounds that falling into the Chinese sphere of cultural influence would mean the ethnic disappearance of Central Asian societies. Despite more than ten years of soft power policy in the region, Beijing struggles to win the hearts and minds of local populations. Central Asian experts and analysts hold views of Chinese influence in Central Asia that remain largely pessimistic, and that contrast significantly with some enthusiasm held by a part of the population engaged or intending to engage in business with China, and which views China as an immediate economic and social opportunity.

CONCLUSION

In two decades, China has made an undeniable and significant inroad into Central Asia. It has emerged as a key economic partner, a factor for political stability, and a strategic ally against potential external terrorist threats. For a segment of the Central Asian population, the big neighbor is viewed through the lens of the opportunities it can provide for finding a job, creating a business, and making a living.

Yet, debates in political and academic circles questioning the Chinese presence, combined with increasing Sinophobic narratives in local media, suggest that Beijing may be struggling to effectively turn its charm offensive into soft power. The difficulties China has faced in its attempts to win the hearts and minds of people in other countries is not specific to Central Asia. Shambaugh's book *China Goes Global*, as well as surveys carried out by the Pew Research Center, has demonstrated the relatively low impact of Chinese soft power on a global scale, including on the African and South American continents, where Beijing has not spared efforts to invest and promote its alternative model of development.

This hitherto lukewarm impact is not to say that China's soft power policy is doomed to fail in Central Asia or globally. However, its success will flow from the Chinese authorities' capacity to combine responses to imponderables with the ability to learn from experience and mistakes, and, as a result, revise their strategy.

First, the effectiveness of China's use of soft power will rely on its ability to make its own economic system sustainable and to secure its image as a purported success story. The continuation of the economic slowdown that China has been experiencing since the second half of the 2010s, could reveal the contrast between the official Chinese narrative lauding its economic progress and the much darker reality on the ground; it would also damage the image of Beijing's model of development. This may already be occurring in the global market of increasingly competitive economic models, as governments in Central Asia have made positive references to other economic systems, particularly other Asian ones such as those of Singapore, Japan, or South Korea.

On the other hand, China's ostentatious display of its economic power on the international stage since the 2000s has increasingly contrasted with the narrative it presented in the 1990s about its status as a developing country. The BRI project that China has presented as providing an unprecedented opportunity for regional development might conversely appear as the ultimate step of its ostentatious economic offensive beyond its borders.[82] Many experts and analysts report that this initiative might serve mainly China's own interests, could deepen the gap between Chinese power and countries in transition, and could reveal economic and political ambitions of domination.[83]

Second, the authoritarian and repressive nature of the Chinese political system, shown even more openly by Xi Jinping than by his predecessor Hu Jintao, is likely to hamper significantly China's soft power through the anxiety it generates abroad. In 2018, the disclosure of re-education camps in Xinjiang with between 800,000 and 2 million Muslims including tens of thousands of Kazakhs and Kyrgyz, widely reported in local media,[84] and the Chinese administration's ban on several hundred persons of Central Asian ethnicity from leaving the country,[85] have damaged significantly the image of China in the region.[86]

Raising the image of China in Central Asia is all the more difficult as the local relays are few. Local Sinologists are few, and the field of research on China (*Kitaevedenie*) remains underdeveloped.[87] This led the director of the Institute of Silk Roads in Kazakhstan to conclude that "we do not yet have Sinophiles, but we already have Sinophobia . . . because we lack knowledge about China." The development of knowledge about China is all the more scant, in that the Central Asian governments have been reluctant to push the development of research on China. Sinology is conducted almost exclusively in institutions closely supervised by the state, for example, departments of the Academy of Sciences and the Center for Strategic Studies in Tajikistan, as well as several leading universities such as the Tajik-Slavic University and the Tajik National University. Moreover, Central Asian proponents of China within governments and administrations are often Sinophilic less by conviction and more by pragmatism. All Central Asian governments have economic, security, political and, in a number of cases, personal financial interests, as reasons to develop and maintain good relations with China. However, while the growth of Sinophobic sentiment has so far been channeled and offset by the authoritarianism of governments in the region, upcoming presidential successions and possible policy or regime changes could call into question the conspicuous Chinese presence, as has happened in Southeast Asia. For example, in Indonesia, Suharto's authoritarianism had for three decades prevented the expression of anti-Chinese sentiment. From 1998, as he loosened his grip on power, violent demonstrations started against the Chinese minorities living in the country and against China's policy in Indonesia.[88] In Central Asia, most public displays of anti-Chinese sentiment have been prevented by restrictive legislation that makes it difficult to hold demonstrations, as well as by outright repression. It is not a coincidence that the most violent demonstrations against the Chinese presence have occurred in least authoritarian Kyrgyzstan.

Beyond this negative impact on its international image, China's political authoritarianism and centralism, by hindering the engagement of most private and civil society actors, could be the main obstacle to the effectiveness of its soft power over the long term. Since its inception, China's soft power policy has been initiated, designed, and implemented almost exclusively by its political authorities and state structures. On the positive side, state authoritarianism is likely to give China more capacity than democratic regimes to coordinate its activities abroad. Yet, by using this approach, China has confused public diplomacy, initiated by governments, with soft power which is generally inclusive of civil society.[89] As demonstrated by Nye, soft power is much less about the ability of political authorities to charm foreign societies, than of civil society to do the same. Public diplomacy may contribute to the promotion of soft power, however, its impact is likely to be significantly weakened if it is not supported and relayed by private and independent actors. As candidly recognized by a former minister of foreign affairs, the Chinese government has used the terms *soft power*, *public diplomacy*, and *external publicity* interchangeably.[90] Moreover, through near-monopolization of initiatives by the state, Beijing has conducted its soft power policy in the same numeric way it has managed its economic relations abroad,[91] that is, by counting the number of Confucius Institutes, or conferences it has sponsored, as it has counted its investments, roads, or railways which allegedly contributed to businesses and local development projects. Yet, counting is not enough; soft power, like identity, is a social construction[92] which cannot be bought but must be earned. The impact of China's propaganda is likely to remain limited as long as it will not be relayed by autonomous civil actors, who will be crucial to promoting an image of China that is not—or not anymore—associated with political authoritarianism and potentially threatening economic ambitions.

Such relays are all the more important in Central Asia, in that China's geographical contiguity, demographic weight, and military power multiply local phobias in Central Asia.[93] Some of the diplomacy and soft power initiatives welcomed in other parts of the world, such as the funding of political parties in Southeast Asia, the sending of the Chinese Peace Corps to Laos, Ethiopia, and Burma,[94] or the promotion of the Mandarin language by making it mandatory in Thailand's primary schools could provoke adverse reactions within local Central Asian populations, and possibly from governments. Several violent confrontations with Chinese traders and interests in Kyrgyzstan and, in 2017, demonstrations in Kazakhstan against the government's plan to rent land to Chinese farmers have been warning signs for Central Asian authorities, who as a result are increasingly anxious about potential popular unrest due to China's conspicuous presence.[95]

So far, Beijing's main achievement in Central Asia has been its ability to show what is unique about China, such as its economic power, or its political authoritarianism and centralism presented as a model for rapid development and stability. Beijing's next step should be to go beyond showing what is unique about China and convincingly demonstrate what is or can be universal about it. The conversion of its public diplomacy into soft power and its sustainability will depend on Beijing's willingness and ability to respond to elements that have so far hindered its goal of winning the hearts and minds of its Central Asian neighbors and on its ability to universalize its values and assets, which to date have created more anxiety and tension than admiration.

NOTES

1. Marlene Laruelle and Sebastien Peyrouse, *The "Chinese Question" in Central Asia: Domestic Order, Social Changes and the Chinese Factor* (London, New York: Hurst and Columbia University Press, 2012).
2. "President Xi's Statements on the Belt and Road Initiative," *China Daily,* April 15, 2017, http://www.chinadaily.com.cn/china/2017-04/15/content_28940829.htm.
3. Julie Yu-Wen Chen and Soledad Jiménez Tovar, "China in Central Asia: Local Perceptions from Future Elites," *China Quarterly of International Strategic Studies* 3, no. 3 (2017): 442.
4. Aleksandr Shustov, "Miagkaia sila drakona: kak Kitaj pytaetsja zavoevat' vliianie v Central'noj Azii," *Evraziia Ekspert*, January 9, 2018, http://eurasia.expert/myagkaya-sila-drakona-kak-kitay-pytaetsya-zavoevat-vliyanie-v-tsentralnoy-azii/.
5. "V chem prichiny kazahstanskoi sinofobii," *Caravan*, September 17, 2018, https://www.caravan.kz/gazeta/v-chem-prichiny-kazahstanskojj-sinofobii-480057/.
6. These fears have been relayed in the media as well as think tanks and academic circles debating Chinese influence on a global scale. See Laruelle and Peyrouse, *The "Chinese Question" in Central Asia.*
7. Zheng Bijian, *China's Peaceful Rise, Speeches of Zheng Bijian 1997–2005* (Washington DC: Brookings, 2005).
8. Beston Husen Arif, "The Role of Soft Power in China's Foreign Policy in the 21st Century," *International Journal of Social Sciences & Educational Studies* 3, no. 3 (2017): 97.
9. William A. Callahan, "Identity and Security in China: The Negative Soft Power of the China Dream," *Politics* 35, no.3–4 (2015): 216–29; Osamu Sayama, "China's Approach to Soft Power Seeking a Balance between Nationalism, Legitimacy and International Influence," (RUSI Occasional Paper, Royal United Services Institute for Defence and Security Studies, March 2016), https://rusi.org/sites/default/files/201603_op_chinas_soft_power.pdf; "Hu Urges Enhancing Soft Power of Chinese Culture," *China Daily,* October 15, 2007, http://www.chinadaily.com.cn/china/2007-10/15/content_6175308.htm.
10. David Shambaugh, "China's Soft-Power Push: The Search for Respect," *Foreign Affairs* 94, no. 4 (July/August 2015): 99–107.
11. Joseph S. Nye Jr., *Soft Power. The Means to Success in World Politics* (New York: Public Affairs, 2004).
12. Joseph S. Nye Jr., "Public Diplomacy and Soft Power," *The Annals of the American Academy of Political and Social Science* 616, no 1 (2008): 96.

13. David Shambaugh, *China Goes Global: The Partial Power* (New York: Oxford University Press, 2013), 169.
14. Shambaugh, *China Goes Global,* 167.
15. Parviz Mullojanov, "Kogda Tadzhikistan nachnët izuchat' Kitaj," *Cabar,* January 15, 2019, https://analytics.cabar.asia/ru/kogda-tadzhikistan-nachnyot-izuchat-kitaj/.
16. Ibid.
17. Joshua Kurlantzick, *Charm Offensive: How China's Soft Power is Transforming the World* (New Haven: Yale University Press, 2007), 38.
18. Bates Gill, *Rising Star: China's New Security Diplomacy* (Washington, DC: Brookings Institution Press, 2007).
19. Thierry Kellner, "Le Dragon et la tulipe. Les relations sino-afghanes dans la période post-9/11," *Asia Paper* 4, no. 1 (2009).
20. James A. Millward, *Eurasian Crossroads: A History of Xinjiang* (New York: Columbia University Press, 2007). See also M. Dickens, *The Soviets in Xinjiang, 1911–1949,* http://www.oxuscom.com/sovinxj.htm (accessed January 6, 2011).
21. On the migration flows between Xinjiang and Kazakhstan, see G. M. Mendikulova, and B. Zh. Atanbaeva, *Istoriia migratsii mezhdu Kazakhstanom i Kitaem v 1860-1960-e gg* [History of migrations between Kazakhstan and China 1869-1960] (Almaty: Institut Vostokovedeniia, 2008).
22. Nadège Rolland, "China's 'Belt and Road Initiative': Underwhelming or Game-Changer?" *The Washington Quarterly* 40, no. 1 (2017): 127–42.
23. Callahan, "Identity and Security in China," 221.
24. Colin Mackerras and Michael Clarke (eds), *China, Xinjiang and Central Asia: History, Transition and Crossborder Interaction into the 21st Century* (New York: Routledge, 2009).
25. Vera Exenerova, "Transnational Ties and Local Society's Role in Improving the PRC's Image in Central Asia," in *China Belt and Road Initiative and Its Impact in Central Asia,* ed. Marlene Laruelle (Washington, DC: The George Washington University, Central Asia Program, 2018), 131.
26. Ibid., 133.
27. Arif, "The Role of Soft Power in China's Foreign Policy," 4.
28. Shustov, "Miagkaia sila drakona"; Ruslan Izimov, "'Miagkaia sila' Kitaia—na pricele Central'naia Aziia," *Regnum.ru,* January 28, 2014, https://regnum.ru/news/1759411.html.
29. Denis Berdakov, "Mehanizmy 'miagkoi sily' Kitaia v Kyrgyzstane," *Ekpsert Evraziia,* February 28, 2018, http://eurasia.expert/mekhanizmy-myagkoy-sily-kitaya-v-kyrgyzstane/
30. Ibid.
31. Shustov, "Miagkaia sila drakona."
32. Falk Hartig, *Chinese Public Diplomacy: The Rise of the Confucius Institute* (New York: Routledge, 2016); Joe Tin-yau Lo and Suyan Pan, "Confucius Institutes and China's Soft Power: Practices and Paradoxes," *Compare: A Journal of Comparative and International Education* 46, no. 4 (2016): 512–32; Randy Kluver, "Chinese Culture in a Global Context: The Confucius Institute as a Geo-Cultural

Force," in *China's Global Engagement: Cooperation, Competition, and Influence in the 21st Century*, ed. Jacques Delisle and Avery Goldstein (Washington, DC: Brookings Institution Press, 2017).

33. Diana Gurbanmyradova, "The Sources of China's Soft Power in Central Asia: Cultural Diplomacy" (Masters Thesis, Central European University, Budapest, 2015), 29.

34. "V tadzhikistane otkrylsia vtoroi Institut Konfuciia," *Sputnik*, August 21, 2015, https://ru.sputnik-tj.com/education/20150821/1016503961.html.

35. "Raschet I pramatizm: Eksperty o vklade Kitaia v tadzhikskoe obrazovanie," *Stanradar.com*, January 24, 2018, https://stanradar.com/news/full/28127-raschet-i-pragmatizm-eksperty-o-vklade-kitaja-v-tadzhikskoe-obrazovanie.html.

36. Gurbanmyradova, *The Sources of China's Soft Power in Central Asia*, 33–5.

37. Shustov, "Miagkaia sila drakona."

38. Izimov, "'Miagkaia sila' Kitaia."

39. Berdakov, "Mehanizmy 'miagkoi sily' Kitaia v Kyrgyzstane."

40. "Obshhie svedeniia o fakul'tete," *Kyrgyz National University*, April 28, 2017 https://www.knu.kg/ru/index.php?option=com_content&view=article&id=5885:2014-02-05-12-17-28&catid=926:2014-02-05-12-16-16&Itemid=555.

41. "V Bishkeke otkrylas' pervaia kyrgyrsko-kitaiskaia shkola," *Radio Azattyk*, September 1, 2017, https://rus.azattyk.org/a/28709414.html.

42. "V Tashkente otkroetsia Shanhaisjaia shkola mezhedunarodnogo biznesa," *Podrobno.uz*, January 5, 2018, https://www.podrobno.uz/cat/obchestvo/v-tashkente-otkroetsya-shankhayskaya-shkola-mezhdunarodnogo-biznesa/.

43. Kurlantzick, *Charm Offensive*, 90.

44. Shambaugh, "China's Soft-Power Push," 100.

45. Celal Bayari, "Chinese Economy and Central Asia," *Academy of Taiwan Business Management Review* 11, no. 3 (2015): 5.

46. Daniel C. Lynch, *China's Futures: PRC Elites Debate Economics, Politics, and Foreign Policy* (Stanford: Stanford University Press, 2015), 170; Kurlantzick, *Charm Offensive*, 52.

47. Wei Liang, "China's Soft Power in Africa: Is Economic Power Sufficient?" *Asian Perspective* 36, no. 4 (2012): 669.

48. Christopher Walker, "The Authoritarian Threat: The Hijacking of 'Soft Power'," *Journal of Democracy* 27, no. 1 (2016): 51.

49. Tolganay Umbetaliyeva, Botagoz Rakisheva, and Peer Teschendorf, *Youth in Central Asia: Kazakhstan—Based on a Sociological Survey* (Almaty: Friedrich Ebert Foundation Kazakhstan, 2016), 158.

50. Joseph S. Nye Jr. and Wang Jisi, "The Rise of China's Soft Power and Its Implications for the United States," in *Power and Restraint: A Shared Vision for the U.S.–China Relationship*, ed. Richard Rosecrance and Gu Guoliang (New York: Public Affairs, 2009).

51. Jean-Marc F. Blanchard and Fujia Lu, "Thinking Hard About Soft Power: A Review and Critique of the Literature on China and Soft Power," *Asian Perspective* 36, no. 4 (2012): 565–89.

52. Callahan, "Identity and Security in China" 2.

53. Thierry Kellner, *L'Occident de la Chine : Pékin et la nouvelle Asie centrale (1991–2001)* (Paris: PUF, 2008), 539–588.

54. Kurlantzick, *Charm Offensive,* 45.

55. Alan Hunter, "Soft Power: China on the Global Stage," *Chinese Journal of International Politics* 2, no. 3 (2009): 388.

56. Mariya Y. Omelicheva, *Asia in the New Millennium: Democracy in Central Asia, Competing Perspectives and Alternative Strategies* (Lexington: The University Press of Kentucky, 2015), 63.

57. Ibid., 64.

58. See for example Alexander Cooley, "Countering Democratic Norms," *Journal of Democracy* 26, no. 3 (2015): 49–63.

59. Christopher Walker, "What is 'Sharp Power'?" *Journal of Democracy* 29, no. 3 (2018) 9–23.

60. Alexander Cooley, "The League of Authoritarian Gentlemen," *Foreign Policy*, January 30, 2013, https://foreignpolicy.com/2013/01/30/the-league-of-authoritarian-gentlemen/.

61. "SCO Issues Statement following Parliamentary Election in Turkmenistan," *Azernews*, March 28, 2018, https://www.azernews.az/region/129327.html.

62. Umbetaliyeva, Rakisheva, and Teschendorf, *Youth in Central Asia,* 158; 193.

63. "Glava Minproma Tadzhikistana: Segodnia tol'ko kitaicy sposobnyinvestirovat'," *Kabar*, February 12, 2019, http://www.kabar.kg/news/glava-minproma-tadzhikistana-segodnia-tol-ko-kitaitcy-sposobny-investirovat/; "Luchshe–drug horoshevo: Uzbekistan I Kitai planiruiut realizovat' desiatki proektov na milliardy dollarov," *Podrobno.uz*, February 1, 2019, https://podrobno.uz/cat/uzbekistan-i-kitay-klyuchi-ot-budushchego/luchshee-drug-khoroshego-u/.

64. Umbetaliyeva, Rakisheva and Teschendorf, *Youth in Central Asia,* 90.

65. Tat'iana Kiseleva, "Kakie riski neset razvitie Kitaia dlia Kazakhstana?—Satpaev," *Info.kz*, April 20, 2018, https://365info.kz/2018/04/kakie-riski-neset-razvitie-kitaya-dlya-kazahstana-satpaev/; Ravshan Radzhab, "Tadzhik I kitaec—ne brat'ia navek. Chem opasny kontrakty s Podnebesnoi dlia odnoi iz bedneishih stran SNG," *FerganaNews,* February 1, 2019, https://fergana.agency/articles/104786/; "Sinofobiia po-kyrgyzski: 700 dollarov dolzhen kazhdyi grazhdanin Kyrgyzstana Kitaiu," *Rezonans.kz*, January 25, 2019, https://rezonans.kz/vse-o-politike/9008-kyrgyzstan-sinofobiya-kitaj-igor-shestakov-denis-berdakov-olga-kartashjova.

66. See the Kazakhstanese political specialist's opinion, A. Arzygulov in G. Ashakeeva and A. A. Eshmatov, "Kitai—Central'naia Aziia: Kto za kem?" *Radio Azattyk*, March 12, 2013, http://rus.azattyk.org/content/kyrgyzstan_china_central_asia/24926252.html; "Zheleznaia doroga KNR – KR – Ruz: 'Naimenee bygodnyi variant dliia Kitaia I sovershenno nevygodnyi dliia nas'," *Vesti.kg*, February 6, 2019, https://vesti.kg/analitika/item/58420-zheleznaya-doroga-knr-kr-ruz-naimenee-vygodnyj-variant-dlya-kitaya-i-sovershenno-nevygodnyj-dlya-nas.html.

67. Andrei Korolev, "Kitaiskie investicii pogloshaiut ekonomiku Kazakhstanan," *Info.kz*, May 29, 2018, https://365info.kz/2018/05/kitajskie-investitsii-pogloshhayut-ekonomiku-kazahstana/.

68. Interview conducted from 2008 to 2018, among 120 experts.

69. Mullojanov, "Kogda Tadzhikistan nachnët izuchat' Kitaj."
70. Bhavna Dave, "Silk Road Economic Belt: Effects of China's Soft Power Diplomacy in Kazakhstan," in *China Belt and Road Initiative and Its Impact in Central Asia*, ed. Marlene Laruelle (Washington, DC: The George Washington University, Central Asia Program, 2018), 100. Interviews in Uzbekistan, Kazakhstan, Kyrgyzstan and Tajikistan.
71. Roman Ivanov, "Chem zakonchit'sia kitaiskaia ekspansiia v Tadzhikistan?—issledovanie," *Info.kz*, January 28, 2019, https://365info.kz/2019/01/chem-zakonchit-sya-kitajskaya-ekspansiya-v-tadzhikistan-issledovanie/.
72. Wei Liang, "China's Soft Power in Africa," 682.
73. Laruelle and Peyrouse, *The "Chinese Question."*
74. Gaukhar Nursha, "Chinese Soft Power in Kazakhstan and Kyrgyzstan: A Confucius Institutes Case Study," in *China Belt and Road Initiative and Its Impact in Central Asia*, ed. Marlene Laruelle (Washington, DC: The George Washington University, Central Asia Program, 2018), 140.
75. Ibid., 140.
76. Umbetaliyeva, Rakisheva and Teschendorf, *Youth in Central Asia*, 62.
77. "Ucheba v Kitae: Chego hotiat i chto poluchaiut nashi studenty," *Zona.kz*, March 2, 2017, https://www.zakon.kz/4846930-ucheba-v-kitae-chego-khotjat-i-chto.html.
78. Nursha, "Chinese Soft Power in Kazakhstan and Kyrgyzstan," 139.
79. See for example "Ne slishkom li mnogo Kitaia?": Aktivisty aposaiutsia 'tihoi ekspansii'," *Stanradar.com*, August 6, 2018, http://www.stanradar.com/news/full/30541-ne-slishkom-li-mnogo-kitaja-aktivisty-opasajutsja-tihoj-ekspansii-kazahstana.html; "Tihaia ekspansiia Kitaia," *Belyi Parus*, August 18, 2016, https://paruskg.info/glavnaya/135211-135211.html; A. Baraev, "Tihaia ekspansiia. Kitaizaciia Tadzhikistana," *Centrasia.ru*, July 21, 2016, www.centrasia.ru/newsA.php?st=1469122500.
80. Radzhab, "Tadzhik I kitaec."
81. Kurlantzick, *Charm Offensive*, 115.
82. Chen and Tovar, "China in Central Asia."
83. Personal interviews Almaty (June 2018), Astana (June 2019) and Bishkek (May and September 2018).
84. Megan Keller, "State Dept. Official: China Holding 800k Muslim Minorities in Internment Camps," *The Hill*, May 12, 2018, https://thehill.com/homenews/administration/419855-state-dept-official-china-holding-800k-uighurs-others-in-internment.
85. "*Kazahstan* na zashhite etnicheskih kazahov v Kitae. Ob''iasniaem situaciu," *Kaktakto*, October 5, 2018, https://kaktakto.com/analitika/kazaxstan-na-zashhite-etnicheskix-kazaxov-v-kitae-obyasnyaem-situaciyu/; Evgeniia Kim, "KNR proigryvaet SSHA bor'bu za informacionnoe pole Turkestana," *Regnum.ru*, December 12, 2018, https://regnum.ru/news/polit/2536399.html.
86. Anar Musabaeva, "Antikitaiskaia tema v Kyrgyzstane priobrela novyi impul's," *Central Asia Analytical Network*, January 21, 2019, http://caa-network.org/archives/15113.

87. Vladislav Iurycyn, "Kitaevedenie v Kazahstane : specialisty est', no shkoly net," *Zona.kz,* February 28, 2019, https://zonakz.net/2019/02/28/kitaevedenie-v-kazaxstane-specialisty-est-no-shkoly-net/.
88. Kurlantzick, *Charm Offensive,* 122.
89. Shambaugh, *China Goes Global,* 167.
90. Ibid., 168.
91. Ibid., 213–14.
92. Callahan, "Identity and Security in China," 216.
93. Botagoz Seidahmetova, *"Kazahstan skoro zapolniat kitaicy,"* Exclusive.kz, April 2, 2018, http://www.exclusive.kz/expertiza/obshhestvo/113550/; "'To, chto kitajcy rvutsiav Kazahstan,—mif' Abaev o sinofobii,"* Tengrinews, June 19, 2018, https://tengrinews.kz/kazakhstan_news/to-chto-kitaytsyi-rvutsya-v-kazahstan-mif-abaev-o-sinofobii-346889/; "Hundreds Protest in Bishkek against Chinese Migrants," *Radio Free Europe/Radio Liberty* RFE/RL, January 17, 2019; "Real'noe chislo iz Kitaiav Kyrgyzstane vdvoe bol'she oficial'nogo," *Vesti.kg*, January 10, 2019, https://vesti.kg/politika/item/57710-realnoe-chislo-nelegalov-iz-kitaya-v-kyrgyzstane-vdvoe-bolshe-ofitsialnogo.html; "Tenevoi' turizm: kak grazhdane Kitaia nelegal'no rabotaiut v Kirgizii?" *Centrasia,* January 11, 2019, *https://centrasia.org/newsA.php?st=1547157000.*
94. Kurlantzick, *Charm Offensive,* 63.
95. "Vlasti *Kirgizii* obespokoeny antikitaiskimi nastroeniiami," *Kommersant,* January 9, 2019, https://www.kommersant.ru/doc/3850141?fbclid=IwAR36mBWwUv16VVHr7WlNs5Z0kyuOwAuWw0a_p-ZOIgNw4koV2Jm2an0qzpU; "Kyrgyzstan asks China for Grant instead of Loan: Authorities are Stepping more Carefully as Sinophobic views get more Exposure," *Eurasianet,* February 28, 2019, https://eurasianet.org/kyrgyzstan-asks-china-for-grant-instead-of-loan.

REFERENCES

Arif, Beston Husen. "The Role of Soft Power in China's Foreign Policy in the 21st Century." *International Journal of Social Sciences & Educational Studies* 3, no. 3 (2017): 94–101.
Ashakeeva, G., and A. A. Eshmatov. "Kitai—Central'naia Aziia: Kto za kem?" *Radio Azattyk*, March 12, 2013. http://rus.azattyk.org/content/kyrgyzstan_china_central_asia/24926252.html.
Azernews. "SCO Issues Statement following Parliamentary Election in Turkmenistan," March 28, 2018. https://www.azernews.az/region/129327.html.
Baraev, A. "Tihaia ekspansiia. Kitaizaciia Tadzhikistana." *Centrasia.ru*, July 21, 2016. www.centrasia.ru/newsA.php?st=1469122500.
Bayari, Celal. "Chinese Economy and Central Asia." *Academy of Taiwan Business Management Review* 11, no. 3 (2015): 1–14.
Belyi Parus. "Tihaia ekspansiia Kitaia," August 18, 2016. https://paruskg.info/glavnaya/135211-135211.html

Berdakov, Denis. "Mehanizmy 'miagkoi sily' Kitaia v Kyrgyzstane." *Ekpsert Evraziia*, February 28, 2018. http://eurasia.expert/mekhanizmy-myagkoy-sily-kitaya-v-kyrgyzstane/.
Bijian, Zheng. *China's Peaceful Rise, Speeches of Zheng Bijian 1997–2005*. Washington DC: Brookings, 2005.
Blanchard, Jean-Marc F., and Fujia Lu. "Thinking Hard About Soft Power: A Review and Critique of the Literature on China and Soft Power." *Asian Perspective* 36, no. 4 (2012): 565–89.
Callahan, William A. "Identity and Security in China: The Negative Soft Power of the China Dream." *Politics* 35, no. 3–4 (2015): 216–29.
Caravan. "V chem prichiny kazahstanskoi sinofobii," September 17, 2018. https://www.caravan.kz/gazeta/v-chem-prichiny-kazakhstanskojj-sinofobii-480057/.
Centrasia. "Tenevoj' turizm: kak grazhdane Kitaja nelegal'no rabotajut v Kirgizii?" January 11, 2019. *https://centrasia.org/newsA.php?st=1547157000*.
Chen, Julie Yu-Wen, and Soledad Jiménez-Tovar. "China in Central Asia: Local Perceptions from Future Elites." *China Quarterly of International Strategic Studies* 3, no. 3 (2017): 429–45.
China Daily. "Hu Urges Enhancing Soft Power of Chinese Culture," October 15, 2007. http://www.chinadaily.com.cn/china/2007-10/15/content_6175308.htm.
China Daily. "President Xi's Statements on the Belt and Road Initiative," April 15, 2017. http://www.chinadaily.com.cn/china/2017-04/15/content_28940829.htm.
Cooley, Alexander. "Authoritarianism goes Global: Countering Democratic Norms." *Journal of Democracy* 26, no. 3 (2015): 49–63.
Cooley, Alexander. "The League of Authoritarian Gentlemen." *Foreign Policy*, January 30, 2013, https://foreignpolicy.com/2013/01/30/the-league-of-authoritarian-gentlemen/.
Dave, Bhavna. "Silk Road Economic Belt Effects of China's Soft Power Diplomacy in Kazakhstan." In *China Belt and Road Initiative and Its Impact in Central Asia*, edited by Marlene Laruelle, 97–108. Washington, DC: The George Washington University, Central Asia Program, 2018.
Dickens, M. *The Soviets in Xinjiang, 1911–1949*. http://www.oxuscom.com/sovinxj.htm. Accessed January 6, 2011.
Eurasianet. "Kyrgyzstan asks China for Grant instead of Loan: Authorities are Stepping more Carefully as Sinophobic views get more Exposure," February 28, 2019. https://eurasianet.org/kyrgyzstan-asks-china-for-grant-instead-of-loan.
Exenerova, Vera. "Transnational Ties and Local Society´s Role in Improving the PRC's Image in Central Asia." In *China Belt and Road Initiative and Its Impact in Central Asia*, edited by Marlene Laruelle, 126–34. Washington, DC: The George Washington University, Central Asia Program, 2018.
Gill, Bates. *Rising Star: China's New Security Diplomacy*. Washington, DC: Brookings Institution Press, 2007.
Gurbanmyradova, Diana. "The Sources of China's Soft Power in Central Asia: Cultural Diplomacy." Master's thesis, Central European University, Budapest, 2015.
Hartig, Falk. *Chinese Public Diplomacy: The Rise of the Confucius Institute*. New York: Routledge, 2016.

Hunter, Alan. "Soft Power: China on the Global Stage." *Chinese Journal of International Politics* 2, no. 3 (2009): 373–98.

Iurycyn, Vladislav. "Kitaevedenie v Kazahstane : specialisty est', no shkoly net." *Zona.kz*, February 28, 2019. https://zonakz.net/2019/02/28/kitaevedenie-v-kazaxstane-specialisty-est-no-shkoly-net/.

Ivanov, Roman, "Chem zakonchit'sia kitaiskaia ekspansiia v Tadzhikistan?—issledovanie," *Info.kz*, January 28, 2019, https://365info.kz/2019/01/chem-zakonchitsya-kitajskaya-ekspansiya-v-tadzhikistan-issledovanie/.

Izimov, Ruslan. "'Miagkaia sila' Kitaia—na pricele Central'naia Aziia." *Regnum.ru*, January 28, 2014. https://regnum.ru/news/1759411.html.

Kabar. "Glava Minproma Tadzhikistana: Segodnia tol'ko kitaicy sposobnyinvestirovat'," February 12, 2019. http://www.kabar.kg/news/glava-minproma-tadzhikistana-segodnia-tol-ko-kitaitcy-sposobny-investirovat/.

Kaktakto. "Kazahstan na zashhite etnicheskih kazahov v Kitae. Ob''iasniaem situaciu," October 5, 2018. https://kaktakto.com/analitika/kazaxstan-na-zashhite-etnicheskix-kazaxov-v-kitae-obyasnyaem-situaciyu/.

Keller, Megan. "State Dept. Official: China Holding 800k Muslim Minorities in Internment Camps." *The Hill*, May 12, 2018. https://thehill.com/homenews/administration/419855-state-dept-official-china-holding-800k-uighurs-others-in-internment.

Kellner, Thierry. "Le Dragon et la tulipe. Les relations sino-afghanes dans la période post-9/11." *Asia Paper* 4, no. 1 (2009).

Kellner, Thierry. *L'Occident de la Chine : Pékin et la nouvelle Asie centrale (1991–2001)*. Paris: PUF, 2008.

Kim, Evgeniia. "KNR proigryvaet SSHA bor'bu za informacionnoe pole Turkestan." *Regnum.ru*, December 12, 2018. https://regnum.ru/news/polit/2536399.html.

Kiseleva, Tat'iana. "Kakie riski neset razvitie Kitaia dlia Kazahstana?—Satpaev." *Info.kz*, April 20, 2018. https://365info.kz/2018/04/kakie-riski-neset-razvitie-kitaya-dlya-kazahstana-satpaev/

Kluver, Randy. "Chinese Culture in a Global Context: The Confucius Institute as a Geo-Cultural Force." In *China's Global Engagement: Cooperation, Competition, and Influence in the 21st Century*, edited by Jacques Delisle and Avery Goldstein, 389–416. Washington DC: Brookings Institution Press, 2017.

Kommersant. "Vlasti Kirgizii obespokoeny antikitaiskimi nastroeniiami," January 9, 2019. https://www.kommersant.ru/doc/3850141?fbclid=IwAR36mBWwUv16VVHr7WlNs5Z0kyuOwAuWw0a_p-ZOIgNw4koV2Jm2an0qzpU.

Korolev, Andrei. "Kitaiskie investicii pogloshaiut ekonomiku Kazahstanan." *Info.kz*, May 29, 2018. https://365info.kz/2018/05/kitajskie-investitsii-pogloshhayut-ekonomiku-kazahstana/.

Kurlantzick, Joshua. *Charm Offensive: How China's Soft Power is Transforming the World*. New Haven: Yale University Press, 2007.

Kyrgyz National University. "Obshhie svedeniia o fakul'tete," April 28, 2017. https://www.knu.kg/ru/index.php?option=com_content&view=article&id=5885:2014-02-05-12-17-28&catid=926:2014-02-05-12-16-16&Itemid=555.

Laruelle, Marlene, and Sebastien Peyrouse. *The "Chinese Question" in Central Asia: Domestic Order, Social Changes and the Chinese Factor*. London, New York: Hurst and Columbia University Press, 2012.

Liang, Wei. "China's Soft Power in Africa: Is Economic Power Sufficient?" *Asian Perspective* 36, no. 4 (2012): 667–92.

Lynch, Daniel C. *China's Futures: PRC Elites Debate Economics, Politics, and Foreign Policy*. Stanford: Stanford University Press, 2015.

Mackerras, Colin, and Michael Clarke, eds. *China, Xinjiang and Central Asia: History, Transition and Crossborder Interaction into the 21st Century*. New York: Routledge, 2009.

Mendikulova, G. M., and B. Zh. Atanbaeva. *Istoriia migratsii mezhdu Kazakhstanom i Kitaem v 1860-1960-e gg* [History of migrations between Kazakhstan and China 1869-1960]. Almaty: Institut Vostokovedeniia, 2008.

Millward, James A. *Eurasian Crossroads: A History of Xinjiang*. New York: Columbia University Press, 2007.

Mullojanov, Parviz. "Kogda Tadzhikistan nachnët izuchat' Kitaj." *Cabar*, January 15, 2019. https://analytics.cabar.asia/ru/kogda-tadzhikistan-nachnyot-izuchat-kitaj/.

Musabaeva, Anar. "Antikitaiskaia tema v Kyrgyzstane priobrela novyi impul's." *Central Asia Analytical Network*, January 21, 2019. http://caa-network.org/archives/15113.

Nursha, Gaukhar. "Chinese Soft Power in Kazakhstan and Kyrgyzstan: A Confucius Institutes Case Study." In *China Belt and Road Initiative and Its Impact in Central Asia*, edited by Marlene Laruelle, 135–42. Washington, DC: The George Washington University, Central Asia Program, 2018.

Nye, Joseph S. Jr. "Public Diplomacy and Soft Power," *The Annals of the America's Academy of Political and Social Science* 616, no 1 (2008): 94–109.

Nye, Joseph S. Jr. *Soft Power. The Means to Success in World Politics*. New York: Public Affairs, 2004.

Nye, Joseph, and Wang Jisi. "The Rise of China's Soft Power and Its Implications for the United States." In *Power and Restraint: A Shared Vision for the U.S.–China Relationship*, edited by Richard Rosecrance and Gu Guoliang, 23–34. New York: Public Affairs, 2009.

Omelicheva, Mariya Y. *Asia in the New Millennium: Democracy in Central Asia, Competing Perspectives and Alternative Strategies*. Lexington: The University Press of Kentucky, 2015.

Podrobno.uz. "Luchshe–drug horoshevo: Uzbekistan I Kitai planiruiut realizovat' desiatki proektov na milliardy dollarov," February 1, 2019. https://podrobno.uz/cat/uzbekistan-i-kitay-klyuchi-ot-budushchego/luchshee-drug-khoroshego-u/.

Podrobno.uz. "V Tashkente otkroetsia Shanhaisjaia shkola mezhedunarodnogo biznesa," January 5, 2018. https://www.podrobno.uz/cat/obchestvo/v-tashkente-otkroetsya-shankhayskaya-shkola-mezhdunarodnogo-biznesa/.

Radio Azattyk. "V Bishkeke otkrylas' pervaia kyrgyrsko-kitaiskaia shkola," September 1, 2017. https://rus.azattyk.org/a/28709414.html.

Radzhab, Ravshan. "Tadzhik I kitaec—ne brat'ia navek. Chem opasny kontrakty s Podnebesnoi dlia odnoi iz bedneishih stran SNG." *FerganaNews,* February 1, 2019, https://fergana.agency/articles/104786/.

Rezonans.kz. "Sinofobiia po-kyrgyzski: 700 dollarov dolzhen kazhdyi grazhdanin Kyrgyzstana Kitaiu," January 25, 2019. https://rezonans.kz/vse-o-politike/9008-kyrgyzstan-sinofobiya-kitaj-igor-shestakov-denis-berdakov-olga-kartashjova.

RFE/RL. "Hundreds Protest in Bishkek against Chinese Migrants," January 17, 2019.

Rolland, Nadège. "China's 'Belt and Road Initiative': Underwhelming or Game-Changer?" *The Washington Quarterly* 40, no. 1 (2017): 127–42.

Sayama, Osamu. "China's Approach to Soft Power Seeking a Balance between Nationalism, Legitimacy and International Influence." RUSI Occasional Paper, Royal United Services Institute for Defence and Security Studies, March 2016. https://rusi.org/sites/default/files/201603_op_chinas_soft_power.pdf.

Seidahmetova, Botagoz. "Kazakhstan skoro zapolniat kitaicy." *Exclusive.kz,* April 2, 2018. http://www.exclusive.kz/expertiza/obshhestvo/113550/.

Shambaugh, David. *China Goes Global: The Partial Power.* New York: Oxford University Press, 2013.

Shambaugh, David. "China's Soft-Power Push: The Search for Respect." *Foreign Affairs* 94, no. 4 (July/August 2015): 99–107.

Shustov, Aleksandr. "Miagkaia sila drakona: kak Kitaj pytaetsja zavoevat' vliianie v Central'noj Azii." *Evraziia Ekspert,* January 9, 2018. http://eurasia.expert/myag-kaya-sila-drakona-kak-kitay-pytaetsya-zavoevat-vliyanie-v-tsentralnoy-azii/.

Sputnik. "V tadzhikistane otkrylsia vtoroi Institut Konfuciia," August 21, 2015. https://ru.sputnik-tj.com/education/20150821/1016503961.html.

Stanradar.com. "Ne slishkom li mnogo Kitaia?" Aktivisty aposaiutsia 'tihoi ekspan-sii'," August 6, 2018. http://www.stanradar.com/news/full/30541-ne-slishkom-li-mnogo-kitaja-aktivisty-opasajutsja-tihoj-ekspansii-kazahstana.html.

Stanradar.com. "Raschet I pramatizm: Eksperty o vklade Kitaia v tadzhikskoe obra-zovanie," January 24, 2018. https://stanradar.com/news/full/28127-raschet-i-prag-matizm-eksperty-o-vklade-kitaja-v-tadzhikskoe-obrazovanie.html.

Tin-yau Lo, Joe, and Suyan Pan. "Confucius Institutes and China's Soft Power: Practices and Paradoxes." *Compare: A Journal of Comparative and International Education* 46, no. 4 (2016): 512–32.

Umbetaliyeva, Tolganay, Botagoz Rakisheva, and Peer Teschendorf. *Youth in Central Asia: Kazakhstan—Based on a Sociological Survey.* Almaty: Friedrich Ebert Foundation Kazakhstan, 2016.

Vesti.kg. "Real'noe chislo iz Kitaiav Kyrgyzstane vdvoe bol'she oficial'nogo," January 10, 2019. https://vesti.kg/politika/item/57710-realnoe-chislo-nelegalov-iz-kitaya-v-kyrgyzstane-vdvoe-bolshe-ofitsialnogo.html.

Vesti.kg. "Zheleznaia doroga KNR – KR – Ruz: 'Naimenee bygodnyi variant dliia Kitaia I sovershenno nevygodnyi dliia nas'," February 6, 2019. https://vesti.kg/analitika/item/58420-zheleznaya-doroga-knr-kr-ruz-naimenee-vygodnyj-variant-dlya-kitaya-i-sovershenno-nevygodnyj-dlya-nas.html.

Walker, Christopher. "The Authoritarian Threat: Hijacking of 'Soft Power'." *Journal of Democracy* 27, no. 1 (2016): 49–63.
Walker, Christopher. "What Is 'Sharp Power'?" *Journal of Democracy* 29, no. 3 (2018): 9–23.
Zona.kz. "Ucheba v Kitae: Chego hotiat i chto poluchaiut nashi studenty," March 2, 2017. https://www.zakon.kz/4846930-ucheba-v-kitae-chego-khotjat-i-chto.html.

Chapter 4

The European Union and Central Asia
Absent Soft Power in a Far Neighborhood
Emilian Kavalski

Soft power appears to have become one of those essentially contested concepts the meaning and practices of which are anything but clear cut and universally accepted. In his introduction of the concept, Joseph Nye defined it as "when one country gets other countries to want what it wants."[1] He positioned this framing of soft power in direct "contrast with the hard or command power of ordering others to do what it wants."[2] Soft power, thereby, reflects a capacity for the socialization of other actors to support ideas and positions which they did not previously share. As such, soft power reflects specific skills for cooptation as indicated by the "ability of a nation to structure a situation so that other nations develop preferences or define their interests in ways consistent with one's own nation."[3] Yet, while this understanding of the concept appears to be generally accepted when applied to the explanation and understanding of American influence, the contestation emerges when the concept of soft power begins to be exported to the interactions of other international actors.

It is often overlooked that Nye developed the concept of soft power in the context of his broader preoccupation with Japan's growing economic preponderance in international life during the 1980s.[4] As such, soft power came to suggest that even if the material capabilities of the United States were indeed waning, this will not lead to a loss of hegemonic position. American soft power—as evidenced through cultural products, ideas, and norms—will continue to outstrip anything that Japan could ever offer. In this respect, American preponderance over the international system will remain unchallenged.[5] Consequently, soft power is essentially a tool of containment, prevaricating challenges from rising powers. This intellectual history is generally occluded from the application of this term to the foreign policy practices of other international actors.

This lineage is befuddled further when deployed in understanding the external affairs of complex and idiosyncratic international actors such as the European Union (EU). Usually, the claim is that its soft power capabilities are reflected in its unique ability to pacify the continent through the practices of economic and political integration, which then spilled over into global aid programs, preferential trade agreements, educational exchanges, and so on. Commentators also tend to stress the novelty of the EU's interdependent politico-economic framework and flaunt the resilience of its liberal democratic institutions. Labeled as "Europeanization," such a context informs the EU's intent to promote a transformative pattern of international affairs premised on transparent forms of governance, viable market mechanisms, and strong civil society. In fact, it is these very objectives that have led many to refer to the Brussels-based bloc as not just any kind of actor, but as a "legitimate, universal, successful, and desirable model for appropriate international behavior."[6] Hence, the EU's promotion of its own model is intimately connected to the attempts to validate its own international identity by emphasizing the value-rationality of making policy choices based on EU norms.[7]

In the context of the post–Cold War EU-enlargement process, there was little reason to doubt the veracity of this framing of the EU's soft power. Yet, as the EU extended its outreach beyond the countries involved in the accession process, the accepted explanation and understanding of its soft power began to be tested. Thus, in terms of the EU's relations with the Central Asian states (Kazakhstan, Kyrgyzstan, Tajikistan, Turkmenistan, and Uzbekistan), the query is whether its soft power has been *catalyzed* (i.e., given impetus and direction) or *constrained* (i.e., subject to a process of external or self-limitation).[8] The pertinence of such analytical enquiry derives from the apparent sense of inevitability about the international influence of the EU. Bearing in mind the experience of the "big bang" enlargement of 2004, the claim is that the post-communist countries of Eastern Europe are adjusting to the rules and norms of a continent wide "new political system."[9] Even in the context of the deepening Eurozone debt crisis in 2011, the accession of Croatia and the ongoing commitment to the project of membership by the countries from the Western Balkans appears to reaffirm the continuing appeal of the EU's lodestone.[10] Thus, it seems only natural to some that such a "civilizing" project will be expanded to the countries on the other side of the enlarged EU.

Owing to the dominant focus on enlargement, the EU's external policy has been treated largely as coterminous with the transformative potential underwriting the dynamics of accession-driven conditionality. Thereby, it was only recently that the relevance of the EU's ability to Europeanize the practices of states (outside the purview and the prospect of membership) has been given serious consideration. It seems, however, that the bulk of popular and policy attention has been captured by the development of the European

Neighbourhood Policy (ENP).[11] Stretching from the former European provinces of the Soviet Union, through the Caucasus, the Middle East, and North Africa, the ENP is hailed as a novel development in the field of EU external relations.[12] In particular, the relationship with Belarus, Moldova, and, especially, Ukraine tend to attract the limelight of commentaries on the ENP development.[13] Such fixation neglects the examination of the EU's soft power in the countries of Central Asia, which are excluded from the ENP process.

The following section outlines the key takes on the EU's soft power. In particular, the attention is on the strategic ambiguity that appears to frame Brussels' exercise of soft power. The point then is that such ambivalence then provides a counterproductive environment for extending the influence of the EU in a "Far Neighborhood" such as Central Asia. Consequently, the EU's engagement in the region seems to confront Brussels with the need "to design a real foreign policy beyond the enlargement paradigm."[14] Such framing draws attention to the EU's ability to project its soft power to "out-of-Europe" areas.[15] As the following sections will demonstrate, such a development reflects a failure to develop deliberate and meaningful programs for the Central Asian states. Instead, the process-tracing of the EU's external outreach reveals reactive, inconsistent, and disconnected interactions with Central Asia. In this respect, the concluding section indicates that if the EU is to catalyze the global relevance of its soft power, Brussels has to offer a meaningful operationalization of its Central Asian strategic discourse.

THE EU—AN AMBIGUOUS OR ABSENT SOFT POWER IN OUT-OF-EUROPE AREAS

As the largest provider of official development assistance in the world, a beacon of democracy and human rights, and a model for successful regional integration, the EU has long been touted as a global norm-setter. The assumption has been that the appeal of its original politico-economic framework offers sufficient incentives to convince other countries to act "appropriately" on the international stage—that is, in line with the EU's demands and expectations. The argument went, that in this way, the EU not only made other actors "do what Brussels wanted them to do," but that it made them internalize the EU's position as their own. As such, the EU has been called a normative power—an appellation signaling not merely "soft power plus," but designating a novel international actor with the idiosyncratic capacities to define what is "normal" in international life.[16] In confirmation of this status and as an indication of its unique contribution to the maintenance of peace and security in Europe, the EU was awarded the 2012 Nobel Peace Prize.

In a major departure from the current conversations on soft power in general and the EU in particular, this chapter claims that the EU has both normative power and soft power components in its external relations toolkit (alongside many others). In other words, rather than the usual either–or debate, the point made here is that the EU has a number of approaches in its foreign policy arsenal and the normative and soft power are only two of those. As such normative power and soft power are not contradictory, but complementary forms of external relations. Thus, while this chapter focuses on the soft power of the EU, this should not be misunderstood as an indication that the Brussels-based bloc has only one foreign policy practice. Instead, the claim is that soft power is part of a much wider set of external relations repertoires of the EU, all of which are utilized (depending on the contingencies of context and circumstance) to position it as a viable "expert," "teacher," "role model," and an "honest broker."[17]

In this respect—and, perhaps, even paradoxically—many have argued that at the heart of the success of the soft power of the EU has been its nonlinearity. While conditionality and thresholds of compliance have long been considered the key ingredients of its transformative agenda (especially, as reflected in its accession and partnership programs), the specific forms that the EU's soft power takes have always been contingent on particular spatiotemporal arrangements and issue areas. Consequently, and unlike its normative power, the EU's soft power is a descriptive rather than a solely ideational category.[18] The point is that soft power—both in general and the case of the European Union in particular—is inherently context-dependent: the constitution of attractive values is invariably "a subjective matter in the eye of the beholder, and not dependent on supposed inherent traits or predispositions."[19] As a result, what appears to be idiosyncratic about the EU's soft power is its seeming lack of coherence and consistency, owing to its constant flux and ongoing adaptation to new contexts and changing circumstances. In other words, "sensitivity to contingency" becomes the defining feature of the EU's "principled pragmatism" in global life.[20]

In this setting, many have pointed to the content and practices of the EU's strategic ambiguity as an underlying characteristic of its soft power. In particular, Bettina Ahrens has outlined in great detail the ways in which the ambivalence framing the character and policies of the EU's soft power provides the critical ingredient of its transformative impact.[21] As she suggests, this characteristic is not coincidental and has emerged in response to the permanent sense of crisis plaguing the evolution of European integration. Ahrens insists that at its core, the ambiguity of the EU's soft power entails "an inevitable *undecidability* between two different options."[22] On the one hand, is the structural quandary for the Brussels-based bloc of overcoming state-centrism in international life, while remaining profoundly embedded in and playing by the rules of a global order pivoted on nation states. On the other hand, is the normative tension implicit in (any call for) changing the fundamentals of international relations, which would involve unpredictable realignments, random power transitions, and unintended reconfigurations. In this respect, the structural and normative ambiguity of the EU's soft power breeds "the parallel existence of particular structures, principles, and ideas," which is the very source of its transformative role on the global stage.[23] In other words, the ambivalence of this framing of soft power facilitates the articulation of grand visions, while allowing the EU the flexibility to implement them in a contingent fashion.

The relevant point here is that while such ambiguity might have been beneficial for the EU in its relations with the countries of Central and Eastern Europe, the Western Balkans, and perhaps, some states involved in the ENP, where Brussels' ongoing commitments are formalized both through regional and bilateral programs, when it comes to Central Asia such an approach proves to be counterproductive (at least for the time being). In fact, such ambiguity tends to be interpreted as an indication of the EU's absence from regional affairs, not least, because of Central Asia's own ambivalent positioning as both distant and proximate to Brussels, all at the same time.[24] According to Olga Spaiser, such framing puts the region in the unique position of a "Far Neighborhood"—that is, "'a neighbor of neighbors' or what the EU's Special Representative, Pierre Morrel, used to refer to as a 'Third European Space'."[25] As a result, the EU structures the ambiguity of its soft power along "circles of influence" or "zones of order." According to Spaiser, each of these circles or zones has a specific role in extending and exercising the influence of the EU. These start with the circle of candidate countries, go through "the ring of friends" of the ENP, and, finally, reach out to Central Asia as a "further circle of influence."[26] The suggestion is that such strategic positioning reveals not only the growing levels of ambiguity in the EU's outreach with each of these circles, but the very constitution of buffer zones that "the EU necessitates in order to hold back the spillover of threats."[27] Perhaps paradoxically, such understanding of the EU's soft power seems to bring it closer to Nye's original definition—as a tool of containment.[28] However, rather than containing potential rivals as was the case with the United States, in the EU's instance it is warding off threats. Yet, in the context of a multitude of international actors vying for influence in Central Asia, the ambiguity of the EU's soft power stands in stark contrast with the bespoke strategies that most other international actors are extending to the region. The following section details the practices of the EU's soft power in Central Asia.

LOOKING FOR THE EU'S SOFT POWER IN CENTRAL ASIA

In line with its positioning as a "Far Neighborhood," the EU's relations with Central Asia reflect the complex mosaic of its external relations.[29] On the one hand, the region is involved in Brussels' interactions with Asia. On the other hand, the Central Asian states have been included in the EU's assistance for the democratic transitions of the countries in the post-Soviet and post-communist space.[30] In this respect, in the jigsaw of the EU's post–Cold War foreign policy, Central Asia does not seem to fit neatly with the other projects of Brussels. For instance, Central Asia has been gradually excluded from the EU's approaches to the other post-Soviet states—the region is neither fully incorporated into the ENP initiatives nor is it a partner to Brussels' relations with Russia. At the same time, Central Asia is not included in the explicitly "Asian" initiatives of the EU—such as the Asia–Europe Meeting (ASEM).[31]

Brussels insists that the positioning of Central Asia on the fringes of its other initiatives reflects the region's unique role as a *bridge*, with a "centuries-old tradition of bringing Europe and Asia together [because] it lies at a strategically important intersection between the two continents."[32] However, the ambiguity of this balancing act appears lost and instead a more cynical view emerges—one, which suggests that Central Asia is merely a bridge (if not—quite literally—a mere refueling station) between the EU's other and strategically more important commitments. Some observers have noted that Central Asia appears as either a "non-existent region, or as a merely forgotten one."[33] In this respect, Central Asia presents an idiosyncratic case of the temporal-and-spatial othering implicit in the EU's exercise of soft power.[34] In particular, the region emerges as a geopolitical locale, whose Europeanization does not seem to be positioned as the EU's "moral obligation."[35] Some have argued that the context of a "Far Neighborhood" makes it "easier" for Brussels to engage Central Asia as it is "free from having to think where the borders of Europe lie, with all of the constraints this question imposes on EU thinking and action."[36]

In particular, such detachment from Central Asian affairs has left the EU with the option to insist on the internalization of certain norms of appropriateness by regional states (as demanded by its strategic culture), without the support of its soft power (as exemplified by its various instruments for socialization). Consequently, one of the most conspicuous legacies of this period is the location of Central Asia in the EU's strategic imagination as *outside of its area of responsibility*. In an attempt to reinforce its position in Central Asia, the EU promulgated the Partnership and Cooperation Agreements (PCAs) at the end of the 1990s. While intent on enhancing its visibility in Central Asia by providing regular annual fora for interaction between the EU and the Central Asian states, the PCAs did not offer a demonstrable change in the EU's framing of the region. The key innovation in terms of the EU's soft power has been the implicit differentiation of the Central Asian states between potentially promising pupils (Kazakhstan and Kyrgyzstan) and problematic cases (Uzbekistan, Tajikistan, and Turkmenistan). Overall, however, the PCAs made obvious that the EU did not expect to play the same role in Central Asia as it did in other post-communist countries. These patterns also reassert the pervasive ambivalence of Brussels' soft power, which lacked the means to provide a veritable lodestone for the region.

It was only the terrorist attacks in the United States on September 11, 2001, that both intensified the discussions of Brussels' engagement in "out-of-Europe" areas and backstopped the nascent articulation of the idea and practices of "circles of influence." In particular, there has been greater attention to the EU's interactions with regions that are not subject to enlargement initiatives (and enlargement-like projects, such as the ENP). Most commentators interpreted these developments as a qualitative change in the EU's strategic outlook, which revealed a growing preoccupation with "controlling the processes by which vulnerable societies slide towards the wrong camp" and ensuring that such societies act "as protectors of the EU."[37] To that effect, in 2002 the European Union advanced the rudiments of a far-reaching and comprehensive policy tailored specifically to the five Central Asian states under the aegis of separate Regional Strategy Paper (RSP). Furthermore, in terms of increasing its visibility, in 2005, the EU appointed its own Special Representative (EUSR) to Central Asia.[38] The appointment of the EUSR indicated the activation of the European Security and Defence Policy (ESDP) in Central Asia.[39]

The EUSR activities have been framed by the ongoing evolution of the RSP initiative, which is undergoing its third iteration—the first RSP (2002–2006), the second RSP (2007–2013), and the third RSP (2014–2020).[40] The second and third RSPs have been administered by the new Development Cooperation Instrument (DCI), which came to substitute the Technical Assistance to the Commonwealth of Independent States (TACIS) program. In policy terms, the RSP initiative has to indicate that the EU is recognizing the idiosyncrasies of the five Central Asian states as well as the need to project distinct and contextual policies in the region. Intent on reinforcing its commitment to Central Asia, during the German presidency of the European Council (2007), the EU launched (after a protracted lobbying by Berlin) its "Strategy for a New Partnership" with the region. This new strategy reiterates the EU's "strong interest in a peaceful, democratic, and economically prosperous Central Asia."[41] Yet, as already indicated, it perpetuates the unquestioning promotion of the norms of the EU's strategic culture. Hence, Brussels is explicit that,

> The development of a stable political framework and functioning economic structures are dependent on respect for the rule of law, human rights, good governance, and the development of transparent, democratic political structures.... [Such a] task calls for the active involvement of civil society. A developed and active civil society and independent media are vital for the development of a pluralistic civil society. The EU will cooperate with Central Asian states to this end and promote enhanced exchanges in civil society.[42]

Such articulations suggest that even though the EU does not intend the same level of integration with Central Asia as it did in other post-communist areas, Brussels still anticipates that its regional outreach will provide sufficient leverage to push for democratic reforms that would lead to political pluralism and social modernization. To that effect, the EU has explicitly indicated that 70 percent of its regional assistance will be directed toward programs for bilateral (as opposed to region-wide) assistance.[43] While further reinforcing the differentiation of the region between promising pupils and problematic cases, this approach has also been criticized for its lack of "instinctive understanding" of the "systemic reality" of Central Asia.[44] As such, the regional states that tend to be characterized by a predilection for "paternalistic heads of state and a hierarchical and centralized conception of authority, find the multitude of European identities and actors difficult to grasp."[45] At the same time, the growth of a "politically driven anti-Western sentiment" further compromises the EU's standing in the region.[46] This loss of appeal also reflects the social conservatism in the region where the EU's association with issues such as LGBTI rights has come to confirm "post-Soviet narratives of decadent Western values and the need for a so-called Eurasian civilization to safeguard the region's traditional values."[47] Such a context curtails the "usages of Europe" in Central Asia—that is, the existence of domestic actors willing to adopt the EU model as a mechanism for the justification (or rejection) of specific policy ideas.[48] There are almost no governmental and fewer non-governmental actors who would be willing to validate their actions by aligning with EU templates.

In fact, many commentators have argued that the EU needs to adopt a more pragmatic approach for implementing its value-based agenda by building relationships that take into account the complex interaction between energy, security, and development in Central Asia. The EU's cultural instinct to position itself as an idiosyncratic actor tasked with the promotion of democracy, human rights, and the rule of law has very little purchase in the region, despite the popularity of European cultural products—especially, education. Such an approach should assist the operationalization of Brussels' soft power by providing tangible benchmarks for measuring the involvement and influence of the EU. As such, it is through the identification and engagement with the key challenges plaguing Central Asia that the EU can play to the strengths of its soft power. In this respect, the call for the promotion of "security by meeting the practical day-to-day needs of the population" seemed to offer a meaningful strategy for overcoming the ambiguity of the EU's soft power.[49] The advice has been that the EU "should be concise and practical in its objectives, without abandoning the overriding concept of political, social, and economic stability through democratic change."[50] More significantly, such a linkage could facilitate the emergence of a more focused Europeanizing strategy for Central Asia that can both lift the EU from its foreign policy impasse in the region and meaningfully catalyze its soft power in global life.

Yet, in the absence of such nuance and contextualization, Central Asian elites have resisted European pressures to reform not only because they fear a "deconcentralization" of their power, but also because such initiatives amount to "a call for revolutionary transformation."[51] At the same time, once Germany ceded the presidency of the European Council at the end of June 2007, no other Member State seemed interested to follow through on Berlin's commitments to the region. Moreover, with the continuing volatility as a result of the European debt crisis, compounded by the rise of populist and anti-establishment sentiments and formations across the continent, as well as the unpredictability caused by Brexit, Brussels appears to be paying increasingly scant attention to its "near abroad" and even less so to the "far neighborhood" of Central Asia. In this setting, both the EU and its soft power appear increasingly "small, worn out, and offer just a weak echo of the real master."[52] Such context lends support to the allegations of a convivial tension (if not clash) between the values and interests of the EU's soft power. As one EU official acknowledged, "the EU has yet to figure out new ways to advance its interests without damaging its fundamental values and to promote its values without compromising its long-term interests."[53]

The ambiguity backstopping such strategic attitudes has urged some to suggest that the EU's preoccupation with its soft power is merely a distraction from the confrontation with "the reality of Europe's provincialization in world politics."[54] It should not be surprising therefore that none of the images that dominate the EU's perception in Central Asia—as part of "the West," as "patronizing," and as a "geopolitical counterbalance"[55]—dovetail with Brussels' own understanding of its soft power. As a result, the ambiguity of the EU's soft power in the Central Asian "far neighborhood" bespeaks the failure of its transformative agency. Ambiguity in this setting is quickly interpreted as an indication of vaguely defined priorities. Furthermore, the ambivalence charactering Brussels' presence in the region falls far short of conceptualizing (let alone validating) the role of its soft power both in the region and in "out-of-Europe" areas more generally. In particular, it fails to account for the willingness of Central Asian states to cooperate with other, more proximate international actors, such as China and Russia. In this respect, the European Parliament has urged the EU to become more attentive to the complex realities of Central Asia by recognizing that "Russia and China are the only completely invested actors in the region. They have the capacity to engage virtually on all fronts, ranging from military action to trade and energy."[56] The suggestion here is that without a meaningful operationalization of the strategic narratives of its soft power, the EU's "ability to shape events" in Central Asia will remain "very limited."[57]

CONCLUSION

The overview of the EU's relations with Central Asia provided in this chapter demonstrates Brussels' struggle to articulate not merely a meaningful strategy for its relations with the region, but more generally an effective external affairs strategy able to project its soft power outside the framework of enlargement (or enlargement-like initiatives). More generally, such development confirms Nye's observation that soft power is "hard to use, easy to lose, and costly to re-establish."[58] Central Asia confronts the EU with the reality where it not only is not a magnet for regional states, but also is in a situation where Brussels has to vie for the attention of regional states that appear spoilt for choice by the many suitors participating in the "new Great Game." Such setting also demonstrates that the soft power of the EU is conditioned by domestic understandings of legitimate political authority.[59] Thus, used to the Europeanization of post-communist countries compliant with its soft power, the EU appears confused and uncertain by the lack of appeal of its rules and values. This is a qualitatively new situation for Brussels and its soft power—one, which baffles the EU and which it is still to address convincingly.[60]

In particular, what appears striking about the EU's agency in Central Asia is the consistent lack of initiatives that engage regional states in the deliberate practice of regular interactions with Brussels. Thus, in response to the question with which this chapter began—whether the EU's soft power in the Central Asian states is *constrained* or *catalyzed*—the answer is the former rather than the latter. In spite of its significant commercial involvement in the region, the EU emerges as both unable and unwilling to extend a dedicated and meaningful practice for the Europeanization of Central Asia. This, in turn, prevents Brussels from becoming a full-fledged soft power in Central Asia. Instead of a soft power, the EU emerges as a "bit player"—an actor with a very limited impact and leverage on regional affairs.[61] In this respect,

> The status of the EU as a continental model of economic and social organization might be seen as giving a strong basis for the development of European

foreign policy, but in many ways the strengths that give the EU a major role in the European order do not export easily; they are less immediately appropriate to a fluid and often chaotic world, and this means that the attempt to project "Europe" into the global arena brings with it new risks and potential costs.[62]

The claim here is that the cultural instincts of the EU's soft power entrap its agency in Central Asia and make it difficult for Brussels to develop contextual approaches to the region.[63] Such policy trend does not bode well for the EU's influence in Central Asia. It seems that deprived of the lure of membership or privileged partnership, the EU's soft power cannot develop resonance in Central Asia. In this respect, the EU's search for a "new" strategy not only in Central Asia, but also in its external affairs (beyond enlargement and enlargement-like initiatives) demands a serious reflection upon the impact of its own normativity. Without such questioning, the EU is unlikely to project its soft power beyond the geographical confines of Europe and its immediate neighborhood and, as recent developments reveal, its credibility might even lose a foothold in the member states, itself.

NOTES

1. Jospeh S. Nye Jr, *Bound to Lead: The Changing Nature of American Power* (New York: Basic Books, 1990).
2. Ibid., 5–80.
3. Ibid., 191.
4. Emilian Kavalski, "Normative Power beyond the Eurocentric Frame," in *Oxford Bibliographies of International Relations*, ed. Patrick James (Oxford: Oxford University Press, 2018).
5. Emilian Kavalski, "Community of Values or Community of Practice," *East Asian Community Review* 1, no. 1 and 2 (2018): 15.
6. Finnemore, Martha and Sikkink, K. 1998. "International Norm Dynamics," *International Organization* 52, no. 4: 887–917.
7. Emilian Kavalski, "Whom to Follow? Central Asia between the EU and China," *China Report* 43, no. 1 (2007): 43–55.
8. Michael Smith, "Between Soft Power and a Hard Place: European Union Foreign and Security Policy between the Islamic World and the United States," *International Politics* 46, no. 5 (2009): 596; Emilian Kavalski, "The Struggle for Recognition of Normative Powers: Normative Power Europe and Normative Power China in Context," *Cooperation & Conflict* 48, no. 2 (2013): 237.
9. Simon Hix, "The EU as a New Political System," in *Comparative Politics*, ed. Daniele Caramani (Oxford: Oxford University Press, 2008).
10. Kavalski, "The Struggle for Recognition."
11. "European Neighbourhood Policy," (strategy paper, COM 373 final, Commission of the European Communities, Brussels, May 12, 2004).

12. "NSLA Strategy Paper," (strategy paper, Commission of the European Communities, Brussels, 2007).

13. Emilian Kavalski, "From the Western Balkans to the Greater Balkans Area: The External Conditioning of "Awkward" and 'Integrated' States," *Mediterranean Quarterly* 17, no. 3 (2006): 86–100.

14. Anna Matveeva, *EU Stakes in Central Asia* (Paris: EUISS, 2006), 110.

15. Emilian Kavalski, *The "New" Central Asia: The Regional Impact of International Actors* (Singapore: World Scientific, 2009).

16. Ian Manners, "Normative Power Europe: A Contradiction in Terms?" *Journal of Common Market Studies* 40, no. 2 (2002): 235–58; Emilian Kavalski, *The Guanxi of Relational International Theory* (London: Routledge, 2018).

17. Olga Alinda Spaiser, *The European Union's Influence in Central Asia: Geopolitical Challenges and Responses* (Lanham: Lexington, 2018), 69; Emilian Kavalski and Young Chul Cho, "Governing Uncertainty in Turbulent Times," *Comparative Sociology* 14, no. 3 (2015): 429–44.

18. Joseph S. Nye Jr., *The Future of Power* (New York: Public Affairs, 2011), 23.

19. Kristian L. Nielsen, "EU Soft Power and the Capability-Expectations Gap," *Journal of Contemporary European Research* 9, no. 5 (2013): 728. Emilian Kavalski, "The European Union and India: A Reluctant Partnership between Aspiring Global Powers," in *The European Union's Strategic Partnerships*, ed. L.Ferreira-Pereira and M. Smith (London: Palgrave, 2021), 202.

20. "Shared Vision, Common Action: A Stronger Europe," (report, European Commission, Brussels, June 2016), 18; Emilian Kavalski, "The European Union in the Heartland," in *Afghanistan and Its Neighbors after the NATO Withdrawal*, ed. Amin Saikal and Kirill Nourzhanov (Lanham: Lexington Books, 2016), 198.

21. Bettina Ahrens, "Normative Power Europe in Crisis? Understanding the Productive Role of Ambiguity for the EU's Transformative Agenda," *Asia Europe Journal* 16, no. 2 (2018): 199–212.

22. Ibid., 201, emphasis in original.

23. Ibid.

24. Emilian Kavalski, *Central Asia and the Rise of Normative Powers: Contextualizing the Security Governance of the EU, China, and India* (New York: Bloomsbury, 2012), 85.

25. Spaiser, *The European Union's Influence in Central Asia*.

26. Ibid. Emilian Kavalski, "Quo Vadis Cooperation," *World Affairs* 184, no. 1 (2021): 41.

27. Ibid., 59–61.

28. Nye, *Bound to Lead*.

29. Emilian Kavalski, *World Politics at the Edge of Chaos: Reflections on Complexity and Global Life* (Albany: State University of New York Press, 2015).

30. Emilian Kavalski and Magdalena Zolkos, *Defunct Federalisms: Critical Perspectives on Federal Failure* (London: Routledge, 2008).

31. "Strategy Paper 2002–2006 and Indicative Program 2002–2004 for Central Asia, (strategy paper, EEAS, Brussels, October 30, 2002); Emilian Kavalski and Magdalena Zolkos, "The Hoax of War: The Foreign Policy Discourses of Poland and

Bulgaria on Iraq, 2003–2005," *Journal of Contemporary European Studies* 15, no. 3, (2007): 377–93.

32. "The EU and Central Asia: Strategy for a New Partnership" (annex QC-79-07-222-29-C, Council of the European Union, Brussels, May 31, 2007).

33. Laure Delcour, *Shaping the Post-Soviet Space? EU Policies and Approaches to Region-Building* (Farnham: Ashgate, 2011), 9.

34. Emilian Kavalski, "The Shadows of Normative Power in Asia: Framing the International Agency of China, India, and Japan," *Pacific Focus* 29, no. 3 (2014): 303–28.

35. Will Myer, *Islam and Colonialism: Western Perspectives on Soviet Asia* (Abingdon: Routledge, 2002), 224–7.

36. Matveeva, *EU Stakes in Central Asia*, 8.

37. Alexandra Gheciu, "*Securing Civilization: The EU, NATO and the OSCE in the Post-9/11 World* (Oxford: Oxford University Press, 2008), 53; "Country Progress Reports," (report, European Commission, Brussels, 2013), http://eeas.europa.eu/central_asia/index_en.htm, accessed June 23, 2020.

38. "Council Joint Action 2005/588/CFSP," *Official Journal of the European Union* 199 (2005): 100–101; "EU SSR Concept, 12566/5/05," (report, European Council, Brussels, 2005).

39. Emilian Kavalski, *Stable Outside, Fragile Inside? Post-Soviet Statehood in Central Asia* (London: Routledge, 2010).

40. "EU-CADAP. 14182/13+COR1," (paper, European Council, Brussels, 2013); Georgiy Voloshin, *The European Union's Normative Power in Central Asia: Promoting Values and Defending Interests* (London: Palgrave, 2014).

41. "The EU and Central Asia," Council of the European Union, 4.

42. "The EU and Central Asia," Council of the European Union, 7.

43. Ibid. Emilian Kavalski, "Universal Values and Geopolitical Interests," in *Global Trends and Regional Development*, ed. N. Genov (London: Routledge, 2012), 285.

44. David Lewis, *Temptations of Tyranny in Central Asia* (London: Hurst, 2008), 25–26; Sebastien Peyrouse, "How Does Central Asia View the EU?" (working paper, Europe Central Asia Monitoring, June 11, 2014).

45. Marlene Laruelle and Sebastien Peyrouse, *Globalizing Central Asia: Geopolitics and the Challenges of Economic Development* (Armonk: M.E. Sharpe, 2013), 59.

46. Nargis Kassenova, "Projecting Soft Power as an Imperative for the EU in Central Asia," *EUCAM Watch* 18 (February 2018): 5.

47. Marlene Laruelle and Eric McGlinchey, "Renewing EU and US Soft Power in Central Asia," *EUCAM Commentary* 28 (October 27, 2017).

48. Cornelia Woll and Sophie Jacquot, "Using Europe: Strategic Action in Multi-Level Politics," *Comparative European Politics* 8, no.1 (2010): 110.

49. "Draft Paper on the State of the Implementation of the EU Strategy for Central Asia," (paper, Committee on Foreign Policy, European Parliament, Brussels, August 2011), 11.

50. "The EU in Central Asia: The Regional Context," (report, Policy Department, European Parliament, January 2016), 11.

51. Stephen Blank, "Democratic Prospects in Central Asia," *World Affairs* 166, no. 1 (2004): 133–40.

52. Ole Wæver, "A Post-Western Europe: Strange Identities in a Less Liberal World Order," *Ethics & International Affairs* 32, no. 1 (2018): 75. Emilian Kavalski, "Inside/Outside and Around," *Global Society* 34, no. 4 (2020): 471

53. Quoted in Voloshin, *The European Union's Normative Power*, 60.

54. Peter Seeburg, "Provincialization of Europe and the Middle East? Migration, Regional Competition and the Global Perspective," (report, Center for Mellemøststudier, Syddansk Universitet, Odense, May 2012), 2; David Walton and Emilian Kavalski, *Power Transition in Asia* (London: Routledge, 2017), 56.

55. Spaiser, *The European Union's Influence in Central Asia*, 83.

56. "The EU in Central Asia," European Parliament, 16

57. Emilian Kavalski and Young Chul Cho, "European Union in Central Eurasia: Still Searching for Strategy," *Asia Europe Journal* 16, no. 1 (2018): 58.

58. Nye, *The Future of Power*, 83.

59. Gergana Noutcheva, "Whose Legitimacy? The EU and Russia in Contest for the Eastern Neighbourhood," *Democratization* 25, no. 2 (2018): 324; Emilian Kavalski and Young Chul Cho, "Worlding the Study of Normative Power: Assessing European and Chinese Definitions of the 'Normal'," *Uluslararası İlişkiler* 15, no. 57 (2018): 49–65.

60. Kavalski, "Whom to Follow?"

61. S. Neil MacFarlane, "Caucasus and Central Asia: Towards a Non-Strategy" (paper, *Occasional Paper Series* 37, Geneva Centre for Security Policy, Geneva, August 2004), 14.

62. Smith, "Between Soft Power and a Hard Place," 603.

63. Emilian Kavalski, "Venus and the Porcupine: Assessing the EU–India Strategic Partnership," *South Asian Survey* 15, no. 1 (2008): 63–81.

REFERENCES

Ahrens, Bettina. "Normative Power Europe in Crisis? Understanding the Productive Role of Ambiguity for the EU's Transformative Agenda." *Asia Europe Journal* 16, no. 2 (2018): 199–212.

Blank, Stephen. "Democratic Prospects in Central Asia." *World Affairs* 166, no. 1 (2004): 133–147.

Delcour, Laure. *Shaping the Post-Soviet Space? EU Policies and Approaches to Region-Building*. Farnham: Ashgate, 2011.

EEAS. "Strategy Paper 2002-2006 and Indicative Program 2002-2004 for Central Asia." Strategy paper, European Union External Action (EEAS), Brussels, October 30, 2002.

European Commission. "Country Progress Reports." Report, European Commission, Brussels, 2013. http://eeas.europa.eu/central_asia/index_en.htm. Accessed June 23, 2020.

European Commission. "European Neighbourhood Policy." Strategy paper, COM 373 final, Commission of the European Communities, Brussels, May 12, 2004.
European Commission. "NSLA Strategy Paper." Strategy paper, European Commission, Brussels, 2007.
European Commission. "Shared Vision, Common Action: A Stronger Europe." Report, European Commission, Brussels, June 2016.
European Council. "Council Joint Action 2005/588/CFSP." *Official Journal of the European Union* 199 (2005): 100–101.
European Council. "The EU and Central Asia: Strategy for a New Partnership." Annex, QC-79-07-222-29-C, Council of the European Union, Brussels, May 31, 2007.
European Council. "EU-CADAP. 14182/13+COR1." Paper, European Council, Brussels, 2013.
European Council. "EU SSR Concept, 12566/5/05." Report, European Council, Brussels, 2005.
European Parliament. "Draft Paper on the State of the Implementation of the EU Strategy for Central Asia." Paper, Committee on Foreign Policy, European Parliament, Brussels, August 2011.
European Parliament. "The EU in Central Asia: The Regional Context." Report, Policy Department, European Parliament, January 2016.
Finnemore, Martha, and Kathryn Sikkink. "International Norm Dynamics." *International Organization* 52, no. 4 (1998): 887–917.
Gheciu, Alexandra. *Securing Civilization: The EU, NATO and the OSCE in the Post-9/11 World*. Oxford: Oxford University Press, 2008.
Hix, Simon. "The EU as a New Political System." In *Comparative Politics*, edited by Daniele Caramani, 387–406. Oxford: Oxford University Press, 2008.
Kassenova, Nargis. "Projecting Soft Power as an Imperative for the EU in Central Asia." *EUCAM Watch* 18 (February 2018): 4–6.
Kavalski, E. *Central Asia and the Rise of Normative Powers: Contextualizing the Security Governance of the EU, China, and India*. New York: Bloomsbury, 2012.
Kavalski, E. "Community of Values or Community of Practice." *East Asian Community Review* 1, no. 1 and 2 (2018): 5–17.
Kavalski, E. "The European Union in the Heartland." In *Afghanistan and Its Neighbors after the NATO Withdrawal*, edited by Amin Saikal and Kirill Nourzhanov, 195–210. Lanham: Lexington Books, 2016.
Kavalski, Emilian. "From the Western Balkans to the Greater Balkans Area: The External Conditioning of "Awkward" and 'Integrated' States." *Mediterranean Quarterly* 17, no. 3 (2006): 86–100.
Kavalski, E. *The Guanxi of Relational International Theory*. London: Routledge, 2018.
Kavalski, E. "Inside/Outside and Around." *Global Society* 34, no. 4 (2020): 467–86.
Kavalski, Emilian. *The "New" Central Asia: The Regional Impact of International Actors*. Singapore: World Scientific, 2009.
Kavalski, E. "Normative Power beyond the Eurocentric Frame." In *Oxford Bibliographies of International Relations*, edited by P. James. Oxford: Oxford University Press, 2018.

Kavalski, E. "Quo Vadis Cooperation." *World Affairs* 184, no. 1 (2021): 33–56.
Kavalski, E. "The Shadows of Normative Power in Asia: Framing the International Agency of China, India, and Japan." *Pacific Focus* 29, no. 3 (2014): 303–28
Kavalski, E. *Stable Outside, Fragile Inside? Post-Soviet Statehood in Central Asia.* London: Routledge, 2010.
Kavalski, E. "The Struggle for Recognition of Normative Powers: Normative Power Europe and Normative Power China in Context." *Cooperation & Conflict* 48, no. 2 (2013): 247–67.
Kavalski, E. "Universal Values and Geopolitical Interests." In Global Trends and Regional Development, edited by N. Genov, 280-296. London: Routledge, 2012.
Kavalski, Emilian. "Venus and the Porcupine: Assessing the EU–India Strategic Partnership." *South Asian Survey* 15, no. 1 (2008): 63–81.
Kavalski, Emilian. "Whom to Follow? Central Asia between the EU and China." *China Report* 43, no. 1 (2007): 43–55.
Kavalski, E. *World Politics at the Edge of Chaos: Reflections on Complexity and Global Life.* Albany: State University of New York Press, 2015.
Kavalski, Emilian, and Magdalena Zolkos. *Defunct Federalisms: Critical Perspectives on Federal Failure.* London: Routledge, 2008.
Kavalski, Emilian, and Magdalena Zolkos. "The Hoax of War: The Foreign Policy Discourses of Poland and Bulgaria on Iraq, 2003–2005." *Journal of Contemporary European Studies* 15, no. 3, (2007): 377–93.
Kavalski, Emilian, and Young Chul Cho. "European Union in Central Eurasia: Still Searching for Strategy." *Asia Europe Journal* 16, no. 1 (2018): 51–63.
Kavalski, Emilian, and Young Chul Cho. "Governing Uncertainty in Turbulent Times." *Comparative Sociology* 14, no. 3 (2015): 429–44.
Kavalski, Emilian, and Young Chul Cho. "Worlding the Study of Normative Power: Assessing European and Chinese Definitions of the 'Normal'." *Uluslararası İlişkiler* 15, no. 57 (2018): 49–65.
Laruelle, Marlene, and Eric McGlinchey. "Renewing EU and US Soft Power in Central Asia." *EUCAM Commentary* 28, October 27, 2017.
Lewis, David. *Temptations of Tyranny in Central Asia.* London: Hurst, 2008.
MacFarlane, S. Neil. "Caucasus and Central Asia: Towards a Non-Strategy." Paper, Occasional Paper Series 37, Geneva Centre for Security Policy, Geneva, August 2004.
Manners, Ian. "Normative Power Europe: A Contradiction in Terms?" *Journal of Common Market Studies* 40, no. 2 (2002): 235–58.
Matveeva, Anna. *EU in Central Asia.* Paris: EUISS, 2006.
Myer, Will. *Islam and Colonialism: Western Perspectives on Soviet Asia.* Abingdon: Routledge, 2002.
Nielsen, Kristian L. "EU Soft Power and the Capability-Expectations Gap." *Journal of Contemporary European Research* 9, no. 5 (2013): 723–39.
Noutcheva, Gergana. "Whose Legitimacy? The EU and Russia in Contest for the Eastern Neighbourhood." *Democratization* 25, no. 2 (2018): 312–30.
Nye, Joseph S. Jr. *Bound to Lead: The Changing Nature of American Power.* New York: Basic Books, 1990.

Nye, Joseph S. Jr. *The Future of Power*. New York: Public Affairs, 2011.
Peyrouse, Sebastien. "How does Central Asia View the EU?" *Eucam Working Paper*, no. 18 (2014), http://www.eucentralasia.eu/uploads/tx_icticontent/EUCAM-WP18-How-does-Central-Asia-view-the-EU-1.pdf.
Peyrouse, Sebastien, and Marlene Laruelle. *Globalizing Central Asia: Geopolitics and the Challenges of Economic Development*. New York: Routledge, 2015.
Seeberg, Peter. "Provincialization of Europe and the Middle East? Migration, Regional Competition and the Global Perspective." Report, Center for Mellemøststudier, Syddansk Universitet, Odense, May 2012.
Smith, Michael. "Between Soft Power and a Hard Place: European Union Foreign and Security Policy between the Islamic World and the United States." *International Politics* 46, no. 5 (2009): 596–615.
Spaiser, Olga Alinda. *The European Union's Influence in Central Asia: Geopolitical Challenges and Responses*. Lanham: Lexington Books, 2018.
Voloshin, Georgiy. *The European Union's Normative Power in Central Asia: Promoting Values and Defending Interests*. London: Palgrave, 2014.
Wæver, Ole. "A Post-Western Europe: Strange Identities in a Less Liberal World Order." *Ethics & International Affairs* 32, no. 1 (2018): 75–88.
Walton, David, and Emilian Kavalski. *Power Transition in Asia*. London: Routledge, 2017.
Woll, Cornelia, and Sophie Jacquot. "Using Europe: Strategic Action in Multi-Level Politics." *Comparative European Politics* 8, no. 1 (2010): 110–12.

Chapter 5

Trajectory of Turkish Soft Power in Central Asia after the Collapse of the Soviet Union

M. Murat Yurtbilir

It is widely acknowledged that Turkey is a bridge-country located strategically at the juncture of continents, a meeting point of different cultures and religions. For this reason, Turkish Foreign Policy (TFP) has faced numerous opportunities and challenges to test the efficiency of its soft and hard power instruments. Three pivotal moments in the last three decades of TFP were the collapse of the Soviet Union in 1991, the rise of the Justice and Development Party (AKP) to power in 2002, and the ongoing Syrian Civil War that started in 2011. The independence of Central Asian and Caucasian states in 1991 opened an era of Janus-faced TFP: in the West, the disheartening and unending wait for membership to the EU; and to the East, elder brother syndrome filled with pan-Turkic romanticism, commercial adventurism, and Gülenist missionary ambitions during the 1990s. In 2002, the ascension of the AKP to power resulted in the major reorientation of TFP first toward the neo-Ottomanist soft power discourse and then to old-style conquest rhetoric. Lastly, the start of the Syrian Civil War in 2013 resulted in a return to the utilization of hard power.

Ibrahim Kalin, spokesperson to Turkish President Erdoğan, once claimed that Turkey had a "rich, multi-layered and multidimensional 'new story,' a new geopolitical imagination and a notion of common memory, conscience and cultural depth" backing its effective soft-power relations.[1] Federico Donelli was also positive that Turkish cultural diplomacy made "indisputable progress and constituted an essential asset for Turkish foreign policy."[2] Aylin Aydın Çakır and Gül Arıkan Akdağ concur, noting that the fruitful use of soft power instruments in environmental, cultural, and educational fields has considerably increased under the AKP.[3] Likewise Bayram Balcı claimed that after overcoming the initial "romanticized vision through wider prism of Turkism" of the 1990s, Turkish Foreign Policy toward Central Asia scored many successes.[4] On the other hand, most of the previous scholarship on Turkish soft power was not as optimistic as Kalin. Jana Jabbour depicted Turkish soft power as "an illusionary power of seduction," attracting the public interest with limited political impact.[5] Likewise, Sinan Ülgen claimed that the AKP's normative foreign policy was "fifteen minutes fame" rather than a persistent political reality.[6] The AKP's neo-Ottomanist *soft power* was also defined as a "selective appropriation of Ottoman grandeur" ignoring the undesirable past for pragmatic public and cultural diplomacy.[7]

In the existing scholarship there is consensus that the efficiency of Turkish soft power has become more and more Middle East–oriented after 2013, and that this represented the shrinking of the multidimensional TFP of the 2003–2013 period.[8] Blendi Lami agrees that with the challenge of ISIS and the Syrian Civil War since 2010, all of Turkey's soft power capacities have declined significantly.[9] E. Fuat Keyman agrees that in the 2002–2010 period, Ahmet Davutoğlu's proactive foreign policy applied soft power coupled with civilizational multilateralism. However, according to Keyman, the humanitarian moral realism of the post-Davutoğlu years inclined toward hard power.[10] On the other hand, Yohanan Benhaïm and Kerem Öktem argued that the discourse on the Turkish model and soft power could not be sustained due to the lack of real power capabilities of Turkey.[11]

There is a wide array of conflicting arguments on the success of TFP's use of soft power in Central Asia in different periods since 1991. To this end, this chapter is an attempt to understand the evolution of Turkey's soft power policy in Central Asia from 1991 to 2019. For the purposes of the chapter, the research will be limited to five former Soviet countries, Kazakhstan, Kyrgyzstan, Tajikistan, Turkmenistan, and Uzbekistan. Joseph Nye defined the concept of *soft power* as "the intangible power resources such as culture, ideology, and institutions"[12] that maintain the "ability to get what you want through attraction rather than coercion or payments."[13] For this reason, this chapter will emphasize Turkey's engagement in the fields of education, religion, development aid, and culture.

The first section will focus on the activities of the Diyanet and Diyanet Foundation in Central Asia, from 1991 to 2019. The second and third sections will discuss the activities primarily in the field of education by the Turkish Ministry of National Education, Presidency for Turks Abroad and Related Communities, and also the Gülen movement. The overview of the official development aid to Central Asian countries by the Turkish Cooperation and Development Agency will constitute the fourth section. Lastly, the cultural aspect of Turkish soft power in Central Asia will be summarized.

DIYANET

The Presidency of Religious Affairs (Diyanet), which was founded as the replacement of the Office of Sheikh al-Islam of the bygone Ottoman Empire, has always been a useful political tool for state elites. Since its foundation in 1924, it served to limit religious activity outside the control of the state by dissemination of a particular "mild" version of Islam, convenient to the secularizing founders. This would require providing a "pro-state interpretation of Islamic tenets":[14] an Islam operating inside the boundaries demarcated by the political power. Diyanet as an instrument proved to be useful for the regime as an "ideological state apparatus for the justification and consolidation" in domestic politics to monopolize the religious domain.[15]

"Turkish Muslimness,"[16] as the minister Mehmet Aydın once labeled it, or "Turkish projection of a moderate perception of Islam,"[17] in the words of the president of Diyanet, Ali Bardakoglu, faced the first transnational challenge in Europe after the early 1960s. Following the mass migration of the Turkish guest workers, initially to Germany and then to other major European countries such as Austria, Netherlands, and Switzerland, Diyanet's operation had to spread to Europe. For the recipient European governments Diyanet's politically limited, mild Islam was preferable to the alternatives of more radical sects, which were also existent among migrant workers.[18] In 1971, the Foreign Services branch under Diyanet's Religious Services Directorate was founded, and later in 1976 it was elevated to a separate unit of the Foreign Relations Directorate. Furthermore, the Diyanet Foundation was founded on March 13, 1975 as a semi-autonomous organization by the high-ranking officials of Diyanet,[19] to provide necessary extra-government funding for Diyanet operations.

The collapse of the Soviet Union in 1991 opened a new field of overseas operation for Diyanet. Similar to their European counterparts, the political elite of the newly independent ex-Soviet Muslim states in Central Asia found the Diyanet version of Islam more desirable, when compared to the Wahhabism of the Saudis, the Shiism of Iran, or other external Islamist movements such as Hizb ut-Tahrir. Consequently, the Turkish discourse to "sell" Diyanet as a "model of religion-state relations in Eurasia,"[20] was perpetuating a status quo Islam similar to Diyanet's in Turkey. According to this propaganda, the threat was that different understandings of Islam could be exploited in a region where stability was the bread and butter during the post-Soviet transition. Thus the Diyanet model for Central Asia[21] was presented as the prophylactic against any possible radicalization.

In the decade preceding the collapse of the Soviet Union, Diyanet had already sent several delegations to the Muslim regions of Central Asia and Caucasus, which were mostly exploratory expeditions limited to the distribution of a few Diyanet publications for special occasions.[22] After the collapse of the Soviet Union in 1991, the most important periodic activity of the Diyanet has been Eurasian Islamic Councils. After the first convened in Ankara in 1995, the organization's most recent Ninth Council was summoned in October 2016. The councils were set as a wide platform for Diyanet and for the so-called Turkish version of Islam. The topics included cooperation in religious education, renovation of historical mosques and construction of new ones, student exchanges, scholarships, methods to produce and spread a modern understanding of Islam, and harmonization of the Eid and Ramadan timetables. Although the summits typically eschewed political issues, in the last summit of 2016, three months after the July 15 coup attempt, condemnation of the Gülen movement and denunciation of its global activities were a recurrent topic in the panels. Representatives from Kazakhstan, Kyrgyzstan, and Tajikistan were regular attendees in the summits, together with delegations from different republics of the Russian Federation. Turkmenistan stopped sending delegations after the third council of 2000. In addition Uzbekistan never sent a delegation to any of the Councils due to the strained political relations between Turkey and Uzbekistan.

In all Eurasian Islamic Councils, Diyanet activity in Central Asia has focused on education, training, and publication, and the Diyanet Foundation has prioritized the construction of mosques, libraries, and service buildings for local religious bodies. In the first two decades of their independence and particularly until the AKP's ascension to power in Turkey, the Diyanet framework was more active in the ex-Soviet field and among the usual Turkish-Muslim base in Europe.

Commencing in 1992, Diyanet started to appoint religious service counselors to the Turkish Embassy in Tashkent, Uzbekistan,[23] although after 2000 no counselors were sent as a part of the diplomatic mission. Between 1992 and 1997, Diyanet sent fifty-one imams to serve at Uzbek mosques during Ramadan, as can be seen in Table 5.1; but this practice was also postponed due to "lack of demand" in Diyanet's words. In the first ten years after its

Table 5.1 Diyanet Activities in the First 12 Years after Independence 1992–2004

Countries	Students to Turkey	Publications sent	Imams sent during Ramadan	Eid sacrifices (third-party delegations)
Kazakhstan	619	789,316	41	1,574
Kyrgyzstan	1166	445,003	74	2,189
Uzbekistan	184	425,096	51	485
Tajikistan	85	6,000	20	-
Turkmenistan	386	108,1145	2	1454

Source: Ruşen Çakır and İrfan Bozan, *Sivil, Şeffaf ve Demokratik Bir Diyanet İşleri Başkanlığı Mümkün mü?* (İstanbul: TESEV Yayınları, February 2005): 94–97. *Note* that after 2002, Uzbekistan has not allowed any Diyanet activities on her soil.

independence, 184 Uzbek students were brought to Turkey by Diyanet; twenty to the Manisa training center as boarding students and sixty-nine provided with Diyanet scholarships. After 2003, all educational exchanges with Uzbekistan came to a halt; only three students in the 2008–2009 education year and four in the 2009–2010 academic year came to Turkey for university training. All seven were from the Turkish minority in Uzbekistan. During the 1993–2001 period, around 425,000 various religious publications and copies of the Quran in the Uzbek language were distributed by Diyanet. Financial aid was provided for the restoration of the Imam Bukhari Mosque in Samarkand and for basic utilities at the Tashkent Madrasah.

In the period of 1992–2005, 396 Turkmen students were brought to Turkey through Diyanet scholarships; ninety-five to Quran courses, five to imam high schools, 276 to undergraduate programs at the Faculty of Divinity, and an additional fifteen for MA and five for PhD studies.[24] Later between 2005 and 2009, no student from Turkmenistan came to Turkey through Diyanet; instead, ninety-one students were provided scholarships for their religious education in their home country. In 2010, only one student was provided a scholarship for a Masters in Islamic Law in Bursa, at the Uludağ University, Faculty of Divinity. In cooperation with the Uludağ University, Diyanet Foundation invested two million USD in 1994 to open a faculty of divinity and dormitory buildings at the Turkmen State University, named after Magtymguly. When this faculty was shut down by Turkmen authorities in 2005, 140 students had already graduated. Up until 1996, Diyanet sent nine religious officers in total for the month of Ramadan and between 1998 and 2000, it sent a permanent officer to Ashgabat. Later, the organization ceased sending Diyanet imams to Turkmenistan. Approximately 600,000 religious publications and schoolbooks were sent in the Latin alphabet, when Turkmen President Turkmenbashi attempted to switch from Cyrillic. The Ashgabat Ertuğrul Gazi Mosque and Cultural Centre, the Kipchak Mosque, and a Quran training center building, all financed by the Diyanet Foundation, were opened in 1998.[25]

Similar to Uzbekistan and Turkmenistan, Diyanet ceased to deliver imams to Kazakhstan after 2003, after sending forty-five members for Ramadan every year.[26] In the 1992–2010 period, around 1,318 Kazakh nationals came to Turkey on Diyanet scholarships; 842 of whom attended Quran courses, sixty-two to imam high schools, 261 to various faculties of divinity, nineteen for MA studies, nine for PhDs, and 103 local imams, including twenty-two to the Istanbul Haseki religious training center. Following the Turkmenistan case, Diyanet initiated a partnership to build a faculty of divinity, this time with Selçuk University of Konya and World Languages University in Almaty. This faculty started teaching in 1998, however at the start of the 2001–2002 academic year, Kazakh authorities closed the faculty while there were ninety-eight enrolled students. Diyanet sent and distributed around 1,569,896 religious publications to Kazakhstan until 2010, including the Quran, booklets such as *Reading the Quran, Prayer in Pictures, The Islamic Belief System, The Path to Happiness: Islam, Life of the Prophet*, and children's booklets such as *I am Learning My Religion and Children's Stories*. Furthermore the Diyanet Foundation constructed or renovated four mosques in Michurin, Tolgar, Nikolaevka, and central Almaty.

In Kyrgyzstan,[27] Osh State University Faculty of Divinity was opened as early as 1993 with the sponsorship of the Diyanet Foundation. Later in the 2000–2001 academic year, a second faculty of divinity was inaugurated in Arashan at southern Bishkek. There are approximately 400 students in these institutions as of 2019. Compared to other Central Asian countries, the activities of Diyanet were the most widespread and generous in Kyrgyzstan and consisted of distributing meat from Eid sacrifices, sister city projects,[28] providing financial help to local imams, constructing several mosques, course buildings, libraries, accommodation for local students and imams, and sending Turkish imams to Kyrgyz cities for different occasions.

Over 700,000 free publications were sent to Kyrgyzstan by Diyanet including the Quran, *Introduction to Reading the Quran, Prayer in Pictures, Islam in Summary, Fundamentals of Islamic Belief*, and *Diyanet Eurasia Journal*. From Kyrgyzstan more than 1,900 students came to Turkey with the Diyanet scholarship for the Quran courses, Imam Hatip High Schools, theological education at various Turkish universities, and local religious training until 2009.[29]

Tajikistan being the only non-Turkic ex-Soviet Central Asian state and due to the civil war of 1992–1997, Diyanet's initiatives have been limited in the decade after independence.[30] Just around ninety-five Tajik citizens were funded to attend short religious trainings in Turkey between 1992 and 2003, and later until 2008 no religious scholarships were provided to Tajik students or religious officials. Starting from the 2009–2010 academic year, a limited number of Tajik students were given Diyanet scholarships, eight to Quran courses, fourteen for Imam Hatip High Schools, and seven for university education. Regarding the construction, only small reparations at the Dushanbe Central Mosque and Shah Mansur Mosque were financed by Diyanet.

As the AKP has firmly established itself in power in Turkey after the 2007–2011 period of transition and as the focus of Turkish foreign policy has shifted toward the Middle East and then to the Islamic world as a whole, particularly during the Syrian Civil War, Central Asia lost its prominence in Diyanet's activities.

In September 2018, a giant religious complex including the Central Imam Serahsi Mosque with a capacity of 20,000 worshippers was opened in the

Kyrgyz capital by the Turkish and Kyrgyz presidents. In the 2018 report of the Diyanet Foundation it is obvious that while the institution was transformed into a global network with operations in eighty-four countries, the focus of the funding shifted away from Central Asia toward the Middle East and Africa. The first priority for Diyanet in 2018 was the Syrian territory under the control of Turkish forces. In the 2012–2018 period, Diyanet spent around 45 million USD for mosque reparations, education, religious services, and aid in cash in Syria, while the Arakan region of Myanmar, as well as Palestine, and Yemen happened to be other areas of substantial Diyanet funding.[31] Diyanet activities in Central Asia in 2018 seemed to be narrowed to Kazakhstan and Kyrgyzstan. In Kyrgyzstan, Diyanet continued to sponsor Osh State University Faculty of Divinity which had 145 continuing students and 549 graduates by 2018. In addition Osh Imam High School, opened in 2013, and was operational in 2018 with 140 students and sixty-six graduates.[32] In Kazakhstan, Almaty University of Foreign Languages and Professional Career (Turk Kazakh University) continued education with 117 students and 489 graduates in 2018. Diyanet's 29 May University in Istanbul has an active student exchange program with the Ahmet Yesevi University in Turkistan.[33]

In Diyanet Foundation reports of 2015, 2016, and 2017 the same trend is trackable: while Diyanet provided funding to Osh State University and Osh Imam Hatip High School in Kyrgyzstan and Almaty University of Foreign Languages in Kazakhstan, in other countries of Central Asia there seemed to be no Diyanet activity, excepting sending some religious publications from Turkey. In Kyrgyzstan the construction of Bishkek Muftiate and Counsellor Complex continues[34] and KOMAŞ, Diyanet's construction and commercial company, opened a permanent office in Bishkek.[35] In 2016, 20,000 USD funding for the construction of Chimkent Quran course was one of the rare contributions in Central Asia for the year.[36] In 2015, short courses were arranged by Diyanet in Turkey for religious officials, twenty-eight of whom were from Kyrgyzstan, seventy-six from Kazakhstan, and only one from Tajikistan.[37] Additionally in 2015, a small cohort of students—twenty-one Kazakh, twenty-three Kyrgyz, and eleven Tajik nationals—were sponsored for their Quran courses in Turkey.[38] Only one mosque complex was opened in the region in 2015 named Ahmed Yesevi Mosque in the city of Turkistan of Kazakhstan.[39]

Concerning publications, introductory books on the basics of Islam and children's books were the main bulk of the booklets sent to Central Asia in the last four years. Diyanet publication activity has concentrated on Kazakhstan and Kyrgyzstan, the only exception being 2,000 Uzbek language Qurans.[40] However the total number of publications sent to Central Asia was significantly less compared with the first ten years after independence. In the last four years the books published in Kazakh, Kyrgyz, and Uzbek were less than 100,000 in total.

EDUCATION

Imam Hatip high schools are the religious vocational high schools in the Turkish education system. In 2006, the Turkish government launched the project of International Imam Hatip Anatolian High Schools (IIHAHS),[41] as an attempt to reinvigorate the then declining Turkish soft power with new initiatives.[42] The project consisted of the transnationalization of the Turkish Imam Hatip schools as a model of religious education and aimed to establish a Turkish-speaking religious segment in the respective societies.[43] Thirteen IIHAHS are in operation in nine different cities as of 2018; nine of them were built in cooperation with the Diyanet Foundation and the Ministry of National Education; and nine of the schools started education after 2016, while one of them was designed as a girls' school.[44]

According to the 2015–2016 teaching year statistics, around 1,068 foreign students from seventy-three different countries were attending IIHAHS.[45] The distribution of the nationalities of the guest students however shows a clear picture of the declining importance of Central Asian countries in the Turkish soft power projection. In 2016, thirty-eight of the seventy-three origin countries were the Sub-Saharan African countries and 411 of the 1,068 students were from Africa.[46] Only eighty-one students were from Central Asia; forty-two Kazakh, thirty-three Kyrgyz, four Uzbek, two Tajik students, and none from Turkmenistan. As of 2018, at the IIHAHS there were around 2,749 students and 7,729 graduates from 111 countries, and more than half of the students were still from Sub-Saharan Africa and less than 8 percent were Central Asian.[47]

As can be seen in Table 5.2, the Turkish Ministry of National Education operates nine schools and three Turkish language education centers in four of the Central Asian countries, apart from Kazakhstan. These schools follow the Turkish curriculum and were initially aimed at the children of Turkish citizens, although a substantial portion of the students are local, non-Turkish students with the exception of Uzbekistan. In Kyrgyzstan, a Girls' Vocational School and a Talented Children Anatolian High School were opened on March 3, 1992, just two months after Kyrgyz independence. Later in June 1999, Bishkek Turkish Pre-School and Primary School, Secondary School, and Imam Hatip Secondary School were opened by the Ministry. One year after Uzbekistan became independent, the Ministry opened two schools in Tashkent, a Turkish primary school and secondary school in October 1993. In June 1999, the Uzbek government banned the Turkish schools from enrolling Uzbek citizens. In the Turkmenistan capital Ashgabat, Turkish primary, secondary, and the Anatolian high schools were founded in April 1993, in the very early years of Turkmen independence. Near these schools in Ashgabat, Bishkek and Dushanbe Turkish language education centers

Table 5.2 Number of Students and Teachers in Turkish Education Institutions under the Control of the Turkish Ministry of National Education—2017–2018

Countries and Schools	No. of students	Republic of Turkey	Other	No. of Teachers
Kyrgyzstan (in total)	2,438	490	1,948	79
Bishkek Turkish Pre-School and Primary School	363	245	118	
Bishkek Turkish Secondary School and Imam-Hatip Secondary School	232	159	73	
Cumhuriyet Talented Children Kyrgyz-Turkish Anatolian High School	209	86	123	
Kyrgyz-Turkish Anatolian Girls' Vocational High School	194	-	194	
Bishkek Turkey Turkish Education Centre	1,440	-	1,440	
Uzbekistan (in total)	193	182	11	16
Tashkent Turkish Primary School	105	99	6	
Tashkent Turkish Secondary School	88	83	5	
Turkmenistan (in total)	787	455	332	46
Ashgabat Turkish Primary School	274	230	44	
Ashgabat Turkish Secondary School	372	147	225	
Ashgabat Turkish Anatolian High School	141	78	63	
Ashgabat Turkey Turkish Education Centre	-	-	-	
Tajikistan (in total)	523	-	523	4
Dushanbe Turkey Turkish Education Centre	523	-	523	

Source: Author, data derived from "National Education Statistics: Formal Education 2017/18," *Republic of Turkey Ministry of National Education* (Ankara: MEB, 2019): 237.

were still operational in 2020. In Kazakhstan, the Turkish language education center was closed due to visa problems of language teachers from Turkey, and the constant demand by the Turkish Embassy to build a primary school in Almaty has not been successful. According to 2018 Ministry statistics, in Kyrgyzstan around 1,948 and in Turkmenistan around 332 local students were being educated at the Turkish Ministry Schools. In Tajikistan, around 523 students were learning Turkish at the Turkish language education centers in 2018.[48]

There have been two major frameworks for the scholarships for foreign students pursuing studies in Turkey after the collapse of the Soviet Union in 1991. The first framework was the hastily initiated Great Student Project which was designed exclusively for students from the Turkic and relative communities. This project was launched in 1992, for the six newly independent states of Central Asia and the Caucasus, Kazakhstan, Kyrgyzstan, Uzbekistan, Tajikistan, Turkmenistan, and Azerbaijan. Despite the scope of the scheme it was expanded to include other communities such as Turkic groups living in Bulgaria, Kosovo, Greece, Crimea, and Iraq; the quotas have had a declining trajectory after starting with 8,100 in the 1992–1993 academic year. In 1993–1994 the quota declined to 5,200 students, then from 1994 to 1998 it further declined to an annual quota of 2,500 students and after 1998 to around 1,500 scholarships per year.[49] Nevertheless, the Great Student Project proved to be the main framework for the Central Asian student influx to Turkish universities in the first two decades of independence.

The Great Student Project was a comprehensive scheme that pays for up to one-year Turkish language education, accommodation, free transport in many cities, health costs, book and stationery payment, clothes money, as well as a monthly stipend. However, in the period from 1992 to 2011, of the 42,318 quota, around 31,037 were used and only 8,914 students could graduate from their programs. After 6,255 ongoing students were considered, 52 percent of the scholarships were cut without graduation.[50] The project was successful in attracting a sizable number of students to come to Turkey for tertiary education. Nevertheless the success ratio of the project has been remarkably low with regard to the graduation figures even though 1,282 Uzbek students had to leave the country after Uzbekistan recalled them in 2000.[51]

The second framework is the government scholarships[52] that have been provided since 2012 under the supervision of the Presidency for Turks Abroad and Related Communities. Contrary to what the supervising institution's name indicates, the scholarship scheme is open to citizens of any country. In fact this scheme is an extension of the Great Student Project to a global level and can be seen as a manifestation of a more global foreign policy with less focus on specific regions such as Central Asia. In the academic year of 2018–2019, around 14,866 students attended Turkish universities with government scholarships. As can be seen in Table 5.3, just around 1,021 students from Central Asia benefitted from the program, only 6.86 percent of all scholarship students. The largest recipient countries reflect shifting priorities of Turkish policy makers, with around 3,320 Syrian, 944 Afghan, 333 Azerbaijani, 338 Iraqi, and 443 Yemeni students.[53] In general, in the 2017–2018 academic year, around 125,138 foreign students attended Turkish universities; 17,735 were from the Central Asian countries, 12,248 from Turkmenistan, 2,065 from Kazakhstan, and 1,926 from Kyrgyzstan, together with 840 Uzbek and 656

Table 5.3 Number of Foreign Students Given Government Scholarships According to Their Countries and Levels of Education in Academic Year 2017–2018

Countries	Total	Total	Total	Total
Kazakhstan	371	190	76	105
Kyrgyzstan	279	164	89	26
Tajikistan	114	87	20	7
Turkmenistan	90	81	8	1
Uzbekistan	167	105	20	41
Total	1021	627	213	180

Source: Author, data derived from "National Education Statistics: Formal Education 2017/18," *Republic of Turkey Ministry of National Education* (Ankara: MEB, 2019): 238–241.

Tajik students. Thus 14.1 percent of all foreign students were from Central Asia, while 20,701 Syrian and 17,088 Azerbaijani students were enrolled at Turkish universities.[54]

There are two special status universities in Central Asia which were established in the peaks of the Turkish rush to the region in the 1990s and both are still operated jointly by Turkey and Kazakhstan and Kyrgyzstan, respectively. Ahmet Yesevi University (AYU) in the city of Turkistan was founded with the "Agreement on Founding International Hoca Ahmet Yesevi Turkish-Kazakh University" on October 31, 1992 and started education in the 1994–1995 academic year.[55] AYU is governed by a board of trustees which is appointed by the Turkish president and the Kazakh government. Turkish students have the option to enroll in the AYU through the national university entrance examination and until 2018, around 1,171 Turkish citizens graduated from the university. In the 2018–2019 academic year, around 1,372 students from the Turkic world are attending programs.[56] Manas University (MU) in Bishkek is the other joint state university in Central Asia where the language of education is Turkish and Kyrgyz, together with several supporting courses in Russian and English. MU is also listed in the national university entrance preference list of Turkey. In the 2019–2020 academic year, MU has around 5,711 undergraduate students, 4,896 from Kyrgyz, 313 Turkish, 167 Tajik, and 115 Kazakh. Furthermore, among the 359 postgraduate students that enrolled in the university in 2019, 248 were from Kyrgyzstan and ninety-five from Turkey.[57]

THE GÜLEN MOVEMENT IN CENTRAL ASIA

In March 2013, the then Deputy Foreign Minister Naci Koru gave an interview to the Gülen movement's admiral newspaper *Zaman* and referring to Gülen schools said that the Turkish schools were the most important actors of

TFP. Koru went on to claim that while the Foreign Ministry was once the sole actor concerning foreign affairs, nonetheless at that moment civil society initiatives and the Turkish schools by the volunteers were crucial foreign policy actors.[58] This interview was just a few months before the stiff breakdown in the relations between the governing the AKP and the Gülen group which became known to the public after the government's announcement to shut down the private cram schools in August 2013. The year 2013 also marked a change in Turkish government attitude toward the Gülen schools in Central Asia and elsewhere, which went from total support to a sworn enemy.

Fethullah Gülen initially had a career as a preacher and imam at Diyanet and served at different mosques around Turkey throughout the 1960s and 1970s. Inspired by the Nur movement the main strategy of Gülen was the creation of a new generation of young Muslims through education, while staying away from daily politics due to the perceived weakness of the Islamists in a secular state. At first small in size, by the mid-1980s and 1990s medium-sized businessmen affiliated with Gülen had organized around business associations, and opened cram schools and private schools all around Turkey.[59] This "multi-sector network"[60] which included banks, endowments, television stations, and newspapers, had already turned into a self-supporting and ever-growing juggernaut by 1991.

The Gülen movement was perhaps the most organized and complex structure that came into the Central Asian countries after 1991. They already had the means and the motive, and with the Central Asian independence the movement found the opportunity for their first transnational large-scale endeavor. The means were thousands of affiliated small and medium-sized businessmen, numerous teachers at the Gülen schools in Turkey, and a mode of operation tested successfully in Turkey. The motives of the movement were both the missionary activity based on Turkish Islam[61] and some business concerns as well. For the Central Asian leaders the Gülen version of Turkish Islam seemed less threatening compared to Saudi- or Iranian-inspired versions. The operation of Gülenists in Central Asia was the same as their *modus operandi* in Turkey, and although transnational at this time, enjoyed the extensive support of the Turkish state till 2012.[62]

The Gülenist infiltration was swift; Balcı noted that in 2000, just nine years after the rush started, about 100 Gülenist institutions existed in Muslim-majority countries of the former Soviet Union.[63] In Kazakhstan, by 1998, there were twenty-eight high schools under the umbrella company KATEV International (Kazakh Turk Education Foundation).[64] The first Kazak-Turkish High School opened in 1992 in Turkistan and most Kazakh cities had a Gülen-affiliated school within five years, including Almaty, Astana (Nur-Sultan), Akmesjit, Aktobe, Aktau, Kyzylorda Jambul, Semey, Pavlodar, Kostanay, Chimkent, Taraz, and Turgan. A few of these high schools were specialized schools in technical subjects or physics, math, or oriental studies, but mostly they were general high schools tutoring in Kazakh, Russian, English, and Turkish. In addition in 1996 in Almaty, the movement launched a university, financed by the Gülenist-dominated Kazakh-Turkish Businessmen Association (KATIAD), which was named after the then president of Turkey.[65] According to Turkish state news agency Anadolu, KATIAD had approximately 300 members in its heyday before 2016.[66]

Just after the July 2016 coup attempt, the Turkish government instigated an alternate business chamber, Turkish-Kazakh Businessmen Alliance (TÜKİB) to replace KATIAD. As of 2019, TÜKİB has thirty-seven members including several large Turkish companies such as Anadolu Efes, Alarko, and Eczacıbaşı. Meanwhile the Kazakh government had declined ceaseless Turkish demands to take over the control of the Gülen schools. The Kazakh Minister of Education declared that Kazakhstan would not transfer the Kazakh-Turkish High Schools to the Turkish government. After Nazarbayev's announcement that the Kazakh-Turkish High Schools belong to Kazakhstan, the Kazakh government decided, on September 14, 2017, to change the names of the schools to Science and Innovation High Schools. Kazakhstan gave permission to the Maarif Foundation to open schools in Kazakhstan and the management of the former Gülen-affiliated Talgar High School was transferred to the Maarif.

In Kyrgyzstan, Sebat Education Company signed a cooperation agreement with the Kyrgyzstan Education Ministry on May 2, 1992. Consequently the movement opened sixteen high schools in Bishkek, Jalalabad, Osh, Talas, Tokmok, and Issyk-Köl in six years. Sebat was able to open four university dormitories, Cambridge Silk Road International School (CSRIS), and SECOM Centre for Language and Computer Studies with an estimated 60 million USD investment in the first fifteen years.[67] In 1996, the signing of another cooperation agreement with Kyrgyz authorities paved the way to open a university; Ala-Too International University had 2,412 students in 2019.[68] The university had students from eleven different countries and 22 percent of the students were international students.[69] In total it is estimated that in an academic year 13,000 students are educated in Gülen schools as a whole.

Similar to Kazakhstan, the movement pioneered and dominated the Kyrgyz-Turk Businessmen Association (KITIAD) which had nearly 250 active members and 300 million USD investment in Kyrgyzstan by 2019.[70] The Young Businessmen Association (JIA) was established in 2006 and has over 1,000 members in 2019. Pro-AKP Turkish newspapers and the Turkish Embassy in Bishkek have repeatedly claimed that JIA is dominated by Gülen sympathizer Kyrgyz businessmen. After the 2016 coup attempt the Turkish government has been exerting considerable pressure on Kyrgyz authorities to break down the influence of the Gülen movement in the country with little success. The name of the umbrella company Sebat was changed to Sapat in March 2017 and the management positions in these schools were assigned to Kyrgyz nationals. Likewise the name of the CSRIS has become United World International School at the start of the 2019–2020 academic year. However, all these institutions were still under Gülenist control in disguise, as of 2019. The Turkish government was only able to challenge the business structure through the creation of the alternative Turkish-Kyrgyz Businessmen Association with the MÜSİAD[71] representative in Kyrgyzstan, Muammer Akkaya, the president.[72]

In Turkmenistan, the umbrella organization for the Gülen movement's schools was Bashkent Education. Hulusi Turgut noted that after opening of Turgut Ozal Turkmen/Turk High School in 1992, Bashkent was managing thirteen high schools and a primary school by 1998.[73] Victoria Clement, an instructor at the International Turkmen-Turk University, observed that the Gülen movement schools were providing "a secular curriculum partnered with a strong moral framework without threatening the state."[74] This observation perfectly mirrors the movement's tenet to secure the expansion of the network through strictly eschewing any conflict with the state elite. In Turkmenistan, some Turkish citizens affiliated with the Gülen movement were appointed to high-level government posts. Muammer Turkyılmaz from the close circle of Gülen was appointed as the Deputy Education Minister and Seyit Embel as the head of the Bashkent Educational Centre.[75] In addition, businessman Ahmet Çalık was serving as advisor to President Niyazov. Particularly Turkyılmaz who was reappointed by new Turkmen President Berdymukhammedov in 2007 was very crucial in the success of the Gülen schools in Turkmenistan.[76]

Despite every attempt by the movement to survive in tune with the Turkmen government, in August 2011 the Turkmen state decided to take over the management of the schools.[77] In 2005, increasing frustration with the Turkmen leadership about the version of Islam spread by Turkish-funded institutions became apparent in the sacking of whole teaching staff in the Divinity Faculty at the Magtymguly Turkmen State University.[78] The only school which remained under Gülenists was the Turgut Ozal Turkmen-Turk High School which was also transferred to Turkmen authorities in August 2016 after the coup attempt in Turkey. This was declared to be an educational reform which included secularization of the system, but obviously Berdymukhammedov wanted to be on good terms with the Turkish government after the July 15 coup attempt. Since then Turkmen government's measures against Gülen sympathizers have been harsh consisting of allegations of unfair trial and torture.[79]

In Uzbekistan, the Gülen movement's strategy was identical with the other Central Asian countries: to open as many schools as part of a larger network without provoking the leaders and the political elites of the countries. The movement's educational operation was managed by the Silm Company and the Association of Uzbek and Turkish Businessmen.[80] Harboring of the Uzbek opposition leader Mohammed Salih in Turkey after 1993 and the Uzbek President Karimov's allegation of a Turkish connection in the assassination attempt on February 1999 against him escalated the tension. As a result, together with all other Turkish aspects of soft power, Gülen network became the victim of the heightened tension in Turkish–Uzbek relations in 1999–2000. The Uzbek government closed all sixteen Gülen high schools and arrested several affiliated people; even an anti-Gülenist documentary was prepared by the Uzbek National Security Service, titled "The Light that Brings Darkness."[81] Dozens of Gülenist businessmen were arrested, many convicted for years, and their properties expropriated.[82]

Similar to Uzbekistan, Tajik authorities were suspicious of Gülen schools long before the coup attempt in Turkey, believing they promoted a combination of Turkish nationalism and Ottomanism.[83] At the outset, in Tajikistan, the Gülen movement had opened six schools in Dushanbe and four in other cities under Shelale Education. But in August 2015, Tajik President Rahmon signed off on the decision to take control of all schools under Shelale and rename them as the "Talented Children High Schools."[84] There are also claims that the Tajik closure of the Gülen schools was "part of a wider campaign against Islamic groups in Tajikistan that are not totally subservient to the government."[85]

TURKISH COOPERATION AND DEVELOPMENT AGENCY (TIKA)

The Turkish government created the Economic, Cultural, Education, and Technical Cooperation Directorate under the Ministry of Foreign Affairs in January 1992.[86] In the first article of the founding decree the aim of the directorate was explained as helping the developing countries but particularly the countries speaking the Turkish language and the neighboring countries. This was a prompt response to the collapse of the Soviet Union and the objective was to create an institutional framework for the Turkish involvement in the post-Soviet space. In 1999, the Directorate was attached directly to the office of the PM and the name was changed to the Turkish Cooperation and Development Administration, in 2001.[87] In the 2001 decree the operation area of the organization was again specified as the neighboring and Turkish-speaking countries. As Güner Özkan and Mustafa Turgut Demirtepe noticed, the main target was to enhance Turkey's position in the newly independent states;[88] so most of TIKA's spending for the development aid went to the Turkic states until 2003. Three Central Asian countries, Kazakhstan, Kyrgyzstan, and Turkmenistan were constantly among the top four aid receivers, alongside Azerbaijan another Turkic ex-Soviet state, throughout the period of 1992–2003.[89] Projects in Uzbekistan could not benefit, because much aid from Turkey had to be diverted elsewhere, due to the tense political situation following the 1999 assassination attempt on Uzbek President Karimov.[90]

The shift of focus in TFP that became evident after the AKP's consolidation of power following the 2011 elections was reflected in TIKA's mission statement document. The organization's name was changed again, as part of restructuring in November 2011 but more importantly the government decree on Turkish Cooperation and Development Agency (TİKA) had not identified Central Asia or the Turkic-speaking countries as the priority areas. TİKA came to operate four regional sub-units, Central Asia and Caucasus; Balkans and Eastern Europe; Middle East and Africa; and East and South Asia and Latin America.[91] Turkish foreign policy indeed downgraded Central Asia in its priorities and TIKA designed a global outreach framework, not limited to Turkic speaking countries. The agency opened sixty-two program coordination offices in sixty countries, in addition to five central Asian countries.[92]

According to figures in the latest *Development Assistance Report* of 2017, TIKA provided 7,950.45 million USD in bilateral official development aid and 170.5 million USD in multilateral aid worldwide in 2017. Central Asian countries obtained only 0.62 million USD. Kazakhstan and Kyrgyzstan were the top Central Asian countries with 20.38 million and 18.16 million, respectively. However the amount for remaining Central Asian countries was rather limited: 5.68 million to Uzbekistan; 2.98 million to Tajikistan; and 2.28 million to Turkmenistan.[93] Among the top ten recipient countries only two were Central Asian; Kazakhstan was sixth and Kyrgyzstan was seventh. The top three countries are Syria with 7.2 billion USD, Somalia with 60.6 million USD, and Palestine with 40.6 million USD in aid. As Table 5.4 summarizes, the figures of 2017 reflected a tremendous change in the priorities of the official development aid. The share of five countries in Central Asia from the TIKA aid has fallen from 27.34 percent to a negligible 0.62 percent in 2017.

On the other hand, TIKA aid was provided to a wide range of projects for different sectors in Central Asia. For instance TIKA sponsored several activities of Turkic Republics Ophthalmology Society such as Kyrgyzstan International Diabetes and Eye Symposium from June 1–3, 2017,[94] and Tashkent International Cataract and Refractive Surgery Course from May 25–27, 2018.[95] TIKA annually sponsors Turkish–Uzbek Health Week and approximately 4,000 Uzbek patients were examined, and more than 1,000 surgeries were performed since 2009.[96] In 2017, during the Turkish–Uzbek Health Week, 222 doctors and health staff were trained, 180 people were treated, and eighty surgeries were performed.[97] In 2017, TIKA has also

Table 5.4 Bilateral Official Development Aid to Central Asian Countries

Bilateral Official Development Aid	2004	2005	2015	2016	2017
Kazakhstan	27.17	44.51	24.44	18.96	20.38
Kyrgyzstan	34.74	55.56	98.36	25.39	18.16
Tajikistan	6.48	3.20	0.70	1.58	2.98
Turkmenistan	18.82	13.08	3.18	4.87	2.28
Uzbekistan	5.48	3.33	4.65	4.26	5.68
Total Bilateral OAD Central Asia	92.69	119.68	131.33	55.06	49.48
Total Bilateral OAD World	339.1	532.4	3845.9	6237.5	7950.4
% in total OAD	27.34	22.47	3.41	0.88	0.62

Source: "Turkish Development Assistance Report 2017," (report, TIKA Department of Strategy Development, Ankara, 2018).

renovated water systems and pipelines in several villages of Kyrgyzstan, such as Ak-Car village of Talas, Krasnorechka in Chuy.[98] TIKA funded the restoration of the History Museum in Bishkek and the Bishkek Turkish Kyrgyz Friendship Hospital, both were completed in 2018.[99]

TIKA pledged 4 million USD for the salaries of the personnel to be employed at the hospital and 15 million USD for the operational costs for three years. After three years of management by the Turkish side, the hospital will be transferred to the Kyrgyz government.[100] In cooperation with Turkish Radio Television Corporation (TRT) TIKA has regularly sponsored training programs on camera techniques, light, montage, television production, and directing for professionals from Kazakhstan, Kyrgyzstan, and Uzbekistan.[101]

Turkish official development aid (ODA) was only 85 million USD in 2002, 339 million USD in 2004, and by 2017 it reached 8.1 billion. Although the 2002 figures were low due to the 2001 economic collapse and mismanagement,[102] the ODA increased massively in the AKP era.[103] The major reason for the continual drop in the share of the Central Asian region in the Turkish ODA has been the Syrian Civil War which absorbed the lion's share of the Turkish aid programs after 2013. The second reason was the reorientation of the Turkish foreign policy. Kerim Can Kavaklı claimed that international alignments and ethno-linguistic ties lost their weight as criteria, while the AKP aid policy consisted of "more economic aid to trade partners and more humanitarian aid to Muslim countries."[104]

CULTURE

Presidency for Turks Abroad and Related Communities under the Ministry of Culture was established in 2010 in order develop the social and cultural status of Turks living abroad and also of the linguistically and ethnically related communities.[105] Since then, the Presidency has initiated several cultural projects alongside its management of the Turkey Scholarship programs. In 2018, the Presidency provided funding for seventy-five cultural and social projects which included conferences, summer schools, training, symposium, research, and publications. Thirty of these projects were aimed at the Central Asia and Caucasus regions. However, the total amount spared specifically for five Central Asian countries was limited. Kyrgyz projects obtained only 20,000 TL, while Kazakh and Tajik could get 111,562 TL and 27,000 TL, respectively. Some of the projects in 2018 consisted of the "Intangible Cultural Heritage of Uyghurs in Kazakhstan," which produced two publications *Uyghur Oral Heritage* and *Catalogue of Uyghur Language Books in Kazakhstan*. Furthermore, the Presidency organized a Turkic World Youth Summer School in Kazakhstan's Turkistan city between June 18 and July 15, 2018, and also International Turkic Culture and Civilization Congress in Balıkesir, Turkey from September 5–8, 2018.[106] Previous projects included "Soviet Era Religion-Politics: Soviet Atheism Literature in Kazakhstan and Kyrgyzstan and Tajikistan Country Profile Report,"[107] in 2017 and "Civil Society Capacity Development" training, in 2012.[108]

Independence of specifically Turkic-speaking countries in 1991 triggered the subsequent global expansion of the Turkish film sector. Just after Central Asian independence, Turkish film companies were among the business ventures rushing to the region for profit and they started to market international documentaries, cartoons, and Latin American soap operas to Central Asian channels. Later Turkish producers started to export Turkish drama series, first to Kazakhstan with *Deli Yürek*[109] in 2001 and later to all Central Asia and global markets. After *Deli Yürek*, forty-two Turkish series were broadcast on Kazakh televisions until 2011.[110] In 2012, Kazakh televisions were reportedly broadcasting ten hours of Turkish series on average per day.[111] Not only did the number of Turkish soap operas exported to Central Asia increase, but also the profitability for the film industry. One Turkish producer commented about the increased profitability "in 2001 we hardly sold *Deli Yürek* to Kazakhstan for $30 per episode, but this time (2011) for *Muhteşem Yüzyıl*,[112] we received over $200,000 per episode."[113]

Muhteşem Yüzyıl was indeed a huge success even in Uzbekistan in 2011. The star of *Muhteşem Yüzyıl* featured in the adverts of the Guli perfumes owned by President Karimov's daughter, Gulnara Karimova. Later, three Uzbek channels had to take Turkish soap operas off the air in February 2012 following the government's ban due to the "rebellious nature" of some characters and "inappropriate scenes incompatible with the Uzbek people's mentality."[114] The ban was lifted in 2017 and in December 2017 six different Turkish series were being aired on Uzbek television. Yet again, in 2017, protests from the Islamists alleging that "immoral"[115] *Kara Sevda*[116] has been "threatening the role of family in Uzbek society" forced President Mirziyoyev to ban the series.[117] In Kyrgyzstan and Tajikistan, Turkish soap operas found a sizable audience. Contrary to neighboring Uzbekistan, Turkish series are enjoying support from the political elite in Kyrgyzstan, allegedly many serials are provided free to Kyrgyz television.[118] In Tajikistan even though the national Tajikkino Corporation announced a ban on Turkish serials owing to extremism and violence, in the Tajik black market Turkish series and films are among the most popular.[119]

Turkish Radio Television (TRT) started broadcasts aiming at Central Asia with TRT-Avrasya on April 28, 1992.[120] TRT first replaced TRT-Avrasya with TRT-Turk in 2001 and later, with TRT-Avaz on March 21, 2009. Since all these channels have used the satellite and paid TV platforms and not the terrestrial free-to-air broadcast, their reach are limited to the local stations. The major issue with TRT channels is the language of the broadcasts. Most programs are in Istanbul Turkish and not with subtitles all the time. This prevented the TRT channels from reaching a wider audience, particularly in Kazakhstan and Kyrgyzstan.

CONCLUSION

This chapter has examined the most important areas of Turkish soft power in Central Asia which have been concentrated in the fields of religion, education, and culture. In order to understand the evolution of Turkish soft power in the region, the instruments analyzed were the Diyanet and its financial wing the Diyanet Foundation, the Ministry of National Education, the Gülen movement, the Turkish Cooperation and Development Agency, the Presidency for Turks Abroad and Related Communities, and the film sector. The analysis of these instruments' policies in the last three decades attained several conclusions.

First, there is no central institutional framework managing Turkish soft power, but several government and non-government institutions cooperating and competing with each other at different times, as can be seen in the oscillating relations between the state and the Gülen movement. Second, the rationale of the Turkish approach to Central Asia has been completely transformed. Major objectives have switched from filling the political and social vacuum, trade opportunities, and Turkic romanticism of the 1990s, toward Islam and religion, particularly after the AKP rose to power in 2002. Third, as TFP has become busier with Middle Eastern problems and also searches for easier markets in Africa, Central Asia has turned into a region of secondary importance especially after the start of Syrian Civil War in 2011.

Fourth, the chapter concludes that in Kyrgyzstan and Kazakhstan, Turkish soft power was more effective compared to Turkmenistan, Uzbekistan, and Tajikistan. Fifth, after thirty years of engagement with Central Asia, Turkey has been able to create a human capital among the local population which is sympathetic to Turkish policies mainly in the religious and educational environments. However, limited economic hard power is still the vulnerability of Turkish influence in the region to date.

NOTES

1. Ibrahim Kalin, "Soft Power and Public Diplomacy in Turkey," *Perceptions* 16, no. 3 (2011): 11.
2. Federico Donelli, "Persuading through Culture, Values, and Ideas: The Case of Turkey's Cultural Diplomacy," *Insight Turkey* 21, no. 3 (2019): 129.
3. Aylin Aydın Çakır, and Gül Arıkan Akdağ, "An Empirical Analysis of the Change in Turkish Foreign Policy under the AKP Government," *Turkish Studies* 18, no. 2 (2017): 352.
4. Bayram Balci and Thomas Liles, "Turkey's Comeback to Central Asia," *Insight Turkey* 20, no. 4 (2018): 24–25.
5. Jana Jabbour, "An Illusionary Power of Seduction?" *European Journal of Turkish Studies* 21 (2015): 2, http://journals.openedition.org/ejts/5234.
6. Sinan Ülgen, "A Place in the Sun or Fifteen Minutes of Fame? Understanding Turkey's New Foreign Policy" (paper number 1, Carnegie Papers, Carnegie Endowment for International Peace, Brussels, 2010), 21–22.
7. Edward Wastnidge, "Imperial Grandeur and Selective Memory: Re-Assessing Neo-Ottomanism in Turkish Foreign and Domestic Politics," *Middle East Critique* 28, no. 1 (2019): 24.
8. Muharrem Ekşi and Mehmet Seyfettin Erol, "The Rise and Fall of Turkish Soft Power and Public Diplomacy," *Gazi Akademik Bakis Dergisi* 11, no. 23 (2018): 40–42.
9. Blendi Lami, "Recalibration of Turkish Foreign Policy during AKP Era," *Central European Journal of International & Security Studies* 12, no. 3 (2018): 50.
10. E. Fuat Keyman, "A New Turkish Foreign Policy: Towards Proactive 'Moral Realism'," *Insight Turkey* 19, no. 1 (2017): 56.
11. Yohanan Benhaïm and Kerem Öktem, "The Rise and Fall of Turkey's Soft Power Discourse," *European Journal of Turkish Studies* 21 (2015): 19, http://journals.openedition.org/ejts/5275.
12. Joseph S Nye Jr., "Soft Power," *Foreign Policy* 80, Twentieth Anniversary (Autumn, 1990): 167.
13. Joseph S Nye Jr., "Soft Power and American Foreign Policy," *Political Science Quarterly* 119, no. 2 (2004): 256.
14. İstar B. Gözaydın, "Diyanet and Politics," *The Muslim World* 98, no. 2–3 (2008): 222.

15. Ahmet Erdi Öztürk, "Turkey's Diyanet under AKP Rule: From Protector to Imposer of State Ideology?" *Southeast European and Black Sea Studies* 16, no. 4 (2016): 620.

16. Mehmet Aydın, "Diyanet's Global Vision," *The Muslim World* 98, no. 2–3 (2008).

17. Ali Bardakoglu, "'Moderate Perception of Islam' and the Turkish Model of the Diyanet: The President's Statement," *Journal of Muslim Minority Affairs* 24, no. 2 (2004): 367–74.

18. Zana Çitak, "Between 'Turkish Islam' and 'French Islam': The Role of the Diyanet in the Conseil Français Du Culte Musulman," *Journal of Ethnic and Migration Studies* 36, no. 4 (2010): 620.

19. "Hakkımızda," Türkiye Diyanet Vakfı, https://tdv.org/tr-TR/kurumsal/, accessed February 3, 2019. The Foundation was founded by the then President of Diyanet Dr. Lütfi Doğan, his deputies Dr. Tayyar Altıkulaç (future president), and Yakup Üstün. The aim was to provide a less-controlled platform outside the state realm for the donations and the funds to be used for internal and external operations of Diyanet.

20. Şenol Korkut, "The Diyanet of Turkey and Its Activities in Eurasia after the Cold War," *Acta Slavica Iaponica* 28 (2010): 122.

21. Mustafa Ünver, "Orta Asya'ya 'Diyanet' Modeli" in *Orta Asya'da İslam* ed. Muhammet Savaş Kafkasyalı (Ankara: Ahmet Yesevi Üniversitesi, 2012), 461.

22. Those special occasions included the 200th anniversary of the creation of the All-Russian Muslim Religious Board and 100th anniversary of the adoption of Islam by the Volga Tatars, both were in 1989. For Diyanet official Halit Güler's travel memoirs see, Halit Güler, *Orta Asya'da İslam'ın Yeniden Doğuşu*, (Ankara: TDV Yayınları, 1994).

23. Kemal Hakkı Kılıç, *Diyanet Avrupa Dergi,* 14/4737, September 2010.

24. Kemal Hakkı Kılıç, *Diyanet Avrupa Dergi,* 16/5972, July 2010.

25. Ekrem Özbay, *Türkmenistan Tarihinde Eğitim-Bağımsızlık-Din* (İstanbul: Hiperlink Yayınları, 2019), 123. Kipchak is the birthplace of the then Turkmen President Turkmenbashi.

26. Kemal Hakkı Kılıç, *Diyanet Avrupa Dergi,* 19/6014, June 2010.

27. Fahri Sağlık, *Diyanet Avrupa Dergi* 45/6861, August 2010.

28. Several cities of Krygyzstan were matched with a Turkish city and many religious activities were organized between the paired cities.

29. Kemal Hakkı Kılıç, *Diyanet Avrupa Dergi* 46/6862, August 2010.

30. Kemal Hakkı Kılıç, *Diyanet Avrupa Dergi* 18/7932, October 2010.

31. "TDV 2018 Faaliyet Raporu," (Ankara: TDV, 2019): 23–34.

32. Ibid., 40.

33. Ibid., 70.

34. "TDV 2017 Faaliyet Raporu," (Ankara: TDV, 2018): 56.

35. "TDV 2017 Faaliyet Raporu," (Ankara: TDV, 2018): 76.

36. "TDV 2016 Faaliyet Raporu," (Ankara: TDV, 2017): 55.

37. "TDV 2015 Faaliyet Raporu," (Ankara: TDV, 2016): 31.

38. Ibid., 32.

39. "Hoca Ahmet Yesevi Camii ibadete hazır," *Anadolu Ajansı*, April 12, 2015, https://www.aa.com.tr/tr/turkiye/hoca-ahmet-yesevi-camii-ibadete-hazir/58309.

40. "TDV 2015 Faaliyet Raporu," 74.

41. In the jargon of the Turkish national education, "Anatolian" refers to English language education and "international" refers to the mixed education of Turkish and non-Turkish citizens.

42. Fatih Bayezit, "Yumuşak Güç Unsuru Olarak Uluslararası İmam Hatip Liseleri," *Talim: Journal of Education in Muslim Societies and Communities* 1 (2017): 301.

43. In the first year twenty-six hours of the forty hour weekly class program is Turkish language, four is Arabic, and four is Quran. Ministry of National Education DÖGM, *Uluslararası İmam Hatip Liseleri*, (Ankara: DÖGM, 2019) 24.

44. Ibid., 30.

45. "TDV 2017 Faaliyet Raporu," 27.

46. Ibid.

47. "TDV 2018 Faaliyet Raporu," 37.

48. All the data regarding Turkish schools in Central Asia were derived from the internet page of the External Schools Directorate of the Turkish Ministry of National Education: https://yyegm.meb.gov.tr/www/yurt-disi-okullarimiz/icerik/366.

49. Bekir S. Gür, Murat Ozoglu, and Ipek Coskun, *Küresel Eğilimler Işığında Türkiye'de Uluslararası Öğrenciler* [International Students in Turkey in the Light of Global Trends] (Ankara: SETA, 2012), 63.

50. Hacı Murat Terzi, *Türkiye'nin Büyük Öğrenci Projesi / The Great Student Project of Turkey* (MA Thesis, Ufuk University, Ankara, 2013): 27–28.

51. Gür, Ozoglu, and Coskun, *Küresel Eğilimler Işığında Türkiye'*, 64-65.

52. Turkey Scholarships.

53. "National Education Statistics," *Ministry of National Education*.

54. Derived from Higher Education Council (YOK) data https://www.drdatastats.com/turkiyedeki-universitelerde-okuyan-yabanci-uyruklu-ogrencilerin-ulkelere-gore-dagilimlari-2017-2018/.

55. A. Işıdan and H. İ. Şanverdi, "Lisans ve Lisansüstü Eğitimde Hoca Ahmet Yesevi Üniversitesinin Yeri," *Uluslararası Güncel Eğitim Araştırmaları Dergisi (UGEAD)* 2, no. 1 (June 2016): 62.

56. https://www.ayu.edu.tr/sayilar. The Turkic world here refers to the students except those from Turkey and Kazakhstan.

57. Manas University Student Affairs Directorate, http://oidb.manas.edu.kg/.

58. Sezai Kalaycı, "Dışişleri Bakan Yardımcısı Koru: Türk okulları, dış politikanın en önemli aktörü," *Zaman Amerika*, March 17, 2013, http://zamanamerika.com/haberler/dunya/disisleri-bakan-yardimcisi-koru-turk-okullari-dis-politikanin-en-onemli-aktoru/.

59. For an idea of the size of the network in Turkey: Turkish Minister of National Education responded to the Parliament motion and stated that 2,284 institutions of education were shut down after the 2016 July coup attempt with the allegation of being linked to the Gülen group. Turkish Parliament motion number 7/13079,

responded to the Minister of National Education on July 24, 2019, https://www2.tbmm.gov.tr/d27/7/7-13133sgc.pdf.

60. Gabrielle Angey, "The Gülen Movement and the Transfer of a Political Conflict from Turkey to Senegal," *Politics, Religion & Ideology* 19, no. 1 (2018): 53.

61. Turkish Islamism is a blend of ideology, Turkish nationalism, and market Islam.

62. Bayram Balci, "Turkey's Religious Outreach in Central Asia and the Caucasus," *Current Trends in Islamist Ideology* 16 (2014): 81.

63. Bayram Balci, "Education, Nationalism, and Hidden Da'wa: Turkish Missionary Movements in Central Asia and the Caucasus," in *Proselytization Revisited: Rights Talk, Free Markets and Culture Wars* ed. Rosalind I. J. Hackett (Sheffield: Equinox Publishing, 2008): 370.

64. Hulusi Turgut, "Fethullah Gülen ve Okullar," *Yeni Yüzyıl*, January 15, 1998.

65. Süleyman Demirel University.

66. "FETÖ'nün Kazakistan'daki faaliyetleri", *Anadolu Ajansı,* July 29, 2016 https://www.aa.com.tr/tr/dunya/fetonun-kazakistandaki-faaliyetleri/618025.

67. Ibrahim Keles, "Contributions of the Gülen schools in Kyrgyzstan," (paper, Gulen Movement Conference, London, October 2007), 364–65, https://www.gulen-conference.org.uk/userfiles/file/Proceedings/Prcd%20-%20Keles,%20I.pdf.

68. "Gateway to the World," (brochure, Ala-Too International University, Bishkek, 2019), http://iaau.edu.kg/booklets-brochures.pdf, accessed December 12, 2019.

69. L. Sagbansua and I. Keles, "Managerial and Educational Features of a Turkish University in Central Asia," *Bulgarian Journal of Science and Education Policy* 1, no. 1 (2007): 193.

70. "FETÖ Kırgızistan'da imparatorluk kurmuş," *Milliyet*, August 15, 2016, http://www.milliyet.com.tr/dunya/feto-kirgizistanda-imparatorluk-kurmus-2295149.

71. MÜSİAD is the pro-AKP businessmen association in Turkey.

72. "Türk-Kırgız İşadamları Derneğinden Tika'ya Teşekkür Plaketi," *Haberler.com*, June 14, 2018, https://www.haberler.com/turk-kirgiz-isadamlari-derneginden-tika-ya-10948954-haberi/.

73. Turgut, "Fethullah Gülen ve Okullar."

74. Victoria Clement, "Turkmenistan's New Challenges: Can Stability Co-exist with Reform? A Study of Gülen Schools in Central Asia, 1997–2007," (paper, Gulen Movement Conference, London, October 2007), https://fgulen.com/en/gulen-movement/conference-papers/contributions-of-the-gulen-movement/25892-turkmenistans-new-challenges-can-stability-co-exist-with-reform-a-study-of-gulen-schools-in-central-asia-19972007.

75. Victoria Clement, "Central Asia's Hizmet Schools," in *The Muslim World and Politics in Transition: Creative Contributions of the Gülen Movement*, ed. Greg Barton, Paul Weller, and Ihsan Yilmaz (London, New York: Bloomsbury, 2013): 165.

76. Naz Nazar, "The Tragic Echoes of Turkey's Anti-Gülen Campaign in Turkmenistan," *Open Democracy*, April 9, 2018, https://www.opendemocracy.net/en/odr/anti-gulen-campaign-in-turkmenistan/.

77. Victoria Clement, "Central Asia's Hizmet Schools," 165–66.

78. Aram Karamyan, "Growing Turkish Influence in Central Asian Countries in the Post-Cold War Era: Tentative Implications for China," *Leidschrift 28*, no. 1, (2013): 154. This school was being supported by Diyanet.

79. "Turkmenistan: 18 Men Tortured, Sentenced in Unfair Trial," *Human Rights Watch*, June 9, 2017, https://www.hrw.org/news/2017/06/09/turkmenistan-18-men-tortured-sentenced-unfair-trial.

80. Süleyman Elik, *Iran-Turkey Relations, 1979–2011: Conceptualising the Dynamics of Politics, Religion and Security in the Middle-Power States* (Oxon: Routledge, 2012): 121.

81. David Tittensor, "The Gülen Movement and the Case of a Secret Agenda: Putting the Debate in Perspective," *Islam and Christian–Muslim Relations* 23, no. 2 (2012): 168. In Uzbekistan and Turkmenistan, the Gülen movement is widely known as "Nurcu" referring to Said Nursi founder of the Nur movement, which Gülen initially belonged.

82. Ece Göksedef, "Özbekistan'da 16 yıl sonra Türk Cumhurbaşkanı," *Al Jazeera*, November 17, 2016, http://www.aljazeera.com.tr/al-jazeera-ozel/ozbekistanda-16-yil-sonra-turk-cumhurbaskani.

83. Sarfaroz Niyozov, "Islamic Education in Post-Soviet Tajikistan: A Tool in Creating and Sustaining a Nation-State," in *Religion and Education: Comparative and International Perspectives*, ed. Malini Sivasubmaniam and Ruth Hayhoe (Oxford: Symposium Books, 2018), 96.

84. "Gülen Cemaati'nin Tacikistan'daki okulları kapatıldı," *Sputnik*, August 6, 2015, https://sptnkne.ws/daTd.

85. Bruce Pannier, "The Gulen Schools in Central Asia," *RFE/RL*, August 13, 2016, https://www.rferl.org/a/majlis-podcast-gulen-schools/27919459.html.

86. Official Gazette of the Republic of Turkey, *KHK 480*, vol: 21124, January 27, 1992.

87. Official Gazette of the Republic of Turkey, *Kanun 4668*, vol: 24400, May 12, 2001.

88. Güner Özkan and Mustafa Turgut Demirtepe, "Transformation of a Development Aid Agency: TİKA in a Changing Domestic and International Setting," *Turkish Studies* 13, no. 4 (2012): 649.

89. Ibid., 650–51.

90. Karimov accused Turkey of having links with the assassination attempt in February 1999 and of supporting the Uzbek opposition.

91. Official Gazette of the Republic of Turkey, *KHK 656*, vol: 28103, February 11, 2011.

92. "62nd Coordination Office of TIKA was Inaugurated in Lefkoşa", *TIKA*, https://www.tika.gov.tr/tr/haber/tika_nin_62_nci_yurt_disi_ofisi_lefkosa_da_acildi-54851, accessed on December 17, 2019.

93. "Turkish Development Assistance Report 2017," (report, TIKA Department of Strategy Development, Ankara, 2018), 28–29.

94. Ibid., 48.

95. "Özbekistan Kursu," *Turkish Republics Ophthalmology Society*, http://tcod-tros.org/ozbekistan-kursu/, accessed December 12, 2018.

96. "Özbekistan-Türkiye Sağlık Haftası sona erdi," *TRT Avaz*, November 10, 2018, https://www.trtavaz.com.tr/haber/tur/avrasyadan/ozbekistan-turkiye-saglik-haftasi-sona-erdi/5be67b6a01a30a177006bac9.

97. "Turkish Development Assistance Report 2017," TIKA, 49.

98. Ibid., 51.

99. "TİKA'nın Kırgızistan'daki Faaliyetleri Anlatıldı," *Media Manas*, March 9, 2017, http://mediamanas.kg/lang-tr/1402-tkann-krgzistandaki-faaliyetleri-anlatld.html.

100. Parliament of Turkey, Approval Decision 2/1602, March 27, 2019, https://www2.tbmm.gov.tr/d27/2/2-1602.pdf.

101. "Turkish Development Assistance Report 2017," TIKA, 66.

102. Musa Kulaklıkaya and Rahman Nurdun, "Turkey as a New Player in Development Cooperation," *Insight Turkey* 12, no. 4 (2010): 138. Kulaklıkaya and Nurdun argued that lack of coordination among Turkish government institutions, unavailability of complete data on development assistance, underreporting of in kind support, and the lack of awareness of the international criteria for aid calculations were the other major reasons of low figures of ODA before 2004.

103. "Turkish Development Assistance Report 2017," TIKA, 15. There were slight decreases only in 2007 and 2009 but particularly after 2011 ODA increased tremendously due to the Syrian Civil War.

104. Kerim Can Kavakli, "Domestic Politics and the Motives of Emerging Donors: Evidence from Turkish Foreign Aid," *Political Research Quarterly* 71, no. 3 (2018): 615.

105. Official Gazette of the Republic of Turkey, *Kanun 5678*, vol: 27544, March 24, 2010.

106. "İdare Faaliyet Raporu 2018" (report, Presidency for Turks Abroad and Related Communities Activity Report, Ankara, YTB, 2019), 48–49.

107. "İdare Faaliyet Raporu 2017" (report, Presidency for Turks Abroad and Related Communities Activity Report, Ankara, YTB, 2018), 70.

108. "İdare Faaliyet Raporu 2013" (report, Presidency for Turks Abroad and Related Communities Activity Report, Ankara, YTB, 2014), 36.

109. "Crazy Heart" sold by Calinos Entertainment was the first export of the Turkish soap opera sector.

110. Mehmed Said Arbatlı and İhsan Kurar, "Türk Dizilerinin Kazak-Türk Kültürel Etkileşimine ve Türkçe'nin Yaygınlaşmasına Etkisi," *Turkish Studies* 10, no. 2 (2015): 40.

111. "Kazaklar her gün 10 saat Türk dizisi izliyor," *Cumhuriyet*, June 5, 2012, http://www.cumhuriyet.com.tr/haber/diger/347978/Kazaklar_her_gun_10_saat_Turk_dizisi_izliyor....html.

112. "Magnificent Century."

113. Aysu Biçer, "Turkey Targets $2B from Exports of Television Series," *Anadolu Ajansı*, December 22, 2016, https://www.aa.com.tr/en/culture-and-art/turkey-targets-2b-from-exports-of-television-series/712548.

114. As reported in "Turkish Soap Operas Taken Off Air In Uzbekistan," *RFE/RL*, February 24, 2012, https://www.rferl.org/a/turkish_soap_operas_taken_off_air_in_uzbekistan/24494989.html

115. "No Turkish Soaps Please, We're Uzbek," *Eurasianet*, June 20, 2019, https://eurasianet.org/no-turkish-soaps-please-were-uzbek.
116. "Endless Love."
117. Constantinos Constantinou and Zenonas Tziarras, "TV Series in Turkish Foreign Policy: Aspects of Hegemony and Resistance," *New Middle Eastern Studies* 8, no. 1 (2018): 32.
118. Kanykei Tursunbaeva, "Central Asia's Rulers View Turkish 'Soap Power' with Suspicion," *Global Voices*, August 7, 2014, https://globalvoices.org/2014/08/07/central-asias-rulers-view-turkish-soap-power-with-suspicion/.
119. "Tacikistan'da Türk dizileri yasaklandı" [Turkish serials banned in Tajikistan], *CNN Turk*, May 16, 2012, https://www.cnnturk.com/2012/dunya/05/16/tacikistanda.turk.dizileri.yasaklandi/661314.0/index.html.
120. S. Tongut and C. Yavu, "Sovyetler Birliği'nin Dağılmasından Sonra Kırgızistan ile İlişkilerde Türk Medyası: TRT-Avrasya, TRT-Türk ve TRT-Avaz," *Manas Sosyal Araştırmalar Dergisi* 3 no. 3. (2014): 135.

REFERENCES

Ala-Too International University. "Gateway to the World." Brochure, Bishkek, 2019. http://iaau.edu.kg/booklets-brochures.pdf. Accessed December 12, 2019.
Anadolu Ajansı. "FETÖ'nün Kazakistan'daki faaliyetleri," July 29, 2016. https://www.aa.com.tr/tr/dunya/fetonun-kazakistandaki-faaliyetleri/618025.
Anadolu Ajansı, "Hoca Ahmet Yesevi Camii ibadete hazır," April 12, 2015. https://www.aa.com.tr/tr/turkiye/hoca-ahmet-yesevi-camii-ibadete-hazir/58309.
Angey, Gabrielle. "The Gülen Movement and the Transfer of a Political Conflict from Turkey to Senegal." *Politics, Religion & Ideology* 19, no. 1 (2018): 53–68.
Arbatlı, Mehmed Said, and İhsan Kurar. "Türk Dizilerinin Kazak-Türk Kültürel Etkileşimine ve Türkçe'nin Yaygınlaşmasına Etkisi." *Turkish Studies* 10, no. 2 (2015): 31–48.
Aydın Çakır, Aylin, and Gül Arıkan Akdağ. "An Empirical Analysis of the Change in Turkish Foreign Policy under the AKP Government." *Turkish Studies* 18, no. 2 (2017): 334–57.
Balci, Bayram. "Education, Nationalism, and Hidden Da'wa: Turkish Missionary Movements in Central Asia and the Caucasus." In *Proselytization Revisited: Rights Talk, Free Markets and Culture Wars*, edited by Rosalind I. J. Hackett, 365–88. Sheffield: Equinox Publishing, 2008.
Balci, Bayram. "Turkey's Religious Outreach in Central Asia and the Caucasus." *Current Trends in Islamist Ideology* 16 (2014): 65–85.
Balci, Bayram, and Thomas Liles. "Turkey's Comeback to Central Asia." *Insight Turkey* 20, no. 4 (2018): 11–26.
Bardakoglu, Ali. "'Moderate Perception of Islam' and the Turkish Model of the Diyanet: The President's Statement." *Journal of Muslim Minority Affairs* 24, no. 2 (2004): 367–74.

Bayezit, Fatih. "Yumuşak Güç Unsuru Olarak Uluslararası İmam Hatip Liseleri." *Talim: Journal of Education in Muslim Societies and Communities* 1 (2017): 293–309.

Benhaïm, Yohanan, and Kerem Öktem. "The Rise and Fall of Turkey's Soft Power Discourse." *European Journal of Turkish Studies* 21 (2015). http://journals.openedition.org/ejts/5275.

Biçer, Aysu. "Turkey Targets $2B from Exports of Television Series." *Anadolu Ajansı*, December 22, 2016. https://www.aa.com.tr/en/culture-and-art/turkey-targets-2b-from-exports-of-television-series/712248.

Çakır, Ruşen, and İrgan Bozan. *Sivil, Şeffaf ve Demokratik Bir Diyanet İşleri Başkanlığı Mümkün mü?* İstanbul: TESEV Yayınları, February 2005.

Çitak, Zana. "Between 'Turkish Islam' and 'French Islam': The Role of the Diyanet in the Conseil Français Du Culte Musulman." *Journal of Ethnic and Migration Studies* 36, no. 4 (2010): 619–34.

Clement, Victoria. "Central Asia's Hizmet Schools." In *The Muslim World and Politics in Transition: Creative Contributions of the Gülen Movement*, edited by Greg Barton, Paul Weller, and Ihsan Yilmaz, 154–67. London, New York: Bloomsbury, 2013.

Clement, Victoria. "Turkmenistan's New Challenges: Can Stability Co-exist with Reform? A Study of Gülen Schools in Central Asia, 1997–2007." Paper, Gulen Movement Conference, London, October 2007. https://fgulen.com/en/gulen-movement/conference-papers/contributions-of-the-gulen-movement/25892-turkmenistans-new-challenges-can-stability-co-exist-with-reform-a-study-of-gulen-schools-in-central-asia-19972007.

CNN Turk. "Tacikistan'da Türk dizileri yasaklandı" [Turkish serials banned in Tajikistan], May 16, 2012. https://www.cnnturk.com/2012/dunya/05/16/tacikistanda.turk.dizileri.yasaklandi/661314.0/index.html.

Constantinou, Constantinos, and Zenonas Tziarras. "TV Series in Turkish Foreign Policy: Aspects of Hegemony and Resistance," *New Middle Eastern Studies* 8, no. 1 (2018): 23–41.

Cumhuriyet. "Kazaklar her gün 10 saat Türk dizisi izliyor," June 5, 2012. http://www.cumhuriyet.com.tr/haber/diger/347978/Kazaklar_her_gun_10_saat_Turk_dizisi_izliyor....html

Donelli, Federico. "Persuading through Culture, Values, and Ideas: The Case of Turkey's Cultural Diplomacy." *Insight Turkey* 21, no. 3 (2019): 113–34.

Ekşi, Muharrem and Mehmet Seyfettin Erol. "The Rise and Fall of Turkish Soft Power and Public Diplomacy." *Gazi Akademik Bakis Dergisi* 11, no. 23 (2018): 15–45.

Elik, Süleyman. *Iran-Turkey Relations, 1979–2011: Conceptualising the Dynamics of Politics, Religion and Security in the Middle-Power States*. Oxon: Routledge, 2012.

Eurasianet. "No Turkish Soaps Please, We're Uzbek," June 20, 2019. https://eurasianet.org/no-turkish-soaps-please-were-uzbek.

Göksedef, Ece. "Özbekistan'da 16 yıl sonra Türk Cumhurbaşkanı." *Al Jazeera*, November 17, 2016. http://www.aljazeera.com.tr/al-jazeera-ozel/ozbekistanda-16-yil-sonra-turk-cumhurbaskani.

Gözaydın, İstar B. "Diyanet and Politics." *The Muslim World* 98, no. 2–3 (2008): 216–27.
Güler, Halit. *Orta Asya'da İslam'ın Yeniden Doğuşu.* Ankara, TDV Yayınları, 1994.
Gür, Bekir S., Murat Ozoglu, and Ipek Coskun. *Küresel Eğilimler Işığında Türkiye'de Uluslararası Öğrenciler* [International Students in Turkey in the Light of Global Trends]. Ankara: SETA, 2012.
Haberler.com. "Türk-Kırgız İşadamları Derneğinden Tika'ya Teşekkür Plaketi," June 14, 2018. "https://www.haberler.com/turk-kirgiz-isadamlari-derneginden-tika-ya-10948954-haberi/.
Human Rights Watch. "Turkmenistan: 18 Men Tortured, Sentenced in Unfair Trial," June 9, 2017, https://www.hrw.org/news/2017/06/09/turkmenistan-18-men-tortured-sentenced-unfair-trial.
Işıdan A., and Şanverdi H. İ. "Lisans ve Lisansüstü Eğitimde Hoca Ahmet Yesevi Üniversitesinin Yeri." *Uluslararası Güncel Eğitim Araştırmaları Dergisi (UGEAD)* 2, no. 1. (June 2016): 60–5.
Jabbour, Jana. "An Illusionary Power of Seduction?" *European Journal of Turkish Studies* 21 (2015). http://journals.openedition.org/ejts/5234.
Kalaycı, Sezai. "Dışişleri Bakan Yardımcısı Koru: Türk okulları, dış politikanın en önemli aktörü," *Zaman Amerika*, March 17, 2013. http://zamanamerika.com/haberler/dunya/disisleri-bakan-yardimcisi-koru-turk-okullari-dis-politikanin-en-onemli-aktoru/.
Kalin, Ibrahim. "Soft Power and Public Diplomacy in Turkey." *Perceptions* 16, no. 3 (2011): 5–23.
Karamyan, Aram. "Growing Turkish Influence in Central Asian Countries in the Post-Cold War Era: Tentative Implications for China." *Leidschrift* 28, no. 1 (2013): 143–59.
Kavakli, Kerim Can. "Domestic Politics and the Motives of Emerging Donors: Evidence from Turkish Foreign Aid." *Political Research Quarterly* 71, no. 3 (2018): 614–27.
Keyman, E. Fuat. "A New Turkish Foreign Policy: Towards Proactive "Moral Realism"." *Insight Turkey* 19, no. 1 (2017): 55–70.
Keles, Ibrahim. "Contributions of the Gülen schools in Kyrgyzstan." Paper, Gulen Movement Conference, London, October 2007, 362–76. https://www.gulenconference.org.uk/userfiles/file/Proceedings/Prcd%20-%20Keles,%20I.pdf.
Kılıç, Kemal Hakkı. *Diyanet Avrupa Dergi* 46/6862. August 2010.
Kılıç, Kemal Hakkı. *Diyanet Avrupa Dergi.* 14/4737. September 2010.
Kılıç, Kemal Hakkı. *Diyanet Avrupa Dergi* 18/7932. October 2010.
Korkut, Şenol. "The Diyanet of Turkey and Its Activities in Eurasia after the Cold War." *Acta Slavica Iaponica* 28 (2010): 117–39.
Kulaklıkaya, Musa, and Rahman Nurdun. "Turkey as a New Player in Development Cooperation." *Insight Turkey* 12, no. 4 (2010): 131–45.
Lami, Blendi. "Recalibration of Turkish Foreign Policy during AKP Era." *Central European Journal of International & Security Studies* 12, no. 3 (2018): 35–56.

Media Manas. "TİKA'nın Kırgızistan'daki Faaliyetleri Anlatıldı." Accessed December 22, 2018. http://mediamanas.kg/lang-tr/1402-tkann-krgzistandaki-faaliyetleri-anlatld.html

Milliyet. "FETÖ Kırgızistan'da imparatorluk kurmuş," August 15, 2016. http://www.milliyet.com.tr/dunya/feto-kirgizistanda-imparatorluk-kurmus-2295149.

Nazar, Naz. "The Tragic Echoes of Turkey's Anti-Gülen Campaign in Turkmenistan," April 9, 2018. https://www.opendemocracy.net/en/odr/anti-gulen-campaign-in-turkmenistan/.

Niyozov, Sarfaroz. "Islamic Education in Post-Soviet Tajikistan: A Tool in Creating and Sustaining a Nation-State." In *Religion and Education: Comparative and International Perspectives,* edited by Malini Sivasubmaniam and Ruth Hayhoe, 85–109. Oxford: Symposium Books, 2018.

Nye, Joseph S. Jr. "Soft Power." *Foreign Policy* 80, Twentieth Anniversary (Autumn, 1990): 15–171.

Nye, Joseph S. Jr. "Soft Power and American Foreign Policy." *Political Science Quarterly* 119, no. 2 (2004): 255–70.

Özbay, Ekrem. *Türkmenistan Tarihinde Eğitim-Bağımsızlık-Din.* İstanbul: Hiperlink Yayınları, 2019.

Özkan, Güner, and Mustafa Turgut Demirtepe. "Transformation of a Development Aid Agency: TİKA in a Changing Domestic and International Setting." *Turkish Studies* 13, no. 4 (2012): 647–64.

Öztürk, Ahmet Erdi. "Turkey's Diyanet Under AKP Rule: From Protector to Imposer of State Ideology?" *Southeast European and Black Sea Studies* 16, no. 4 (2016): 619–35.

Pannier, Bruce. "The Gulen Schools in Central Asia." August 13, 2016. https://www.rferl.org/a/majlis-podcast-gulen-schools/27919459.html.

RFE/RL. "Turkish Soap Operas Taken Off Air In Uzbekistan," February 24, 2012. https://www.rferl.org/a/turkish_soap_operas_taken_off_air_in_uzbekistan/24494989.html.

Sagbansua, L., and I. Keles. "Managerial and Educational Features of a Turkish University in Central Asia." *Bulgarian Journal of Science and Education Policy* 1, no. 1 (2007): 191–203.

Sağlık, Fahri. *Diyanet Avrupa Dergi,* 45/6861. August 2010.

Sputnik. "Gülen Cemaati'nin Tacikistan'daki okulları kapatıldı," August 6, 2015. https://sptnkne.ws/daTd.

TDV. "2015 Faaliyet Raporu." Ankara: TDV, 2016.

TDV. "2016 Faaliyet Raporu." Ankara: TDV, 2017.

TDV. "2017 Faaliyet Raporu." Ankara: TDV, 2018.

TDV. "2018 Faaliyet Raporu." Ankara: TDV, 2019.

Terzi, Hacı Murat. "Türkiye'nin Büyük Öğrenci Projesi / The Great Student Project of Turkey." Master's thesis, Ufuk University, Ankara, 2013.

TIKA Department of Strategy Development. "Turkish Development Assistance Report 2017." Report, TIKA Department of Strategy Development, Ankara, 2018.

Tittensor, David. "The Gülen Movement and the Case of a Secret Agenda: Putting the Debate in Perspective." *Islam and Christian–Muslim Relations* 23, no. 2, (2012):163–79.
Tongut, S., and C. Yavuz. "Sovyetler Birliği'nin Dağılmasından Sonra Kırgızistan ile İlişkilerde Türk Medyası: TRT-Avrasya, TRT-Türk ve TRT-Avaz." *Manas Sosyal Araştırmalar Dergisi* 3 no. 3. (2014): 132–5.
TRT Avaz. "Özbekistan-Türkiye Sağlık Haftası sona erdi." November 10, 2018, https://www.trtavaz.com.tr/haber/tur/avrasyadan/ozbekistan-turkiye-saglik-haftasi-sona-erdi/5be67b6a01a30a177006bac9.
Turgut, Hulusi. "Fethullah Gülen ve Okullar." *Yeni Yüzyıl*, January 15, 1998.
Turkey, Ministry of National Education, Republic of. *National Education Statistics: Formal Education 2017/18*. Ankara: MEB, 2019).
Turkey, Official Gazette of the Republic of. *Kanun 4668*, Volume 24400. May 12, 2001.
Turkey, Official Gazette of the Republic of. *Kanun 5678*, Volume 27544. March 24, 2010.
Turkey, Official Gazette of the Republic of. *KHK 480*, Volume 21124. January 27, 1992.
Turkey, Official Gazette of the Republic of. *KHK 656*, Volume 28103. February 11, 2011.
Turkey, Official Gazette of the Republic of. Volume 27544. March 24, 2010.
Turkey, Parliament of. Reply to Motion, 7/13079. Responde by Minister of National Education on July 24, 2019. https://www2.tbmm.gov.tr/d27/7/7-13133sgc.pdf.
Turkey, Parliament of. Approval of Treaty, Decision 2/1602. March 27, 2019. https://www2.tbmm.gov.tr/d27/2/2-1602.pdf.
Turkish Cooperation and Development Agency. "62nd Coordination Office of TIKA was Inaugurated in Lefkoşa." https://www.tika.gov.tr/tr/haber/tika_nin_62_nci_yurt_disi_ofisi_lefkosa_da_acildi-54851. Accessed December 17, 2018.
Turkish Ministry of National Education. "Yurtdışı Okullarımız," https://yyegm.meb.gov.tr/www/yurt-disi-okullarimiz/icerik/366. Accessed December 3, 2019.
Turkish Republics Ophthalmology Society. "Özbekistan Kursu," http://tcod-tros.org/ozbekistan-kursu/. Accessed December 12, 2018.
Türkiye Diyanet Vakfı. "Hakkımızda," https://tdv.org/tr-TR/kurumsal/. Accessed February 3, 2019.
Tursunbaeva, Kanykei. "Central Asia's Rulers View Turkish 'Soap Power' with Suspicion." *Global Voices*, August 7, 2014. https://globalvoices.org/2014/08/07/central-asias-rulers-view-turkish-soap-power-with-suspicion/.
Ulgen, Sinan. "A Place in the Sun or Fifteen Minutes of Fame? Understanding Turkey's New Foreign Policy." Paper number 1, Carnegie Papers, Carnegie Endowment for International Peace, Brussels, 2010.
Ünver, Mustafa. "Orta Asya'ya 'Diyanet' Modeli." In *Orta Asya'da İslam*, edited by Muhammet Savaş Kafkasyalı, 459–83. Ankara: Ahmet Yesevi Universitesi, 2012.
Wastnidge, Edward. "Imperial Grandeur and Selective Memory: Re-Assessing Neo-Ottomanism in Turkish Foreign and Domestic Politics." *Middle East Critique* 28, no. 1 (2019): 7–28.

YTB. "İdare Faaliyet Raporu 2013." Report, Presidency for Turks Abroad and Related Communities Activity Report 2017. Ankara: YTB, 2014.
YTB. "İdare Faaliyet Raporu 2017." Report, Presidency for Turks Abroad and Related Communities Activity Report 2017. Ankara: YTB, 2018.
YTB. "İdare Faaliyet Raporu 2018." Report, Presidency for Turks Abroad and Related Communities Activity Report 2017. Ankara: YTB, 2019.

Chapter 6

Israel in Southern Eurasia
The Legitimacy Quest of a Contested Entity
Bruno De Cordier

This chapter examines the relations and channels of interaction between Israel and southern Eurasia—as this author prefers to call the formerly Soviet Central Asian space—through the lens of the soft power paradigm. In line with the starting point of this volume, soft power is understood here as the ability to shape the preferences of others and to affect others to obtain the outcomes one wants through attraction rather than coercion or payment. It is not merely influence, though it is one source of influence, and rests primarily on three resources: culture (in places where it is attractive to others), political values (when it lives up to them at home and abroad), and foreign policies (when they are seen as legitimate and having moral authority).[1] Although regular reference will be made to the southern Eurasia region in general, this contribution will focus on Kazakhstan and Kyrgyzstan, where the author had the opportunity to carry out some field research.[2]

SOUTHERN EURASIA, ISRAEL, AND THE JEWISH WORLD

No doubt, few countries raise as much controversy and as many emotions as Israel, and examining its relations with southern Eurasia is no exception. This was clear when the author presented the idea for this chapter at a seminar in early 2018: "Be careful that you don't write anything that can be construed as anti-Semitic," "Merely speaking about Israeli soft power is a godsend for conspiracy theorists." Such comments reflect the fact that this topic is challenging and is sufficiently complex and controversial to be worth pursuing. Although Israel as a country, the world's Jewish population, and Judaism are not synonymous and do not form a homogenous whole, Israel, as the sole modern Jewish polity, is a crucial component of a Jewish civilization that is historically and sociologically not at all alien to southern Eurasia. [3]

Our region of interests undeniably and directly occupies a not unimportant place in Jewish history, just as Jews and Judaism do in the history of the region and its societies. Take the peculiar example of the semi-nomadic Turkic Khazar kingdom, which existed on the northern Caspian between 650 and 959, and the at times fierce controversy around the role that its reportedly Judaist-influenced culture—rather than ancient tribes of Israel—played in the formation of Eastern European Jewry or, at least, some subgroups of it;[4] or the presence of Oriental Jews—more specifically Judeo-Iranian populations—in southern Eurasia's sedentary-urban core areas since the fifteenth century. In the twentieth century, as we will see in more detail later on, the region and its societies saw the arrival of Jewish populations from Belarus, Ukraine, and Russia, in the context of processes of radical social transformation of the region and its societies after they were incorporated into the USSR. Finally, despite a dramatic decrease due to emigration over the past decades, there are still residual populations of both European and Oriental Jews in the region.

What characteristics of Israel as a distinct polity should be taken into account when examining its current interaction, through soft power and other channels, with southern Eurasia? Although Israel reportedly holds just one-third of the world's enlarged Jewish population of 20.37 million (see Figure 6.1), it is the beacon state of Jewish-Judaist civilization. How to understand the terms "civilization" and "beacon state"? *Civilization* is understood here as Marcel Mauss defined it back in 1929: a sufficiently large and ample whole of qualitatively as well as numerically important and characteristic social phenomena and the different societies in which they occur(red) and which are characterized by them, so that one can speak of families of societies. By definition, civilizations possess more or less common characteristic forms which consist of all their specific aspects in terms of ideas, practices, and products; a territorial and non-territorial area; as well as layers which are a civilization's form within a given timeframe.[5]

A *beacon state* is a state or polity that champions, steers, or sets the standards through various channels which do not necessarily have to be classical state institutions, for a cultural civilization and an ideological project.[6] Israel has the peculiarity of being one of the world's few ideological states in the sense that its raison d'être is one of a homeland for the followers of a confession—that is, an ideological community—and that its conception and existence are anchored in Judaist tradition and political theology. It encompasses the geographic areas that form the cradle of Judaism and the Jewish nation and where Judaism's religious centers are situated. It is the only country where Jews are in the majority and where, in a number of ways, Judaism regulates social and political life.

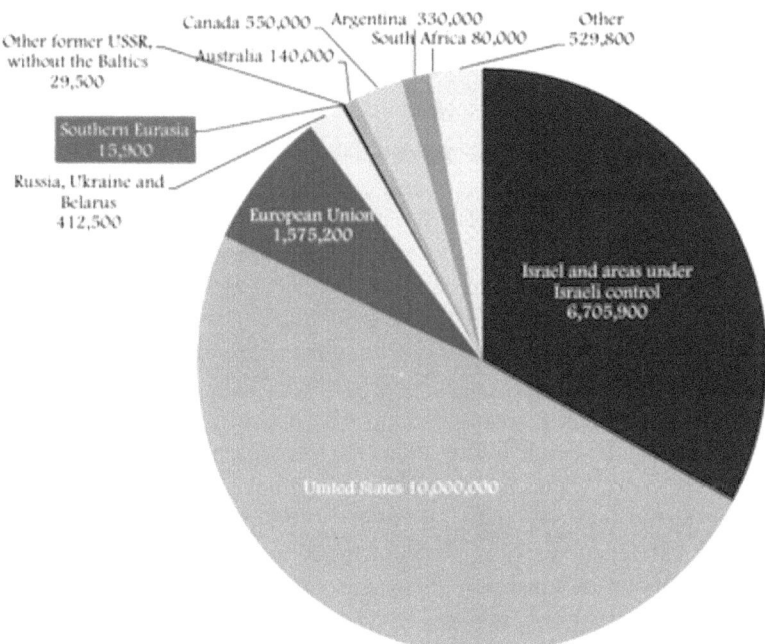

Figure 6.1 The Global Geographic Distribution of the Enlarged Jewish Population and the Place of Israel and Southern Eurasia Therein (2016, in number of persons).
Source: Author, April 2018, on the basis of figures from Sergio Della Pergola, "World Jewish Population 2016," Current Jewish Population Reports, Berman Jewish Databank 17 (2016): 57–59.

Israel is both the space and the central protagonist of the Israeli-Palestinian conflict, the strong symbolic-emotional significance and effects of which go well beyond the geographic spaces where it actually occurs. Further, Israel's right to exist as an entity is heavily contested by a range of political movements as well as in popular Islamic opinion in both the Arab and non-Arab Muslim realm, by Leftist groups in Western Europe and elsewhere, for which "Palestine" is a cause célèbre, as well as, for theological reasons, certain Haredi Judaist factions. And finally, pretty much as is the case with Germany, Korea, and Armenia, all of whom had sizable or still have residual or returnee ethnic kin and "compatriots" in southern Eurasia, Israel's capacity of a beacon state also connects it to a diaspora paradigm.

A PERIPHERY AXIS?

Against this background, is there a specific Jewish framework and approach to foreign policy (including soft power), and to interaction with other nations and peoples in general? According to Shmuel Sandler, 3,000 years of Jewish history indeed shaped a foreign policy that is defensive rather than expansive, and rooted in an idea of uniqueness in the sense that Jews collectively stand alone when push comes to shove.[7] In that respect, Jewish foreign policy and interaction with other nations and peoples are not so much driven "by the Jewish state" as it is by "the state of the Jews." More concretely, it includes four characteristics. First and foremost, it is geared toward the physical and cultural survival of the Jews, not only from anti-Semitism, persecution, or assimilation, but also from famines, and social and natural disasters in places where Jews live. The aspect of survival includes the survival of Israel as a country and polity, the existential right and the space of which are defined in Biblical tradition and by modern Zionist thought.

Robert Frank thereby makes a distinction between "existential Zionism" (both Jews and non-Jews, living within or outside Israel, defending Israel's right to exist) and "power Zionism" (Israel's territorial expansion, seen by its advocates as security- and survival-driven rather than aggressive expansionism).[8] The second driving force in Sandler's view is the strengthening of Jewish power beyond survival, to sustain an alleged Jewish uniqueness as well as deter external threats. The importance of state and state power and of weak and strong states thereby varies, and is determined in an ad hoc manner. Jewish and Israeli power thus transcends national boundaries, comparable to the influence and soft power of the Holy See in the Catholic world and beyond.[9]

Third, in order to realize the first two, there is a clear emphasis on alliance-seeking between equal, independent polities, with unequal partners or in the form of vassal alliances, as well as between Jewish minorities and local rulers or host polities. Since 1958, this is reflected in Israel's so-called periphery doctrine. This doctrine proposes a foreign policy strategy of alliances with non-Arab countries that neighbor—and minorities that reside within—countries which are at war or have otherwise a conflictual relationship with Israel. Originally designed to frame Israel's ties with Turkey, imperial Iran, and the Ethiopian empire, some authors believe it to now apply to some extent to Israel's interaction with southern Eurasia, Azerbaijan, and the Kurdish separatists in the Arab countries.[10]

Fourth, there is the concept of interdependence and diaspora politics. This interdependence manifests itself at two levels. One level is at the relationship between the Jewish diaspora and Israel. As Ilan Zvi Baron emphasizes in his work on Israel-diaspora relations, certainly not all diaspora Jews identify with Israel or are directly attached to it. Nonetheless, for many if not most diaspora Jews, Israel is exceptional as it is the only state where Jews form a majority and where Jewish cultural norms and Judaism frame life.[11] As a result, its interaction with the Jewish diaspora is much stronger and more intensive than is the case with other countries with large diasporas, with the exception perhaps of Armenia.[12] The other level of interdependence is the quest for common interests between Jewish minorities and the host polities, which allows the Jewish diaspora to function—also in southern Eurasia as we will see later in this chapter—as an international player, despite not being a nation-state.

Image (Re-)Building

Are these applicable here? And what are Israel's actual and practical interests and reasons to be in southern Eurasia? To start with, Israel's relations with southern Eurasia, as suggested earlier, clearly fits within *a move to look for allies in the wider Islamic sphere and with majority Muslim countries*. Practically, it seeks to foster friendly, or at least neutral, relations with the countries and those in power, and promote a positive image of Israel in the respective societies and in public opinion. So how does a country like Israel and its representatives attempt to build its image in a region like southern Eurasia? A first approach consists of an active *cultural and public diplomacy* for general audiences and especially for decision makers and future decision makers. This includes the intensive use of the usual, popular social media, both international and Russian, for public relations in the broad sense, on topics such as bilateral relations, innovation and startups, both leisure and medical tourism, investment, sports, and Israeli and to some extent Jewish-Judaist culture. [13]

In the realm of culture, the Israeli embassy to Kazakhstan and Kyrgyzstan has been active in supporting a range of cultural events, such as the organization of Israeli cultural days, the Israeli film festivals in Almaty and Chimkent, and support of the participation of Israeli bands in the Almaty and Bishkek jazz festivals and of Jewish folk ensembles in world music fests in Almaty.[14] During the international exposition in Astana in summer 2017, the embassy also helped to organize performances of klezmer music, an Ashkenazi-Yiddish musical tradition, on the expo premises. The embassy organized commemorations for Jewish victims of Stalinist repression at the Akmolinsk and Karaganda gulag memorial sites—in line with similar initiatives by other embassies for their kin and compatriots, and a historiographic project about people and families in Kazakhstan who hosted or otherwise helped Jewish evacuees during the Second World War.

Contrary to the way the promotion of the French and German languages, to pick just two examples among many, form core components in the cultural diplomacy and soft power of France and Germany, respectively, the promotion of Hebrew, Israel's official idiom and the main Jewish language nowadays, is no main preoccupation of Israel's official cultural diplomacy in southern Eurasia. As we will see later on, the organization of Hebrew courses and language events is rather a specific activity of nongovernmental organizations and of parastatal agencies not attached to the embassy that offer support to the residual Jewish populations in the region and to Jewish citizens of Kazakhstan and Kyrgyzstan who plan to emigrate to Israel. Israel does not promote, either directly or through party foundations, non-governmental organizations (NGOs) and local civil society, democracy causes, and liberal values in the region—a position which may, as a matter of fact, yield goodwill in a region that is increasingly weary of outside patronizing in this field.

The Approach of Development Assistance

A second approach is *development cooperation*, which along with humanitarian assistance, is generally a very important channel of soft power and image building for the donor countries (the United States, the European Commission, and European Union countries, as well as Persian-Arab Gulf countries) and those organizing such aid. Israel, which is a member of the Organization for Economic Co-operation and Development (OECD) since 2010 and is an observer at the OECD's Development Assistance Committee, globally spent some 220 million USD on official development and humanitarian assistance in 2016, which makes it a smaller donor, comparable to Greece.[15] Surprising as it may sound, but not illogical, about half of that global amount was destined for Cis-Jordan and Gaza, Jordan, and Syria. Israeli development cooperation has been deployed in southern Eurasia since 1993, yet with Kazakhstan receiving some 950,000 USD in aid in 2016 (390,000 USD in 2012) and Kyrgyzstan 70,000 USD (280,000 USD in 2012), the region is really no top destination of Israeli aid.[16]

MASHAV, Israel's official development cooperation agency, has an official discourse which is partly embedded in universal development discourse and official working principles that abide to mainstream development aid and OECD recommendations, while also evolving partly out of Israel's own historical development experience and partly adhering to a secular practice of *tikkun olam*, the Judaist concept of improving the world and humanity.[17] Quite clearly, development cooperation is also a manner to enhance recognition and bilateral relations. "This is no secret," stated the Israeli ambassador to Kazakhstan and Kyrgyzstan. "If we do this, it is also with the purpose that Israel gets something back politically. In some countries this has worked. In others, like Kyrgyzstan, which so far [at the time of research] has not nominated a permanent representative to Israel, less so."[18]

In southern Eurasia, its project activities, which are managed from the Israeli embassy, have been primarily focusing on agriculture and horticulture—sectors where the agency clearly seeks to promote Israel's own experience in developing them in arid environments—and on health care.

In Kazakhstan, for example, the agency funded horticulture and greenhouse projects in Aqmola Province and five other regions, a fish hatchery close to the northern Aral Sea, and greenhouses for orphanages in Atyrau and Almaty. Another, still on-going example of a project is a drop irrigation demonstration center in Uç Qongır in Almaty Province. Since 1993, about 300 nurses and other medical and paramedical staff also undertook various sorts of training in Israel. In Kyrgyzstan, MASHAV supported, among other activities, an agribusiness consulting center focusing on female agricultural entrepreneurs with demonstration farms now reported to be self-sustaining. [19]

Many of these activities in Kazakhstan and Kyrgyzstan are or were carried out in cooperation with specialized UN agencies and with the development cooperation institutions of the United States, Japan, and Germany.[20] In general, classical on-the-ground project activities in Kazakhstan, Kyrgyzstan, and the rest of southern Eurasia were more extensive between 1998 and 2011. Today, the emphasis of Israel's development cooperation in southern Eurasia lies in training. Currently twenty to thirty people per year from Kyrgyzstan and about sixty people from Kazakhstan are sent for training in agricultural techniques, health, and entrepreneurial skills and management, to training centers near Haifa, Jerusalem, and Beit Dagan. In Kazakhstan, which has become a donor country itself in the meantime, at the time of research Israeli cooperation also focused on support to private companies as well as to the foreign ministry's attempts to set up a development cooperation agency of its own.[21]

"Israel–Palestine" and Southern Eurasia

Third, there is the regional attitude toward the Israeli-Palestinian conflict, which globally largely determines the international image of Israel. All five southern Eurasian states recognize Palestine. In addition, all support the 1988 UN General Assembly's resolution no. 43/177 calling to respect the pre-1967 borders of Palestine (although they are not original signatories), approved the fall 2012 resolution no. 67/19 upgrading Palestine to non-member observer state status in the United Nations, and all, except Turkmenistan which was absent at the vote, supported the UN General Assembly's late 2017 resolution no. ES10-L.22 urging the United States to cancel the transfer of its embassy in Israel to Jerusalem.[22] In practice, they keep a more actively neutral stance. All also recognize Israel, and Kazakhstan and Uzbekistan have diplomatic relations with both Israel and Palestine and host embassies of both.[23]

On the whole, the Israeli-Palestinian conflict is not really a core issue in Israel's official public diplomacy in the region. Rather than take a defensive or self-justifying stance in the matter, it is, as we have seen, geared toward promoting an image of Israel as a functioning, dynamic, and creative country in a region affected by general chaos since the beginning of the Arab unrest in late 2010. The Israeli-Palestinian conflict is also not a much a key cause and as emotionally mobilizing among southern Eurasian Muslims, as it is in majority Muslim Arab countries and among Arab migrant communities in Western Europe for example. This does not mean, however, that it is completely absent from southern Eurasian opinion, especially not during heavy and internationally mediatized flare-ups such as the so-called "stabbing intifada" in Jerusalem in 2016 or the tragic "return march" in Gaza in 2018.

The USSR's anti-Zionist and pro-Arab line held between 1967 and 1989, for example, still resonates in the reporting of such events in Russian audiovisual and social media, which also reach wide audiences in southern Eurasia. Individual members and representatives of the Jewish communities in Bishkek and Karaganda also stated that if the war with the Palestinians negatively affects the image of Israel among street opinion in southern Eurasia, it is mostly this way, or because the media often copy international media coverage, "which," as one respondent puts it, "has always largely been unsympathetic towards Israel no matter what."[24] The growing Islamic identification and consciousness that can be observed in certain sectors of society in Kazakhstan and Kyrgyzstan, also sees to it that the issue remains on the mental map there. In any case, Islam and Islamic practice in southern Eurasia are in full reconstruction, and the outside resources and influences and transnational channels which contribute to this process, unavoidably bring in transnational issues that were not present in ethnic-traditional Islam before.

INVESTMENT AND TRADE AS SOFT POWER?

One of the claimed priorities of Israeli diplomacy in southern Eurasia is to support and promote the Israeli private sector and investment in the region.[25] Tables 6.1 and 6.2 give an overview, at least as far as open source statistics are available, on the trade volumes between southern Eurasia and Israel between

Table 6.1 Exports to Israel from Southern Eurasia (1996–2016, in million USD)

	Kazakhstan	Uzbekistan	Tajikistan	Kyrgyzstan	Turkmenistan
2016	235.6	n/a	n/a	0.065	n/a
2011	1.418	n/a	n/a	0.023	n/a
2006	622.43	n/a	n/a	0.070	n/a
2001	3.6	n/a	n/a	0.25	0.34[1]
1996	0.89	n/a	n/a	0.094	0.414[2]

Source: Author, March 2018, on the basis of figures from the World Integrated System Database, The World Bank Group, and UNCTAD, wits.worldbank.org.
[1] Figure for 2000.
[2] Figure for 1997.

Table 6.2 Imports from Israel into Southern Eurasia (1996–2016, in million USD)

	Kazakhstan	Uzbekistan	Tajikistan	Kyrgyzstan	Turkmenistan
2016	66.1	n/a	n/a	2.43	n/a
2011	125.9	n/a	n/a	3.75	n/a
2006	76.24	n/a	n/a	0.99	n/a
2001	23.65	n/a	n/a	0.24	1.35
1996	16.3	n/a	n/a	0.71	1.9

Source: Author, March 2018, on the basis of figures from the World Integrated System Database, The World Bank Group, and UNCTAD, wits.worldbank.org.
[1] Figure for 2000.
[2] Figure for 1997.

the years 1996 and 2016. Kazakhstan is clearly the focus for Israeli trade and economic investment in the region, for reasons related to Israeli energy security, the often-overlooked capacity of Kazakhstan as a major agro-industrial and especially grain and wheat producer, and the opportunities for the Israeli private sector in the country's growing economy, particularly in the fields of energy, agriculture, telecommunications, and health care.[26] In 1995, seventy-six Israeli businesses or business ventures with Israeli capital allegedly operated in the country.[27] In 2011, this was reported to be 176, while the number for 2016 was 270. They are active in construction, cable production, agro-industry hydrocarbons and mining, pharmaceutics, and real estate.[28]

Even if the trade and investment volumes are rather volatile, subject to Israel's energy security policies, and have also been affected by the financial crisis and the impact of the oil price slump, Israel as such figures among Kazakhstan's main trade partners in the Near East. It figures in that position next to Turkey (851 million USD exports and 618.14 million USD imports to Kazakhstan in 2016), Iran (550.9 million USD exports, 46.5 million imports), and the United Arab Emirates (UAE) (305.19 million USD exports, 69 million USD imports). Kazakhstan's extensive trade and neutral relations with Iran has at the same time been a bone of contention with Israel, especially when it comes to sales of uranium of which Kazakhstan is a major producer and exporter globally. In Kyrgyzstan, with which, as one can see, reported trade is much more modest in both scope and volume, Israel does not figure among the country's largest Near Eastern trade partners, which at 2016 are Turkey (90 million USD exports and 190.77 million USD imports in 2016), the UAE (36.4 million USD exports, 3.7 million USD imports), and Iran (8.1 million USD exports, 6.58 million USD imports).[29]

Not surprisingly, Kazakhstan's main export commodity to Israel consists of oil, which makes up 85 to 97 percent of its exports to the country. Israel's domestic oil production being limited and its relations with the OPEC and Arab oil producers strained at best, it largely relies on imports from non-OPEC, non-Arab oil suppliers such as Russia, Azerbaijan, Kazakhstan, and the Kurdish entity in northern Iraq, the latter of which was reported to provide three-quarters of Israeli oil imports in mid-2015.[30] Over the last ten years (i.e., until fall 2018), 15 to 25 percent of Israel's oil import is reported to come from Kazakhstan.[31] Besides hydrocarbons, Kazakhstan also exports coal, wheat, and, more recently, mutton to Israel. Imports from Israel mostly consist of agricultural and other machinery, electro-technical and telecommunications equipment, defense equipment, seeds and chemicals, and transportation equipment.[32]

Israeli businesses are also quite prominently active in the field of health care, with the imports of medical equipment, pharmaceutics, and, not in the least, medical treatment tourism to Israel, the latter boosted, among others, by the fact that not a few physicians and surgical specialists in Israel speak Russian or originally come from the former Soviet Union.[33] Finally, since 2017, in the wake of the Astana expo, Israeli companies have tried to position themselves in the Kazakhstan and southern Eurasian market of solar power and other forms of "green energy."[34] Having said all this, can trade and investment be considered a typical channel of soft power, or just a generic way of interaction between economies and societies? Probably it is a bit of both. As is the case with Israeli development cooperation, the country's own historical development experience in a hostile environment is instrumental in the promotional approach that goes with trade and investment. And what there is of soft power comes in when it is needed to smooth the obstacles in doing business in southern Eurasia and obtaining access to regional and local markets, where much stands or falls with connections and patronage.

THE DIASPORIC ANGLE

A last and very important aspect which we will now examine is that related to the diaspora, something, as said earlier, that Israel has in common with countries such as Germany, Korea, and Armenia. What we are talking about more specifically is the role of Israel and its representatives in protecting, supporting, and "repatriating" southern Eurasia's residual Jewish population. Officially, Israeli diplomatic representations do not see this as their primary raison d'être in the region. "The priorities are fostering relationships with the countries, their states and general societies rather than specifically with the Jewish communities here," the Israeli ambassador to Kazakhstan and Kyrgyzstan stressed. "Of course, we maintain active ties with them and closely follow up on their situation and on Jewish life here. After all, Israel and the Jews here are culturally close. It's geographically relatively close to this region. And we are aware that a good image of Israel also positively affects the Jewish citizens here. But social support for the Jews in Kazakhstan and Kyrgyzstan is not among the core tasks of the embassy, and neither is the organization of emigration to Israel."[35]

Southern Eurasia's Contemporary Jewish Demography

According to the Berman Jewish Databank, in 2016 the *enlarged* Jewish population (see Table 6.3 and the remarks below it), in the five countries of southern Eurasia numbered around 15,900 people. At once, though, this number is contested. Representatives of Jewish organizations in Kazakhstan, for instance, claim that there are more than 50,000 Jews in the country alone.[36] Similarly, in Karaganda Province, the number of Jews who are registered with the provincial Jewish association amount to some 1,300, whereas the actual number is believed to be around 4,000.[37] The figure cited for Kyrgyzstan to this author during personal contacts and interviews ranged from 200 or 250 to around 1,500.[38]

In general, figures starkly differ depending on whether they are provided by the synagogues (who usually only count the actively practicing Judaist congregation), by the national Jewish associations (who also count in the larger secular Jewish population), and by the Tashkent and Almaty branches of the Jewish Agency for Israel (who rather focus on the population eligible for "repatriation" to Israel).[39]

There is allegedly a quite high number of so-called *skrytie yevrei* or "hidden Jews," people who do self-identify as being (partly) Jewish and as personally connected to Jewish culture, but who prefer, for various personal and social reasons, to say that they are a member of (usually) one of the Slavic minorities in censuses or in public life.[40] Some believe that there is interest in minimalizing the size and portion of minorities in general in the censuses. And in some of the region's countries, Jews are no longer listed as a separate nationality in the censuses and are categorized under the designation "others" instead.

Who are southern Eurasia's Jewish populations? The first and historically largest component is the Ashkenazi or Central and Eastern European Jews, to which the near-totality of Kazakhstan's and Kyrgyzstan's Jewish population belong. Originally using Yiddish as their lingua franca, they gradually became predominantly Russian speaking. It is at once also its most recently established population in the sense that its presence in any critical mass in the region goes back only a few generations. Confined since 1791 to the Pale of Settlement between the Baltic and the Black Sea, small numbers of Ashkenazi Jews did move into southern Eurasia either illegally or after the relaxation of movement restrictions for Jews between 1859 and 1880. The existence of a permanent Ashkenazi Jewish community in Verny, present-day Almaty, was reported as early as 1870. By 1897, there were also established Ashkenazi

Table 6.3 The Jewish population in Southern Eurasia in 2016 or Latest Year Available

	Core Jewish population (number of individuals)[1]	Enlarged Jewish population[2]		Total "Law of Return population" (number of individuals)[3]
		Number of individuals	Population share (in %)	
Kazakhstan	2,900	6,500	0.037	9,600
Kyrgyzstan	400	1,000	0.016	1,500
Uzbekistan	3,500	8,000	0.025	10,000
Tajikistan[4]	n/a	n/a	n/a	n/a
Turkmenistan	200	400	0.074	600
Regional total	7,400	15,900	0.023	21,700

Source: Author, March 2018, on the basis of figures from Sergio Della Pergola, "World Jewish Population 2016," Current Jewish Population Reports, Berman Jewish Databank 17 (2016): 58–59.
[1] Defined as "all persons who, when asked, identify themselves as Jews, or, if the respondent is a different person in the same household, are identified by him or her as Jews, and do not have another religion" as well as all persons "with a Jewish parent who claim no current religious or ethnic identity."
[2] Defined in Della Pergola, "World Jewish Population 2016," as "the sum of .... the core Jewish population; persons reported as partly Jewish; all others not currently Jewish with a Jewish parent; and all other non-Jewish household members (spouses, children [etc.])."
[3] Defined in Della Pergola, "World Jewish Population 2016," as "the sum of the core Jewish population, children and grandchildren of Jews and their respective spouses regardless of their Jewish identification," who are eligible for "return" to Israel. Israel's "Law of Return" gives Jews worldwide, as well as their non-Jewish kin, the right to come and live in Israel and to gain Israeli citizenship. It was adopted in summer 1950.
[4] According to the 2010 official population census of Tajikistan, the joint number of Ashkenazi and Central Asian Jews in the country that year amounted to thirty-six people. Non-official estimates informally shared with the author go up to ten times that number.

communities and synagogues in Semipalatinsk (Semei), Akmolinsk, and Tashkent.

The bulk of Ashkenazi settlement in southern Eurasia, however, took place during the previous century, through dynamics pretty much embedded in the general evolution and functioning of the USSR as a state and as a societal project. The 1928–1939 period, for example, saw the arrival of young Jewish pioneers and skilled workers (often from Belarus and Ukraine), Communist Party workers, and civil servants to help develop industries and large infrastructure during the first Five-Year Plan, especially in Kazakhstan and Tashkent. The number of Ashkenazi Jews in Kazakhstan thus increased fivefold from reportedly 3,600 in the year 1926 to 19,200 by 1939.[41] The Karaganda and Akmolinsk areas also received Jewish deportees and gulag inmates, a number of whom were charged with involvement in "nationalist-Zionist" activity and espionage. Not a few remained in the region even after serving their sentences.

Another contingent of European Ashkenazi Jews arrived especially in the Tashkent area and in various parts of Kazakhstan, Turkmenistan, and Kyrgyzstan after the invasion of the USSR by Germany and its allies in summer 1941. They came as evacuees from the occupied or threatened parts of the

Western USSR during 1941–1942.[42] Between summer 1941 and early 1942, for instance, some 24,000 evacuees arrived in Kazakhstan of which one-third were Jewish. Many more, among them a high percentage of children, women, skilled workers, and intelligentsia, were to follow. When the war ended, some Jewish evacuees returned to their places of origin. Others moved on from southern Eurasia to Israel, often via Iran. And yet others remained and settled in the region. In the postwar USSR, large-scale economic projects such as the Virgin Lands campaign (1954–1962), the outlay of new, multiethnic industrial towns, and the expansion of educational and social infrastructure, continued to attract various professionals and skilled workers and their families, among whom were Jews from Ukraine, the Baltics, and Belarus.

The second Jewish component in southern Eurasia consists of Oriental Jews who are native to the region or to certain sub-regions, in the sense that their presence there dates back well into the medieval period. The "Bukhara Jews," as they are better known, are of Judeo-Iranian descent and are historically concentrated in Uzbekistan and in Dushanbe, where jointly there are reportedly some 3,000 to 3,300 persons left. They predominantly speak a Judeo-Tajik dialect.[43] Third, there are residual populations, numbering no more than a few hundred, of (descendants of) non-Ashkenazi Jews who settled in the region during the postwar population transfers and through internal labor mobility in the USSR from the 1950s to 1980s. Examples are small groups of Caucasian "mountain Jews" and Crimean Karaite Jews in Kazakhstan and Turkmenistan.

Both the Ashkenazi and Oriental Jewish populations have always been predominantly city dwellers. Regional cities that had sizable Jewish populations back in 1989 included Tashkent, Samarkand, Alma-Ata (Almaty), Chimkent, and Dushanbe. In informal conversations, non-Jewish inhabitants of these cities with active memories of life in the USSR, often recall how local Jews invigorated cultural and intellectual life back then, adding to an urban diversity that has since been on the wane because of the departure of minorities and the influx of members of the titular majority from the provinces and the countryside. Another consequence of this ingrained Jewish presence in the region, dating back to times well before the coming into being of Israel, is, that in wider opinion, Jews are generally not equated with Israel or seen to be an extension of the latter. In society as well as by state bureaucracies, Jews are generally perceived as an ethnic and not a religious minority.

Israel and the Jews in Kazakhstan and Kyrgyzstan

When we take a closer look at the Jewish populations of Kazakhstan and Kyrgyzstan, eight social and cultural characteristics and dynamics come forward. To start with, the near-totality of the Jews in both Kazakhstan and

Kyrgyzstan are Ashkenazi Jews who speak Russian as their mother tongue. Although Yiddish is still present in Jewish folklore and in some slang, it is no longer a general idiom as it used to be a couple of generations ago. Second, in line with their historical settlement pattern in the region, the near-totality of the Jewish population is urban. In Kyrgyzstan, for example, over 90 percent live in the capital. In Kazakhstan, the largest group of Jews lives in Almaty. There are also populations in Karaganda (where three-quarters were said to live in Karaganda city itself and the rest in the province's smaller industrial cities),[44] Chimkent, and some of the northern cities such as Semipalatinsk and Pavlodar.

Third, although there are officially no population pyramids for minorities, on the basis of the author's own observations and what was reported by respondents, we see that due to both birth rates and substantial emigration, the share of pensioners is higher than the national average and, certainly, than the share of pensioners among both the titular Muslim majorities and the Muslim minorities. This does not mean that there is no base of youth and young adults left. There certainly is. But in general, the average age is rather high. Fourth, professionally, most Jews in Kazakhstan and Kyrgyzstan belong to an urban middle class, if not sociologically then at least in terms of self-identification. Many hold higher education degrees. And those who are professionally active are usually so in management either of their own company or in an office of a foreign private company, in trade, accounting, in the so-called liberal professions such as physicians and dentists, in the educational sector (although in Kyrgyzstan reportedly less so than before), and sometimes in regional offices of international development organizations (though in Kyrgyzstan, again, reportedly less so than seven to ten years ago).[45]

Unlike, for example, Uyghurs and Koreans who are prominently present in specialized agriculture and food production, technical professions, or sections of the bazaar economy, there are no specific economic sectors where Jews hold a dominant position. Few are government civil servants because Jews, like other minorities, usually do not have the patronage and family networks necessary to obtain government positions. Fifth, as was also already the case in the USSR, there is a very high degree of intermarriage between Jews and other ethnicities. In 1993, the percentage of children born from a Jewish mother and non-Jewish father in Kazakhstan and Kyrgyzstan was 65.2 and 47.1 percent, respectively.[46] According to respondents, "over 90 percent" of the Jewish families in Kazakhstan and Kyrgyzstan are, to one or another extent, mixed or of mixed ancestry and, as such, demographically, culturally, and psychologically closely intertwined with other ethnicities, especially the Slavic groups (and, more rarely, with the titular majorities).[47]

Sixth comes the level and nature of social organization of the said communities. In Kazakhstan, at the time of research there were reportedly some twenty local Jewish ethnic-cultural associations which resort under Mitvsa, the national Jewish umbrella organization which liaises with the authorities and formally represents the Jewish minority at official occasions. In Kyrgyzstan, the Jewish cultural center Menorah has a similar function. There are a couple of private Jewish schools in both countries, which are not exclusively reserved for Jewish pupils. A very important component of social organization are the Jewish social welfare centers or Hesed, of which there were, again at the time of research, thirteen in Kazakhstan and one in Kyrgyzstan.[48] Mostly run by volunteers, and some professional staff, the Hesed (which is Hebrew for "compassion") provide winter relief, medical assistance, food parcels, and other social and humanitarian support to Jewish pensioners and impoverished families.

The main external supporter of these, and the main provider of humanitarian assistance to Jews in the region, is not the Israeli government, but the American-Jewish Joint Distribution Committee (JDC). Globally one of the largest Jewish nongovernmental humanitarian organizations, the JDC was founded in the United States (where it is still based) in the fall of 1914 to organize humanitarian assistance and, later, agricultural development support to Jewish settlements in Palestine, Ukraine, Belarus, Russia, and the Crimea. It still focuses on humanitarian assistance and welfare and social support to precarious or impoverished Jewish populations in the former Soviet Union (a region which was allocated 43.7 percent of its 299 million USD global operations budget in 2016), in Israel (30.5 %), and in Central and Eastern Europe (15%).[49] In Karaganda province, for example, 381 people, mostly pensioners, receive assistance from a JDC-supported Hesed. In Aqmola Province, the number of recipients at time of research was ninety-six.[50] The Hesed in Bishkek also received JDC support at the time of research.

Seventh, in terms of primary identification, most self-identify as Jews or as Kazakhstani or Kyrgyzstani citizens of Jewish ethnicity.[51] Jewish identity is largely understood in a secular way, shaped as it is by ancestry and genealogy, a large extent of assimilation in the secular pan-Soviet culture in the USSR, a high degree of intermarriage with mostly Slavic groups, and the attribution, both by the in-group, by others, and by popular lore, of a number of specific Jewish social characteristics, such as urbanity, high levels of education, a certain pattern of leisure activities and lifestyle, with a tendency toward a particular kind of humor and nonconformity, prominence in scientific and artistic life, and diminishing presence in official life.[52] The post-1991 exposure to Jewish and Judaist influences from beyond the former USSR and from Israel and the United States in particular, reinvigorated or added layers to the relevant population's identity patterns.

Although the portion of Jews in Kazakhstan and Kyrgyzstan who regularly and actively practice Judaism and especially its more orthodox interpretation, is rather small, a clear increase in religiosity has been observed since 1991, similar to what has been happening in the Muslim and Christian parts of society. There are two synagogues in Almaty and one each in Karaganda, Pavlodar, Bishkek, and some other cities. The synagogue—one of the few generally visible and tangible signs of Jewish presence—and Judaist traditions and holidays, are claimed to be important for Jewish identity, community life, and community symbolism.[53] Contrary to what some may think, Judaist religious infrastructure and confessional life in the countries of interest are not sponsored and organized by Israel's chief rabbinate or religious affairs ministry.

Instead, almost all synagogues in Kazakhstan and Kyrgyzstan were built or refurbished with support of business philanthropists and ethnic entrepreneurs. A prominent example is the Kazakhstani metallurgy, mining, and banking magnate and philanthropist Alexander Mashkevich. Born in what is now Bishkek and having started his ascension in business from Pavlodar, Mashkevich's net worth at the time of research was estimated at 2.3 billion USD, the eleventh largest fortune in Israel where he both resides and also holds citizenship.[54] He is an active supporter of Jewish communities and causes in Kazakhstan and Kyrgyzstan, and funded the construction of half a dozen synagogues, charitable activities, and Jewish schools in the two countries. Mashkevich seems to be a unique case, however, in the sense that there are no other Jewish businessmen from the region who offer similarly substantial support to their community, apart from some ad hoc charity by local Jewish entrepreneurs or by Jewish business expatriates either from Israel or from other former Soviet countries.[55] The maintenance of the central synagogue building in Almaty, for example, is partly funded by a group of local Jewish building contractors.[56]

Furthermore, all except one of the synagogues in both Kazakhstan and Kyrgyzstan are headed by rabbis belonging to the Chabad-Lubavitch movement. This movement, which originated in Belarus but has been based in the United States since 1940, is globally the largest orthodox Hasidic-Judaist movement. It is very active in trying to reinvigorate Judaist consciousness and practice among the Jewish populations in the former USSR. As such, it has a section in Kyrgyzstan and four in Kazakhstan, where Chabad rabbis head all of the synagogues except one, as well as the country's chief rabbinate.[57] Most Chabad rabbis are emissaries from abroad. The rabbi of the Karaganda synagogue, for example, is from Odessa.[58] The movement's presence and the position it holds in Judaist religious life in the region is not uncontroversial among local Jews themselves. Yet in general, the way in which Chabad and its emissaries try to inform and steer Judaist religious practice objectively bears similarity to the way emissaries of extraneous Islamic movements such as the Fethullah Gülen movement and the Salafists, for example, try (or tried) to inform and steer the renewed Islamic consciousness among parts of the southern Eurasian Muslim populations.[59]

The eighth and final point, in terms of community characteristics, is that a large majority of the Jews in Kazakhstan and Kyrgyzstan have first- and second-degree relatives in Israel.[60] In Kazakhstan in general, according to one respondent, the share of Jewish families with relatives in Israel amounts to 65 to 70 percent.[61] In Karaganda, about four-fifths of the twenty or so participants in the group discussions confirmed they had Israeli-based relatives.[62] This is, of course, the outcome of several waves of Jewish emigration to Israel. Southern Eurasia's current enlarged Jewish population is one-ninth of the size of 137,950 that it had in 1989 and one-twelfth of the 197,700 Jews who reportedly lived in the region in 1970.[63] Between 1970 and 2009, some 1.92 million Jews left the USSR and its successor states for Israel, the United States, and Western-Central Europe (especially to German-speaking countries), with peaks in 1971–1978 and 1989–1999.[64]

Confronted, as Jews and other minorities were, with the unraveling or collapse of the social-educational institutions and industries where many were employed, uncertain about their socioeconomic position in the successor states, and also concerned that unrest like the Tajik civil war might spill over to the rest of region, the post-1989 migration phase was primarily socioeconomically driven. Moreover, Jews, like the region's ethnic Germans, also had a beacon state with an active "repatriation" policy as well as kin who had already emigrated there in the 1970s. Table 6.4 below offers an overview of Jewish emigration from southern Eurasia to Israel, the United States, and Germany (or West Germany before 1990). As we can see, the large majority

Table 6.4 Jewish Emigration from Southern Eurasia and its Destinations 1959–2006 (in Number of Persons)[1]

	Israel			US		Germany
	1959–1978	1979–1989	1990–2006	1979–1989	1990–2005	1989–2001
Kazakhstan	600	200	19,700	200	2,100	1,500
Uzbekistan	11,300	4,900	82,100	6,300	24,800	2,100
Kyrgyzstan	100	100	5,300	100	400	800
Tajikistan	2,200	900	10,700	600	3,000	100
Turkmenistan	100	–	2,700	–	300	100

Source: Author, April 2018, on the basis of Vyacheslav Konstantinov. *Yevreiskoe naselenie byvshego SSSR v XX veke—sotsial'no-demograficheskii analiz*. Jerusalem: Lira, 2007, 272.

[1] Present day states or the corresponding constituent Soviet republic prior to 1991.

[2] No breakdown per destination available, although it can be assumed that the majority went to Israel, at least until 1975–76. See Toltz, "Yevreiskaya emigratsia iz byvshego SSR," Table 1; Fred A. Lazin, "Refugee Resettlement and 'Freedom of Choice': The Case of Soviet Jewry," (report, Backgrounder, Center for Immigration Sudies, Washington DC, 2005).

of the Jews who emigrated from Kazakhstan and Kyrgyzstan in the 1990–2006 period went to Israel.

Much has been written about the motives and the push and pull factors behind the Soviet and post-Soviet Aliyah movements.[65] The most important to retain is that the different migration waves resulted in a strong transnationalization of Soviet and former Soviet Jewry, including that from southern Eurasia. The interpersonal ties and contacts which resulted from this, eased and intensified by the proliferation of low-cost communication technology, created what is by far the main channel of interaction between Israel-as-a-society and southern Eurasia's residual Jewish populations and à priori their non-Jewish in-laws and relatives. It brings what happens in Israel in the political-security sphere but also in the field of popular culture on the mental map among southern Eurasia's Jewish population.

Connecting back to Israel, one institution which is actively involved in diaspora policy and in emigration to Israel, more so than the embassy itself, is the Jewish Agency for Israel. Founded as an arm of World Zionist Organization in 1929 to support Jewish immigration to what was then Mandate Palestine, it is now an autonomous, parastatal Israeli agency based in Jerusalem. Its global income in 2016 was 449 million USD, not funded from the Israeli state budget but by private donations (much from the Jews in the United States), grants (particularly from the U.S. government), and self-generated income. The agency's core activities focus on fostering and strengthening ties between the Jewish diaspora and Israel, the organization of Jewish education and Hebrew language courses outside Israel, and offering practical support to Jews outside Israel who want to do Aliyah.[66]

The agency's branch in Almaty, which is accountable to its regional headquarters in Tashkent and as well as Kazakhstan also covers Kyrgyzstan, is registered as a local NGO and operates independently from the Israeli embassy. There also used to be branches in Karaganda, Ust-Kamenogorsk (Öskemen), and a couple of other places, but with the stagnation of the number of departures for Israel as compared to ten or fifteen years ago, these have now been closed. All applicants for Aliyah now have to go through the Almaty office.[67] Aliyah emigration from Kazakhstan and Kyrgyzstan has indeed been over its zenith for a number of years now, although flare-ups could be observed after the unrest in southern Kyrgyzstan in Spring 2010 and during the financial crisis and oil price slump that affected Kazakhstan.[68]

To conclude this section, we will examine a couple of relevant factors related to the way the interaction with Israel impacts the identity and the position in society of the Jews in Kazakhstan.

One important aspect of a diaspora paradigm which can translate into soft power is the presence of a remittance economy—in this case the Israeli citizens who immigrated from Kazakhstan and Kyrgyzstan that send money to relatives in the country of origin. According to available open source data, in 2016, Kazakhstan reportedly received 1 million USD of remittances from Israel, and Kyrgyzstan 8 million USD, which is actually quite limited as compared to other countries.[69] Remittances were, in any case, not claimed to be a survival line by most of the people questioned about this, especially not in Kazakhstan, where living conditions and social support were said to be sufficient.[70]

And then there are the movements of returnees. In Kazakhstan, for instance, reportedly, about 10 percent of the Jews or non-Jewish kin who immigrated to Israel return to the country either for certain periods or definitively, to care for elderly or dependent parents who stayed behind, because of difficulties with social adaptation in Israel, or to do business and invest.[71] The question is if, and to what extent, the cultural changes and societal experiences they went through in Israel will leave an impact among local Jews. Contrary to the first-generation Jewish immigrants from the former USSR, in Israel, for example, there is apparently a stronger religiosity among the second generation, where 60 percent claims to be Hiloni or secular as compared to 81 percent among the first-generation immigrants, and where 14 percent now identifies as Haredi or orthodox Jews as compared to 4 percent among the first generation.[72] Whether returnees will contribute to a stronger religiosity and Judaist identity remains to be seen.

CONCLUDING REMARKS

Having observed and examined all this, and coming back to the definition of *soft power* used as a departure point for this book—the ability to shape the preferences of others and to affect others to obtain the outcomes one wants through attraction rather than coercion or payment—how to characterize Israel in this regard? Do we have a case of extensive soft power at all, or, rather, a classical policy of bilateral interaction and influence, with elements of soft power contained in it? The key question is what Israel wants, in and from the region. Israel as an entity is a key component and beacon state of a cultural-civilizational sphere. But, at least in southern Eurasia, it does not seek to propagate or win converts for that culture and civilization among non-Jews, nor promote a specific societal-developmental model among overall society, starting with its elites and opinion makers.

It rather seeks to create goodwill and mobilize support in a peculiar part of the wider Islamic realm so as to enhance its own legitimacy and hence survival. Another important driving factor is to secure hydrocarbon resources, and boost trade and hence opportunities for the Israeli private sector and economy. Israel's representatives thereby highlight and promote a number of the country's achievements in agricultural development, agro-industry, technology, and health care, as well as promote an image of Israel as a society where social, cultural, and creative life continues to function and blossom, despite being situated in a hostile and very turbulent region. But Israel's official soft power approach is certainly not as extensive and multidimensional as that of the United States, Russia, or the European Union, and its individual core member countries such as Germany and France, or even of some of the Gulf countries.

Israeli diplomats and government representatives follow up closely on the state of the Jews living in southern Eurasia and actively maintain contacts with them. Social support and attempts to reinvigorate Jewish and Judaist life and an identification with Israel, however, come from a range of actors and channels from the wider Jewish sphere. Most important, the interaction between the Jewish population of southern Eurasia (in this case Kazakhstan and Kyrgyzstan) and Israel, occurs through interpersonal and family-based diaspora networks, and is oriented toward Israel-as-a-society rather than Israel-as-a-state. Material and political support for the Jewish minorities and its social institutions in Kazakhstan and Kyrgyzstan largely comes from regional business philanthropists, U.S.-based Jewish aid agencies and movements, and from Israeli parastatal organizations, rather than from the Israeli government and its representatives. What eventually comes up then is an interaction pattern between southern Eurasia and the Jewish world in which Israel is an important component, but not the sole linchpin.

NOTES

1. Joseph S. Nye Jr., "Public Diplomacy and Soft Power," *The Annals of the American Academy of Political and Social Science* 616, no. 1 (2008): 94–97.

2. The author wishes to thank Marie Skłodowska-Curie CASPIAN Research Fellow Maira Zeinilova for the useful suggestions and contacts; Irina Kozhanovskaya of the Shemesh Jewish cultural center for organizing the group discussions in Karaganda; Arkady Divinsky for his kind advice, and to all who were willing to share their insights and experiences.

3. My interest in the Jewish history of the former USSR came up while researching a short article on the attempts, during the early Soviet period, to establish Jewish autonomy in the Crimean peninsula. Bruno De Cordier, "Un 'Israël soviétique' en Mer noire," *Les Courrier du Maghreb et de l'Orient* 4, no. 3 (2017), https://lecourr ierdumaghrebetdelorient.info/israel/israel-un-israel-sovietique-en-mer-noire

4. For sources and various views on this, see Schlomo Sand, "Comment fut inventé le peuple juif," *Le Monde diplomatique* 8 (2008): 3, https://www.monde -diplomatique.fr/2008/08/SAND/16205. The book, especially its fourth chapter, by the same author, Schlomo Sand, *The Invention of the Jewish People* (London: Verso,

2009); and Shaul Stampfer, "Did the Khazars Convert to Judaism?" *Jewish Social Studies* 19, no. 3 (2013): 1–72.

5. Marcel Mauss, "Les civilisations: éléments et formes," Les classiques des sciences sociales, *CÉGEP–Université du Québec*: 10-12, classiques.uqac.ca/classiques/mauss_marcel/oeuvres_2/oeuvres_2_13/les_civilisations.html.

6. The term "beacon state" (*État-phare*) comes from Hugues de Jouvenel and Geoffrey Delcroix, "Le choc des identités? Cultures, civilisations et conflits de demain," *Futuribles—Perspectives* (2008): 11.

7. Shmuel Sandler, 'Toward a Theory of World Jewish Politics and Jewish Foreign Policy," *Hebraic Political Studies* 2, no. 3 (2007): 331–52.

8. Robert Frank, "Religion(s): enjeux internationaux et diplomatie religieuse," in *Pour l'histoire des relations internationals*, ed. Robert Frank, (Paris: Presses Universitaires de France—Le nœud gordien, 2012): 421–22.

9. Sandler, "Toward a Theory of World Jewish Politics."

10. Jean-Loup Samaan, "Israël et l'Eurasie: le retour de la doctrine de la périphérie?" *Géoéconomie* 72, no. 5 (2014): 139–41; Vladimir Mesamed, *Izrail v Tsentralnoi Azii: grezy i realnost* (Moscow: Institut Blizhnego Vostoka, 2012), 28; and Pierre Razoux, "Quel avenir pour le couple Turquie-Israël?" *Politique étrangère* 1 (2010): 25–39.

11. Ilan Zvi Baron, "The Contradictions of Diaspora: A Reflexive Critique of the Jewish Diaspora's Relationship with Israel," *Journal of International Political Theory* 14, no. 1 (2018): 95. For perceptions of Israel in the diaspora, in this case American Jewry, see "A Portrait of Jewish Americans," *Pew Research Center*, 2013. Especially Chapter 5: "Connection with and Attitudes toward Israel," www.pewforum.org/2013/10/01/chapter-5-connection-with-and-attitudes-towards-israel/.

12. There are probably over twice as many Armenians or people of Armenian descent in the diaspora (the largest groups residing in Russia, the United States, and Lebanon, as well as in France and other parts of the European Union) than the some 3.25 million in the Armenian ethnographic concentration areas in the southern Caucasus. Consisting of a formerly Ottoman and a more recently-formed formerly Soviet Armenian diasporas, there has been no massive "repatriation" policy to the two Armenian entities (or declared entities) of Armenia and Nagorno-Karabakh, even if Armenia has been taking in ethnic-Armenian refugees from Aleppo since 2011. Both diasporas, however, form a considerable lifeline in terms of aid, investment and remittances. The maintenance of historical memory and collective identity and policy priorities in Armenia often collide with those propagated by the former Ottoman Armenian diaspora. See Martine Hovanessian, "Diaspora arménienne et patrimonialisation d'une mémoire collective: l'impossible lieu du témoignage?" *Les Cahiers de FRAMESPA—Nouveaux champs de l'histoire sociale* 3, Patrimoine et immigration (2007), journals.openedition.org/framespa/314.

13. The promotion of Israel as an open and dynamic society has its limits in this region, however. Highlighting an issue like the liberal climate towards homosexuality and sexual minorities in Israel, as is regularly done in public relations efforts to improve Israel's image in Western Europe for example, would actually have a totally opposite effect in much of southern Eurasia.

14. Interview with Michael Brodsky, ambassador of Israel to Kazakhstan and Kyrgyzstan, Astana, April 10, 2018, and the author's verification of local online press coverage in Russian on these events.

15. "Development Co-operation Report 2017: Data for Development" (report, Organization for Economic Cooperation and Development, Paris, 2017), 289–90.

16. "ODA Disbursements to Countries and Regions," *OECD stats database*, https://stats.oecd.org.

17. MASHAV was founded in late 1957 as a division of the Israeli foreign ministry. Its name is a Hebrew acronym for "Centre for International Development Cooperation," the agency's official name. "About MASHAV: Guiding Principles," MASHAV—Israel's Agency for International Development Cooperation, https://mfa.gov.il/mfa/mashav/aboutmashav/pages/guiding_principles.aspx, accessed June 24, 2020.

18. Interview with Michael Brodsky, ambassador of Israel to Kazakhstan and Kyrgyzstan, Astana, April 10, 2018.

19. Author's analysis of the annual reports available at "Publications: Annual Reports," MASHAV—Israel's Agency for International Development Cooperation, https://mfa.gov.il/mfa/mashav/publications/annual_reports/pages/default.aspx.

20. Interview with Michael Brodsky, ambassador of Israel to Kazakhstan and Kyrgyzstan, Astana, April 10, 2018.

21. Ibid.; "MASHAV: About MASHAV," *Israeli Embassy to Kazakhstan*, https://embassies.gov.il/astana/departments/mashav/pages/aboutmashava.aspx, accessed June 24, 2020.

22. "Resolution adopted by the General Assembly—no. 43/177, Question of Palestine," General Assembly of the United Nations, A/RES/43/177, December 15, 1988, *UNISPAL*, https://unispal.un.org/DPA/DPR/unispal.nsf/0/146E6838D505833 F852560D600471E25; "Resolution adopted by the General Assembly—no. 67/19, Status of Palestine in the United Nations," General Assembly of the United Nations, A/RES/67/19, December 4, 2012, *UNISPAL*, https://unispal.un.org/DPA/DPR/unispal.nsf/0/19862D03C564FA2C85257ACB004EE69B.

23. Michael Bishku, "The Relations of the Central Asian Republics of Kazakhstan and Uzbekistan with Israel," *Journal of Middle Eastern Studies* 48, no. 6 (2012): 928. Region-wise, Israel currently has embassies in Kazakhstan, Uzbekistan, and Turkmenistan.

24. Group discussion with members of Karaganda's Jewish community at the Shemesh Jewish cultural center, Karaganda, April 11, 2018, and interview with Vladimir Kritsman, chairman of the Menorah Jewish cultural center, Bishkek, April 30, 2018.

25. Interview with Michael Brodsky, ambassador of Israel to Kazakhstan and Kyrgyzstan, Astana, April 10, 2018.

26. Gil Feiler and Kevjin Lim, "Israel and Kazakhstan: Assessing the State of Bilateral Relations," (report, Mideast Security and Policy Studies no.107, The Begin-Sadat Center for Strategic Studies, Bar Ilan University, Ramat Gan, 2014), 24–28.

27. Ruzanna Avestisian, "Faktor Kazakhstana v israilskoi vneshnei politiki v Tsentralnoi Azii", *Teoria i praktika obshestvennogo razvitie*, no. 8 (2011): 279.

28. Feiler and Lim, "Israel and Kazakhstan," 28; Yulia Mager, "Kazakhstan-Izrail: po puti diversifikatsii dyelovogo partnyorstva," *Kazakhstanskaya Pravda*, December 15, 2016, www.kazpravda.kz/articles/view/kazahstan--izrail--po-puti-diversifikatsii-delovogo-partnerstva; "Kazakhstansko-Izrailskie otnosheniya (spravka)," *Embassy of Kazakhstan to Israel* (2017), 3. By comparison, in early 2016, there were officially 5,800 Russian, 1,600 Turkish, 845 German, 429 Korean, and 164 Iranian companies, or companies with capital participation from these respective economies, operating in Kazakhstan. Alibi Sarwar, "Skolko innostrannykh kompanii rabotayut v Kazakhstane—infografika," *LS News*, January 25, 2016, https://lsm.kz/skol-ko-inostrannyh-kompanij-rabotaet-v-kazahstane-infografika.

29. These figures are drawn variously from The World Integrated System Database, The World Bank Group, and UNCTAD.

30. John Reed, "Israel turns to Kurds for three-quarters of its Oil Supplies," *The Financial Times*, August 23, 2015, www.ft.com/content/150f00cc-472c-11e5-af2f-4d6e0e5eda22.

31. Feiler and Lim, 26.

32. Author's analysis of data from the World Integrated System Database, The World Bank Group, and UNCTAD, wits.worldbank.org and Feiler and Lim, 31–33. The active role of Israeli companies and investors in the agricultural sector can also bring up an image issue at some point, namely the participation of Israeli companies and investors in the purchase of land, as some Israeli investors did in Ukraine and Russia for example. Seen Oane Visser and Max Spoor, "Land Grabbing in post-Soviet Eurasia: The World's Largest Agricultural Land Reserves at Stake," *Journal of Peasant Studies* 38, no. 2 (2011): 302–303). A very sensitive and explosive issue both in politics and society, land sales affected the image of not a few investor countries.

33. Feiler and Lim, 29; Interview with Michael Brodsky, ambassador of Israel to Kazakhstan and Kyrgyzstan, Astana, April 10, 2018.

34. Elena Tumashova, "Kak Israilskie kompanii vnyedryayut 'zelyonie' tekhnologii," *Kapital* May 9, 2017, https://kapital.kz/business/59523/kak-izrailskie-kompanii-vnedryayut-zelenye-tehnologii.html.

35. Interview with Michael Brodsky, ambassador of Israel to Kazakhstan and Kyrgyzstan, Astana, April 10, 2018.

36. Communication with Alexander Baron, chairman of the Mitsva association of Jewish organizations in Kazakhstan, Almaty, March 13, 2018.

37. Personal communication with Irina Kozhanovskaya, director of the Shemesh Jewish cultural center, Karaganda, April 11, 2018.

38. Personal communication with Daniel Vainerman, Bishkek, May 11, 2018; Interview with Vladimir Kritsman, chairman of the Menorah Jewish cultural center, Bishkek, April 30, 2018.

39. Interview with Anastassiya Borovikova, Jewish Agency for Israel—Kazakhstan office, Almaty, May 7, 2018.

40. Apart from some incidents with an anti-Semitic undertone, Jews, Jewish properties, and Judaist infrastructure were not specifically targeted during past unrest in the region like the Jeltoqsan riots in Alma-Ata (1986), the communal-ethnic unrest in Novii Uzen (1989) and in Uzgen (1988–90), the Tajik Civil War (1991–97, with

sporadic localized flare-ups until 2001), and the violent uprising in Kyrgyzstan in spring 2010 and the subsequent ethnic-communal unrest in the south of the country. Nonetheless, there is somehow an unease among the remaining Jews that this can rapidly change during future unrest in the region.

41. For data and in-depth discussions of the place and share of Jews (or at least of persons of Jewish origins) in Soviet governance and Communist Party structures, see Benjamin Pinkus, *The Jews of the Soviet Union: The History of a National Minority* (Cambridge and New York: Cambridge University Press, 1988), 235; Benjamin Pinkus, *The Soviet Government and the Jews (1948–67): A Documented Study* (Cambridge and New York: Cambridge University Press, 1984), 341–63, Everett M. Jacobs, "A Note on Jewish Membership of the Soviet Communist Party," *Soviet Jewish Affairs* 6, no. 2 (1976): 114–15; Vyacheslav Konstantinov, *Yevreiskoe naselenie byvshego SSSR v XX veke—sotsial'no-demograficheskii analiz* (Jerusalem: Lira, 2007), 238–48. During the prewar Stalinist period, the party branches of the Kazakh (one, 1925–33), Kyrgyz (one, 1933–37), Tajik (one, 1933–34), and Turkmen (three, 1928–37) SSR had first secretaries of Jewish origin. By 1976, persons of Jewish nationality formed the sixth-largest (and eleventh-largest population-wise) group among the membership of the Communist Party of the USSR, although shares varied considerably per republic and at one time only exceeded the Jewish population shares in the Kazakh and Turkmen SSR.

42. Evguéni V. Abdullaev, "Les Juifs ashkénazes d'Ouzbékistan," *Cahiers d'Asie centrale* 15–16 (2007): 307–21.

43. Cathérine Poujol, "Juifs boukhariotes en Asie centrale: fin de partie," *Revue Regard sur l'Est,* Dossier no. 58, Le renouveau du monde juif en Europe centrale et orientale (2011), http://www.regard-est.com/home/breve_contenu.php?id=1234.

44. Group discussion at the Shemesh Jewish cultural center, Karaganda, April 11, 2018; Interview with Vladimir Kritsman, chairman of the Menorah Jewish cultural center, Bishkek, April 30, 2018.

45. Ibid.

46. Konstantinov, "Yevreiskoe naselenie byvshego SSSR v XX veke," 52; 71. See especially Table 2.11.

47. Group discussion at the Shemesh Jewish cultural center, Karaganda, April 11, 2018; Interview with Vladimir Kritsman, chairman of the Menorah Jewish cultural center, Bishkek, April 30, 2018; Interview with Anastassiya Borovikova, Jewish Agency for Israel, Kazakhstan office, Almaty, May 7, 2018.

48. Communication from Alexander Baron, chairman of the Mitsva association of Jewish organizations in Kazakhstan, Almaty, March 13, 2018; Interview with Vladimir Kritsman, chairman of the Menorah Jewish cultural center, Bishkek, April 30, 2018.

49. American-Jewish Joint Distribution Committee, "JDC on the Frontlines: 2016–17 Annual Report," (report American-Jewish Joint Distribution Committee), 28–90, www.jdc.org/wp-content/uploads/2017/10/ar_2017.pdf.

50. Personal communication by Irina Kozhanovskaya, director of the Shemesh Jewish cultural center, Karaganda, April 11, 2018.

51. Group discussion at the Shemesh Jewish cultural center, Karaganda, April 11, 2018; Interview with Vladimir Kritsman, chairman of the Menorah Jewish cultural center, Bishkek, April 30, 2018.

52. See Igor Krupnik, "Soviet Cultural and Ethnic Policies towards Jews: A Legacy Reassessed," in *Jews and Jewish life in Russia and the Soviet Union*, ed. Yaacov Ro'i (London: Frank Cass, 1995), 78–80; Zvi Gitelman, 'The Evolution of Jewish Culture and Identity in the Soviet Union," in *Jewish Culture and Identity in the Soviet Union, ed.* Yaacov Ro'i and Avi Beker (New York: New York University Press, 1991), 10–17.

53. Group discussion at the Shemesh Jewish cultural center, Karaganda, April 11, 2018; Interview with Vladimir Kritsman, chairman of the Menorah Jewish cultural center, Bishkek, April 30, 2018; Personal communication with Daniel Vainerman, Bishkek, May 11,2018.

54. For updated data, see Alexander Mashkevich's Forbes profile, www.forbes.com/profile/alexander-machkevich, last accessed June 29, 2020. For more on the position and role of Jews in late- and post-Soviet business circles, see Marshall I. Goldman, "Russian Jews in Business," in *Jewish Life after the USSR*, ed. Zvi Gitelman, Musya Glants, and Marshall I. Goldman (Bloomington and Indianapolis: Indiana University Press, 2003), 76–98.

55. Group discussion at the Shemesh Jewish cultural center, Karaganda, April 11, 2018; Interview with Vladimir Kritsman, chairman of the Menorah Jewish cultural center, Bishkek, April 30, 2018.

56. Interview with Anastassiya Borovikova, Jewish Agency for Israel, Kazakhstan office, Almaty, May 7, 2018.

57. See Chabad Lubavitch, Kazakhstan at www.chabad.kz.

58. Personal communication at the Shemesh Jewish cultural center, Karaganda, April 11, 2018. The author's attempts to contact the Chabad leadership in Kazakhstan during the period of research were unsuccessful.

59. For an examination of how Western-based Jewish organizations try to reconstruct and model a Jewish life in the former USSR, see Sara Brachman Shoup, "From Leadership to Community: Laying the Foundations for Jewish Community in Russia," in *Jewish Life after the USSR*, ed. Zvi Gitelman, Musya Glants, and Marshall I. Goldman (Bloomington and Indianapolis: Indiana University Press, 2003): 127–40.

60. For an in-depth study on settlement patterns among Jews from the former USSR in Israel, see William Berthomière, "L'Aliya d'ex-URSS: repères démogéographiques sur une décennie d'immigration," *Bulletin du Centre de recherche français à Jérusalem* 8 (2001): 86–120, openedition.org/bcrfj/2152.

61. Interview with Anastassiya Borovikova, Jewish Agency for Israel, Kazakhstan office, Almaty, May 7, 2018.

62. Group discussion at the Shemesh Jewish cultural center, Karaganda, April 11, 2018.

63. "Vsyesoyuznaya perepis' naseleniya 1989 goda. Natsional,nii sostav po respublikam SSSR" *Demoscope* 753–54, 2017, www.demoscope.ru/weekly/ssp/sng_nac_89.php?reg=7.

64. Mark Toltz, "Yevreiskaya emigratsia iz byvshego SSR c 1970 goda sostavila pochti 2 milliona chelovyek," *Demoscope* 479–98, 2012, www.demoscope.ru/weekly/2012/0497/tema01.php

65. See, for instance, William Berthomière, "L'immigration des Juifs d'ex-URSS : un nouveau défi pour Israël ?" *Revue Européenne des Migrations Internationales* 11, no. 3 (1995): 19–41; Anatoli Vichnevski and Jeanne Zayontchkovskaia, "L'émigration de l'ex-Union soviétique : prémices et inconnues," *Revue Européenne des Migrations Internationales* 8, no. 1 (1992): 41–65.

66. *Aliyah* (Hebrew for "ascension") is the immigration of Jews from the diaspora to Israel.

67. "Every one of us, together—Performance Report 2016-17," (report, The Jewish Agency for Israel, 2017) 6–7, http://lln-websites.com/pdf/performance_report/files/downloads/performance_report_2016-2017.pdf , "Financial Report 2016," (report, The Jewish Agency for Israel, 2017), 9, http://www.jewishagency.org/sites/default/files/2016_financial_report.pdf; Interview with Anastassiya Borovikova, Jewish Agency for Israel, Kazakhstan office, Almaty, May 7, 2018.

68. Interview with Anastassiya Borovikova, Jewish Agency for Israel, Kazakhstan office, Almaty, May 7, 2018.

69. By comparison, Kazakhstan received 175 million USD of remittances from Russia and Kyrgyzstan 1.53 billion USD that same year. The reported total of remittances from Israel to the rest of the world was 2.7 billion USD. "Migration Remittances Data," *The World Bank Group*, www.worldbank.org/en/topic/migrationremittancesdiasporaissues/brief/migration-remittances-data, accessed June 24, 2020.

70. Group discussion with members of Karaganda's Jewish community at the Shemesh Jewish cultural center, Karaganda, April 11, 2018. Interview with Vladimir Kritsman, chairman of the Menorah Jewish cultural center, Bishkek, April 30, 2018.

71. Interview with Anastassiya Borovikova, Jewish Agency for Israel, Kazakhstan office, Almaty, May 7, 2018.

72. "Israel's Religiously Divided Society," (Pew Forum on Religion and Public Life, Pew Research Center, Washington DC, March 8, 2016), 105, www.pewforum.org/2016/03/08/israels-religiously-divided-society.

REFERENCES

Abdullaev, Evguéni V. "Les Juifs ashkénazes d'Ouzbékistan." *Cahiers d'Asie centrale* 15–16 (2007): 307–21.

Avestisian, Ruzanna. "Faktor Kazakhstana v israilskoi vneshnei politiki v Tsentralnoi Azii," *Teoria i praktika obshestvennogo razvitie*, no. 8, 2011.

Baron, Ilan Zvi. "The Contradictions of Diaspora: A Reflexive Critique of the Jewish Diaspora's Relationship with Israel." *Journal of International Political Theory* 14, no. 1 (2018): 85–106.

Berthomière, William. "L'Aliya d'ex-URSS: repères démo-géographiques sur une décennie d'immigration." *Bulletin du Centre de recherche français à Jérusalem* 8 (2001): 86–120, openedition.org/bcrfj/2152.

Berthomière, William. "L'immigration des Juifs d'ex-URSS: un nouveau défi pour Israël?" *Revue Européenne des Migrations Internationales* 11, no. 3 (1995): 19–41.

Bishku, Michael. "The Relations of the Central Asian Republics of Kazakhstan and Uzbekistan with Israel." *Journal of Middle Eastern Studies* 48, no. 6 (2012): 927–40.
Brachman Shoup, Sara. "From Leadership to Community: Laying the Foundations for Jewish Community in Russia." In *Jewish Life after the USSR*, edited by Zvi Gitelman, Musya Glants, and Marshall I. Goldman, 127–40. Bloomington and Indianapolis: Indiana University Press, 2003.
De Cordier, Bruno. "Un 'Israël soviétique' en Mer noire." *Les Courrier du Maghreb et de l'Orient* 4, no. 3 (2017), https://lecourrierdumaghrebetdelorient.info/israel/israel-un-israel-sovietique-en-mer-noire.
Della Pergola, Sergio. "World Jewish Population 2016," Current Jewish Population Reports. *Berman Jewish Databank* 17 (2016): 57–9.
Feiler, Gil, and Kevjin Lim. "Israel and Kazakhstan: Assessing the State of Bilateral Relations." Report, Mideast Security and Policy Studies no.107, The Begin-Sadat Center for Strategic Studies, Bar Ilan University, Ramat Gan, 2014.
Forbes. "#962 Alexander Machkevich: 2019 Billionaires Net Worth." www.forbes.com/profile/alexander-machkevich. Accessed June 24, 2020.
Frank, Robert. "Religion(s): enjeux internationaux et diplomatie religieuse." In *Pour l'histoire des relations internationals*, edited by Robert Frank, 421–22. Paris: Presses Universitaires de France—Le nœud gordien, 2012.
Gitelman, Zvi. 'The Evolution of Jewish Culture and Identity in the Soviet Union," In *Jewish Culture and Identity in the Soviet Union*, edited by Yaacov Ro'i and Avi Beker, 3–26. New York: New York University Press, 1991.
Goldman, Marshall I. "Russian Jews in Business." In *Jewish Life after the USSR*, edited by Zvi Gitelman, Musya Glants, and Marshall I. Goldman, 76–98. Bloomington and Indianapolis: Indiana University Press, 2003.
Hovanessian, Martine. "Diaspora arménienne et patrimonialisation d'une mémoire collective: l'impossible lieu du témoignage?" *Les Cahiers de FRAMESPA—Nouveaux champs de l'histoire sociale* 3, Patrimoine et immigration (2007), journals.openedition.org/framespa/314.
Israeli Embassy to Kazakhstan. "MASHAV: About MASHAV." https://embassies.gov.il/astana/departments/mashav/pages/aboutmashava.aspx. Accessed June 24, 2020.
Jacobs, Everett M. "A Note on Jewish Membership of the Soviet Communist Party." *Soviet Jewish Affairs* 6, no. 2 (1976): 114–15.
JDC. "JDC on the Frontlines: 2016–17 Annual Report." Report, American-Jewish Joint Distribution Committee, www.jdc.org/wp-content/uploads/2017/10/ar_2017.pdf.
Jewish Agency for Israel. "Every one of us, together—Performance Report 2016-17." Report, The Jewish Agency for Israel, 2017. http://lln-websites.com/pdf/performance_report/files/downloads/performance_report_2016-2017.pdf , Jewish Agency for Israel. "Financial Report 2016." Report, The Jewish Agency for Israel, 2017. http://www.jewishagency.org/sites/default/files/2016_financial_report.pdf;
Jouvenel, Hugues de, and Geoffrey Delcroix. *Le choc des identités? Cultures, civilisations et conflits de demain*. Paris: Futuribles—Perspectives, 2008.

Kazakhstan, Embassy of, to Israel "Kazakhstansko-Izrailskie otnosheniya (spravka)," 2017.
Konstantinov, Vyacheslav. *Yevreiskoe naselenie byvshego SSSR v XX veke—sotsial'no-demograficheskii analiz*. Jerusalem: Lira, 2007.
Krupnik, Igor. "Soviet Cultural and Ethnic Policies towards Jews: A Legacy Reassessed." In *Jews and Jewish life in Russia and the Soviet Union*, edited by Yaacov Ro'i, 67–86. London: Frank Cass, 1995.
Lazin, Fred A. "Refugee Resettlement and 'Freedom of Choice': The Case of Soviet Jewry." Report, Backgrounder, Center for Immigration Sudies, Washington DC, 2005.
MASHAV. "About MASHAV: Guiding Principles." *MASHAV—Israel's Agency for International Development Cooperation*. https://mfa.gov.il/mfa/mashav/aboutmashav/pages/guiding_principles.aspx. Accessed June 24, 2020.
MASHAV. "Publications: Annual Reports." *MASHAV—Israel's Agency for International Development Cooperation*, https://mfa.gov.il/mfa/mashav/publications/annual_reports/pages/default.aspx. Accessed July 1, 2020.
Mauss, Marcel. "Les civilisations: éléments et forms." Les classiques des sciences sociales, *CÉGEP–Université du Québec*: 10–12, classiques.uqac.ca/classiques/mauss_marcel/oeuvres_2/oeuvres_2_13/les_civilisations.html.
Mesamed, Vladimir. *Izrail v Tsentralnoi Azii: grezy i realnost*. Moscow: Institut Blizhnego Vostoka, 2012.
Nye, Joseph S. Jr. "Public Diplomacy and Soft Power," *The Annals of the America's Academy of Political and Social Science* 616, no 1 (2008): 94–109.
OECD. "Development Co-operation Report 2017: Data for Development." Report, Organization for Economic Cooperation and Development, Paris, 2017.
OECD. "ODA Disbursements to Countries and Regions." *OECD stats database*. https://stats.oecd.org. Accessed July 1, 2020.
Pew Research Center. "Israel's Religiously Divided Society." Report, Pew Forum on Religion and Public Life, Washington DC, March 8, 2016. www.pewforum.org/2016/03/08/israels-religiously-divided-society.
Pew Research Center. "A Portrait of Jewish Americans," *Pew Forum*, October 1, 2013. www.pewforum.org/2013/10/01/chapter-5-connection-with-and-attitudes-towards-israel/.
Pinkus, Benjamin. *The Jews of the Soviet Union: The History of a National Minority*. Cambridge and New York: Cambridge University Press, 1988.
Pinkus, Benjamin. *The Soviet Government and the Jews (1948–67): A Documented Study*. Cambridge and New York: Cambridge University Press, 1984.
Poujol, Cathérine. "Juifs boukhariotes en Asie centrale: fin de partie." *Revue Regard sur l'Est*, Dossier no. 58, Le renouveau du monde juif en Europe centrale et orientale (2011), http://www.regard-est.com/home/breve_contenu.php?id=1234.
Razoux, Pierre. "Quel avenir pour le couple Turquie-Israël?" *Politique étrangère* 1 (2010): 25–39.
Reed, John. "Israel turns to Kurds for three-quarters of its Oil Supplies." *The Financial Times*, August 23, 2015. www.ft.com/content/150f00cc-472c-11e5-af2f-4d6e0e5eda22.

Samaan, Jean-Loup. "Israël et l'Eurasie: le retour de la doctrine de la périphérie?" *Géoéconomie* 72, no. 5 (2014): 139–41.
Sand, Schlomo. "Comment fut inventé le peuple juif." *Le Monde diplomatique* 8 (2008), https://www.monde-diplomatique.fr/2008/08/SAND/16205.
Sand, Schlomo. *The Invention of the Jewish People*. London: Verso, 2009.
Sandler, Shmuel. 'Toward a Theory of World Jewish Politics and Jewish Foreign Policy." *Hebraic Political Studies* 2, no. 3 (2007): 331–52.
Sarwar, Alibi. "Skolko innostrannykh kompanii rabotayut v Kazakhstane—infografika." *LS News*, January 25, 2016. https://lsm.kz/skol-ko-inostrannyh-kompanij-rabotaet-v-kazahstane-infografika.
Stampfer, Shaul. "Did the Khazars Convert to Judaism?" *Jewish Social Studies* 19, no. 3 (2013): 1–72.
Toltz, Mark. "Yevreiskaya emigratsia iz byvshego SSR c 1970 goda sostavila pochti 2 milliona chelovyek." *Demoscope* 479–98, 2012, www.demoscope.ru/weekly/2012/0497/tema01.php.
Tumashova, Elena. "Kak Israilskie kompanii vnyedryayut 'zelyonie' tekhnologii." *Kapital* May 9, 2017. https://kapital.kz/business/59523/kak-izrailskie-kompanii-vnedryayut-zelenye-tehnologii.html.
UN General Assembly. "Resolution adopted by the General Assembly—no. 43/177, Question of Palestine." *General Assembly of the United Nations*, A/RES/43/177, December 15, 1988. https://unispal.un.org/DPA/DPR/unispal.nsf/0/146E6838D505833F852560D600471E25;
UN General Assembly. "Resolution adopted by the General Assembly—no. 67/19, Status of Palestine in the United Nations." *General Assembly of the United Nations*, A/RES/67/19, December 4, 2012. https://unispal.un.org/DPA/DPR/unispal.nsf/0/19862D03C564FA2C85257ACB004EE69B.
Vichnevski, Anatoli, and Jeanne Zayontchkovskaia. "L'émigration de l'ex-Union soviétique: prémices et inconnues." *Revue Européenne des Migrations Internationales* 8, no. 1 (1992): 41–65.
Visser, Oane, and Max Spoor. *"Land Grabbing in post-Soviet Eurasia: The World's Largest Agricultural Land Reserves at Stake." Journal of Peasant Studies* 38, no. 2 (2011): 299–323.
World Bank Group. "Migration Remittances Data," www.worldbank.org/en/topic/migrationremittancesdiasporaissues/brief/migration-remittances-data. Accessed June 24, 2020.

Part II

Chapter 7

Russian and Chinese Hard/Soft Power Projection in Kazakhstan

Challenge and Response

Reuel R. Hanks

Soft power, Joseph Nye informs us, appears in three distinctive guises: culture, political values, and policies.[1] He draws a clear distinction between "hard power," which effects political change through force, and its counterpart "soft power," an influence that eschews force and coercion (or the threat of them), and instead seeks to alter the political equation between two or more states through the instruments of reputation, persuasion, moral rectitude, and popular culture. To borrow a phrase from a bygone era, soft power aims to "win the hearts and minds" of those a state wishes to co-opt into viewing that state in a positive light. The three incarnations of soft power identified by Nye are not mutually exclusive, certainly work in coordination to some degree, and often overlap. However, if one of these instruments carries a greater potential for effecting behavioral change among states, "getting others to want the outcomes that you want," as Nye puts it, it would appear to be culture, broadly defined. Political values and policies are frequently the extensions of the cultural and social values of a state, and are rooted in an ideology that expresses the core of the state's identity. Ideology and core identity are what frames the desired "outcomes" that Nye describes.

This aspect of soft power is of critical importance in understanding the nature of the beast in a post-colonial context. If "culture" is the superior lever for the exercise of soft power, then it would seem to follow that in a post-imperial context, the culture of the former empire would represent an ideal conduit for soft power influence. Moreover, geographic proximity is an aspect of the success or failure of soft power that scholars of foreign relations have seldom considered. Even in the era of the internet, globalized commerce, and instantaneous communication across the planet, the concept of "distance decay" developed by geographers in the 1960s continues to have relevance. Spatial interaction theory and gravity modeling not only remain relevant, but recent research has suggested that space directly dictates the magnitude of social influence.[2]

While soft power may appear in many guises, the discussion here will focus on cultural expressions of soft power. This chapter offers a brief comparative survey of the two states which are geographically contiguous with Kazakhstan and are attempting to wield cultural influence via soft power: Russia and China. The argument presented here is that while Russia enjoys great advantage over China in terms of soft power potential, both states have failed to develop a soft power strategy that maximizes their influence in Kazakhstani policy making. For different reasons, neither has utilized soft power in the most effective way, given the advantages and disadvantages each experiences. An analysis of the soft power strategies and initiatives of Russia and China follows, which attempts to contextualize the challenges each faces in Kazakhstan's political and cultural landscape, as well as offering some perspective on Kazakhstani responses to the projection of soft power.

RUSSIAN SOFT POWER

Russia's relatively poor showing on global soft power indices belies its potential to exercise soft power in the regional setting of Central Eurasia. In the competition for soft power influence in Central Eurasia, Russia possesses enormous historical advantages over China, the West, and other competitors. As the former imperial hegemon in the region for the past two centuries, Russia established its language and culture in Kazakhstan from the 1820s, a process that culminated with the implementation of a universal educational system during the Soviet era that emphasized the acquisition of Russian language and absorption of Russian culture. Russian customs and cultural awareness became the foundation for the cultural identity of the Kazakh elite, and indeed many Kazakhs in the second half of the twentieth century spoke Russian as their first language, all but abandoning their eponymous language. Russian literature, music, sport, and many other aspects of everyday culture, including drinking customs, were adopted as the norm for a large percentage of the Kazakh nation.

Geographically, the fact that the Russian culture area was contiguous with the Kazakh lands facilitated (and continues to do so) the integration of Russian culture into Kazakh identity. The Russian Federation and the Republic of Kazakhstan today share the longest continuous border between two states, a boundary 4,254 miles (6,846 kilometers) in length. Ethnic Russians comprise

20 percent of the population, and the Russian language remains a recognized language of administration in the country. The Russian minority is clustered in the oblasts that adjoin Russia (with a large Russian population in the southern city of Almaty as well), and cross-border ties remain strong between northern and eastern Kazakhstan and southern Russia.[3]

Kazakhstan's large Russian minority has not shown a propensity for separatism except in a few isolated cases in the early 1990s. Yet both the government and the public are aware of the demographic similarities between the Crimea and northern Kazakhstan, and many in Kazakhstan watched Russia's annexation of the former with considerable alarm in 2014,[4] although public opinion surveys in Kazakhstan taken early in the conflict showed solid support for Russia's actions, at least among those who received most of their information from Russian media.[5] Russia's use of hard power in its dispute with Kiev certainly tarnished its image and set back efforts to cultivate "softer" influence, but the cultural advantages Moscow enjoys in projecting soft power in Kazakhstan appear to outweigh any damage that might accrue from its aggressive policy toward Ukraine.

Russia's Cultural Advantages

As mentioned above, Russia enjoys enormous advantage over any competitor state for soft power influence in Kazakhstan. Russian language, especially in the northern tier of oblasts in Kazakhstan, is as widely spoken as Kazakh, and Russian continues to function as the *lingua franca* among Kazakhstan's elite. The near ubiquitous Russian language fluency among educated Kazakhs age fifty and up confers a messaging advantage that easily overwhelms the competing strategies of China and the West. Russian language media, both broadcast and via the internet, are viewed by literally hundreds of thousands of Kazakhstani citizens on a daily basis. Moreover, social media platforms widely used in Kazakhstan frequently use Russian and are influenced from Russia, allowing Russian commentators to widely disseminate Moscow's policy objectives among the younger generation of Kazakhstanis. A recent study reveals that social media is emerging as a major platform for the extension of Russia's soft power influence in much of the post-Soviet space.[6] Interestingly, in the capital of Nur-Sultan perceptions of America are much more positive, with about 35 percent of the young people living there supporting the United States as an example Kazakhstan should follow in its development.

The Russian advantage in broadcast and print media is also massive. A large percentage of the Kazakhstani public receives the majority of their political information from sources in Russia, especially Russian newscasts. Survey data from April 2010 illustrate that over 60 percent of Kazakhstanis listed "Russian TV" as a major source of their political knowledge, with Russian newspapers and radio broadcasts also contributing a significant portion of information.[7] It should be noted that many "Kazakhstani" channels, the leading source of political information, often re-broadcast programming that was produced by Russian sources, and even some channels that broadcast primarily in Kazakh are in fact bilingual, featuring occasional programs in Russian. Other foreign sources (TV, print, radio, and internet) were important to less than 5 percent of the respondents.[8] The data reinforce the fact that Russia holds an enormous advantage in projecting its image to the Kazakhstani public.

A recently published extensive study of Russia's informational footprint in Kazakhstan divides Russian media into three vectors.[9] The first is Russian information sources that are government-sponsored and directed at shaping a positive view of Russia in Kazakhstan. Russia Today (RT) is an example, although the channel ceased broadcasting in Kazakhstan in 2018. The influence of RT in Kazakhstan was limited as the channel and related internet presence are more focused toward projecting Russian soft power onto the global stage, with the majority of programming offered in English. A Moscow-sponsored internet news channel, Sputnik, also falls within this category. But these sources directed at public diplomacy do not probably have the greatest impact on Kazakhstani public opinion regarding Russia. Rather, the second "vector," Russian programming that is state-controlled but not specifically directed at the Kazakhstani audience, very likely has a greater role in projecting Russia's soft power. While this programming is not geared to promote Russia's official political positions, the more subtle presentation of Russian views may be more effective at shaping Kazakhstani attitudes. This type of programming is pervasive across the spectrum of TV broadcasting in Kazakhstan, as many channels typically offer Russian-produced features, although as Marlene Laruelle and her coauthors observe, the share of broadcast time devoted to these programs is declining. Indeed, they argue that the Kazakhstan government is currently curtailing imported Russian language broadcasting in favor of domestically produced broadcasts, giving Nur-Sultan more control over public perception.[10] The impact of this shift on Russia's soft power in Kazakhstan is not likely to be immediate, however, as Moscow has a twenty-year head start and Russian-produced broadcasts remain popular.

Russian soft power efforts appear to be effective among the younger generation of Kazakhstanis. A survey of Kazakhstani youth conducted in 2016 showed a marked preference for Russia. When asked about their interest in political events "internationally" and in Russia, Central Asia, China, and Europe, 72 percent of respondents indicated that they were "very interested" or "interested" in political events in Russia, only slightly less than the percentage who were "very interested" or "interested" in such events internationally, and significantly greater than those who were "very interested" or "interested" in politics in Central Asia. When asked to rank countries and organizations with which Kazakhstan should pursue closer relations, more distant relations, or maintain the status quo, Russia was the overwhelming favorite, with the same proportion, 72 percent, believing that Kazakhstan should pursue closer relations with Russia.[11] The Eurasian Economic Union was a distant second, with 49 percent of young people desiring closer relations with the relatively new economic entity (the survey was conducted in 2016). Only Iran, Afghanistan, and NATO drew lower percentages for "closer relations" than the United States at 18 percent, with the EU garnering a somewhat higher percentage at about 30 percent.[12] Perhaps even more revealing, a far larger percentage of youth in Kazakhstan chose the United States as a country Kazakhstan should distance itself from than any other entity, including China, with 40 percent of the respondents seeing a more distant relationship with the United States as desirable, an indicator perhaps of the success of Russian media in casting the United States in a negative light.[13]

CHINESE SOFT POWER IN KAZAKHSTAN

China does not enjoy the same historical or cultural advantages as Russia in exercising a soft power strategy in Kazakhstan. China never colonized any significant territory in Central Asia beyond its present control of Xinjiang, and the imprint of Chinese culture in the region has been far fainter than that of Russia for the past three centuries. Although the percentage of foreign exchange students from Kazakhstan attending Chinese universities has increased greatly since the mid-2000s, the numbers remain quite modest when compared to those attending institutions in Russia and neighboring Kyrgyzstan. In 2015, more than 80 percent of all Kazakhstani students studying abroad were studying in those two countries, with the lion's share in Russia.[14] Moreover, during the last three decades of the Soviet period China was viewed as a potential, or in some cases, real adversary of the USSR, a position inculcated in the psyche of Kazakhstanis via official media and Communist Party propaganda. Sensitive policy disputes between Nur-Sultan (Astana) and Beijing have also damaged the Chinese "brand" in Kazakhstan, especially the controversies over Chinese treatment of the Uyghur and Kazakh minorities in Xinjiang, and the control and use of water resources in the same region. Some former Kazakh officials with intimate knowledge of China are harshly critical of Chinese motives toward the country.[15]

Survey and interview data indicate that China has an image problem with the Kazakhstani public in comparison to Russia. Possibly the most widely known case illustrating negative attitudes toward China is the proposal floated in 2010 by President Nursultan Nazarbayev to lease up to a million hectares in southern Kazakhstan to Chinese guest farmers. In January 2010, a month after the plan had been publically presented, opponents staged a large protest challenging the proposal. A national survey conducted in April 2010 found that 81 percent of respondents opposed the plan to lease the land to the Chinese farmers, with only 5 percent supporting the plan.[16] The Nazarbayev regime later withdrew the proposal. Other data also reinforce the perception that a sizable section of the Kazakhstani population views China with suspicion, if not outright trepidation.

For example, surveys distributed by a prominent Kazakh sociologist, Yelena Sadovskaya in 2007 and 2012 disclosed widespread stereotyping and prejudice toward the Chinese in Kazakh society, with the level of anti-Chinese sentiment actually *increasing* in her sample.[17] Articles frequently appear in print and online calling attention to the number of Chinese labor migrants in the country.[18] Interestingly, it appears there is an ethnic distinction among Kazakhstanis regarding attitudes toward the Chinese, with ethnic Russians harboring less nationalistic attitudes than their Kazakh counterparts.[19] Yet the number of Chinese working legally in Kazakhstan continues to grow at a steady pace. In 2013, the number of Chinese citizens holding work visas in Kazakhstan was 5,300,[20] rising to 12,700 in 2016. Even as the number of Chinese guest workers climbs, their agency in the dissemination of Chinese soft power seems curtailed, as most of the workers are employed in the petroleum industry in Western Kazakhstan located in a relatively few locations, and communication with local people are limited to occasional business interactions.[21] The number of Kazakhstani students studying in China has indeed increased dramatically over the past decade, but the ramifications of larger numbers of students attending Chinese universities are not clear. Some Kazakhstani commentators are skeptical that this exchange is building influence for the Chinese in Kazakhstan. Aidar Amrebayev, a specialist in Almaty, suggests that Kazakh students who study in China find few opportunities when they return to Kazakhstan, and the benefits of the expended student exchange have mostly fallen to China.[22]

Natalie Koch's study of public attitudes and geographic imaginaries conducted at about the same time as the land leasing controversy in 2010 revealed that while around 55 percent of respondents viewed China "ambivalently," only 25 percent of respondents viewed China favorably; yet 68 percent held a favorable opinion of Russia.[23] A relatively small but vocal segment perceive an actual threat of invasion or occupation of Kazakhstan by China, while others see the "threat" of a Chinese takeover as more subtle and insidious, with China slowly but inexorably taking control of Kazakhstan's resources and economy. Some of this concern is based in the simple geographic and demographic imbalance between the countries: some Kazakhstanis view China as an overpopulated teeming mass of humanity that seeks to extend control into more "empty" adjoining space, with Kazakhstan presenting an attractive target for this ambition.

Koch expresses some skepticism in her analysis that the perception of a Chinese "threat" is pervasive among Kazakhstanis. Yet evidence has mounted in the past decade that China and its citizens are in fact viewed by a substantial portion of Kazakhstanis with unease, if not fear. If capturing the "hearts and minds" is a milestone of soft power advancement, China has a great deal of work to do among the Kazakhstani public. An investigation of print media in Kazakhstan carried out in 2015 indicated that among non-government newspapers in the state, those published in the Kazakh language tended to present a negative image of China, and while independent Russian language publications also evinced a negative bias toward China, though not as directly as their Kazakh language counterparts.[24] Aziz Burkhanov and Yu-wen Chen found significant levels of "Sinophobia" in the media regarding several aspects of the Kazakhstan–China relationship, including the location of Chinese-owned factories in Kazakhstan and tourism. Interestingly, their study revealed a distrust of China woven throughout the social strata of the country. Regarding the controversial changes to the visa regime with China, the former Kazakh Ambassador to China Murat Auezov had flatly stated that "China is not a pet dog, it is a tiger" and argued against simplifying the visa requirements for Chinese tourists visiting Kazakhstan.[25]

Leveraging Soft Power via CIs and the BRI

Beijing has clearly recognized the disadvantages it must overcome in Kazakhstan and the larger Central Asian region in building soft power through cultural linkages, especially in comparison to Russia. In the mid-2000s, the Chinese government initiated a global strategy to expand knowledge of Mandarin and Chinese culture by the establishment of "Confucius Institutes" (CIs). The Confucius Institutes have a global reach and as of 2019 there were over 480 in over 120 countries; they are clearly intended to function as instruments of Chinese soft power.[26] In some Western countries since 2014 the CIs have become quite controversial, primarily due to problems of censorship and the lack of academic freedom alleged by their detractors. Since 2018 at least ten CIs in the United States have been shuttered.[27] In Kazakhstan, the first CI was opened at Eurasian National University in Astana in 2007, and has been followed by others in Aktobe, Karaganda, and Almaty. However, the ability of these centers to advance Chinese cultural soft power in Kazakhstan appears to be quite limited. Ainur Nogayeva suggests that the CIs in Kazakhstan are limited in their outreach ability, as the

Kazakhstani public perceives them to be politicized instruments of Chinese foreign policy.[28] While she notes that "the CIs will likely be a venue for, and geopolitical actor in, these ongoing geopolitical dynamics," China's support of its network of CIs in Kazakhstan seems to have produced little progress in increasing Beijing's soft power there.

The discounting of the Chinese "brand" in Kazakhstan may be seen in recent public demonstrations. In 2016, the Nazarbayev regime revisited the proposal to lease land to foreigners in Kazakhstan. Large public demonstrations in the country, many featuring overt anti-China rhetoric, forced the government to crackdown on the demonstrations, but also to once again retreat from the plan to streamline the leasing process for foreign investors. Three years later anti-Chinese protests erupted in Western Kazakhstan in the city of Zhanaozen, rallies that had smaller counterparts in cities across the country.[29] Interestingly, the demonstrations were in response to reports that Chinese firms would invest in a host of new factories in the region; a development that should be welcome news in Kazakhstan where the economy has faltered with the collapse of global petroleum prices since 2014. Some speakers at the protest stated that they "did not want jobs, just keep them (the Chinese) out."[30] This would appear to undermine the argument that Beijing's soft power strategy in Kazakhstan is working because the massive economic investment China is pouring into the country will overcome persistent anti-China views among Kazakhstanis.[31] Indeed, the strategy of pursuing soft power via economic investment rather than through improving the cultural image of China among Kazakhstanis may be counterproductive, as the public views the former as a means to seize control of Kazakhstan's economy.

China's massive investment project, the "Belt and Road Initiative" (BRI) has been touted as not only integrating Eurasia, but embedding Chinese soft power influence in partner states.[32] It is beyond the scale of this brief commentary to delve deeply into all the possible ramifications of the BRI regarding Chinese soft power in Kazakhstan, but it should be noted that investing in Kazakhstan may not be enough to significantly increase China's influence. As Bhavna Dave observes:

> Soft power emanates not only from the ideational and normative orientation of the state, but also from the engagement of civil society and non-state actors—including universities, educational and charitable foundations, religious and cultural institutions, NGOs, business, and commercial interests—in defining this vision and bringing it to fruition. China's record of censorship and monitoring civil society groups, NGOs, and trade unions is a major limitation. Nye notes that the CPC has not accepted that "soft power springs largely from individuals, the private sector, and civil society."[33]

KAZAKHSTANI RESPONSES TO CHINESE AND RUSSIAN SOFT POWER

Neither the Kazakhstani government nor the general population are passive recipients of soft power influence; both possess independent agency in their response to the cultural and economic leverage of external actors. Considerable evidence is mounting that despite the economic advantages China enjoys, and the cultural/historical advantages of Russia in the region, the soft power strategies of both are losing market share in the broader context of official and public attitudes. Surveys, anecdotal evidence, and other material used to evaluate the efficacy and nature of soft power of course offer only a static snapshot of conditions, but cumulatively these sources may indicate longer-term modifications in the soft power environment of Kazakhstan.

As Dave and others have observed, economic development does not always bring with it significant benefits of public diplomacy and soft power. China has now been investing heavily in Kazakhstan for nearly twenty years, yet surveys indicate that anti-Chinese sentiment among the Kazakhstani public may be rising. Certainly there is little evidence that China has made measurable progress in advancing its interests in Kazakhstan through the mechanism of soft power. A recent survey, conducted in April 2020, yielded quite negative results for China's soft power ambitions in Kazakhstan. Fifty-five percent of the Kazakhstanis surveyed indicated that they would prefer *less* presence of China in Kazakhstani society, a remarkably high figure given the enormous investment that China has made in the country since the early 2000s.[34] China has invested close to twenty-eight billion USD in a total of fifty-five joint projects in recent years.[35] Yet despite this princely sum, a *majority* of the Kazakhstani people want a diminished imprint of China in their country. In contrast, Russia has invested a fraction of the Chinese amount in Kazakhstan, with one recent estimate from 2019 placing Russian investment in Kazakhstan at around 650 million USD annually.[36] Moreover, among those surveyed who believe that Kazakhstan has a "primary enemy" among the world's nations, China was chosen by the largest percentage, at 10 percent. Less than 4 percent of the respondents viewed China as a model for Kazakhstan to emulate, despite China's rising reputation as a global economic power and regional hegemon.[37]

Indeed, China's efforts to broaden its profile in Kazakhstan at times are hindered by a crude and overtly aggressive tone, resulting in backlash from official channels. An example is the recent controversy regarding an article that appeared on the Chinese internet blogging site *Sohu.com*. The article, entitled in English translation "Why Does Kazakhstan Wish to Return to China?" propounded the dubious position that a significant number of Kazakhstanis, backed by a secretive, imprecise number of government functionaries, harbor ambitions of joining Kazakhstan to China. Although the piece originally appeared in Chinese, a language only a small number of Kazakhstanis can read, it nevertheless drew an immediate and, by diplomatic standards, vigorous response from the Kazakhstani government. In Nur-Sultan, the Chinese Ambassador was summoned to the Foreign Ministry and apparently presented with a formal note of protest, and the displeasure of the Kazakhstani authorities was shared directly with Beijing as well. A comprehensive, if somewhat tendentious analysis of the article by the Information and Analytical Center at Moscow State University appeared on the Kazakhstani blog site Yvision, which pointed out that Sohu.com is the largest electronic information platform in China and is connected to the government as well as official news agencies.[38] Whatever the motivation for circulating the article might be, the dust up highlights the tone deafness of the Chinese regime regarding the negative impact and subsequent damage to China's efforts to exert soft power in Kazakhstan that such irredentist propaganda evokes.

Yet Russia is not in a position to blithely celebrate the failures of its regional rival in Kazakhstan. The same poll cited above, showing China's lack of progress in winning over the Kazakhstani public, contains some cautionary notes for Moscow. Seventeen percent of those surveyed preferred that Russia have a lower profile in Kazakhstani society, and rather surprisingly, nearly a quarter did not view Russia as a model for Kazakhstan to follow.[39] In 2017, 81 percent of a cohort of Kazakhstanis listed Russia as a "friendly state," with apparently 19 percent feeling otherwise, matching closely the 17 percent who desire less Russian influence in the country.[40] The same study indicated that only 55 percent "trusted Russian goods," and only 39 percent were "grateful for Russian investment" in Kazakhstan. While these figures are higher than for any other country, in the context of Russia's huge advantage in media exposure, cultural ties, and common language, they are lower than one might anticipate. A significant percentage of Kazakhstanis appear to be critically minded, are aware of soft power's influence in their lives, and develop perspectives independently of public diplomacy and cultural dominance.

CONCLUSION: DIRECTIONS OF SOFT POWER IN KAZAKHSTAN

Concerning soft power, Nye has famously written that "the best propaganda is not propaganda," and has emphasized that those projecting soft power must be held to be credible and transparent. It follows that regimes that have failed to develop the institutions of civil society and plurality face structural vulnerabilities when crafting a nation brand via the conduits of soft power. Writing specifically on China's soft power strategy, David Shambaugh makes the case that "Soft power cannot be bought, it must be earned."[41] China has yet to learn this lesson, both in its global strategy toward soft power, and more specifically in Kazakhstan. Indeed, large-scale economic investment without associated progress in promoting cultural soft power appear to have damaged China's image among many in Kazakhstan, who perceive Beijing's motives to be solely resource extraction, economic hegemony, and exportation of surplus labor, rather than a cooperation rooted in mutual respect and the shared goals of development and joint benefit.

In the case of Russia, the concept of soft power in the sense that Nye meant has been distorted into a hybrid somewhat similar to the Soviet concept of "agitprop," wherein image management and public diplomacy are simply an extension of more direct measures. Russia's official defense strategy conceives of soft power as being an "instrument" or arm of Moscow's overall military posture.[42] In this approach, soft power becomes "soft coercion," and is far removed from Nye's concept as applied to free society. Polls of Kazakhstani public opinion and ubiquitous Russian media lead observers to conclude that Russia has a broad, successful soft power profile in the country, but this assessment must be contextualized in the frame of Russia's historical, cultural, linguistic, and demographic advantages; advantages that may be gradually eroding away. As the Kazakhstani regime moves to limit the influence of Russian-produced media and "domesticate" Russian language content, a diminution of Russian soft power may follow. Will Moscow's approach to soft power evolve as well?

NOTES

1. Joseph S. Nye, Jr., "Soft Power," *Foreign Policy* 80, Twentieth Anniversary (Autumn, 1990): 15–171. See also Joseph S. Nye, Jr., *Soft Power: The Means to Success in World Politics* (New York: Public Affairs, 2004).

2. Jannik Meyners et al., "The Role of Mere Closeness: How Geographic Proximity Affects Social Influence," *Journal of Marketing* 81, no. 5 (2017): 49–66.

3. See Reuel R. Hanks, "Directions in the Ethnic Politics of Kazakhstan: Concession, Compromise, or Catastrophe?" *Journal of Third World Studies* XV, no. 1 (Spring 1998) 143–62.

4. The author had occasion to witness this concern firsthand. After delivering a lecture on geopolitics in Eurasia at a university in Kazakhstan in May of 2014, I was approached by approximately a dozen students, some of whom asked me directly if "American will save us" if Russia attempted to absorb some of the country's northern oblasts.

5. Almas Taizhanov, "Manipulating Public Opinion in Kazakhstan," *Global Dialogue: Newsletter for the International Sociological Association* 4, no. 4 (2014): 37.

6. Todd C. Helmus et al., *Russian Social Media Influence: Understanding Russian Propaganda in Eastern Europe* (Santa Monica: RAND Corporation, 2018).

7. "Kazakhstan National Opinion Poll," (report, International Republican Institute, Baltic Survey Ltd. and Gallup Organization, with funding by USAID, Washington DC, April 3–13, 2010).

8. Ibid.

9. Marlene Laruelle, Dylan Royce, and Serik Beyssembayev, "Untangling the Puzzle of 'Russia's Influence' in Kazakhstan," *Eurasian Geography and Economics* 60, no. 2 (2019): 225–26.

10. Ibid., 234.

11. Tolganay Umbetaliyeva, Botagoz Rakisheva, and Peer Teschendorf, *Youth in Central Asia: Kazakhstan. Based on a Sociological Survey* (Almaty: Friedrich Ebert Foundation Kazakhstan, 2016), 158.

12. Ibid.

13. Russian-language media frequently blame the United States, and to a lesser degree European countries, for the political crisis over the Crimea, as well as harshly criticizing American and NATO policy in the region.

14. "Kazakhstan National Opinion Poll," 45–6.

15. See Murat Auezov, "Kitaisko-Kazahstanskie Otnosheniia: Istoriia i Sovremennost'" (Sino-Kazakh Relations: History and Modernity), *Central Asia and the Caucasus Journal* (April 1999). Auezov served as Kazakhstan's first Ambassador to China.

16. "Kazakhstan National Opinion Poll," 19.

17. Yelena Sadovskaya, "The Mythology of Chinese Migration in Kazakhstan," *Central-Asia Caucasus Analyst*, January 7, 2015, https://www.cacianalyst.org/publications/feld-reports/item/13112-the-mythology-of-chinese-migration-in-kazakhstan.html.

18. Migratsiia po-kitaiski. Skol'ko uzhe zhitelei podnebesnoi v Kazakhstane?" *Exclusive.kz*, August 10, 2016, http://exclusive.kz/skolko_kitaicev-v_kazahstane.

19. Aziz Burkhanov and Yu-wen Chen, "Kazakh Perspective on China, the Chinese, and Chinese Migration," *Ethnic and Racial Studies* 39, no. 12 (2016): 2134–8.

20. "Bolee 150 tysiach grazhdan Kitaia priekhali v Kazakhstan za tri goda," *Tengrinews,* September 6, 2013.

21. Sadovskaya, "The Mythology of Chinese Migration in Kazakhstan."

22. Aigerim Toleukhanova, "Kazakhstan and China: Fear, Loathing and Money," *Eurasianet.org*, June 21, 2016, https://eurasianet.org/kazakhstan-china-fear-loathing-and-money.

23. Natalie Koch, "Kazakhstan's Changing Geopolitics: The Resource Economy and Popular Attitudes about China's Growing Regional Influence," *Eurasian Geography and Economics* 54, no. 1 (2013): 119–21. An additional study produced about the same time that confirms many of Koch's conclusions is, Marlene Laruelle and Sebastien Peyrouse, *The Chinese Question in Central Asia: Domestic Order, Social Change and the Chinese Factor* (London: Hurst Publishers, 2012).

24. Burkhanov and Chen, "Kazakh Perspective on China, the Chinese, and Chinese Migration," 2134–8.

25. Ibid., 2143.
26. See James F. Paradise, "China and International Harmony: The Role of Confucius Institutes in Bolstering Beijing's Soft Power," *Asian Survey* 49, no. 4 (2009): 647–69 and Rui Yang, "Soft Power and Higher Education: An Examination of China's Confucius Institutes," *Globalization, Societies and Education* 8, no.2 (2010): 235–45.
27. Elizabeth Redden, "Closing Confucius Institutes," *Inside Higher Education*, January 9, 2019, https://www.insidehighered.com/news/2019/01/09/colleges-move-close-chinese-government-funded-confucius-institutes-amid-increasing.
28. Ainur Nogayeva, "Limitations of Chinese 'Soft Power' in Its Population and Language Policies in Central Asia," *Geopolitics* 20, no. 3 (2015): 596–98.
29. Darkan Umirbekov, "Kazakhstan: Sinophobic Sentiments Trigger Fresh Rallies," *Eurasianet.org*, September 4, 2019, https://eurasianet.org/kazakhstan-sinophobic-sentiments-trigger-fresh-rallies.
30. Ibid.
31. See the comments attributed to Ruslan Izimov in Toleukhanova, "Kazakhstan and China."
32. Nadège Rolland, *China's Eurasian Century? Political and Strategic Implications of the Belt and Road Initiative* (Seattle and Washington DC: The National Bureau of Asian Research, 2017), 64–7.
33. Bhavna Dave, "Silk Road Economic Belt: Effects of China's Soft Power Diplomacy in Kazakhstan," in *China's Belt and Road Initiative and its Impact in Central Asia*, ed. Marlene Laruelle (Washington, DC: The George Washington University, Central Asia Program, 2018), 107.
34. Marlene Laruelle et al., "Kazakhs are Wary of Neighbors Bearing Gifts," *OpenDemocracy*, April 30, 2020, https://www.opendemocracy.net/en/odr/kazakhs-are-wary-neighbours-bearing-gifts/.
35. Eugene Simonov, "Half China's Investment in Kazakhstan is in Oil and Gas," *China Dialogue*, October 29, 2019, https://chinadialogue.net/en/energy/11613-half-china-s-investment-in-kazakhstan-is-in-oil-and-gas-2/.
36. Marat Shibutov, Yuri Solozobov, and Natalya Malyarchuk, *Kazakhstan Russia Relations in the Modern Era* (Almaty: International Institute for Global Analyses, 2019), https://www.vision-gt.eu/wp-content/uploads/2019/01/AD_Kazakhstan-Russia_1.pdf, 27.
37. Laruelle et al., "Kazakhs are Wary of Neighbors Bearing Gifts."
38. See the discussion at: https://yvision.kz/post/854510.
39. Laruelle et al., "Kazakhs are Wary of Neighbors Bearing Gifts."
40. Shibutov, Solozobov, and Malyarchuk, *Kazakhstan Russia Relations in the Modern Era*. Interestingly, only 54 percent of Russians surveyed viewed Kazakhstan as a "friendly country."
41. David Shambaugh, "China's Soft Power Push," *Foreign Affairs* 94, no. 4 (2015): 107.
42. "Kontseptsiya Vneshney Politiki Rossiyskoy Federatsii," Government of the Russian Federation, 2013, http://archive.mid.ru//brp_4.nsf/0/6D84DDEDEDBF7DA644257B160051BF7F.

REFERENCES

Auezov, Murat. "Kitaisko-Kazahstanskie Otnosheniia: Istoriia i Sovremennost'" (Sino-Kazakh Relations: History and Modernity). *Central Asia and the Caucasus Journal* (April 1999).
Burkhanov, Aziz, and Yu-wen Chen. "Kazakh Perspective on China, the Chinese, and Chinese Migration." *Ethnic and Racial Studies* 39, no. 12 (2016): 2129–48.
Dave, Bhavna. "Silk Road Economic Belt Effects of China's Soft Power Diplomacy in Kazakhstan." In *China Belt and Road Initiative and Its Impact in Central Asia*, edited by Marlene Laruelle, 97–108. Washington, DC: The George Washington University, Central Asia Program, 2018.
Exclusive.kz. "Migratsiia po-kitaiski. Skol'ko uzhe zhitelei podnebesnoi v Kazakhstane?" August 10, 2016. http://exclusive.kz/skolko_kitaicev-v_kazahstane.
Hanks, Reuel R. "Directions in the Ethnic Politics of Kazakhstan: Concession, Compromise, or Catastrophe?" *Journal of Third World Studies* XV, no. 1 (Spring 1998) 143–62.
Helmus, Todd C., Elizabeth Bodine-Baron, Andrew Radin, Madeline Magnuson, Joshua Mendelsohn, William Marcellino, Andriy Bega, and Zev Winkelman. *Russian Social Media Influence: Understanding Russian Propaganda in Eastern Europe* (Santa Monica: RAND Corporation, 2018).
International Republican Institute. "Kazakhstan National Opinion Poll." Report, International Republican Institute, Baltic Survey Ltd. and Gallup Organization, with funding by USAID, Washington DC, April 3–13, 2010.
Koch, Natalie. "Kazakhstan's Changing Geopolitics: The Resource Economy and Popular Attitudes about China's Growing Regional Influence." *Eurasian Geography and Economics* 54, no. 1 (2013): 110–33.
Laruelle, Marlene, Dylan Royce, and Serik Beyssembayev. "Untangling the Puzzle of "Russia's influence" in Kazakhstan." *Eurasian Geography and Economics* 60, no. 2 (2019): 211–43.
Laruelle, Marlene, Gerard Toal, John O'Loughlin, and Kristin M. Bakke. "Kazakhs are Wary of Neighbors Bearing Gifts." *OpenDemocracy*, April 30, 2020.
Laruelle, Marlene, and Sebastien Peyrouse. *The "Chinese Question" in Central Asia: Domestic Order, Social Changes and the Chinese Factor*. London, New York: Hurst and Columbia University Press, 2012.
Meyners, Jannik, Christian Barrot, Jan U. Becker, Jacob Goldenberg. "The Role of Mere Closeness: How Geographic Proximity Affects Social Influence," *Journal of Marketing* 81, no. 5 (2017): 49–66.
Nogayeva, Ainur. "Limitations of Chinese 'Soft Power' in Its Population and Language Policies in Central Asia." *Geopolitics* 20, no. 3 (2015): 583–605.
Nye, Joseph S. Jr. "Soft Power." *Foreign Policy* 80, Twentieth Anniversary (Autumn, 1990): 15–171.
Nye, Joseph S. Jr. *Soft Power. The Means to Success in World Politics*. New York: Public Affairs, 2004.

Paradise, James F. "China and International Harmony: The Role of Confucius Institutes in Bolstering Beijing's Soft Power." *Asian Survey* 49, no. 4 (2009): 647–69.
Redden, Elizabeth. "Closing Confucius Institutes." *Inside Higher Education*, January 9, 2019. https://www.insidehighered.com/news/2019/01/09/colleges-move-close-chinese-government-funded-confucius-institutes-amid-increasing.
Rolland, Nadège. *China's Eurasian Century? Political and Strategic Implications of the Belt and Road Initiative*. Seattle and Washington DC: The National Bureau of Asian Research, 2017.
Russian Federation, Government of the. "Kontseptsiya Vneshney Politiki Rossiyskoy Federatsii," 2013. http://archive.mid.ru//brp_4.nsf/0/6D84DDEDEDBF7DA644257B160051BF7F.
Sadovskaya, Yelena. "The Mythology of Chinese Migration in Kazakhstan." *Central-Asia Caucasus Analyst*, January 7, 2015. https://www.cacianalyst.org/publications/feld-reports/item/13112-the-mythology-of-chinese-migration-in-kazakhstan.html.
Shambaugh, David. "China's Soft-Power Push: The Search for Respect." *Foreign Affairs* 94, no. 4 (July/August 2015): 99–107.
Shibutov, Marat, Yuri Solozobov, and Natalya Malyarchuk. *Kazakhstan Russia Relations in the Modern Era*. Almaty: International Institute for Global Analyses, 2019. https://www.vision-gt.eu/wp-content/uploads/2019/01/AD_Kazakhstan-Russia_1.pdf.
Simonov, Eugene. "Half China's Investment in Kazakhstan is in Oil and Gas." *China Dialogue*, October 29, 2019. https://chinadialogue.net/en/energy/11613-half-china-s-investment-in-kazakhstan-is-in-oil-and-gas-2/.
Taizhanov, Almas. "Manipulating Public Opinion in Kazakhstan." *Global Dialogue: Newsletter for the International Sociological Association* 4, no. 4 (2014): 37.
Tengrinews. "Bolee 150 tysiach grazhdan Kitaia priekhali v Kazakhstan za tri goda," September 6, 2013.
Toleukhanova, Aigerim. "Kazakhstan and China: Fear, Loathing and Money." *Eurasianet.org*, June 21, 2016. https://eurasianet.org/kazakhstan-china-fear-loathing-and-money.
Umbetaliyeva, Tolganay, Botagoz Rakisheva, and Peer Teschendorf. *Youth in Central Asia: Kazakhstan—Based on a Sociological Survey*. Almaty: Friedrich Ebert Foundation Kazakhstan, 2016.
Umirbekov, Darkan. "Kazakhstan: Sinophobic Sentiments Trigger Fresh Rallies." *Eurasianet.org*, September 4, 2019. https://eurasianet.org/kazakhstan-sinophobic-sentiments-trigger-fresh-rallies.
Yang, Rui. "Soft Power and Higher Education: An Examination of China's Confucius Institutes." *Globalization, Societies and Education* 8, no.2 (2010): 235–45.

Chapter 8

Less Attraction, More Fear

The Future of China's and Russia's Soft Power in Kyrgyzstan

Aminat Chokobaeva and Drew Ninnis

In the decades since Joseph Nye first articulated his concept of "soft power," the idea has taken on a life of its own. This is partially due to what others have highlighted as a deficiency in traditional theories of states' sources of power; but it is also because the core idea of soft power remains highly alluring for theorists and decision makers. It promises the potential of achieving one's ends in foreign relations with a minimum effort and through the power of attraction alone. It is unsurprising then, that both Russia and China have attempted to make extensive use of it in Central Asia, in order to further their own objectives.

Both Russia and China have identified that cultivating more extensive, effective means of soft power are national priorities. In 2012, President Putin formalized Russia's pursuit of soft power influence in a 2012 election campaign article where he acknowledged it as an essential tool of Russia's foreign policy, but at the same time decried Western use of "illegal instruments of soft power" as destabilizing the rightful sovereignty of nations.[1] Similarly in China, soft power was a key element of the political report to the sixteenth Chinese Communist Party (CCP) Congress in 2002 and the topic of thirteenth collective study session of the Politburo in 2004, with both Presidents Hu and Xi recognizing it as essential in increasing China's influence as a great power.[2] Yet again, Chinese elites remain skeptical of Western soft power as "a surreptitious attempt to undermine the party's legitimacy through the infiltration of Western culture and political values."[3] In short, both Russia and China envy the success of the United States in employing its extensive soft power arsenal, often to their own perceived detriment.

But Russia's and China's attempts to employ soft power within Central Asia have been largely unsuccessful, as this chapter will discuss. The central question is: can soft power truly be soft when its audience is captive? This is the tension that runs through the use of Russia's and China's influence in Central Asia, where the employment of soft power is closely underwritten by the implicit threat of both nations' coercive and harder power capabilities.

This chapter will then seek to problematize the concept of soft power in the context of Central Asia. By looking at the interactions of Moscow and Beijing with Kyrgyzstan, we will argue that the multivector dependence of the small Central Asian state on its more powerful neighbors makes the concept of limited use. To illustrate our argument, this chapter will look at several critical areas of Kyrgyzstan's dependence on Russia and China, including the energy sector, media, investments and aid, military presence, and migration, while examining at the same time instances when Russia and China were able to influence Kyrgyzstan's domestic and foreign policies. As we will see, the separation of both nations' soft power from other more coercive forms quickly becomes difficult to discern—particularly, understanding whether Central Asian leaders are acting out of genuine attraction or simply out of fear of the drastic consequences that come with crossing Russia or China in the region. As this chapter will demonstrate, Russia's and China's influence in Central Asia runs counter to the "legitimacy and moral authority" stipulated by Nye.[4] It blurs the difference between public and private diplomacy (a critical distinction for Nye) and between the intermediate forms of economic power (which may be hard or soft—the attraction of markets, vs. state control and threat).

RUSSIA'S CULTURAL INFLUENCE IS WANING, BUT THEIR HARD POWER REMAINS STRONG

As Nye identifies, soft power frequently rests on sources of culture, political values, and foreign policy.[5] In subsequent publications, he and other theorists have identified the roles that institutions, language, civil society, and other cultural or political sources have played in generating soft power.[6] At first glance, Russia would seem to have these sources of influence within Central Asia in abundance—a common history and the shared political context of the former Soviet Union, the prevalence of Russian as the official language, Russian ethnic enclaves throughout the region, and, in several cases, the continued government of former Soviet party secretaries as leaders of the newly born Commonwealth of Independent States (CIS).[7]

History

Some of the defining moments in modern Russian history resonate strongly in Central Asia too. Memories of joint struggle in WWII and the shared Soviet past constitute a considerable source of Russia's soft power in the region. But as the group of war veterans is quickly dwindling the question arises as to how long the Russian leadership will be able to capitalize on this shared past. Similarly, as Valentina Feklyunina identifies in the relationship between Russia and Ukraine, the resurgence of strongly nationalist identities that emphasize "historical narratives of oppression by Russia" and bad behavior toward states in the region, cuts against the effectiveness of common memory as a source of Russian soft power.[8] This common history is frequently a source of friction for Central Asian nations, with former Russian President Dmitri Medvedev citing it as a justification for Russia's "zone of privileged interest" within the former Soviet sphere.[9] This is a stance accepted, but perhaps not appreciated, among Central Asia's foreign policy elites.[10]

Language

Russian too remains the lingua franca in the region and most adult Central Asians speak Russian to a greater or lesser extent. Russia has sought to capitalize on this by establishing "Russian World" (*Russki Mir*) centers throughout the post-Soviet sphere, reflecting a "desire to maintain the influence of Russian language and culture in the region, including amongst Russian compatriots."[11] As we shall see below, ensuring the wide-spread use of the Russian language is also essential to Russia's soft power media strategy within the region.[12] Given that the language is common across the CIS, it is also pivotal in maintaining business links between the states and Russia.[13]

Yet, as population censuses suggest, the use of Russian has been in steep decline since independence. According to the 2009 population census in Kyrgyzstan, 9 percent of the population eighteen and over spoke Russian as a native language, while 50 percent of Kyrgyz in the same age bracket said they spoke Russian as a second language. In the 1999 census, 14.9 percent of respondents listed Russian as their native tongue, while for 75 percent Russian was their second language. Russian fluency, however, is considerably lower among children between the ages of seven and fifteen, of whom only 5 percent are native Russian speakers, and 26 percent speak it as a second language.

Despite the status of Russian as an official language in Kyrgyzstan and Kazakhstan, the number of people speaking it in all of the Central Asian republics is likely to continue to decline. The same is true of the number of ethnic Russians. This does not however mean that Russia's overall role is likely to diminish greatly in Central Asia. For one, the geographic proximity means that Russia will continue to be a key player in the region. Second, the withdrawal of the United States from Afghanistan and Central Asia leaves Russia and China as primary security guarantors in the region. Finally, even though China has been making forays into the region, Central Asia's dependence on Russia in economic and security terms is unlikely to diminish considerably in the near future. On the example of Kyrgyzstan, let us then examine the key areas of Russia's and China's preponderance in the region.

Ethnicity and Citizenship

A key means of Russian soft power—both in the CIS and other former Soviet states—is the maintenance of an ambiguous definition of Russian ethnicity and citizenship. Russia frequently employs these populations as geopolitical bargaining chips in exerting influence over post-Soviet states. While the history of Russia's citizenship laws after the fall of the Soviet Union is long and tangled, a series of 2008 amendments created a "compatriots resettlement program," while in 2010 the Russian government instituted an ambiguously defined policy of recognizing "people living outside the border of the Russian Federation who made a free choice in favor of spiritual and cultural connection with Russia and who usually (*kak pravilo*) belong to peoples (*narody*) which have historically lived on the territory of the Russian Federation."[14]

This has had two practical consequences. First, Moscow has been able to influence key figures such as businessmen, political elites, and other targets with the promise of citizenship (and implicit protection should things turn sour, such as with Viktor Yanukovych).[15] Second, it has allowed Moscow to plausibly claim that it is protecting the interests of Russian citizens living in the near abroad or post-Soviet space.[16] The latter has formed an implicit threat in dealing with enclaves of Russian citizens, and formed the foundation of Russia's intervention in South Ossetia and Abkhazia in 2008. It was estimated that over 90 percent of them held Russian passports, while a significant number of Abkhazians, Transnistrians, Tajiks, and Kyrgyz also hold Russian passports.[17] This neatly exposes the dual nature of Russian soft power, which makes it so hard to separate from the coercive or "hard" elements of that power—the promise of Russian citizenship or support attracts and persuades, while the threat of Russian interests and protection simultaneously dissuades.[18]

However, this too is fading, as fewer individuals take Russia up on their offer. While there remain pockets of ethnic Russian populations across Central Asia, with the largest one in Kazakhstan, at the same time the Russian population of Central Asian republics has been steadily declining; in Tajikistan, for example, only 50,000 Russians remain of the pre-independence population of 334,000. In Uzbekistan and Kyrgyzstan, the Russian population decreased from 1,665,000 to 800,000 and 916,500 to 500,000, respectively.

Russian Civilization

In the shadow of the ongoing "color revolutions" from the former Yugoslavia in 2000 to Ukraine and Kyrgyzstan in 2005 and beyond, Putin announced the Russian project of "continuing the civilizational role of the Russian nation in Eurasia."[19] Built of a mish-mash of nostalgic readings of Russian history from the origins of the Tsars to the culmination of Soviet culture, the concept was meant to guide the nations of Eurasia through "Christian ideals, trans-ethnic imperial principles, and the model of strong state (*derzhava*) in domestic and international affairs."[20] In the opinion of Andrei Tsygankov, "these values have had a strong appeal in Eurasia . . . [as] Russians relied not only on coercion, but cooptation and co-existence with others . . . [and] not only Slavs, but many Muslims too were willing to submit to the empire's general direction."[21]

A less credulous reading of Putin's rhetoric, and Moscow's increasingly revanchist foreign policy, wonders whether these formulations were meant to attract or repel their intended audience. Scott Radnitz writes that "from the Central Asian perspective, Russian revanchism was as quixotic and perplexing as Western rhetoric on democracy and human rights had been for the previous two decades."[22] Accordingly, it left CIS leaders "unnerved by Putin's precipitous actions . . . because ideological litmus tests would limit their freedom of action, constrain their sovereignty, and possibly threaten their ability to preserve their regimes."[23] Indeed, "Central Asian leaders may wish that this iteration of Putin would disappear, [and] their greater fear is that Russia will self-destruct."[24]

Regardless of which side one comes down on, there is a concerted attempt by Moscow to give a Russian "sphere of privileged interests" a conceptual coherency as a cultural and spiritual union. Yet Moscow has dwindling resources to make this happen—as Jeanne Wilson observes, Russia has been consistently outspent by the United States and China in their own soft power efforts to promote a complete vision of regional and international order.[25] Radnitz also notes that this approach is unlikely to be appealing within the CIS, as their "regimes have embraced a pallid and prosaic legitimating narrative . . . of founding-father political identities and soft (mostly civic) national ideologies as a byproduct of [their] political cautiousness."[26] And Tsygankov himself admits that in the long term this may be more of an effort "of political elites to make use of civilisational values as a means of withstanding either an internal or an external threat."[27]

Doing Business "Russian-style"

At this point, a word needs to be said on the "Russian way of business"—which falls somewhere between Russia's common history and cultural influence, and its economic (predominantly energy) politics. As Agnia Grigas observes:

> In soft power terms, Russia also establishes networks bonded by mutual interest to promote its objectives. Its soft power stems from its ability to attract and co-opt using cultural and political values as well as the compatible business cultures that still prevail in certain spheres.[28]

While Grigas is speaking of the Baltics, again the same Russian tactics are applied extensively within Central Asia and is also "best exemplified by the creation, maintenance and support of Kremlin-friendly networks of influence in the cultural, economic and political sectors."[29]

Grigas additionally observes that the individual elements of Russia's soft power strategies in the post-Soviet sphere are mutually reinforcing—a culture of corruption and permeability between state-private interests is enabled across national boundaries by a common language, culture, and experience of post-Soviet collapse (and the wild days of Yeltsin's "shock therapy") and Russia's compatriot policy generating willing agents. All of this is further enabled through the "creation of loyal interests groups," which "involves co-opting decision-makers through financing and valuable connections and contracts"—frequently backed up by Russian "bribes, financial incentives and the appeal of a Russian business culture that is network-driven rather market driven, and is marked by opaqueness, corruption and political influence."[30]

ENERGY DIPLOMACY

Russia's use of its energy exports as a geopolitical leverage in furthering its strategic interests is well known.[31] Similarly, Central Asian dependency on those exports is also well known—a dynamic that replicates itself across the post-Soviet sphere, although as Grigas points out, "Russia cut off energy exports on around 40 occasions, most often to the Commonwealth of Independent States."[32] While Nye and others might define these as incidents of economic coercion—which they most certainly are—and therefore examples of hard or intermediate forms of power, this is to ignore soft power logic that such incidents inculcate. Quite apart from being individual incidents to bargain for specific, isolated outcomes these energy power plays are specifically designed to shape the behavior of Central Asian states even in the absence of a particular desired outcome for Russia. Rather, they are part of

"Russia's tendency to argue that cooperative relations with Moscow would result in benefits such as lower gas prices, and that tensions would result in higher energy prices for the state in question."[33]

Furthermore, Russia's control of energy exports and infrastructure as part of its larger strategy in seeking influence over the post-Soviet sphere—and even Europe—creates what John Haines describes as "an asymmetric structure of interdependence." Although this asymmetry favors Russia, it comes at a high cost. Haines writes that:

> The extraordinarily high fixed cost associated with constructing energy pipelines gives enterprises like Russia's Gazprom substantial monopoly power. But pipeline owners are subject to a key vulnerability—political disruption—since the independent states these pipelines transit can block gas flow or siphon off gas for their own use. On the other hand, transit countries have a robust self interest to ensure the steady, secure flow of gas for both domestic consumption purposes and for the revenue they receive in the form of transit fees.[34]

Again, the relationship between soft power, economic coercion, and hard power becomes increasingly difficult to untangle in Central Asia, as every engagement plays out against a background of Russian threat. This is such an ever-present dynamic that CIS leaders are even comfortable working within it; as Radnitz points out "by skillfully managing their risk portfolio, they remained comfortably inside Russia's zone of 'privileged interests' even as they secured billions of dollars in Western aid, much of which was siphoned into the pockets of elites" and even growing Chinese investment, while "profiting from great power rivalries and seeking to avoid getting caught in the crossfire."[35] This dynamic makes categorizing the nature of Russia's power in Central Asia very difficult—it is soft until, in the event of a dispute, it is no longer.[36] It is worth examining both the softer and harder elements of this energy diplomacy in detail, with Kyrgyzstan as a prime example.

Kyrgyzstan's energy dependency on Russia is particularly acute in comparison to some of its neighbors, with as much as 97 percent of oil products consumed in the republic imported from Russia.[37] While there are two oil processing plants in the republic, the production capacity of which exceed the country's demand for fuel, Kyrgyzstan does not have sufficient oil reserves and has to import petroleum products from Russia.[38] This gives Russian companies importing petroleum products to Kyrgyzstan an effective control over petroleum prices in Kyrgyzstan. Petroleum prices also fluctuate depending on exchange rate because all financial transactions with Russian companies are conducted in U.S. dollars.[39] The high transportation costs—oil products imported from Russia to Kyrgyzstan are transported through

Kazakhstan—and export tariffs in Kazakhstan, make Russian petroleum a less attractive but unavoidable option.

Some of the costs of Russian petroleum are offset by the duty-free arrangement between the countries. A bilateral free trade agreement first signed by the governments of Kyrgyzstan and Russia in 1992 allowed Kyrgyzstan to receive petroleum from Russia at preferential rates.[40] On several occasions, however, the Kremlin used its control of petroleum exports to Kyrgyzstan to push its political agenda. The political and economic crisis that overthrew Kurmanbek Bakiyev's government in April 2010 is particularly illustrative in this regard.

From early 2010, Bishkek's relationship with the Kremlin grew increasingly tense. The failure of Bakiyev's government to close the Manas air base in exchange for loans and investments in a hydropower station and its willingness to host a U.S.-funded anti-terrorist training center in the south of the country convinced the Russian leadership that the Bakiyev government was an unreliable partner. As the disagreements mounted—the Kyrgyz government failed to pass 48 percent of stocks of Dastan, the Soviet-built torpedo plant in Bishkek, in exchange for the forgiveness of 180 million USD indebtedness—the Russian government imposed a tariff on oil and oil products imported to Kyrgyzstan on April 1, 2010.[41] While Medvedev's government argued that the tariffs on petroleum exports applied to any nation outside the Eurasian Customs Union, observers suggested that the tariffs were a "retaliation" against Bakiyev's government. The report by the Kyrgyz Ministry of Economic Regulations that the Kremlin did not officially inform Bishkek about the introduction of the tariffs strongly points in this direction.[42]

The 30 percent increase in petroleum prices resulting from the imposition of tariffs was particularly damaging for the economy of a country in the throes of political and economic crisis. As Bishkek-based political analyst Alexander Knyazev noted, the increase in gasoline prices would "seriously affect Bakiyev's position. The protest mood based on social-economic reasons is strong and is increasing among ordinary people, and the expected rise [in prices] of basic commodities and products will heighten the anti-Bakiyev mood."[43] The discontent over the higher prices on gasoline certainly fueled popular protests that had already started in the north of the country as early as March 2010. Soon after the spike in prices, protests escalated into a standoff with government forces, forcing Bakiyev to flee the capital on April 9, 2010.

Although, as Evgeny Troitskiy argues, the Russian government intended, in all likelihood, to put pressure on Bakiyev's regime rather than topple it, the Russian government both fueled popular discontent with and criticism of Bakiyev and benefited from his ouster. Omurbek Tekebayev, a former opposition leader, suggested that "the Russian factor was decisive" in giving momentum to the protests. Knyazev added that "Bakiyev was spoiling the relationship, and people saw it. That's how this protest mood got started."[44] Tekebayev also suggested that Russia's actions undermined Bakiyev's support by signaling to Kyrgyz elites and opposition leaders that Bakiyev could not stay in power.[45]

Russia's first actions after the so-called Second Revolution (the first one brought Bakiyev to power in 2005) indicate that the Russian government was keen on seizing the opportunity to influence the new interim government and Kyrgyzstan's dependence on Russian petroleum as one of the means of ensuring loyalty of the fledgling government. In what was a fine show of Russia's soft power built on the promise of aid and concessions, Moscow pledged its support for the interim government a week after Bakiyev's flight from the country. Bishkek would receive 50 million USD in humanitarian aid, 25,000 tons of petroleum products, and the cancellation of oil export tariffs.[46]

Russia further expanded its control of Kyrgyzstan's energy sector in 2014, when the Russian state-owned own company Rosneft signed an agreement to buy 100 percent of Bishkek Oil, which has a wholesale and retail gasoline business in the capital. The same month, Gazprom, the Russian state gas company, paid the symbolic 1 USD for the 100 percent stake in Kyrgyzgas, the state-owned monopolist supplier of natural gas. In return Gazprom assumed more than 41 million USD in Kyrgyzgas's debt. Gazprom is also the dominant provider of aviation fuel in Kyrgyzstan and, as of 2014, had a 70 percent share of the retail gasoline market.[47]

While energy dependency is rightfully seen by many as an example of hard power, Russia's leverage over energy markets builds heavily on investments and rewards to local actors. Over the past ten years, Gazprom invested around 1 billion USD in Kyrgyzstan. The completion of a pipeline in August 2017 has similarly made Kyrgyzstan's gas supply more reliable.[48] Gazprom also committed to investing around 100 billion rubles (1.73 billion USD) in expanding Kyrgyzstan gas grid by 2030, which would provide 60 percent of Kyrgyzstan's territory with gas, as opposed to 26 percent currently.[49]

The dim economic prospects of Kyrgyzstan's energy markets—the failure to pay gas bills remains a significant issue—highlight the political motivations of Gazprom's investments. According to Igor Yushkov, a senior analyst at the Moscow-based National Energy Security Fund, "Moscow is looking to expand the Eurasian Economic Union (EAEU) project, so it needs to offer Kyrgyzstan favourable economic conditions."[50] But there is a downside to these favorable conditions; as Nicolas De Pedro of the Barcelona Centre for International Affairs points out "If Russia takes control of the few strategic assets that Bishkek has at its disposal, the Kyrgyzstan authorities will see their already narrow capacity of maneuver severely diminished."[51]

THE STRANGE CASE OF RUSSIAN CONTROL IN CENTRAL ASIAN MEDIA

Mass media is indispensable to creating and projecting soft power abroad. As Nye has famously argued, "information is power"[52] and "the ability to share information—and to be believed—becomes an important source of attraction and power."[53] In other words, "politics in an information age may ultimately be about whose story wins."[54] Russia is no stranger to recognizing the ability of media to shape favorable public opinion and policy outcomes. In 2011, the then Russian foreign minister Sergey Lavrov acknowledged that defending national interests "without proper use of solid soft power resources" was "impossible." The Russian Foreign Policy Concepts of 2008 and 2013 had similarly pledged to "develop effective means of information influence on public opinion abroad."[55] To that end, the Kremlin funneled considerable resources into domestic and international media outlets and news agencies. In 2017, Russia Today (RT), the state-sponsored TV network which broadcasts in English, Spanish, German, French, and Arabic, received 18.7 billion rubles (around 328 million USD) in government funding.[56]

Despite the obvious soft power implications of Russia's efforts to build a media presence in the near and far abroad, its mode of operation and its interference in elections in the republics of the former Soviet Union[57] raises serious concerns about the harder aspects of the Kremlin's use of media. Furthermore, while Russian state-sponsored outlets are often successful at co-opting public opinion—which Nye considers critical to the functioning of soft power—the means with which these networks come to dominate the media landscape in targeted countries are more suggestive of hard power. Let us consider how Russian media shape favorable public opinions and policy outcomes with the example of Kyrgyzstan.

It is hard to underestimate the influence of public broadcasting in Kyrgyzstan, where 97 percent of the population has access to TV[58] and only 34 percent have access to internet.[59] A considerable share of broadcasters in Kyrgyzstan is either Russian-owned or Russian-based. Sputnik—one of the best known Russian news agencies with close ties to the Russian government-funded Russia Today network—has an office in Bishkek and reports both in Russian and in Kyrgyz.

Even more influential are Russian TV broadcasters, such as ORT and RTR. Both channels are included in the so-called "social package" broadcasting, meaning that they are available free of charge as a part of the public broadcasting services.[60] It is unusual to have a foreign broadcaster included in the public broadcasting services and the Kyrgyz government's decision to give Russian TV broadcasters the same status as national broadcasters was controversial. The initial proposal to give equal status to ORT and RTR-planeta was first made by the Kyrgyz Ministry of Culture, Information and Tourism in January 2016. If implemented, the proposal would eliminate any fees payable by the Russian broadcasters for broadcasting in the territory of Kyrgyzstan. The costs would be effectively transferred onto the Kyrgyz government. The proposal would also lift the legal restrictions which bar foreign-owned media from becoming public broadcasters in Kyrgyzstan and stipulate that more than half of broadcasting content should be in Kyrgyz.[61] It is unclear whether the proposal was implemented—the government had called it off after a public outcry—but the inclusion of three Russian broadcasters in the "social package" broadcasting in May 2017 suggests that it was, this time without any consultation with the public.[62]

The discontent of some public commentators who expressed their reservations about Russian broadcasters is understandable. Russia has in the past used its media to sway popular opinion in Kyrgyzstan. In March 2010, during popular protests against the Bakiyev government, Russian media, including ORT and the leading daily *Izvestia*, both state-funded, launched a campaign against Bakiyev and his family. TV programs and newspapers ran investigations on corruption and nepotism within the Bakiyev government, with some even alleging Bakiyev's involvement in the killing of the journalist Gennadii Pavliuk. The regime attempted to block some Russian websites and TV programs in response.[63] Undoubtedly, the popular discontent against Bakiyev had more to do with local factors, but it is easy to see how the media campaign against him and his family helped stoke the protests.

Moscow used Russian broadcasters again during the parliamentary and presidential elections after the ouster of Bakiyev in 2010. Felix Kulov, Russia's favorite in the presidential elections, received considerable attention in the Russian media. One of the most publicized moments of Kulov's presidential campaign involved his meeting with President Medvedev.[64] In a televised reception, Medvedev said that Russia was "an interested observer" in the elections willing to see "a strong, responsible and authoritative" government in Kyrgyzstan.[65] Kulov's party, Ar-Namys, even signed a well-publicized cooperation agreement with the ruling United Russia party.[66]

Another Kyrgyz politician, who received considerable—and considerably negative— exposure in the Russian media was Tekebayev. Tekebayev, the leader of the Ata-Meken party, was widely seen as pro-American and the main proponent of the parliamentary form of government heavily criticized by the Russian leadership.[67] In what Erica Marat, a Kyrgyz-born political scientist, has described as "Russia's use of its soft power," Russia's NTV television network aired a program on Tekebayev that screened a two-year-old sex tape of Tekebayev's extramarital affair.[68] Tekebayev did not go on to win the presidency, but neither ultimately did Kulov. Nonetheless, Russian media's enormous popularity in Kyrgyzstan and its ability to influence popular opinion are likely to remain a force to contend with. Furthermore, the inclusion of Russian broadcasters into the public broadcasting services package gives Russian media a captive audience of up to 97 percent of Kyrgyzstan's population.

CHINESE AID GENERALLY BENEFITS CHINA

Although investments and development aid do not fall in Nye's definition of power resources, which include culture, political values, and policies that "have moral authority," and is instead tied to payments, or what Nye terms the "carrots" designed to affect others' behavior,[69] its ability to increase countries' attractiveness and bolster legitimacy is impossible to ignore. Yet, as we will show below, the implications of foreign aid and investments both for providers and their recipients are mixed. While intended to boost soft power, foreign aid can facilitate economic and political coercion and alienate domestic audiences. Because China has now replaced Russia as the key provider of grants, loans, and investments in Central Asia, this section will focus on China's development aid to Kyrgyzstan.

Several things need to be said about Chinese aid to countries of the Global South, including Kyrgyzstan. Its attractiveness builds on principles designed to place China apart from Western donors. China is particularly keen on positioning itself as a fellow developing nation through what it calls South-South collaboration. Another element of the Chinese strategy of building soft power through aid is the principle of non-interference and respect for sovereignty;[70] Chinese loans, as a rule, are not attached to specific demands for economic and political reforms. The goal is to convince recipient governments that "they can shape their own development strategies without outside interference."[71]

Often, China is the only source of large-scale investments. Corruption, political and economic instability, as well as difficulties associated with conducting business in Central Asia make the region less attractive for European and North American investors. Loans by international organizations, such as the IMF and World Bank, impose strict conditions on recipient countries, which are required to implement policy reforms, including the highly unpopular austerity measures. Chinese loans, on the other hand, come with fewer restrictions on spending. In the words of the Chinese ambassador to Kyrgyzstan, Xiao Qinghua, "how Kyrgyzstan uses [China's] credits is its internal affair."[72] Another advantage that China has over other creditors is that China can, as Valentin Bogatyrev, the coordinator of a Bishkek-based think tank, noted, "offer Kyrgyzstan significantly more investment than all the other donors put together."[73]

This explains Kyrgyzstan's high rates of indebtedness to China. In 2010, Kyrgyzstan's 150 million USD debt to China was equivalent to 5.7 percent of foreign loans taken by Kyrgyzstan. Within seven years, the share of Chinese loans to Kyrgyzstan grew eleven-fold and reached 41.6 percent, or 1.7 billion USD. Most of this debt is managed by the state-owned Exim (Export Import) Bank of China, whose loans to Kyrgyzstan, by the end of 2016, totaled 1.5 billion USD, or approximately 40 percent of the country's total external debt.[74]

On the other hand, the benefits of Chinese credits to Kyrgyzstan are equivocal at best, as the terms of repayment for Chinese loans are notoriously harsh. To start with, most Chinese loans are denominated in U.S. dollars,[75] which makes Kyrgyzstan more vulnerable to inflation and fluctuations in currency exchange rates. Second, the terms of repayment are very short, meaning that many loans have to be repaid in as little as five years. According to the Kyrgyz Ministry of Finance, terms of repayment on Chinese loans range from five to twenty-five years. In five years, Kyrgyzstan will have to pay its Chinese creditors 320 million USD.[76]

Third, Chinese creditors often require recipient countries to employ Chinese contractors to implement projects funded by their loans. All of the large projects in Kyrgyzstan financed by Chinese loans are completed by Chinese companies. For example, the "North–South" road—the largest road construction project since independence—financed by an 850 million USD loan from the Exim Bank is built by the China Road and Bridge Corporation (CBRC).[77] The 405-kilometer-long Datka-Kemin high-voltage power line financed by a 390 million USD loan from the Exim Bank was built by the Chinese Tebian Electric Apparatus (TBEA) company.[78] The same company completed the modernization of the Bishkek Heat and Power Plant (HPP), which was financed by a 386 million USD loan from the Exim Bank.[79]

In addition to not being able to choose contractors on projects financed by China, Kyrgyzstan is also obliged to hire Chinese workers to work on the projects. During the construction of two roads (Osh-Sarytash-Irkeshtam and Bishkek-Naryn-Torugart), funded in part by a loan from China, only 30 percent of workers working on the project were local, the remaining 70 percent were Chinese. Furthermore, 60 percent of raw materials for the construction were imported from China.[80] The Chinese-built and Chinese-owned Zhongda China Petrol Company oil processing plant in Kara-Balta similarly employs 50 percent Chinese workers, even though the initial agreement required that 80 percent of the workforce should be filled by Kyrgyz nationals.[81] Recent reports by government officials and youth organizations suggest that the company also employed up to 970 illegal Chinese workers to build the plant.[82] In 2016, of the 13,500 guest workers who came to Kyrgyzstan on a government quota, 85 percent were Chinese.[83] Some analysts estimate that as many as 100,000 Chinese labor migrants, both legal and illegal, work in the country.[84]

The issue of greatest concern, however, is how these loans are going to be repaid and what happens if Kyrgyzstan is unable to honor its duties. According to the Chinese ambassador to Kyrgyzstan, Xiao Qinghua, China does not intend to write off its debts to Kyrgyzstan. Speaking in March 2018, Qinghua emphasized that "Chinese credits are given on preferential conditions . . . Kyrgyzstan benefited from them. Credits will have to be repaid in accordance with agreements. The Chinese side does not consider other options."[85]

While the reluctance of the Chinese government to write off debts is understandable, the terms of repayment that China imposed on Kyrgyzstan are highly controversial. One of the loan agreements signed between the government of Kyrgyzstan and the Exim Bank, for example, stipulates that "neither the borrower nor any of its assets is entitled to any right of immunity on the grounds of sovereignty or otherwise from arbitration, suit, execution or any other legal process with respect to its obligations under this agreement."[86] The agreement also requires that any disputes concerning the repayment of loans are settled at the Hong Kong–based International Arbitration Centre in accordance with Chinese laws.[87]

In simple terms, that means that the Chinese government may demand any of Kyrgyzstan's assets. There is a growing fear in all of the Central Asian republics that China may seize land or natural resources if loans are not repaid on time. These fears are not entirely unfounded. There have been precedents where China claimed critical assets in return for loan forgiveness. Countries that transferred their assets to Chinese creditors include Pakistan, which in 2015 leased Gwadar Port to China for forty years in return for a Chinese loan which financed the construction of the port in the first place. In 2017, another port financed by a Chinese loan in Sri Lanka was leased to China by the Sri Lankan government for ninety-nine years. Even more contentious was the transfer of land to China by Tajikistan.[88] In 2011, the Tajik government ceded 1,000 square kilometers of its territory to China in exchange for having some of its debts forgiven.[89]

Central Asia's mineral wealth could provide another means of repaying Chinese loans. Li Lifan, associate research professor at Shanghai Academy of Social Sciences, noted that repayment may be made in the form of mineral concessions. Chinese mining companies are already active in the country. As of June 2013, of the 228 gold deposits in the territory of Kyrgyzstan, 100 were operated by Chinese companies.[90] In 2015, 60 percent of all licenses for exploration and development of Kyrgyz mineral deposits were held by Chinese corporations.[91] According to Jeffrey Reeves, director of Asian Studies at The United States Army War College, China uses loans and aid to secure access to mining sites in Kyrgyzstan in lieu of repayment.[92] Certainly, some of the mineral deposits, such as that of Ishtamberdy, in the south of the country, are seen by local media as concessions in exchange for Chinese assistance.[93] Often, the terms of repayment offered as a part of the debt forgiveness schemes in exchange for resources are highly unequal. In 2012, the Chinese government proposed "Resources for Investment" scheme, which would transfer control over two aluminum and iron ore deposits, valued at $15 and $100 billion, respectively, to Chinese companies in return for a $3 billion loan, which would finance the construction of a railway line connecting Kyrgyzstan with China and Uzbekistan.[94]

China's economic influence in Kyrgyzstan also translates into political influence. Owing to the country's geographic location on the border with China's most volatile province of Xinjiang and its minority Uyghur population, Kyrgyzstan, and the Central Asian region at large, are critical to China's security. Nicolas De Pedro claims the Uyghur issue always figured in China's policies toward the region. "It is a key factor to explain the rapid rapprochement between Beijing and the newly independent republics after the collapse of the USSR. Beijing was interested in putting an end to the Soviet policy of traditional support and sympathy for the Uighur activism, particularly in Kyrgyzstan, Kazakhstan and Uzbekistan."[95]

Today, Uyghurs comprise about 1 percent of Kyrgyzstan's population of 6.2 million people. Although Kyrgyzstan is considered a relative safe haven for Uyghur, the recent crackdown by the Chinese government on its Muslim ethnic minorities, primarily Uyghurs, but also Kazakhs, Kyrgyz, and Hui put increasing pressure on Kyrgyzstan and other Central Asian republics to yield to the demands of their more powerful neighbor.[96] In recent years, Uyghurs of Kyrgyzstan have become a target of increased surveillance and repression by the Kyrgyz authorities. The Kyrgyz government routinely prohibits Uyghur meetings, and, according to the World Uyghur Congress, fifty Uyghurs were extradited from Kyrgyzstan to China in the ten years between 2001 and 2011.[97] According to the World Uyghur Congress, the Kyrgyz authorities "invariably send . . . Uyghurs who flee persecution in China . . . back to face Chinese authorities." Another unnamed source from the George Washington University confirms that "if China requests the arrest or extradition of its Uyghur citizens resident in Kyrgyzstan, the Kyrgyz government is likely to oblige them."[98]

Ultimately, China's role in the region is likely to grow in the coming years. Central Asia is indispensable to the highly ambitious Belt and Road Initiative (BRI) proposed by the Chinese leadership, and the Beijing government will look for ways to integrate the region more firmly within its growing commercial and political networks. Beijing is also likely to use its increasing involvement in Central Asia in order to gain access to mineral resources and ensure the cooperation of Central Asian governments in addressing its Uyghur issue.

CENTRAL ASIA'S CAPTIVE WORKERS

Like foreign aid, immigration does not strictly fall within Nye's definition of *soft power*, but it is highly relevant when measuring soft power in terms of countries' ability to attract. Anholt–Gfk Roper Nation Brands Index, for example, lists immigration among six dimensions of "national competence."[99] By that measure, Russia's soft power in the republics of Central Asia is formidable as it keeps attracting millions of labor migrants from the region. The Kremlin's use of labor migrants to further its political goals, however, is more in line with the conception of hard power, as Russia's leadership leverages migration quotas to put pressure on the governments of Central Asian republics, which are heavily dependent on remittances from labor migrants in Russia. Let us consider how this dynamic plays out in the example of Kyrgyzstan.

Kyrgyzstan ranks among most remittance-dependent countries in the world. Between 2017 and 2018, in fact, it ranked first in the world in terms of remittances to GDP ratio and the situation is unlikely to change in the coming years. There has been a steady and considerable growth in migrant remittances to Kyrgyzstan. While in 2008 remittances made up 20 percent of the country's GDP, in 2018 they hit the 40 percent mark. Most of these remittances are sent by Kyrgyz labor migrants in Russia. As of 2018, there were more than 800,000 registered Kyrgyz migrants in Russia. The actual number—inclusive of illegal migrants—is likely to be higher. In 2017, labor migrants transferred 2.5 billion USD to Kyrgyzstan—a number which exceeds the annual budget of the country.[100]

For a country with a population of roughly six million, the staggering number of labor migrants reflects the lack of opportunities at home. Remittances help the economy of Kyrgyzstan stay afloat, if not develop; without remittances from abroad, as much as 60 percent of Kyrgyzstan's population would live below the poverty line. The obvious implication of the scale of labor migration from Kyrgyzstan to Russia is Kyrgyzstan's dependence on Russia. Just how dangerous this dependence can be, is well illustrated by the sharp drop in remittances during the Russian economic crisis of 2014–2015, when the number of people living below the poverty line in Kyrgyzstan rose by 1.5 percent.[101]

Political implications of Kyrgyzstan's economic dependence on Russia are equally serious. The Russian government has in the past pressured Central

Asian republics by using threats to introduce visa regimes or other regulations to reduce the number of migrants. In 2014, the Russian government added over 600,000 foreigners to the blacklist, according to the head of the Federal Migration Service (FMS). Of these, 60,000 were Kyrgyz citizens. Russian officials cited the economic downturn as the chief reason for the black list. According to Bakhrom Ismailov, an adviser on migration to the Russian parliament, "there was no need for so many labor migrants . . . due to slowing economic growth in the global economy and negative trends in the Russian economy."[102]

For many observers, however, the introduction of the black list was an attempt to pressure the Kyrgyz government into the Customs Union. Kyrgyz opposition parliamentarian Ravshan Djeyenbekov described it as "pressure on our country, which is being pulled by unhealthy economic and political associations like the Customs Union." Djeyenbekov also expressed fear that the Russian leadership would "invent a problem to drag us into the union."[103]

Djeyenbekov's fears were not entirely unfounded. Established in 2010, the Eurasian Customs Union is a Russia-led initiative seen by many as an instrument of consolidating Russian influence in the republics of the former Soviet Union. Kyrgyzstan's accession to the union in 2015 was highly controversial. As a member of the World Trade Organization (WTO), Kyrgyzstan profited from low customs tariffs and proximity with China. Chinese goods were first imported to Kyrgyzstan and later resold to customers in Kazakhstan, Russia, and other republics of the former Soviet Union.[104] Joining the Customs Union, however, made trade with countries outside the union more difficult. As a member of the Customs Union, Kyrgyzstan has to pay much higher tariffs on goods coming from China. Given that China accounts for half of Kyrgyzstan's trade volume, while Russia's share is only 17 percent, it would be safe to argue that the decision to join the Customs Union was a political, not economic one.[105] Moscow's decision to liberalize the movement of goods, services, labor, and capital within the Union was likely a key factor in Kyrgyzstan's decision to join.[106]

Despite Kyrgyzstan's accession to the union, the black list of migrants remains. As of October 2018, there were 70,000 Kyrgyz citizens on the list.[107] The continuing efforts of the Kyrgyz leadership to renegotiate this number with Moscow indicate that the Russian government may again use labor migrants to put pressure on Kyrgyzstan. The Russian military base in Kyrgyzstan could certainly provide sufficient grounds for another round of talks concerning the removal of Kyrgyz migrants from the black list. Precedence has already been established when in 2011 the Russian leadership used threats to close the Russian labor markets to Tajik migrants to force Dushanbe to agree to the terms of extension for the Russian military base near the border with Afghanistan. Despite initial disagreements, which led to the

Russian authorities' crackdown on illegal migrants from Tajikistan, the Tajik government agreed to a thirty-year extension after Moscow promised to ease some of the visa restrictions.[108]

HARD POWER CAN BE SOFT, TOO

Perhaps the most obvious indicator of Russia's hard power in Central Asia is its military bases in Kyrgyzstan and Tajikistan. Yet, as we will discuss in this section, this particular display of hard power has paradoxically soft dimensions. Despite the tensions and hard bargaining between Russia and Kyrgyzstan over the Kant military base, Russia's military presence is seen by the country's political leadership both as a way to enhance security of the republic and as means of counterweighing China's growing influence in the region.[109] The Kyrgyz leadership is keen to keep the Russian military base. Indeed, the Kyrgyz government extended the invitation to the Kremlin to open a second base in the south of the republic in 2017. By all reports, the Russian government declined the offer, due probably to the enormous costs of Russia's engagement in Syria and in Ukraine,[110] but the discussions of a possible second base are ongoing.[111]

As a host country, Kyrgyzstan, too, had some leverage over Russia, which it used in the past to raise the rental fees and to extract debt forgiveness. More importantly, however, Russia's military presence in Kyrgyzstan is seen by the domestic audience as at least legitimate, if not attractive. Furthermore, as we will argue here, Russia is likely to expand its military presence in Kyrgyzstan in future. In practical terms, this means that the Kremlin may use its military to generate soft power as regional security provider, while at the same time enhance its ability to put pressure on the Central Asian republics. This section will discuss the complex nature of Russia's military presence in Kyrgyzstan and the future security arrangements in the region.

The Kant military base, which employed around 600 Russian servicemen and four Su-25 ground-attack aircraft and four Mi-8 transport helicopters in 2012,[112] was established in 2003 as a counterweight to the American Manas Transit Center that opened two years earlier. American military presence gave Kyrgyzstan some leverage in its dealings with Russia. Eager to see Americans leave Kyrgyzstan, the Russian government held several rounds of talks in 2009 with the then Bakiyev government. Russia offered Kyrgyzstan a substantial aid package of 300 million USD and 2 billion USD in investments in hydropower projects in exchange for the closure of the Transit Center and a forty-nine-year extension of the lease on the Russian base.[113] The Kyrgyz authorities accepted 300 million USD from Russia and publicly announced the closure of the Center before reneging on their earlier commitments after the U.S. government raised the annual rental payment to 60 million USD and pledged an additional 117 million USD in aid.[114] The subsequent fallout between Russia and Kyrgyzstan led to Russia's withdrawal from the hydropower project.

In 2010, after Bakiyev's ouster from power, the Russian leadership was given another opportunity to lobby for the closure of the Manas Transit Center. On the other hand, the newly elected government under President Almazbek Atambayev sought to revise the agreement on the lease of the Kant base reached under Bakiyev. In 2012 he threatened to close down the base, saying that Kyrgyzstan "may take a different path."[115] After much negotiation, Kyrgyzstan and Russia agreed to extend Moscow's lease on the base for fifteen years in exchange for a 500 million USD debt write-off. The agreement came in the wake of Bishkek's confirmation of plans to close down the Transit Center after its lease expired in 2014.[116]

In a swift development, the Russian state-owned oil company Rosneft moved in to secure a majority stake in the Manas International Airport as the Transit Center was preparing to vacate the premises. Seeking at least a 51 percent stake in the airport, Rosneft said that the investment was "aimed at the creation of a large-scale international logistics hub." Alexander Cooley, a political scientist specializing in Central Asia at Barnard College in New York, contended that "Rosneft's bid for Manas marks the culmination of Russia's recent methodical acquisition of Kyrgyzstan's key strategic assets. Over the last two years, Moscow has sought to terminate Bishkek's security cooperation with the US and become the Central Asian state's dominant and exclusive strategic partner. It is now clear that Moscow seeks to turn Kyrgyzstan into a client state."[117]

But the Kant airbase and the controlling stake in the Manas International Airport are not the only Russian assets in Kyrgyzstan. In addition to the airbase in Kant, some 40 kilometers away from Bishkek, Russia maintains the torpedo testing center at Issyk-Kul, a seismic station at Maily-Suu, and a communication center in Chui Province.[118] An even more interesting potential asset that Kyrgyzstan may sell to Russia is the Dastan torpedo plant. Sputnik News reports that Russia has been eager to acquire the plant for some time as Dastan produces the world's fastest VA-111 Shkval torpedoes used by the Russian Navy. In 2009, during the negotiations about the extension of lease on the Kant airbase, Russia used the opportunity to propose that Kyrgyzstan trade the controlling stake in the Dastan torpedo plant for a debt write-off. For a 48 percent stake in the plant, Moscow would write off 180 million USD that Kyrgyzstan owed to Russia. The debt forgiveness scheme was developed in 2009 but did not go through because the following year

Bakiyev's government was ousted from power. In 2011, the new government offered the plant to Russia, but Russia was now asking for a 75 percent stake in the torpedo plant, or, as an alternative, to write off a lesser share of the Kyrgyz debt for the previously agreed 48 percent stake in the plant. "Bishkek has been offered to either a write off a lesser debt for the same assets or to increase the stake transferred to Russia," Kommersant said, citing a Russian government source.[119] It seems that no agreement was reached on the plant in 2011 and it is still in Kyrgyzstan's possession, though that may of course change in future.

The U.S. withdrawal from Kyrgyzstan means that Russia and China will play increasingly important roles in the country and in the region in general. General Joseph Votel, the commander of U.S. Central Command, blamed the failure of military cooperation with Kyrgyzstan on the Kyrgyz government, which he contended "has increasingly aligned its interests with Russia and China," citing the closure of the Manas Transit Center and the breakdown of military ties between the two countries.[120] While perhaps a fair assessment, Vogel's criticism of the Kyrgyz leadership belies both Kyrgyzstan's economic and security dependence on Russia and its integration into Russia-led regional military alliances. The Kant airbase, for example, is a part of the Collective Security Treaty Organization (CSTO), the military alliance of six post-Soviet states, where it plays the role of air force component of the Collective Rapid Reaction Forces.[121]

Furthermore, as the United States is preparing to pull out of Afghanistan, Kyrgyzstan will have to look to its more powerful neighbors, China and Russia, for security and aid. After all, security issues affecting Kyrgyzstan are far more likely to affect neighboring states than the far-flung United States. Kyrgyzstan is also a member of several regional security schemes, of which the Shanghai Cooperation Organization (SCO), which was founded by China, Kazakhstan, Kyrgyzstan, Russia, Tajikistan, and Uzbekistan in 2001, is increasingly important.

Equally important is that as China's military assistance to Kyrgyzstan and other Central Asian countries continues to grow so will the region's dependence on China. China has been providing military assistance to Central Asian republics for nearly twenty years. In November 1999, for example, China gave Kyrgyzstan's army clothing for troops. China has also participated in military counterterrorism exercises with troops from Kyrgyzstan, Kazakhstan, and Tajikistan (Uzbekistan usually does not send troops to such drills). In October 2002, China conducted bilateral exercises with Kyrgyz forces. While concerns have been raised by observers about the possibility of growing military tensions between China and Russia in the region, Beijing seems content to allow Russia to be Central Asia's guarantor of security.[122]

CONCLUSION

In this chapter, we sought to investigate the applicability of Nye's conception of soft power to contemporary Kyrgyzstan by looking at several key areas of Russia's and China's influence in the country. We argued that the disparity of capabilities and the highly asymmetric pattern of relations between Kyrgyzstan and the two powers make decoupling soft power from hard power impossible. As we have shown in the example of Kyrgyzstan, soft power can have hard characteristics and hard consequences. For instance, Russia's use of media, a presumably soft power tool, is intended to intervene in and shape the electoral behavior of the Kyrgyzstani electorate. The means with which Russia obtained the extensive media presence in Kyrgyzstani was also coercive. Similarly, the promise of higher earnings, which attracts Central Asian labor migrants to Russia, has given the Russian government an increased leverage against Kyrgyzstan.

On the other hand, hard power can have soft power effects. To give but one example, Russia's military presence—a hard power feature—is seen by the majority of Kyrgyzstan's elites as desirable and having a positive impact on the security of the republic. Kyrgyzstan's energy dependence, another ostensibly hard power instrument, as this chapter has shown, has been premised on the promise of rewards and benefits for the country. Another contentious question we sought to address in this chapter is whether development aid and foreign investments can generate soft power. As the example of China's aid to Kyrgyzstan suggests, despite the possible attraction of China's development models, its aid and investments have acted as instruments of hard power and hold a substantial capacity for political and economic pressure both at present and in future. Put simply, Chinese aid does not so much seek to purchase influence or co-opt local elites, as give the Communist Party levels of power and coercion against its much smaller neighbor. In the final analysis, the complex entanglements of soft and hard power in Kyrgyzstan and the Central Asian region at large call for new conceptions of influence and soft power in the former Soviet space.

NOTES

1. Jeanne L. Wilson, "Soft Power: A Comparison of Discourse and Practice in Russia and China," *Europe-Asia Studies* 67, no. 8 (2015): 1174.

2. Li Mingjiang, "Soft Power in Chinese Discourse: Popularity and Prospects," (working paper no. 165, S. Rajaratnam School of International Studies, Singapore, September 2008), https://www.rsis.edu.sg/wp-content/uploads/rsis-pubs/WP165.pdf.

3. Bonnie S. Glaser and Melissa E. Murphy, "Soft Power with Chinese Characteristics: The Ongoing Debate," in *Chinese Soft Power and Its Implications for the United States: Competition and Cooperation in the Developing World*, ed. Carola McGiffert (Washington DC: CSIS, 2009), 15.

4. Agnia Grigas, "Legacies, Coercion and Soft Power: Russian Influence in the Baltic States," briefing Paper, Chatham House, London, August 2012), https://www.chathamhouse.org/sites/default/files/public/Research/Russia%20and%20Eurasia/0812bp_grigas.pdf.

5. Joseph S. Nye Jr., "Public Diplomacy and Soft Power," *The Annals of the American Academy of Political and Social Science* 616 (2008): 94–109.

6. Tsygankov has a unique description: "Soft power includes all aspects of Russia's attractiveness to foreigners: Russian mass media, a large and efficient economy, familiar language and religion, aspects of historical legacy, family ties, and electronic products." Andrei P. Tsygankov, "If Not by Tanks, Then by Banks? The Role of Soft Power in Putin's Foreign Policy," *Europe-Asia Studies* 58, no. 7 (2006): 1079.

7. As Radnitz highlights, "Given their shared history, common language, and similar regime types, Central Asian security cooperation with Russia is to be expected. Political elites from the post-Soviet space were trained in the same institutions and received the same socialisation in late Soviet practice, discourse, worldview, and behavioural norms. . . . When Central Asian leaders meet, they converse in the lingua franca of the former empire." Scott Radnitz, "Between Russia and a Hard Place: Great Power Grievances and Central Asian Ambivalence," *Europe-Asia Studies* 70, no. 10 (2018): 1603.

8. Valentina Feklyunina, "Soft Power and Identity: Russia, Ukraine and the 'Russian World(s)'," *European Journal of International Relations* 22, no. 4 (2015): 786.

9. Grigas, "Legacies, Coercion and Soft Power."

10. Scott Radnitz remarks: "Though the Central Asian states may bristle at Russian patronising or neo-imperial hubris, they at least know they can 'do business' with Russians, a familiarity that is salient in contrast with China, a country not only with its own great power pretensions, but also a distinctly different culture that tends to alienate locals." Radnitz, "Between Russia and a Hard Place," 1603.

11. Wilson, "Soft Power," 1177.

12. Russian consolidation in the media, along with the launch of new cultural festivals and language centers, testifies to the importance that Moscow attaches to maintaining Russia's traditional cultural influence. Grigas, "Legacies, Coercion and Soft Power."

13. Tsygankov, "If Not by Tanks, Then by Banks?" 1084; Andrei P. Tsygankov, "Moscow's Soft Power Strategy," *Current History*, vol. 112, no. 756 (2013): 260.

14. Oxana Shevel, "The Politics of Citizenship Policy in Post-Soviet Russia," *Post-Soviet Affairs* 28, no. 1 (2012): 139–40.

15. Marlene Laruelle, "Russia's Eurasianist Soft Power in Central Asia," *Analytical Media "Eurasian Studies,"* July 14, 2017, http://greater-europe.org/archives/3190.

16. Tsygankov has a statement on this that has again not aged well: "Evidence of Russia's role in supporting secessionism and applying economic sanctions in Georgia remains inconclusive. One could assert that the Kremlin exploits its soft power in Abkhazia and South Ossetia by granting its residents Russian citizenships in order to preserve its leverage over Tbilisi. Yet the Kremlin's actions could also be viewed as informed by the desire to preserve stability by restraining Georgia's attempts to solve the issue through military force. On this issue, the jury is still out." Tsygankov, "If Not by Tanks, Then by Banks?" 1097. In 2008, the jury came back with a firm verdict.

17. Kristopher Natoli, "Weaponizing Nationality: An Analysis of Russia's Passport Policy in Georgia," *Boston University International Law Journal* 28 (2010): 389–417.

18. Grigas details the policy explicitly in relation to the Baltics: "Lastly, a particularly powerful tool of Russia's influence is its citizenship policy for its 'compatriots' or ethnic Russians living in the near abroad. This is the more powerful and invasive side of Russia's cultural policies that aim to maintain loyalty among compatriots. Russia offers automatic citizenship to people of Russian descent regardless of their domicile and other citizenship status. Crucially, Moscow offers them protection: Russia's National Security Strategy to 2020, approved in 2010 but consistent with the doctrine launched in 2000, declares the intent to protect the rights and interests of Russian citizens and 'compatriots' abroad through political, economic and other means. The strategy also emphasizes that united compatriots are a tool in achieving Russia's foreign policy aims. . . . The compatriot policy is perhaps meant and certainly works to create anticipation of leverage; thus it gives Russia influence without the Russian minority factor having to be invoked explicitly in specific disputes." Grigas, "Legacies, Coercion and Soft Power."

19. Tsygankov, "If Not by Tanks, Then by Banks?" 1088.
20. Tsygankov, "Moscow's Soft Power Strategy," 260.
21. Ibid.
22. Radnitz, "Between Russia and a Hard Place," 1598.
23. Ibid: 1608.
24. Ibid.
25. Wilson, "Soft Power," 1191.
26. Radnitz, "Between Russia and a Hard Place," 1602.
27. As noted by Jeanne L. Wilson, "Russia and China Respond to Soft Power," *Politics*, vol. 35, no. 3–4 (2015): 288.
28. Grigas, "Legacies, Coercion and Soft Power."
29. Ibid.
30. Ibid.
31. See, for example, Nigel Gould-Davies, "Russia's Sovereign Globalization: Rise, Fall and Future," (research paper, Chatham House, London, March 2016), https://www.chathamhouse.org/sites/default/files/publications/research/2016010 6RussiasSovereignGlobalizationGouldDaviesFinal.pdf.

32. Grigas writes: "Russia's coercive use of energy has not been confined to the Baltic states. It has been used as a tool of geopolitical influence in many states of the

former Soviet Union since the early 1990s. Under the leadership of Vladimir Putin, energy has become a consistent means to reach foreign policy goals."

33. Ibid.

34. John R. Haines, "Gazprom's 'Energetic Pliers' and Aspirations of a Eurasian Archipelago: The Geopolitics of Russia's Networked Energy Infrastructure," (The Philadelphia Papers No. 11, Foreign Policy Research Institute, Philadelphia, August 2015, https://www.fpri.org/wp-content/uploads/2015/08/haines_where-the-lions-are_complete.pdf.

35. Radnitz, "Between Russia and a Hard Place," 1604, 1598.

36. As Grigas remarks: "Inherent problems are posed by its economic diplomacy owing to the relationship between Russian business and the Russian state, which work together to achieve Moscow's goals." Grigas, "Legacies, Coercion and Soft Power."

37. "97% ot obshchego importa nefteproduktov v Kyrgyzstan prikhoditsia na Rossiiu," *Kabar*, July 4, 2013, http://old.kabar.kg/economics/full/58606.

38. Experts estimate that Kyrgyzstan needs about 1 million tons of fuel a year. The processing capacity of the oil-processing plants in Tokmok and Kara-Balta is jointly 1.2 million tons a year. "Pochermu Kyrgyzstan ne pokupaet kazakhstanskuiu neft' i kak rossiiskii benzin podryvaet valiutnye zapasy strany," *Belyi Parus*, January 1, 2016, https://paruskg.info/glavnaya/127523-127523.html.

39. "6 glavnykh mifov o rynke GSM v Kyrgyzstane," *Kaktus Media*, February 16, 2017, https://kaktus.media/doc/352511_6_glavnyh_mifov_o_rynke_gsm_v_kyrgyzstane.html

40. David Trilling and Chinghiz Umetov, "Kyrgyzstan: Is Putin Punishing Bakiyev?" *Eurasianet*, April 6, 2010,
https://eurasianet.org/kyrgyzstan-is-putin-punishing-bakiyev.

41. Evgeny Troitskiy, "Turmoil in Kyrgyzstan: A Challenge to Russian Foreign Policy," (UI Occasional Papers, The Swedish Institute of International Affairs, Stockholm, 2012), https://www.ui.se/globalassets/ui.se-eng/publications/ui-publications/turmoil-in-kyrgyzstan-a-challenge-to-russian-foreign-policy-min.pdf.

42. Trilling and Umetov, "Kyrgyzstan: Is Putin Punishing Bakiyev?

43. Ibid.

44. Ibid.

45. Philip P. Pan, "Russia is said to have Fueled Unrest in Kyrgyzstan," *Washington Post*, April 12, 2010, http://www.washingtonpost.com/wp-dyn/content/article/2010/04/11/AR2010041103827.html.

46. Jim Nichol, "The April 2010 Coup in Kyrgyzstan and its Aftermath: Context and Implications for U.S. Interests," (report, The Congressional Research Service, Washington DC, June 2010), https://fas.org/sgp/crs/row/R41178.pdf.

47. "Zavisimost': vse, chto nuzhno znat' kyrgyzstantsam o gaze, Rossii i 'Gazprome'," *Akchabar*, April 29, 2016, https://www.akchabar.kg/ru/article/economy/kyrgyz-gaz-gazprom/.

48. "Kyrgyzstan: Revamped Transnational Gas Pipeline Unveiled," *Eurasianet*, August 30, 2017, https://eurasianet.org/kyrgyzstan-revamped-transnational-gas-pipeline-unveiled.

49. "Gazprom Wraps up Pipeline Overhaul in Kyrgyzstan," *AVIM Center for Eurasian Studies*, September 8, 2017, https://avim.org.tr/en/Bulten/GAZPROM-WRAPS-UP-PIPELINE-OVERHAUL-IN-KYRGYZSTAN.

50. Ibid.

51. Ryskeldi Satke, "Russia Tightens Hold on Kyrgyzstan," *Nikkei Asian Review*, March 27, 2014, https://asia.nikkei.com/Economy/Russia-tightens-hold-on-Kyrgyzstan.

52. Nye, "Public Diplomacy and Soft Power," 99.

53. Joseph S. Nye Jr., "The Benefits of Soft Power," *Harvard Business School Working Knowledge*, August 2004, https://hbswk.hbs.edu/archive/the-benefits-of-soft-power.

54. Nye, "Public Diplomacy and Soft Power," 100.

55. Joanna Szostek, "Russia and the News Media in Ukraine: A Case of 'Soft Power'," *East European Politics & Societies* 28, no. 3 (2014): 463–64.

56. Farida Rustamova, "Biudzhet gosudarstvennykh SMI v Rossii vyrastet na 2,5 mlrd rublei," *BBC*, May 26, 2017, https://www.bbc.com/russian/news-40062877.

57. Russian meddling in elections is not new and had been observed in the early 1990s, after the collapse of the Soviet Union. Lucan Ahmad Way and Adam Casey, "Russia has been Meddling in Foreign Elections for Decades. Has it made a Difference?" *Washington Post*, January 8, 2018, https://www.washingtonpost.com/news/monkey-cage/wp/2018/01/05/russia-has-been-meddling-in-foreign-elections-for-decades-has-it-made-a-difference/?noredirect=on&utm_term=.239b756cf80f.

58. "Media prepdpochteniia naseleniia Kyrgyzstana (8 volna)," (report, M-Vector, Soros Foundation Kyrgyzstan, Bishkek, 2017), https://soros.kg/wp-content/uploads/2017/12/Otchet-Mediapredpochteniya-naseleniya-KR-8-volna.pdf.

59. "Kyrgyzstan profile—Media," *BBC*, June 25, 2019, https://www.bbc.com/news/world-asia-16187183

60. "Spisok kanalov," *RPO RMTR*, http://rpo.kg/channels/, accessed July 1, 2020.

61. Grigorii Mikhailov, "Rossiiskie telekanaly v Kyrgyzstane mogut ostat'sia bez statusa," *InoZpress*, January 12, 2016, http://www.inozpress.kg/news/view/id/48081.

62. "Rossiiskie kanaly ORT i RTR budut translirovat'sia v telesemeistve KTRK," *KTRK*, May 19, 2017, http://www.ktrk.kg/post/13345/ru.

63. Erica Marat, "Russian Mass Media Attack Bakiyev," *Jamestown Foundation*, April 1, 2010, https://jamestown.org/program/russian-mass-media-attack-bakiyev/.

64. Bruce Pannier, "Russia Takes Active Role in Kyrgyz Parliamentary Elections," *Radio Free Europe*, October 5, 2010, https://www.rferl.org/a/Russia_Takes_Active_Role_In_Kyrgyz_Parliamentary_Elections/2177192.html.

65. Troitskiy, "Turmoil in Kyrgyzstan."

66. Ibid.

67. Ibid.

68. Pannier, "Russia Takes Active Role in Kyrgyz Parliamentary Elections."

69. Nye, "Public Diplomacy and Soft Power," 94.

70. Cornelia Tremann, "China's Aid: The Image Boost," *The Interpreter*, September 21, 2018, https://www.lowyinstitute.org/the-interpreter/chinas-aid-image-boost.

71. Dan Banik and Nikolai Hegertun, "Why do Nations Invest in International Aid? Ask Norway. And China," *Washington Post*, October 27, 2017, https://www.washingtonpost.com/news/monkey-cage/wp/2017/10/27/why-do-nations-invest-in-international-aid-ask-norway-and-china/?utm_term=.a06316935e8a.

72. "Kitai obiazatel'no vernet vlozhennye v Kyrgyzstan sredstva. Tol'ko kak?" *Vesti.kg*, April 17, 2018, https://vesti.kg/zxc/item/51244-kitaj-obyazatelno-vernet-vlozhennye-v-kyrgyzstan-sredstva-tolko-kak.html.

73. Chris Rickleton, "Kyrgyzstan: Is Chinese Investment Really Win-Win?," *Eurasianet*, July 23, 2013, https://eurasianet.org/kyrgyzstan-is-chinese-investment-really-win-win.

74. John Hurley, Scott Morris, and Gailyn Portelance, "Examining the Debt Implications of the Belt and Road Initiative from a Policy Perspective," (CGD Policy Paper 121, Center for Global Development, Washington DC, March 2018), https://www.cgdev.org/sites/default/files/examining-debt-implications-belt-and-road-initiative-policy-perspective.pdf.

75. Dirk van der Kley, "Can Central Asia's Poorest States Pay Back Their Debts to China?" *The Diplomat*, December 1, 2017, https://thediplomat.com/2017/12/can-central-asias-poorest-states-pay-back-their-debts-to-china/.

76. Jazgul Masalieva, "Kyrgyzstan must pay down $ 320 million Debt to China in 5 years," *24.kg*, April 16, 2018, https://24.kg/english/81729_Kyrgyzstan_must_pay_down__320_million_debt_to_China_in_5_years_/.

77. Satina Aidar, "Kyrgyzstan's North-South Road to Corruption," *Open Democracy*, August 9, 2018, https://www.opendemocracy.net/od-russia/satina-aidar/kyrgyzstans-north-south-road-to-corruption.

78. "Kyrgyzstan Hails Epoch-Making Power Line," *Eurasianet*, August 31, 2015, https://eurasianet.org/kyrgyzstan-hails-epoch-making-power-line.

79. Both the North-South road project and the modernization of the HPP gained notoriety as documents were uncovered detailing embezzlement scheme and collusion between key Kyrgyz officials and the Chinese contractors. Altogether, it is estimated that $100 million was embezzled during the modernization of the HPPP. Aidar, "Kyrgyzstan's North-South Road to Corruption."

80. Sarah Lain, "China's Silk Road in Central Asia: Transformative or Exploitative?" *Financial Times*, April 27, 2016, https://www.ft.com/content/55ca031d-3fe3-3555-a878-3bcfa9fd6a98.

81. Cholpon Orozbekova, "China Relocating Heavy Enterprises to Kyrgyzstan," *Jamestown Foundation*, June 24, 2016, https://jamestown.org/program/china-relocating-heavy-enterprises-to-kyrgyzstan/.

82. Rickleton, "Kyrgyzstan: Is Chinese Investment Really Win-Win?"

83. Orozbekova, "China Relocating Heavy Enterprises to Kyrgyzstan."

84. Jeffrey Reeves, *Chinese Foreign Relations with Weak Peripheral States: Asymmetrical Economic Power and Insecurity* (London: Routledge, 2015), 67.

85. "Kitai daet kredity razvivaiushchimsia stranam – v tom chisle, Kyrgyzstanu. Ob'iasniaem zachem,"*Kloop*, April 9, 2018, https://kloop.kg/blog/2018/04/09/kitaj-daet-kredity-razvivayushhimsya-stranam-v-tom-chisle-kyrgyzstanu-obyasnyaem-zachem/.

86. Ibid. A nearly identical clause was included in the Chinese-Kenyan agreement for a loan to finance the construction of the Mombasa–Nairobi railway signed in May 2014. Edwin Okoth, "Kenya: SGR Pact with China a Risk to Kenyan Sovereignty, Assets," *Daily Nation*, January 13, 2019, https://allafrica.com/stories/201901140451.html.

87. Masalieva, "Kyrgyzstan must pay down $ 320 million debt to China in 5 years."

88. "Kitai daet kredity razvivaiushchimsia stranam," *Kloop*

89. "Tajikistan, Turkmenistan Submit to Chinese Capture," *Eurasianet*, June 24, 2016, https://eurasianet.org/tajikistan-turkmenistan-submit-chinese-capture.

90. "Chinese Companies have 79 Licenses for Gold Deposits in Kyrgyzstan," *Kabar*, June 23, 2013, http://old.kabar.kg/eng/economics/full/2095.

91. Jeffrey Reeves, "Economic Statecraft, Structural Power, and Structural Violence in Sino-Kyrgyz Relations," *Asian Security* 12, no. 2 (2015): 123.

92. Ibid, 124.

93. Rickleton, "Kyrgyzstan: Is Chinese Investment Really Win-Win?"

94. Reeves, "Economic Statecraft, Structural Power, and Structural Violence in Sino-Kyrgyz Relations," 124. It seems that the government gave the proposal serious consideration, but was ultimately forced to reject it under public pressure.

95. Ryskeldi Satke, "Uighurs in Kyrgyzstan Hope for Peace despite Violence," *Al Jazeera*, January 8, 2017, https://www.aljazeera.com/indepth/features/2016/09/uighurs-kyrgyzstan-hope-piece-violence-160915133619696.html.

96. Gene A. Bunin, "Central Asia Struggles with Fallout from China's Internment of Minorities," *Foreign Policy*, August 15, 2018, https://foreignpolicy.com/2018/08/15/central-asia-struggles-with-fallout-from-chinas-internment-of-minorities/.

97. Cristina Maza, "Kyrgyzstan's Uighurs Cautious, Still Fear Chinese Influence," *Eurasianet*, November 25, 2014, https://eurasianet.org/kyrgyzstans-uighurs-cautious-still-fear-chinese-influence.

98. "Kyrgyzstan: Treatment of the Uyghur [Uighur] minority by society and authorities, including state protection provided to victims of violence and discrimination; Uyghur minority political groups, including activities (2012–2015)," (report, Immigration and Refugee Board of Canada, published by Refworld, UNHCR, February 2015), https://www.refworld.org/docid/560b96564.html.

99. Barry M. Feinberg and Xiaoyan Zhao, "The Anholt–GfK Roper Nation Brands Index SM: Navigating the Changing World," in *International Place Branding Yearbook 2011: Managing Reputational Risk*, ed. Frank H. Go and Robert Covers (London: Palgrave Macmillan, 2011), 64–6.

100. Savia Hasanova and Anna Kapushenko, "Kyrgyzstan Survives on Money Made by Migrant Workers, But It Doesn't Know How To Spend It," *Open Democracy*, November 12, 2018, https://www.opendemocracy.net/od-russia/kyrgyzstan-survives-on-money-made-by-migrant-workers-but-it-doesn-t-know-how-to-spend-it.

101. Ibid.

102. Bakyt Ibraimov and Hamid Tursunov, "Russian Blacklist Keeps Central Asian Migrants Out," *Eurasianet*, March 24, 2014, https://eurasianet.org/russian-blacklist-keeps-central-asian-migrants-out.

103. Ibid.
104. "Kyrgyzstan's Dilemma over Russian-led Customs Union," *BBC*, January 20, 2014, https://www.bbc.com/news/world-asia-25718770.
105. "Remittance Man," *The Economist*, September 7, 2013, https://www.economist.com/asia/2013/09/07/remittance-man.
106. Aizhan Karypova, "Chem obernetsia dlia trudovykh migrantov iz Kyrgyzstana evraziiskaia integratsiia," *Region.kg*, June 3, 2015, http://region.kg/index.php?option=com_content&view=article&id=1491:2015-06-03-07-47-06&catid=42:2014-02-02-11-14-01&Itemid=7.
107. "Migratsiia. Kyrgyzstantsev iskliuchat iz 'chernogo spiska'," *Radio Azattyk*, October 18, 2018, https://rus.azattyk.org/a/kyrgyzstan_migraziya_rossiya/29551254.html.
108. "Russia Gets 30-year Extension for Base in Tajikistan," *BBC*, October 5, 2012, https://www.bbc.com/news/world-asia-19849247.
109. Margarete Klein, "Russia's Military Policy in the Post-Soviet Space: Aims, Instruments and Perspectives," (SWP Research Paper 1, German Institute for International and Security Affairs, Berlin, January 2019. https://www.swp-berlin.org/fileadmin/contents/products/research_papers/2019RP01_kle.pdf.
110. Paul Goble, "Why does Kyrgyzstan want a Second Russian Military Base?," *Jamestown Foundation*, August 3, 2017, https://jamestown.org/why-does-kyrgyzstan-want-a-second-russian-military-base/.
111. Stepan Kravchenko, "Kyrgyzstan may Host Second Russian Military Base, Tass Reports," *Bloomberg*, February 1, 2019, https://www.bloomberg.com/news/articles/2019-02-01/kyrgyzstan-may-host-second-russian-military-base-tass-reports.
112. Gleb Bryanski and Olga Dzyubenko, "Russia cuts Kyrgyz Debt for Military, Power Deals," *Reuters*, September 20, 2012, https://www.reuters.com/article/russia-kyrgyzstan/russia-cuts-kyrgyz-debt-for-military-power-deals-idUSL5E8KK15720120920.
113. Joshua Foust, "Going It Alone: Why Kyrgyzstan Doesn't Want Russian or American Bases," *The Atlantic*, March 23, 2012, https://www.theatlantic.com/international/archive/2012/03/going-it-alone-why-kyrgyzstan-doesnt-want-russian-or-american-bases/254903/; Catherine Putz, "What about that Proposed Second Russian Base in Kyrgyzstan?" *The Diplomat*, March 2018, https://thediplomat.com/2018/03/what-about-that-proposed-second-russian-base-in-kyrgyzstan/.
114. Alexander Cooley, "Manas Hysteria," *Foreign Policy*, April 12, 2010, https://foreignpolicy.com/2010/04/12/manas-hysteria/.
115. "Rossiiskaia voennaia baza v Kante mozhet byt' zakryta – president Kirgizii," *Interfax*, February 25, 2012, https://www.interfax.ru/russia/232576.
116. Bryanski and Dzyubenko, "Russia cuts Kyrgyz Debt."
117. Satke, "Russia Tightens Hold on Kyrgyzstan."
118. "Top Kyrgyz Official Says Russian Military Base Granted 15-Year Extension," *Radio Free Europe (RFE/RL)*, August 16, 2012, https://www.rferl.org/a/kyrgyzstan-gives-russian-base-extension/24678971.html.
119. "Russia, Kyrgyzstan Clash over Torpedo Plant," *Sputnik International*, March 22, 2012, https://sputniknews.com/world/20120322172327934/.

120. Joshua Kucera, "US Military Giving Up on Kyrgyzstan," *Eurasianet*, March 16, 2018, https://eurasianet.org/us-military-giving-up-on-kyrgyzstan.
121. Fabio Indeo, "The Role of Russia in the Central Asian Security Architecture," (Policy Brief no. 48, *OSCE Academy in Bishkek*, Bishkek, June 2018), http://www.osce-academy.net/upload/file/PB48The_Role_of_Russia_in_the_Central_Asian_Security_Architecture.pdf.
122. Bruce Pannier, "A New Chinese Interest in Central Asian Security," *Radio Free Europe*, March 30, 2017, https://www.rferl.org/a/china-central-asia-security-uyghurs-russia/28400327.html.

REFERENCES

Aidar, Satina. "Kyrgyzstan's North-South Road to Corruption." *Open Democracy*, August 9, 2018. https://www.opendemocracy.net/od-russia/satina-aidar/kyrgyzstans-north-south-road-to-corruption.
Akchabar. "Zavisimost': vse, chto nuzhno znat' kyrgyzstantsam o gaze, Rossii i 'Gazprome'," April 29, 2016. https://www.akchabar.kg/ru/article/economy/kyrgyz-gaz-gazprom/.
AVIM. "Gazprom Wraps Up Pipeline Overhaul in Kyrgyzstan." *AVIM Center for Eurasian Studies*, September 8, 2017. https://avim.org.tr/en/Bulten/GAZPROM-WRAPS-UP-PIPELINE-OVERHAUL-IN-KYRGYZSTAN.
BBC. "Kyrgyzstan Profile—Media," June 25, 2019. https://www.bbc.com/news/world-asia-16187183.
BBC. "Kyrgyzstan's Dilemma over Russian-led Customs Union," January 20, 2014. https://www.bbc.com/news/world-asia-25718770.
BBC. "Russia gets 30-year Extension for Base in Tajikistan," October 5, 2012. https://www.bbc.com/news/world-asia-19849247.
Belyi Parus. "Pochermu Kyrgyzstan ne pokupaet kazakhstanskuiu neft' i kak rossiiskii benzin podryvaet valiutnye zapasy strany," January 1, 2016. https://paruskg.info/glavnaya/127523-127523.html.
Bryanski, Gleb, and Olga Dzyubenko. "Russia cuts Kyrgyz Debt for Military, Power Deals." *Reuters*, September 20, 2012. https://www.reuters.com/article/russia-kyrgyzstan/russia-cuts-kyrgyz-debt-for-military-power-deals-idUSL5E8KK15720120920.
Bunin, Gene A. "Central Asia Struggles with Fallout from China's Internment of Minorities." *Foreign Policy*, August 15, 2018. https://foreignpolicy.com/2018/08/15/central-asia-struggles-with-fallout-from-chinas-internment-of-minorities/.
Canada, Immigration and Refugee Board. "Kyrgyzstan: Treatment of the Uyghur [Uighur] Minority by Society and Authorities, including State Protection Provided to Victims of Violence and Discrimination; Uyghur Minority Political Groups, Including activities (2012-2015)." Report, published by Refworld, UNHCR, February 12, 2015. https://www.refworld.org/docid/560b96564.html.
Cooley, Alexander. "Manas Hysteria." *Foreign Policy*, April 12, 2010. https://foreignpolicy.com/2010/04/12/manas-hysteria/.

Economist, The. "Remittance Man," September 7, 2013. https://www.economist.com/asia/2013/09/07/remittance-man.

Eurasianet. "Kyrgyzstan Hails Epoch-Making Power Line," August 31, 2015. https://eurasianet.org/kyrgyzstan-hails-epoch-making-power-line.

Eurasianet. "Kyrgyzstan: Revamped Transnational Gas Pipeline Unveiled," August 30, 2017. https://eurasianet.org/kyrgyzstan-revamped-transnational-gas-pipeline-unveiled.

Eurasianet. "Tajikistan, Turkmenistan Submit to Chinese Capture," June 24, 2016. https://eurasianet.org/tajikistan-turkmenistan-submit-chinese-capture.

Feinberg, Barry M., and Xiaoyan Zhao. "The Anholt–GfK Roper Nation Brands Index SM: Navigating the Changing World." In *International Place Branding Yearbook 2011: Managing Reputational Risk*, edited by Frank H. Go and Robert Covers, 63–76. London: Palgrave Macmillan, 2011.

Feklyunina, Valentina. "Soft Power and Identity: Russia, Ukraine and the 'Russian World(s)'." *European Journal of International Relations* 22, no. 4 (2015): 773–96.

Foust, Joshua. "Going It Alone: Why Kyrgyzstan Doesn't Want Russian or American Bases." *The Atlantic*, March 23, 2012. https://www.theatlantic.com/international/archive/2012/03/going-it-alone-why-kyrgyzstan-doesnt-want-russian-or-american-bases/254903/.

Glaser, Bonnie S., and Melissa E. Murphy. "Soft Power with Chinese Characteristics: The Ongoing Debate." In *Chinese Soft Power and Its Implications for the United States: Competition and Cooperation in the Developing World,* edited by Carola McGiffert, 10–27. Washington DC: CSIS, 2009.

Goble, Paul. "Why Does Kyrgyzstan Want a Second Russian Military Base?" *Jamestown Foundation*, August 3, 2017. https://jamestown.org/why-does-kyrgyz-stan-want-a-second-russian-military-base/.

Gould-Davies, Nigel. "Russia's Sovereign Globalization: Rise, Fall and Future." Research Paper, Chatham House, London, March 2016. https://www.chathamhouse.org/sites/default/files/publications/research/20160106RussiasSovereignGlobalizationGouldDaviesFinal.pdf.

Grigas, Agnia. "Legacies, Coercion and Soft Power: Russian Influence in the Baltic States." Briefing Paper, Chatham House, London, August 2012. https://www.chathamhouse.org/sites/default/files/public/Research/Russia%20and%20Eurasia/0812bp_grigas.pdf.

Haines, John R. "Gazprom's 'Energetic Pliers' and Aspirations of a Eurasian Archipelago: The Geopolitics of Russia's Networked Energy Infrastructure." The Philadelphia Papers No. 11, Foreign Policy Research Institute, Philadelphia, August 2015. https://www.fpri.org/wp-content/uploads/2015/08/haines_where-the-lions-are_complete.pdf.

Hasanova, Savia and Anna Kapushenko. "Kyrgyzstan Survives on Money made by Migrant Workers, but it doesn't know how to Spend it." *Open Democracy*, November 12, 2018. https://www.opendemocracy.net/od-russia/kyrgyzstan-survives-on-money-made-by-migrant-workers-but-it-doesn-t-know-how-to-spend-it.

Hurley, John, Scott Morris, and Gailyn Portelance. "Examining the Debt Implications of the Belt and Road Initiative from a Policy Perspective." CGD Policy Paper 121,

Center for Global Development, Washington DC, March 2018. https://www.cgdev.org/sites/default/files/examining-debt-implications-belt-and-road-initiative-policy-perspective.pdf.

Ibraimov, Bakyt, and Hamid Tursunov. "Russian Blacklist Keeps Central Asian Migrants Out." *Eurasianet*, March 24, 2014. https://eurasianet.org/russian-blacklist-keeps-central-asian-migrants-out.

Indeo, Fabio. "The Role of Russia in the Central Asian Security Architecture." Policy Brief no. 48, OSCE Academy in Bishkek, Bishkek, June 2018. http://www.osce-academy.net/upload/file/PB48The_Role_of_Russia_in_the_Central_Asian_Security_Architecture.pdf.

Interfax. "Rossiiskaia voennaia baza v Kante mozhet byt' zakryta – president Kirgizii," February 25, 2012. https://www.interfax.ru/russia/232576.

Kabar. "97% ot obshchego importa nefteproduktov v Kyrgyzstan prikhoditsia na Rossiiu," July 4, 2013. http://old.kabar.kg/economics/full/58606.

Kabar. "Chinese Companies have 79 Licenses for Gold Deposits in Kyrgyzstan," June 23, 2013. http://old.kabar.kg/eng/economics/full/2095.

Kaktus Media, "6 glavnykh mifov o rynke GSM v Kyrgyzstane," February 16, 2017. https://kaktus.media/doc/352511_6_glavnyh_mifov_o_rynke_gsm_v_kyrgyzstane.html.

Karypova, Aizhan. "Chem obernetsia dlia trudovykh migrantov iz Kyrgyzstana evraziiskaia integratsiia." *Region.kg*, June 3, 2015. http://region.kg/index.php?option=com_content&view=article&id=1491:2015-06-03-07-47-06&catid=42:2014-02-02-11-14-01&Itemid=7.

Klein, Margarete. "Russia's Military Policy in the Post-Soviet Space: Aims, Instruments and Perspectives." SWP Research Paper 1, German Institute for International and Security Affairs, January 2019. https://www.swp-berlin.org/fileadmin/contents/products/research_papers/2019RP01_kle.pdf

Kloop. "Kitai daet kredity razvivaiushchimsia stranam – v tom chisle, Kyrgyzstanu. Ob'iasniaem zachem," April 9, 2018. https://kloop.kg/blog/2018/04/09/kitaj-daet-kredity-razvivayushhimsya-stranam-v-tom-chisle-kyrgyzstanu-obyasnyaem-zachem/.

Kravchenko, Stepan. "Kyrgyzstan May Host Second Russian Military Base, Tass Reports." *Bloomberg*, February 1, 2019. https://www.bloomberg.com/news/articles/2019-02-01/kyrgyzstan-may-host-second-russian-military-base-tass-reports.

KTRK. "Rossiiskie kanaly ORT i RTR budut translirovat'sia v telesemeistve KTRK," May 19, 2017. http://www.ktrk.kg/post/13345/ru.

Kucera, Joshua. "US Military Giving Up on Kyrgyzstan." *Eurasianet*, March 16, 2018. https://eurasianet.org/us-military-giving-up-on-kyrgyzstan.

Lain, Sarah. "China's Silk Road in Central Asia: Transformative or Exploitative?" *Financial Times*, April 27, 2016. https://www.ft.com/content/55ca031d-3fe3-3555-a878-3bcfa9fd6a98.

Laruelle, Marlene. "Russia's Eurasianist Soft Power in Central Asia." *Analytical Media "Eurasian Studies,"* July 14, 2017. http://greater-europe.org/archives/3190.

Marat, Erica. "Russian Mass Media Attack Bakiyev." *Jamestown Foundation*, April 1, 2010. https://jamestown.org/program/russian-mass-media-attack-bakiyev/.

Masalieva, Jazgul. "Kyrgyzstan must pay down $ 320 million Debt to China in 5 years." *24.kg*, April 16, 2018. https://24.kg/english/81729_Kyrgyzstan_must_pay_down__320_million_debt_to_China_in_5_years_/.

Maza, Cristina. "Kyrgyzstan's Uighurs Cautious, Still Fear Chinese Influence." *Eurasianet*, November 25, 2014. https://eurasianet.org/kyrgyzstans-uighurs-cautious-still-fear-chinese-influence.

Mikhailov, Grigorii. "Rossiiskie telekanaly v Kyrgyzstane mogut ostat'sia bez statusa." *InoZpress*, January 12, 2016, http://www.inozpress.kg/news/view/id/48081.

Mingjiang, Li. "Soft Power in Chinese Discourse: Popularity and Prospects." Working paper no. 165, S. Rajaratnam School of International Studies, Singapore, September 2008. https://www.rsis.edu.sg/wp-content/uploads/rsis-pubs/WP165.pdf.

M-Vector. "Media prepdpochteniia naseleniia Kyrgyzstana (8 volna)." Report, Soros Foundation Kyrgyzstan, Bishkek, 2017. https://soros.kg/wp-content/uploads/2017/12/Otchet-Mediapredpochteniya-naseleniya-KR-8-volna.pdf.

Natoli, Kristopher. "Weaponizing Nationality: An Analysis of Russia's Passport Policy in Georgia." *Boston University International Law Journal* 28 (2010): 389–417.

Nichol, Jim. "The April 2010 Coup in Kyrgyzstan and its Aftermath: Context and Implications for U.S. Interests." Report, The Congressional Research Service, Washington DC, June 2010. https://fas.org/sgp/crs/row/R41178.pdf.

Nye Joseph S., Jr. "The Benefits of Soft Power." *Harvard Business School Working Knowledge*, August 2004. https://hbswk.hbs.edu/archive/the-benefits-of-soft-power.

Nye, Joseph S. Jr. "Public Diplomacy and Soft Power," *The Annals of the America's Academy of Political and Social Science* 616, no 1 (2008): 94–109.

Okoth, Edwin. "Kenya: SGR Pact with China a Risk to Kenyan Sovereignty, Assets." *Daily Nation*, January 13, 2019. https://allafrica.com/stories/201901140451.html.

Orozbekova, Cholpon. "China Relocating Heavy Enterprises to Kyrgyzstan." *Jamestown Foundation*, June 24, 2016. https://jamestown.org/program/china-relocating-heavy-enterprises-to-kyrgyzstan/.

Pan, Philip P. "Russia is said to have Fueled Unrest in Kyrgyzstan." *Washington Post*, April 12, 2010. http://www.washingtonpost.com/wp-dyn/content/article/2010/04/11/AR2010041103827.html.

Pannier, Bruce. "Russia Takes Active Role in Kyrgyz Parliamentary Elections." *Radio Free Europe*, October 5, 2010. https://www.rferl.org/a/Russia_Takes_Active_Role_In_Kyrgyz_Parliamentary_Elections/2177192.html.

Pannier, Bruce. "A New Chinese Interest in Central Asian Security." *Radio Free Europe*, March 30, 2017. https://www.rferl.org/a/china-central-asia-security-uyghurs-russia/28400327.html.

Putz, Catherine. "What about that Proposed Second Russian Base in Kyrgyzstan?" *The Diplomat*, March 2018. https://thediplomat.com/2018/03/what-about-that-proposed-second-russian-base-in-kyrgyzstan/.

Radnitz, Scott. "Between Russia and a Hard Place: Great Power Grievances and Central Asian Ambivalence." *Europe-Asia Studies* 70, no. 10 (2018): 1597–611.

Radio Azattyk. "Migratsiia. Kyrgyzstantsev iskliuchat iz 'chernogo spiska'," October 18, 2018. https://rus.azattyk.org/a/kyrgyzstan_migraziya_rossiya/29551254.html.
Reeves, Jeffrey. *Chinese Foreign Relations with Weak Peripheral States: Asymmetrical Economic Power and Insecurity*. London: Routledge, 2015.
Reeves, Jeffrey. "Economic Statecraft, Structural Power, and Structural Violence in Sino-Kyrgyz Relations." *Asian Security* 12, no. 2 (2015): 116–35.
RFE/RL. "Top Kyrgyz Official Says Russian Military Base Granted 15-Year Extension," August 16, 2012. https://www.rferl.org/a/kyrgyzstan-gives-russian-base-extension/24678971.html.
Rickleton, Chris. "Kyrgyzstan: Is Chinese Investment Really Win-Win?" *Eurasianet*, July 23, 2013. https://eurasianet.org/kyrgyzstan-is-chinese-investment-really-win-win.
RPO RMTR. "Spisok kanalov." http://rpo.kg/channels/. Accessed July 1, 2020.
Rustamova, Farida. "Biudzhet gosudarstvennykh SMI v Rossii vyrastet na 2,5 mlrd rublei." *BBC*, May 26, 2017. https://www.bbc.com/russian/news-40062877.
Satke, Ryskeldi. "Russia Tightens Hold on Kyrgyzstan." *Nikkei Asian Review*, March 27, 2014. https://asia.nikkei.com/Economy/Russia-tightens-hold-on-Kyrgyzstan.
Satke, Ryskeldi. "Uighurs in Kyrgyzstan Hope for Peace despite Violence." *Al Jazeera*, January 8, 2017. https://www.aljazeera.com/indepth/features/2016/09/uighurs-kyrgyzstan-hope-piece-violence-160915133619696.html.
Shevel, Oxana. "The Politics of Citizenship Policy in Post-Soviet Russia." *Post-Soviet Affairs* 28, no. 1 (2012): 111–47.
Sputnik International. "Russia, Kyrgyzstan Clash over Torpedo Plant," March 22, 2012. https://sputniknews.com/world/20120322172327934/.
Szostek, Joanna. "Russia and the News Media in Ukraine: A Case of 'Soft Power'." *East European Politics & Societies* 28, no. 3 (2014): 463–64.
Tremann, Cornelia. "China's Aid: The Image Boost." *The Interpreter*, September 21, 2018. https://www.lowyinstitute.org/the-interpreter/chinas-aid-image-boost.
Trilling, David, and Chinghiz Umetov. "Kyrgyzstan: Is Putin Punishing Bakiyev?" *Eurasianet*, April 6, 2010. https://eurasianet.org/kyrgyzstan-is-putin-punishing-bakiyev.
Troitskiy, Evgeny. "Turmoil in Kyrgyzstan: A Challenge to Russian Foreign Policy." UI Occasional Papers, The Swedish Institute of International Affairs, Stockholm, 2012. https://www.ui.se/globalassets/ui.se-eng/publications/ui-publications/turmoil-in-kyrgyzstan-a-challenge-to-russian-foreign-policy-min.pdf.
Tsygankov, Andrei P. "If Not by Tanks, Then by Banks? The Role of Soft Power in Putin's Foreign Policy." *Europe-Asia Studies* 58, no. 7 (2006): 1079–99.
Tsygankov, Andrei P. "Moscow's Soft Power Strategy," *Current History*, vol. 112, no. 756 (2013): 259–64.
Van der Kley, Dirk. "Can Central Asia's Poorest States Pay Back their Debts to China?" *The Diplomat*, December 1, 2017. https://thediplomat.com/2017/12/can-central-asias-poorest-states-pay-back-their-debts-to-china/.
Vesti.kg. "Kitai obiazatel'no vernet vlozhennye v Kyrgyzstan sredstva. Tol'ko kak?" April 17, 2018. https://vesti.kg/zxc/item/51244-kitaj-obyazatelno-vernet-vlozhen-nye-v-kyrgyzstan-sredstva-tolko-kak.html.

Way, Lucan Ahmad and Adam Casey. "Russia has been Meddling in Foreign Elections for Decades. Has it made a Difference?" *Washington Post*, January 8, 2018. https://www.washingtonpost.com/news/monkey-cage/wp/2018/01/05/russia-has-been-meddling-in-foreign-elections-for-decades-has-it-made-a-difference/?noredirect=on&utm_term=.239b756cf80f.

Wilson, Jeanne L. "Russia and China Respond to Soft Power." *Politics* 35, no. 3–4 (2015): 287–300.

Wilson, Jeanne L. "Soft Power: A Comparison of Discourse and Practice in Russia and China." *Europe-Asia Studies* 67, no. 8 (2015): 1171–202.

Chapter 9

The Soft Power of Neoliberal Civil Society

The Case of Post-Communist Tajikistan

Karolina Kluczewska and Payam Foroughi

At first sight, it might seem that we chose to analyze a type of soft power that is intangible and purely ideational.[1] It is based upon an assumption that civil society is a "domain parallel to but separate from the state—where citizens associate according to their own interests and wishes."[2] Unlike several other contributors of this volume, we do not describe soft power developed by a specific agent, such as a country or a particular organization. Our agent refers to multiple organizations which we describe under a common label of development agencies by way of Western donor agencies, international organizations (IOs), international non-governmental organizations (INGOs), and domestic non-governmental organizations (NGOs), which have adopted the idea of "neoliberal civil society" and have been exercising it by utilizing foreign aid or, in turn, providing funding to local activists and civil society entrepreneurs, in our case in post-Soviet Tajikistan. The case of Tajikistan, we believe, is somewhat typical of many other post-communist, but also aid-dependent countries.

BACKGROUND

In the context of post-Soviet and post-communist transitions, the idea of neoliberal civil society has been alleged to hold a potential for general liberalization, democratization, and emergence of the free market.[3] For some development agencies, promotion of the neoliberal civil society has been the main field of activity, while others have integrated it into their respective fields, such as migration, health, or women's rights. In this chapter, we describe how development agencies have been exercising the soft power of neoliberal civil society in independent post-Soviet Tajikistan. In other words, we analyze how through development assistance local activists and NGO entrepreneurs have been turned into neoliberal civil society players, and with what effects. We ask how various state and non-state actors in Tajikistan have reacted and positioned themselves toward this unique form of soft power. There is also a comparative longitudinal dimension in our case study. We attempt to capture differences in how development agencies had been exercising the soft power of neoliberal civil society in the early 1990s and in more recent years, and how reactions of local actors have changed as a result.

Theoretically, like other contributors of this volume, we refer to Joseph Nye's work on soft power,[4] and try to understand what soft power means in the context of Central Asia and, in our particular case, Western donor–induced civil society in Tajikistan. For Nye, "soft power is the ability to affect others to obtain the outcomes one wants through attraction rather than coercion or payment" and, thus, soft power is a potential for and capacity "to entice and attract."[5] Such element of persuasion is particularly relevant in the Central Asian context, a region which following the Soviet collapse has become a meeting point of multiple powers and interests, principally of Russia, China, and the United States, but also the European Union, Japan, Turkey, and Iran.[6] At the same time, we have also witnessed a reluctance to utilize the hard power of military force by actors external to the region. The argument that emerges from this volume is that this unwritten rule of no use of military force in Central Asia has increased the relevance of soft power both in the conduct of international relations and as a way of influencing domestic politics.

Mary Kaldor tells us that by the end of the Cold War and an accelerated globalization, local civil society entities linked up with others worldwide by way of "transnational networks of activists" working on a variety of liberal causes, whether that of human rights, countering landmines, advocating for the formation of the International Criminal Court, or seeking solutions to environmental degradation.[7] This was still the purely "activism version" of civil society. Soon after, however, the term *civil society* was used by the post–Cold War victorious Western governments and Western-dominated international institutions to promote such liberal norms of "market reform" and "parliamentary democracy."[8] This was a de facto taming and institutionalizing of former social movements by way of formation of a global network of "neoliberal civil society" manifested through often formalistic business-minded NGOs. This switch from dominance of social movements to NGOs in the post–Cold War has been anticlimactic. Kaldor quotes Neera Chandhoke who calls this change a "tragedy" as when "people struggling against authoritarian regimes demanded civil society, what they got [instead] were NGOs."[9]

Mahmoud Mamdani, in turn, writes that "NGOs are killing civil society."[10] As a third variety of civil society, Kaldor also tells of the "postmodern version," which can include indigenous institutions such as "religious orders, the bazaar, or religious foundations," which can potentially serve as "a check on state power."[11] Neoliberal civil society is thus part of the broader processes related to the influx of multiple Western actors to the Central Asian region in the early 1990s, using development aid as a soft power tool aimed at influencing and emulating political and economic trajectories of the region in the West's image or in the West's interests.[12]

Methodologically, in this chapter we draw on our long-term fieldworks in Tajikistan. One of us has been in Tajikistan for nearly a decade sporadically since 1995 and the other since 2013. We have been combining roles of analyst and researcher with work in the development sector and having been present in spaces where the neoliberal civil society becomes tangible on the ground. These experiences by way of "political ethnography" and "immersion"[13] in post-Soviet Central Asia and being "observing participants"[14] of foreign aid associated with Tajikistan inform our understanding of the topic. We also heavily rely on interviews with NGO leaders and government officials.[15]

After this introduction, we outline the origins of neoliberal civil society in Tajikistan and explain circumstances in which development agencies started exercising it as a form of soft power in this country. In turn, we proceed with an analysis of initial reactions to the phenomenon among local activists, as well as the central government, local authorities, and the general population. In the following section, we explain why and how this soft power of neoliberal civil society exercised by development actors transformed over time, and how reactions of local actors changed as a consequence. In the conclusion, we offer a holistic explanation regarding the current condition of the soft power of neoliberal civil society in Tajikistan.

NEOLIBERAL CIVIL SOCIETY AS SOFT POWER IN TAJIKISTAN

Various forms of civil society, with distinct modalities, social practices, internal power relations, and relations to the state have always existed across cultures and communities worldwide.[16] In Central Asian societies, for example, the *masjid* (mosque), *choikhona* (teahouse), and bazaar (market) had, over centuries, been traditional and communal places of community discussion and potential launching grounds of social movements that in some ways served as precursors to more modern versions of civil society.[17] The concept of neoliberal civil society as the third sector, balancing the state and the market, can be attributed to late nineteenth-century Scottish and continental

Enlightenment thinkers.[18] While initially such civil society manifested itself in popular movements accompanying the American and French revolutions in the second half of the eighteenth century, throughout the nineteenth century Western countries took up forms of associations of citizens dedicated to promoting public interest through participation in labor unions, student and sports groups, as well as cultural and professional associations.[19] After WWII, NGOs, as a modern means of expression of neoliberal civil society, became integrated in development aid.[20] In the context of the Cold War, neoliberal civil society became the soft power of Western states, and served as means of promotion of specific geopolitical interests through the work of Western development agencies.[21] The neoliberal civil society euphoria was strengthened by prominent cases of "successful" social opposition to the state, such as, for example, Poland's Solidarność (Solidarity) movement in the 1980s.

After the symbolic victory of the Western bloc following the Soviet collapse, NGOs began to rapidly multiply across the post-communist and post-Soviet space with the ideological and indispensably financial support of Western states and associated development agencies.[22] The latter saw the newly emerged Central Asian countries as a *tabula rasa*, an empty space, which with the fall of communism was now devoid of particular political and economic systems.[23] Western development agencies also bypassed traditional—both communal and late-Soviet—forms of civil society, assuming that the "right" civil society, of neoliberal type, could be designed from scratch.[24] Independent Central Asian countries facilitated this process by strategically signing a myriad of international conventions and commitments within the United Nations' (UN) system and the Organization for Security and Co-operation in Europe (OSCE). While Tajikistan has been part of these trends, there are some peculiarities of how the country was integrated into the new world order, which influenced its particular trajectories of neoliberal civil society, as well as local reactions.

Similar to its post-Soviet neighbors, the avowed transition from socialism and centralized economy to democracy and market economy created a condition for the expansion of neoliberal civil society by way of formalistic Western-funded NGOs in Tajikistan. By supporting the formation of domestic NGOs, a largely externally driven process, development agencies turned a nontangible idea of neoliberal civil society into a tangible product. Importantly, NGOs appeared in Tajikistan in times which were marked not only by a beginning of a post-communist transition, similar to other post-Soviet neighbors, but also by an ongoing brutal civil war (1992–1997), which resulted in anywhere between 40,000 and 100,000 deaths,[25] followed by a Peace Accord signed in Moscow in June 1997. Tajikistan was thus exposed to processes of post-conflict quasi-democratic peacebuilding, rather than solely development aid, the profile of which has been strongly influenced by the civil war. Local NGOs became intermediaries of the Western plateau of donors in what John Heathershaw calls "civil society peacebuilding."[26] They were tasked with the delivery of humanitarian aid and services to the population. Because of normative guidance of donors and economic dependence, local NGOs had to operate within the shared, often purely nominal, paradigms of the development community, such as "human rights," "women's empowerment," and "small entrepreneurship."

Drawing on Alexander Vuving's work, Nye explains how agents use "benignity," "competence," and "beauty" (or charisma) when articulating soft power, in order to generate attraction among the "target group."[27] They use benignity when they provoke the feeling of gratitude among the local population. They act in a way which shows competence, and by that generate admiration of the target group. Finally, agents use beauty by showing values or goods which evoke inspiration. We argue that since the early 1990s, development agencies have been using these three features when exercising soft power of neoliberal civil society in Tajikistan, however, primarily toward one specific target group—local activists, mostly Soviet-era *intelligentsia* and/or members of the former Soviet structures, such as *Komsomol* (youth organization) or *zhensovety* (women's councils). To begin with, development agencies in post-communist Tajikistan demonstrated benignity by offering local activists and socioeconomic entrepreneurs a space for action and providing them with decent salaries. They showed competence by teaching them new skills and giving them a chance to become part of regional and international networks and coalitions of NGOs. They also showed beauty and inspiration by offering them a new value system and its associated rhetoric, which included the ideology of neoliberal civil society, thus replacing the ideational vacuum brought about by the collapse of Soviet communism.

The result of this use of soft power was a Tajik neoliberal civil society or NGO sector. Given the numbers and the vast spatial distribution of NGOs in the country, it might seem that the soft power of the neoliberal society has been successfully grounded in the country. In 1993, only two years after the Soviet collapse, there were only thirty-three registered NGOs in Tajikistan,[28] while by 1997, that number had reached 225.[29] Julie Fischer provides data from the Judicial Consortium indicating that in 1999 about 30,000 people worked in the Tajik NGO sector. By the mid-2000s, this number had likely increased substantially as the number of NGOs had risen to 3,500 in 2007.[30]

Apart from the NGO sector, however, there has been no broader spillover of the idea of neoliberal civil society in Tajikistan. This is because, in the first place, when constructing neoliberal civil society, development agencies consciously or unconsciously bypassed the "real political actors," much of it in the state structures.[31] In the second place, it is important to account for the agency of local actors. As mentioned above, in his soft power framework,

Nye consistently refers to local actors as the target group.[32] However, as we show in the next section, local actors are more than just targets. They have their own positions and interests at stake.

INITIAL REACTIONS OF LOCAL ACTORS IN TAJIKISTAN

NGO Activists

By the beginning of post-communism, the core of the Tajik NGO sector was formed by the aforementioned Soviet *intelligentsia*, many of whom previously worked for the Soviet state in academic, cultural and community activities. With the arrival of development agencies to the country in the early 1990s, these activists quickly declared their support for neoliberal civil society. In 1996, a Tajik academic and a new NGO activist, Ashurboy Imomov, expressed his dissatisfaction of the past on pages of a Tajik academic journal:

> The NGO system has become widespread across all developed countries of the world. . . . The [previous, Soviet] totalitarian system could not allow the formation and functioning of coalitions or associations of citizens, which did not fit into the framework of that political system. . . . Unions of youth, women, *kolkhoz*, writers, journalists and others . . . were an appendage of the totalitarian system, an additional branch of state power through which the state guaranteed people's obedience.[33]

This condemnation of the Soviet system and its structures may sound surprising, given that local activists who formed the new NGO sector owed their experience, organizational skills and leadership capacities to the same Soviet period.[34] It can, however, be explained through processes of neoliberal economic co-optation. Against the background of a severe economic decline after the Soviet collapse and the ongoing conflict, the new Western-funded local NGO sector provided activists with employment and salaries which allowed for a dignified life, like few other sectors.[35] According to another NGO worker:

> At that time [in the early 1990s], we [NGO leaders] did not pose questions [to development agencies which provided grants]. We happily did what they asked us to do. You see, a few years before I was an unemployed single mother. Now, suddenly I had a private driver who was taking me around from one seminar to another, I had a big salary which I could never have had if working for the *hukumat* [local government]. I could even afford buying a flat in Dushanbe.[36]

The tendency described by the above activist reveals that under the liberal façade of the neoliberal civil society, there was and is likely little idealistic liberal content, or rather, little normative attraction with the soft power of neoliberal civil society. This does not mean, however, that there had not been and there is no genuine activism within the NGO sector. A side effect of foreign funding of local activists, however, has been a suppression of sociopolitical activism toward change via dressing activism in formalistic liberal, even rhetorical form, instead.

Central Government

During the civil war and in its aftermath, the Tajik government did not interfere in the formation of the local NGO sector. More specifically, it neither created obstacles for the activities of NGOs nor provided extra conditions for their growth. In the words of a Tajik intellectual:

> The 1990s provided a good atmosphere for NGOs to flourish. It looked like a perfect democracy; NGOs could do whatever they wanted. But rather than a product of a natural evolution, "democracy" was an outcome of an absence of [a strong central] government during the war and weakness of government structures right after the conflict.[37]

Once the conflict had officially ended by signing of the 1997 Peace Accord in Moscow, the Tajik government's and the international donor organizations' priorities shifted toward post-conflict rehabilitation, consolidation of newly formed state structures, as well as the return of internally and externally displaced persons. The fact that the government had not provided a detailed legal framework for NGOs' activities is telling of the period. Like in cases of many other laws in Tajikistan, the 1996 Law on Non-Commercial Organizations was a near-copy-paste from a 1995 Russian Law on Public Associations. It was adopted without taking into account the needs of a quickly growing NGO sector and in the absence of other frameworks, the law was regulating activities of Tajik NGOs until 2007.[38]

The relationship between the Tajik NGOs and other sectors was also peculiar. In the neoliberal model, NGOs as the third sector are to ideally balance the state as the first sector and the market. In Tajikistan in the 1990s, however, the market was in a state of collapse and as a result, the NGO sector overlapped, even outshined, the market sector, since it provided employment for thousands of people—managers, assistants, trainers, accountants, lawyers, researchers, procurement officers, interpreters, security guards, drivers, cooks, cleaners, and service providers, such as catering companies, realtors and property owners, hotels, printing houses, phone providers, and many others. The relations of NGOs with the first sector, the state, were even more curious. On the one hand, the NGO sector did not interact with government forces, insofar as during the war the NGOs did not deal directly with politics and armed forces and, as a result, had not necessarily developed any unified political stance on the peacebuilding process, either.[39] On the other hand, NGOs partially substituted the first sector, in that they often took over the state's functions to provide services to the population, especially in rural areas.

Local Government

Overall, in the 1990s, NGOs working in the regions had good relations with local authorities—both the *hukumat* (second-level, district administrative divisions) and *jamoat* (third-level, communal administrative units). Because of Tajikistan's civil war and its devastating effects on rural areas, especially in the south of the country, the presence of NGOs in rural areas was vaster than in other post-Soviet countries, where they were concentrated mainly in urban areas. By 2006, out of the 2,700 registered NGOs in Tajikistan, 1,683 or over 60 percent were based in Dushanbe and surroundings (however, many of them had a republican status and worked across the country), and 1,017 in the regions.[40] Under conditions of ongoing conflict, local authorities lacked basic funding to continue their work in an efficient way, especially in Khatlon and Rasht which were more affected by the war. Parviz Mullojanov writes that during the war, local authorities could not "afford to provide local communities with basic services such as [potable] water and [natural] gas supply, or reconstruction of sewage systems."[41] They were grateful for services that NGOs offered to the local population through funding primarily from Western development agencies.

Furthermore, in comparison with the central government, there was more trust and actual collaboration between local authorities and NGOs, because of high mobility of employees between the two sectors, but also the more tangible results which some NGOs would bring at the local level. An NGO leader from northern Panjakent district explains:

Before the Soviet collapse I was working in the Soviet administration and after 1991 in the (local) *hukumat,* in the division working with women. So before I opened my NGO in 1995, the *hukumat* already knew me and trusted my work. . . . Obviously it makes our work [as an NGO] easier.[42]

Importantly, the basis of this collaboration was not a shared soft power of the ideational concepts of neoliberal civil society, but toward its material component, that is, provision of funding from development agencies which allowed NGOs to provide much needed humanitarian relief and social services to the population.

Population

While there were frequent cases of corruption by way of pilferage and selling of humanitarian aid which was supposed to be distributed to people for free on a grassroots level,[43] overall, local NGOs developed good relations with the population, especially in areas affected by the war and its negative socio-economic effects, where their work was most needed. In particular, women's NGOs were active in assisting women and children, including from among the 25,000 war widows and 55,000 war orphans.[44] An interviewee who witnessed reactions of the population during her work in the Tajikistan's regions explains that:

> From the beginning [the early 1990s], especially people in the regions used to know about NGOs and really respected their work. . . . [But] did people understand the idea of civil society that NGOs represented? Not really. Maybe those who attended trainings and seminars, but even they did not really understand, or care. Those were hard times. People turned to NGOs to get any kind of support, like food or medical services.[45]

As the above quotation reveals, material benefits were the driving force behind a positive reception and attraction of NGOs among the population. The positive reaction of local actors toward neoliberal civil society was thus evoked mainly with economic incentives via Western humanitarian assistance. Based on Nye's framework, the feature of attraction which was successfully received in Tajikistan by the general population was benignity, rather than competence or beauty.[46]

TRANSFORMATIONS WITHIN THE SOFT POWER OF NEOLIBERAL CIVIL SOCIETY

Soft power is not necessarily a stable phenomenon. Its strength depends upon the credibility of actors who exercise it vis-à-vis "targets," and this credibility can fluctuate over time.[47] In Tajikistan, as well, the soft power of neoliberal civil society has not been constant, due to structural changes within the context that produced it, namely development agencies. Naren Chitty's framework which builds on Nye's is useful here, according to which soft power has two vectors: internal and external.[48] The internal vector is related to the circumstances which produced the soft power, while the external concerns relations with the outside world and applications of soft power elsewhere.

What changes in the internal vector put the soft power of neoliberal civil society on a different external tangent in Tajikistan? In the late 2000s, several interrelated changes took place among Western-funded development agencies. First, geographic priorities changed. The end of Tajikistan's civil war, the U.S.-led "war on terror" in neighboring Afghanistan and the end of the transition paradigm in the post-Soviet space had significant impact on the structure of Western development aid to Tajikistan.[49] They resulted in decreased funding for democratization and neoliberal civil society, while the share of hard power security assistance to the country began to rise in Western foreign aid budgets.[50]

Second, Tajik NGOs felt the burden of an increasing conditionality of funding. On the one hand, the so-called Great Aid Debate took place within the community of Western donors and development agencies.[51] This led to signing of the Rome Declaration on Harmonization of Aid in 2003, the 2005 Paris Declaration on Aid Effectiveness, and the 2008 Accra Agenda for Action, which advocated for giving more ownership of aid to local actors. On the other hand, a simultaneous process of projectization of development aid has been taking place—what has also been referred to as "projectosis"—a condition where donor organizations assume that societal problems can be tackled via Western-designed standardized projects, allocation of technical assistance, and material goods, which often ignore the peculiarities of the society at hand and only address symptoms of the problem, rather than in-depth critical reporting and investigations to shed light on real causes of problems.[52]

Ironically, a growing sophistication of Western-designed project frameworks has also implied less—not more—ownership of aims and objectives by local NGOs. In Tajikistan, development agencies began to treat Tajik NGOs like service providers. A Western IO worker in Tajikistan sarcastically referred to such Western-funded NGOs not as civil society but "service society."[53] This label is de facto largely accurate given the contracting nature of such entities and the obligations to deliver a set of pre-established outputs, rather than giving the same NGOs space to develop their own ideas of what *they* understand as development.[54]

Third, in the hope of increasing both sustainability of projects and their own longevity in Tajikistan, in recent years development agencies and IOs started channeling more resources directly to the government through Project Management Centers created by specific ministries.[55] More funds were also spent directly on government-implemented projects, which were often badly managed by the state, poorly monitored, and also lacking proper coordination among the donors. One IO worker recalled, for example, that a specific Tajik government ministry at one point had three to five overlapping committees to deal with different donors funding similar and often overlapping counter-human trafficking projects.[56]

These three changes impacted on the capacities of development agencies to attractively articulate their soft power toward local actors in Tajikistan. They could not demonstrate their benignity like they used to do because grants for Tajik NGOs were shrinking. Decreasing salaries and general financial instability accompanying the NGO work changed attitudes toward neoliberal civil society among local activists, but also influenced reactions and mindsets of other actors, including local activists, the central government, *hukumat*s, and Tajikistan's population at large, as we discuss below.

REACTIONS OF LOCAL ACTORS

NGO activists

While in the early 1990s, interest in liberal norms among local activists in Tajikistan developed mainly due to material benefits accompanying NGO work, starting from the late 2000s, a significant decrease of such benefits resulted in a declining appeal of liberal norms. As of 2018, there were 1,805 officially registered NGOs in Tajikistan.[57] Within a decade, therefore, the sector was substantially reduced in size. Moreover, according to Mullojanov, among those registered NGOs "a few dozen only are operating . . . continually, and only a dozen or so of them are really able to stand on their own feet [presumably, if funding was to be cut off]."[58] Among NGOs which remain active, there has been a growing resentment toward Western donors and development agencies. Negative sentiments are framed both around discontent with lowered funding and growing contestations of development agencies themselves. When present in the NGO community, however, they are rarely expressed aloud, due to fear of losing the few remaining opportunities of funding.[59] Dodarbek Saydaliev from the NGO Shahrvand (Citizen) in Kulob, one of the few outspoken activists in the region, publicly expressed grievances on the wastefulness and self-centeredness of Western donors in the following way:

> International organizations, which [claim] to help our country solve different problems as stated in their mandates, have become places where foreign experts are making money. Despite [their] . . . big projects with huge budgets, every year the results are worse. The reason for this is that big parts of project budgets are not allocated for solving specific problems but for covering the expenses of [international] organizations [themselves]. . . . On a daily basis we see many cars with special [green, red and blue] plates passing around the city [Dushanbe] and regions, but most of the time not with the aim of implementing [meaningful] projects.[60]

It is significant that such contestations are for the most part materially—rather than ideationally—based, that is, concerns are generally framed around issues of funding, rather than differences in understanding of the concepts of development or civil society and its aims by NGOs and development agencies. This is revealing of the material foundations and the links between development agencies and local NGOs. It also shows that the tangible outcome of the soft power of neoliberal civil society, the local NGO sector, has been largely built on material principles—perceived benignity of development agencies—rather than shared values and goals. Nevertheless, the decreasing funding for Tajik NGOs has created an opportunity for local activists to develop their own, critical position toward development and donors, even if the reflection remains largely limited to monetary rather than ideational and normative discontent.

Central Government

In comparison with other local actors, the current position of Tajikistan's central government toward the soft power of neoliberal civil society is the least influenced by changes in the internal vector of how soft power has been exercised by development agencies. Rather, reactions of the government are far more related to two other ongoing processes. The first concerns state and nation-building priorities. With an ongoing process of the government strengthening its institutions and developing a normative framework of national ideology, values, and traditions, as well as a centralized, hierarchical vision of governance, the space for NGOs as an avenue "where citizens associate according to their own interests and wishes"[61] has been automatically shrinking.

Second, broader geopolitical trends related to the wave of color revolutions in the post-Soviet space have been influencing the position of governments in Central Asia toward NGOs and their Western backers. The 2004 Orange Revolution in Ukraine, the 2003 Rose Revolution in Georgia, and the 2005 Tulip Revolution in Kyrgyzstan (in addition to other revolutionary regime changes in that country in 2010 and 2020), have often been locally viewed as Western-manufactured and due to foreign support to NGOs operating in these countries.[62] The so-called "Foreign Agents Law" adopted in Russia in 2014 has also contributed to skepticism toward neoliberal civil society in Tajikistan. Amendments to Tajikistan's own Laws on Public Associations in 2015 gave the government "greater powers to examine NGOs' funding streams, including grants from foreign donors, as well as to track their expenditure."[63] The law also obliges the NGOs "to report how much funding they receive to the authorities."[64] All this has brought about more scrutiny of local NGOs in Tajikistan and other Central Asian states with similar laws in recent years.[65] As a result, some NGO activists (and also journalists) have left the sector, with others relocating to neighboring Kyrgyzstan or Europe and the US, where working conditions are either more liberal or out of reach of Tajik authorities.

There is, however, a caveat which needs to be accounted for. While the government in Tajikistan remains skeptical regarding (the few) NGOs that work on political issues,[66] it is more open to collaborations with NGOs working in politically neutral fields, in particular concerning support to the economically vulnerable groups. According to an NGO employee:

> In my experience, it would not be right to say that the government categorically mistrusts NGOs. Of course, if they work on human rights and are positioned confrontationally towards the government, they can expect problems. . . . but no one will disturb an NGO which works with, for example, children with disabilities. On the contrary, the government will only be supportive of its work.[67]

The above quotation suggests that there is a differentiated strategy of how the Tajik government relates to internationally-funded NGOs. While some NGOs working on purely social issues are allowed to continue "associat[ing] according to their own interests and wishes,"[68] under the government's umbrella, others have been excluded from this process. As a result, changes can be observed in the three-sector model of sociopolitical organization. While the business sector is still developing in Tajikistan and the NGO sector continues substituting or complementing it, in varying degrees, the state or public sector is regulating the work of NGOs.

Local Government

Over the years, local governments (*hukumat*s and *jamoat*s) in Tajikistan have continued to relate to NGOs in a much more positive manner than the central government.[69] As mentioned above, NGOs have carried on with offering some vital services to the population, even if on a more irregular basis due to shortages of funding. Local authorities actively participate in roundtables, seminars, and trainings organized by NGOs in outlying areas.[70] However, an employee of an NGO which works on prevention of domestic violence in the north of the country explains how the collaboration of the two sectors looks in practice:

[NGO worker]: We collaborate closely with the Committee on Women and Family Affairs, *jamoat, hukumat*, the police, the prosecutor's office, and others.
[Author]: What exactly do you mean by collaboration?
[NGO worker]: They usually refer women to us so that we offer them services which they [state institutions] cannot provide; for example specialized health care or help in compiling legal documents.[71]

This indicates that, similarly to the 1990s, the collaboration between local authorities and NGOs today in Tajikistan is once again taking place on pragmatic, material grounds, rather than ideational ones. After nearly three decades of international assistance channeled to the regions through NGOs, at an institutional level local authorities appear to have become used to "outsourcing" to NGOs many services which they, themselves, should normally be offering to the population, but do not do so because of a combination of factors including lack of skilled personnel, insufficient budget, and, often, negligence and corruption. Furthermore, on a personal level, local officials often attempt to benefit from foreign funding. This happens, for example, when they demand unofficial payments from NGO leaders in return for issuing supporting documents and recommendation letters for NGOs, which are required to apply for funding from international donors.[72]

Population

Although the local population in the regions continues to benefit from services which are offered by NGOs on the ground, in comparison with the 1990s the scope of these services is, today, more modest. And the availability of NGO services is dependent on one- or two-year-long project cycles. As explained by a government official from the Rasht Valley, for local populations which are not aware of the logic of funding and project cycles, this process may seem confusing:

> On the one hand, people today are well aware that NGOs exist, but on the other hand, they usually do not know what services they exactly offer. . . . [NGO] services are also changing constantly, depending on what project they implement. So, they might have one project [this year], and then another [totally different project later], or stop working for some time. But people do not understand that well. You know, even for us [local officials] this is sometimes difficult to comprehend.[73]

As in the 1990s, among the local population there is still little awareness of what NGOs stand for and how the Tajik government positions itself toward them in the domestic context. Thus, while the central government and local authorities have developed pragmatic working relations with NGOs based on common areas of interests, the local population is still largely treated as a passive "target" of foreign assistance, both by development agencies and local NGOs. That said some INGOs, such as Oxfam Great Britain and Mountain Societies Development Support Programme (MSDSP), have attempted to engage with the local population and provide incentives for them in taking ownership of Western-funded development projects. Despite this progress, as Anna Cieślewska notices, often such collaborations on the ground are not without problems, as INGOs try to "readjust" local populations by insisting on including special quota for women's participation in community projects or engaging all community members in decision making as equals, despite established local hierarchies based on age, gender, religiosity, family reputation and other factors.[74]

CONCLUSION

Our ambition in this chapter was to draw a bigger picture of the soft power of neoliberal civil society in post-Soviet Tajikistan by depicting a number of its components. We briefly described the origins of neoliberal civil society, as well as why and how the concept was adopted as a form of soft power by Western development agencies operating in the post Soviet space. We explained what was particular about this process in Tajikistan in the context not only of post-Soviet transformations, but also a devastating civil war in the 1990s. We described differences in how development agencies had exercised the soft power of neoliberal civil society in the early 1990s and since the late 2000s, as well as changing reactions of local actors to this soft power.

Nearly three decades after the arrival of neoliberal civil society to Central Asia, the tangible output of its soft power, the ideational components of NGO sector, is in decline, at least in the Tajik case. As previously outlined, Nye defines soft power as "the ability to affect others to obtain the outcomes one wants through *attraction* rather than coercion or payment."[75] Since the early 1990s, foreign development agencies in Tajikistan have been relying on a number of persuasion tools to attractively portray the idea of neoliberal civil society to local actors. They demonstrated benignity, by offering project funding and humanitarian aid; presumed competence, by bringing ready models of neoliberal civil society, projects and funding of NGOs; and beauty by offering new ideas which replaced the post-Soviet vacuum. But why has there been little spillover of the greater ideational components of liberalism in Tajikistan, which has experienced less, not more, democracy, pluralism, and other avowed Western-promoted ideals in the decades following the collapse of the Soviet Union and emergence of various components of civil society in the region?

We argue that this is because, first, development actors directly targeted only one social group with benignity, competence, and beauty: local activists who later formed NGOs. Through Western-funded and often badly designed projects, newly formed local NGOs were presumed to not only uptake liberal norms, but to spread liberal ideas among other actors, including the central government, local authorities, and the population at large. Second, although it remains absent in Nye's framework, the agency of local actors upon the soft power that is projected matters.[76] In the conditions of severe economic decline, local activists reacted mainly to one tool of soft power, benignity, rather than competence and beauty. In other words, their positive reaction toward neoliberal civil society was evoked mainly with its economic and material incentives—which in reality verges on hard not soft power.

Nowadays, the NGO sector, or neoliberal civil society in Tajikistan, is identified nearly across the board with employment and material benefits gained from Western donors. The NGO label has become a curse for genuine local activists. For them, association with NGOs often diminishes the value of their activism in the eyes of other local actors. And for the central government officials, in particular, the association of local NGOs with Western donors carries connotations of a mercenary type of activism. Whether the more idealistic connotations of liberalism and civil society entailing grassroots socioeconomic, political, and environmental activism will eventually dominate in Tajikistan is still indeterminate and likely years away. While resources for NGOs are shrinking, new spaces of more apolitical civic grassroots activism and volunteerism are opening and filling with, inter alia, dedicated journalists, creative bloggers, and passionate animal and eco-activists. Such liberal activism, however, likely has little direct relationship with years of promotion of neoliberal civil society by Western donors in Central Asia.

NOTES

1. Writing of this chapter was supported by the "Tomsk State University Competitiveness Improvement Programme" (Tomsk State University, grant number 8.1.27.2018) and Collaborative Research Center SFB/TRR 138 "Dynamics of Security" (Deutsche Forschungsgemeinschaft, grant number 227068724).

2. Thomas Carothers, "Think Again: Civil Society," *Foreign Policy* 117 (1999–2000): 18.

3. Babken Babajanian, Sabine Freizer, and Daniel Stevens, "Introduction: Civil Society in Central Asia and the Caucasus," *Central Asian Survey* 24, no. 3 (2005): 211–12.

4. Joseph S. Nye, Jr., *Soft Power: The Means to Success in World Politics* (New York: Public Affairs, 2004); Joseph S. Nye, Jr., *The Future of Power* (New York: Public Affairs, 2011); Joseph S. Nye, Jr., "Public Diplomacy and Soft Power," *The Annals of the American Academy of Political and Social Science* 616, no. 1 (2008): 94–109.

5. Nye, "Public Diplomacy and Soft Power," 94–95.

6. Alexander Cooley, *Great Games, Local Rules: The New Power Contest in Central Asia* (Oxford: Oxford University Press, 2012); Marlene Laruelle and

Sebastien Peyrouse, *Globalizing Central Asia: Geopolitics and the Challenges of Economic Development* (New York: Routledge, 2015).
7. Mary Kaldor, "The Idea of Global Civil Society," *International Affairs* 79, no. 3 (2003): 583–93.
8. Ibid., 589.
9. Ibid.
10. Ibid.
11. Ibid.
12. Eric Sievers, *The Post-Soviet Decline of Central Asia: Sustainable Development and Comprehensive Capital* (New York: Routledge, 2003).
13. Edward Schatz, "What Type of Ethnography Does Political Science Need?" in *Political Ethnography: What Immersion Contributes to the Study of Politics*, ed. Edward Schatz (Chicago: The University of Chicago Press, 2009), 303.
14. David Mosse, ed., *Adventures in Aidland: The Anthropology of Professionals in International Development* (New York and London: Berghahn Books, 2011).
15. As a point of acknowledgment, we would like to thank all interviewees for sharing their views and entrusting us with their personal stories.
16. Christopher Michael Hann and Elizabeth Dunn, eds., *Civil Society: Challenging Western Models* (London and New York: Routledge, 1996).
17. Payam Foroughi, "Tajikistan," in *Nations in Transit 2011: Democratization from Central Europe to Eurasia*, ed. Sylvana Habdank-Kolaczkowska and Christopher Walker (New York: Rowan and Littlefield, 2011).
18. Alison Van Rooy, "Civil Society as Idea: An Analytical Hatstand," in *Civil Society and the Aid Industry*, ed. Alison Van Rooy (New York: Routledge, 2013).
19. Michael Edwards, ed., *Civil Society* (Cambridge: Polity Press, 2009).
20. Alan Fowler, "Development NGOs," in *The Oxford Handbook of Civil Society*, ed. Michael Edwards (Oxford: Oxford University Press, 2013).
21. Nye, "Public Diplomacy and Soft Power."
22. Marc Morjé Howard, *The Weakness of Civil Society in Post-Communist Europe* (New York: Cambridge University Press, 2003); Babajanian et al. "Introduction"; Armine Ishkanian, *Democracy Building and Civil Society in Post-Soviet Armenia* (London and New York: Routledge, 2008).
23. Sievers, *The Post-Soviet Decline of Central Asia*.
24. Sabine Freizer, "Central Asian Fragmented Civil Society: Communal and Neoliberal Forms in Tajikistan and Uzbekistan," in *Exploring Civil Society: Political and Cultural Contexts*, ed. Glasius, Marlies, David Lewis, and Hakan Seckinelgin. London and New York: Routledge, 2014; Olivier Roy, "The Predicament of 'Civil Society' in Central Asia and the 'Greater Middle East'," *International Affairs* 81, no. 5 (2005): 1001–12; Anna Cieślewska, *Community, the State and Development Assistance: Transforming the Mahalla in Tajikistan* (Cracow: Księgarnia Akademicka, 2015).
25. Tim Epkenhans, *The Origins of the Civil War in Tajikistan: Nationalism, Islamism, and Violent Conflict in the Post-Soviet Space* (Lanham: Lexington Books, 2016).

26. John Heathershaw, *Post-Conflict Tajikistan: The Politics of Peacebuilding and the Emergence of Legitimate Order* (London and New York: Routledge, 2009), 47.

27. Alexander Vuving, "How Soft Power Works," (paper, American Political Science Association annual meeting, Toronto, September 3–6, 2009), https://bit.ly/2slb3YC; Nye, *The Future of Power*, 92.

28. Freizer, "Central Asian Fragmented Civil Society."

29. Julie Fischer, *Importing Democracy: The Role of NGOs in South Africa, Tajikistan and Argentina* (Dayton: Kettering Foundation Press, 2013).

30. Shamsidin Karimov, *Rol' NPO v formirovanii grazhdanskogo obshestva v Tadzhikistane. Istoriko-politologicheskoe issledovanie* [The role of NGOs in the forming of civil society in Tajikistan: A historical and political science research] (Dushanbe, 2008), 205.

31. Roy, "The Predicament of 'Civil Society'," 1003.

32. Nye, *The Future of Power*.

33. Ashurboy Imomov, "NPO Tadzhikistana," *Izvestiya Akademii Nauk Respubliki Tadzhikistan* 2 (1996). Our translation.

34. Charles Buxton, *The Struggle for Civil Society in Central Asia: Crisis and Transformation* (Sterling: Kumarian Press, 2011), 34–66.

35. Kamoludin Abdullaev, "Tadzhikskie NPO. Kto oni? Agentyvliyaniya Zapada ilistroiteligrazhdanskogoobshestva? [Tajik NGOs. Who Are They? Western Agents of Influence or Builders of Civil Society?]," *Ariana*, March 4, 2006, https://bit.ly/2IQPE0M; Parviz Mullojanov, "25 Years of Independence: Civil Society and the State in Tajikistan," in *Central Asia at 25: Looking Back, Moving Forward. A Collection of Essays from Central Asia*, ed. Marlene Laruelle and Aytolkyn Kourmanova (Washington, DC: Central Asia Program, 2017).

36. Interview with a leader of a women's NGO in the Kulob district, September 17, 2017.

37. Interview with a Tajik intellectual with extensive experience both in the government and the development sector, August 2, 2017.

38. Karimov, *Rol' NPO v formirovanii grazhdanskogo obshestva v Tadzhikistane*, 161.

39. Mullojanov, "25 Years of Independence."

40. Karimov, *Rol' NPO v formirovanii grazhdanskogo obshestva v Tadzhikistane*, 205.

41. Parviz Mullojanov, "Civil Society and Peacebuilding," in *Politics of Compromise: The Tajikistan Peace Process*, Accord Issue 10, ed. Komoludin Abdullaev and Catharine Barnes (London: Conciliation Sources, 2001), 62.

42. Interview with an NGO leader in the Panjakent district, September 11, 2017.

43. Interview with an employee of an NGO in Istaravshan, July 27, 2014.

44. Mullojanov, "Civil Society and Peacebuilding," 63; Viloyat Mirzoeva, "Istoriya razvitiya zhenskogo dvizheniya v Tadzhikistane za gody nezavisimosti" [The History of Development of Women's Movement in Tajikistan after Independence], (PhD thesis, Tajik Academy of Sciences, University of Dushanbe, Dushanbe, 2004); Dilbar Turakhanova, "The Legal Response to Domestic Violence in Tajikistan," in

Gender Based Violence and Public Health: International Perspectives on Budgets and Policies, ed. Keerty Nakray (London: Routledge, 2013).

45. Interview with an NGO leader from Dushanbe, August 19, 2014.

46. Nye, *The Future of Power*.

47. Ibid., 84.

48. Naren Chitty, "Soft Power, Civic Virtue and World Politics (Section Overview)," In *The Routledge Handbook of Soft Power*, ed. Naren Chitty et al. (London and New York: Routledge, 2016), 21–28.

49. Thomas Carothers "The End of the Transition Paradigm," *Journal of Democracy* 13, no. 1 (2002): 5–21.

50. Heathershaw, *Post-Conflict Tajikistan*, 128.

51. Susan Engel, "The Not-so-great Aid Debate," *Third World Quarterly* 35, no. 8 (2014): 1374–89.

52. Payam Foroughi, "The Helsinki Final Act Four Decades On," *Central Asian Survey* 36, no. 3 (2017): 298.

53. Author recollection of an IO worker's comments, Dushanbe, May 2009.

54. Karolina Kluczewska, "Questioning Local Ownership: Insights from Donor-funded NGOs in Tajikistan,"*Journal of Civil Society* 15, no. 4 (2019).

55. Fidokor, "Otchet ekspertnogo issledovaniya dlya podgotovki analiticheskogo doklada o regional'nyh i mezhstranovyh tematicheskih napravleniyah sotrudnichestva OGO Azerbaijana i stran Central'noy Azii. Strana: Tajikistan" [Expert Study Report for the Preparation of an Analysis of Regional and Intercountry Case Studies of Civil Society Organisations in Azerbaijan and countries of Central Asia, Strana: Tajikistan], (unpublished report, Programme Partnership for Innovation, Tajikistan, 2017).

56. Author recollection of an IO worker's comments, Dushanbe, November 2008.

57. Government of Tajikistan, "Fehristi hizbhoi siyosi va ittihodiyahoi jam'iyati" [List of Political Parties and Public Associations], Ministry of Justice of the Republic of Tajikistan, 2018, https://bit.ly/2JgewT0, accessed May 22, 2018.

58. Mullojanov, "25 Years of Independence," 70.

59. Cieślewska, *Community, the State and Development Assistance*, 134.

60. Dodarbek Saydaliev, "Sozmonhoi baynamilali: sud yo ziyon? [International Organizations: Profit or Loss?]," *Impuls* 14 (2014). Our translation.

61. Carothers, "Think Again," 18.

62. Andrew Wilson, "Ukraine's Orange Revolution, NGOs and the Role of the West," *Cambridge Review of InternationalAffairs* 19, no. 1 (2006): 21–32; Theodor Tudoroiu,"Rose, Orange, and Tulip: The Failed Post-Soviet Revolutions," *Communist and Post-Communist Studies* 40, no. 3 (2007): 315–42.

63. "NGO Law Brings Chill Wind to Tajikistan,"*Institute for War and Peace Reporting* (IWPR, Central Asia), November 26, 2015, https://bit.ly/2LaGfSa.

64. Ibid.

65. Fischer,*ImportingDemocracy*,132;Mullojanov,"25YearsofIndependence,"71.

66. Fidokor, "Otchet ekspertnogo issledovaniya," 22.

67. Interview with an employee of a Tajik charity organisation, September 18, 2017.

68. Carothers, "Think Again," 18.

69. Fischer, *Importing Democracy*, 133.
70. Fidokor, "Otchet ekspertnogo issledovaniya," 21.
71. Interview with an employee of a women's NGO in Istaravshan, July 27, 2014.
72. Interview with an NGO leader in the Panjakent district, September 11, 2017.
73. Interview with a government employee in the Rasht valley, July 22, 2014.
74. Cieślewska, *Community, the State and Development Assistance*, 143–44.
75. "Public Diplomacy and Soft Power," 94. Emphasis added.
76. Ibid.

REFERENCES

Abdullaev, Kamoludin. "Tadzhikskie NPO. Kto oni? Agenty vliyaniya Zapada ili stroiteli grazhdanskogo obshestva? [Tajik NGOs. Who Are They? Western Agents of Influence or Builders of Civil Society?]." *Ariana*, March 4, 2006. https://bit.ly/2IQPE0M.

Babajanian, Babken, Sabine Freizer, and Daniel Stevens. "Introduction: Civil Society in Central Asia and the Caucasus." *Central Asian Survey* 24, no. 3 (2005): 209–24.

Buxton, Charles. 2011. *The Struggle for Civil Society in Central Asia: Crisis and Transformation*. Sterling: Kumarian Press.

Carothers, Thomas. "The End of the Transition Paradigm." *Journal of Democracy* 13, no. 1 (2002): 5–21.

Carothers, Thomas. "Think Again: Civil Society." *Foreign Policy* 117 (1999–2000): 29.

Chitty, Naren. 2016. "Soft Power, Civic Virtue and World Politics (Section Overview)." In *The Routledge Handbook of Soft Power*, edited by Naren Chitty, Li Ji, Gary D. Rawnsley, and Craig Hayden, 9–36. London and New York: Routledge.

Cieślewska, Anna. *Community, the State and Development Assistance: Transforming the Mahalla in Tajikistan*. Cracow: Księgarnia Akademicka, 2015

Cooley, Alexander. *Great Games, Local Rules: The New Great Power Contest in Central Asia*. New York: Oxford University Press, 2012.

Edwards, Michael, ed. *Civil Society*. Cambridge: Polity Press, 2009.

Engel, Susan "The Not-so-great Aid Debate." *Third World Quarterly* 35, no. 8 (2014): 1374–89.

Epkenhans, Tim. *The Origins of the Civil War in Tajikistan: Nationalism, Islamism, and Violent Conflict in the Post-Soviet Space*. Lanham: Lexington Books, 2016.

Fidokor. "Otchet ekspertnogo issledovaniya dlya podgotovki analiticheskogo doklada o regional'nyh i mezhstranovyh tematicheskih napravleniyah sotrudnichestva OGO Azerbaidzhana i stran Tsentral'noy Azii. Strana: Tadzhikistan [Expert Study Report for the Preparation of an Analysis of Regional and Intercountry Case Studies of Civil Society Organisations in Azerbaijan and countries of Central]." Unpublished report, Programme Partnership for Innovation, 2017.

Fischer, Julie. *Importing Democracy: The Role of NGOs in South Africa, Tajikistan and Argentina*. Dayton: Kettering Foundation Press, 2013.

Foroughi, Payam. "The Helsinki Final Act Four Decades On." *Central Asian Survey* 36, no. 3 (2017): 293–99.
Foroughi, Payam. "Tajikistan." In *Nations in Transit 2011: Democratization from Central Europe to Eurasia*, edited by Sylvana Habdank-Kolaczkowska and Christopher Walker, 537–56. New York: Rowan and Littlefield, 2011.
Fowler, Alan. "Development NGOs." In *The Oxford Handbook of Civil Society*, edited by Michael Edwards, 42–55. Oxford: Oxford University Press, 2013.
Freizer, Sabine. "Central Asian Fragmented Civil Society: Communal and Neoliberal Forms in Tajikistan and Uzbekistan." In *Exploring Civil Society: Political and Cultural Contexts*, edited by Glasius, Marlies, David Lewis, and Hakan Seckinelgin, 130–40. London and New York: Routledge, 2014.
Hann, Christopher Michael, and Elizabeth Dunn, eds. *Civil Society: Challenging Western Models*. London and New York: Routledge, 1996.
Heathershaw, John. *Post-Conflict Tajikistan: The Politics of Peacebuilding and the Emergence of Legitimate Order*. London and New York: Routledge, 2009.
Howard, Marc Morjé. *The Weakness of Civil Society in Post-Communist Europe*. New York: Cambridge University Press, 2003.
Imomov, Ashurboy. "NPO Tadzhikistana." *Izvestiya Akademii Nauk Respubliki Tadzhikistan* 2 (1996).
Ishkanian, Armine. *Democracy Building and Civil Society in Post-Soviet Armenia*. London and New York: Routledge, 2008.
IWPR Central Asia. "NGO Law Brings Chill Wind to Tajikistan." *Institute for War and Peace Reporting*, November 26, 2015. https://bit.ly/2LaGfSa.
Kaldor, Mary. "The Idea of Global Civil Society." *International Affairs* 79, no. 3 (2003): 583–93.
Karimov, Shamsidin. *Rol' NPO v formirovanii grazhdanskogo obshestva v Tadzhikistane. Istoriko-politologicheskoe issledovanie* [The role of NGOs in the forming of civil society in Tajikistan: A historical and political science research]. Dushanbe, 2008.
Kluczewska, Karolina. "Questioning Local Ownership: Insights from Donor-funded NGOs in Tajikistan," *Journal of Civil Society* 15, no. 4 (2019): 354–372.
Laruelle, Marlene, and Sebastien Peyrouse. *Globalizing Central Asia: Geopolitics and the Challenges of Economic Development*. Armonk: M.E. Sharpe, 2013.
Mirzoeva, Viloyat. "Istoriya razvitiya zhenskogo dvizheniya v Tadzhikistane za gody nezavisimosti" [The History of Development of Women's Movement in Tajikistan after Independence]. PhD thesis, Tajik Academy of Sciences, University of Dushanbe, Dushanbe, 2004.
Mosse, David, ed. *Adventures in Aidland: The Anthropology of Professionals in International Development*. New York and London: Berghahn Books, 2011.
Mullojanov, Parviz. "25 Years of Independence: Civil Society and the State in Tajikistan." In *Central Asia at 25: Looking Back, Moving Forward. A Collection of Essays from Central Asia*, edited by Marlene Laruelle and Aytolkyn Kourmanova, 69–71. Washington, DC: Central Asia Program, 2017.

Mullojanov, Parviz. "Civil Society and Peacebuilding." In *Politics of Compromise: The Tajikistan Peace Process*, Accord Issue 10, edited by Komoludin Abdullaev and Catharine Barnes, 60–63. London: Conciliation Sources, 2001.
Nye, Joseph S. Jr. *The Future of Power*. New York: Public Affairs, 2011.
Nye, Joseph S. Jr. "Public Diplomacy and Soft Power," *The Annals of the America's Academy of Political and Social Science* 616, no 1 (2008): 94–109.
Nye, Joseph S. Jr. *Soft Power. The Means to Success in World Politics*. New York: Public Affairs, 2004.
Rooy, Alison Van. "Civil Society as Idea: An Analytical Hatstand." In *Civil Society and the Aid Industry*, edited by Alison Van Rooy, 8–30. New York: Routledge, 2013.
Roy, Olivier. "The Predicament of 'Civil Society' in Central Asia and the 'Greater Middle East'." *International Affairs* 81, no. 5 (2005): 1001–12.
Saydaliev, Dodarbek. "Sozmonhoi baynamilali: sud yo ziyon? [International Organizations: Profit or Loss?]." *Impuls* 14 (2014).
Schatz, Edward. "What Type of Ethnography Does Political Science Need?" In *Political Ethnography: What Immersion Contributes to the Study of Politics*, edited by Edward Schatz, 303–18. Chicago: The University of Chicago Press, 2009.
Sievers, Eric. *The Post-Soviet Decline of Central Asia: Sustainable Development and Comprehensive Capital*. New York: Routledge, 2003.
Tajikistan, Government of. "Fehristi hizbhoi siyosi va ittihodiyahoi jam'iyati" [List of Political Parties and Public Associations]. Ministry of Justice of the Republic of Tajikistan, 2018. https://bit.ly/2JgewT0. Accessed May 22, 2018.
Tudoroiu, Theodor. "Rose, Orange, and Tulip: The Failed Post-Soviet Revolutions." *Communist and Post-Communist Studies* 40, no. 3 (2007): 315–42.
Turakhanova, Dilbar. "The Legal Response to Domestic Violence in Tajikistan." In *Gender Based Violence and Public Health: International Perspectives on Budgets and Policies*, edited by Keerty Nakray, 137–49. London: Routledge, 2013.
Vuving, Alexander. "How Soft Power Works." Paper presented at the American Political Science Association annual meeting, Toronto, September 3–6, 2009. https://bit.ly/2slb3YC.
Wilson, Andrew. "Ukraine's Orange Revolution, NGOs and the Role of the West." *Cambridge Review of International Affairs* 19, no. 1 (2006): 21–32.

Index

Afghanistan, 9, 11, 12, 28, 30, 32–35, 43–45, 91, 144, 203, 218, 231, 234, 258
Africa, 1, 40, 86, 95, 99, 102, 141, 142, 150, 153; North, 119; Sub-Saharan, 142
agitprop, 16, 209
Ahrens, Bettina, 120
aid, 12, 17, 21n42, 28, 31–33, 43, 44, 65, 73, 118, 136, 138, 141, 149–51, 159n52, 172, 186, 187n12, 216, 221, 223, 226–30, 232–35; military, 38–39. *See also* USAID
Akaev, Askar, 33
Akdağ, Gül Arıkan, 135
Akkaya, Muammer, 148
AKP. *See* Justice and Development Party (AKP)
aliyah, 184, 192n66. *See also* migration
American Corners, 11, 30
American-Jewish Joint Distribution Committee, 181
Amrebayev, Aidar, 204
Andijan massacre, 4, 32–33, 97
Anholt Ipsos Nation Brands Index, 10
Arab Spring, 8, 37, 174
Aral Sea, 173
Armenia, 169, 171, 176, 187n12
Ashgabat, 62, 139, 142, 143

Ashkenazı, 171, 177–80
Asia–Europe Meeting (ASEM), 122
Atambayev, Almazbek, 233
Ata-Meken, 225
Auezov, Murat, 205, 210n15
Austria, 137
Aydın, Mehmet, 137
Azerbaijan, 144, 145, 150, 170, 175

Bakiyev, Kurmanbek, 38, 222–23, 225, 232–34
Balcı, Bayram, 135–36, 146
Balkans, 118, 121, 150
Baltic, 179, 220, 237n18, 237–38n32; Sea, 177
banking, 85, 146, 182
Baron, Ilan Zvi, 170
Beacon state, 168–69
Beijing Consensus, 95
Belarus, 119, 168, 178, 179, 181, 182
Belt and Road Initiative (BRI), 40, 46, 85, 94, 102, 205–6, 229
Benhaïm, Yohanan, 136
Berdymukhammedov, Gurbanguly, 3, 4, 148
Berlin, 57, 123, 125
Berman Jewish Databank, 177
Bijian, Zheng, 86
Bishkek Oil, 223

271

Blank, Stephen, 31
Bogatyrev, Valentin, 226
Brzezinski, Zbigniew, 2, 5, 27–28, 45
Bulgaria, 144
Burkhanov, Aziz, 205
Bush, George H. W., 37

Çakır, Aylin Aydın, 135
Carnegie, 42, 62
Caspian, 27, 168
Caucasus, 34, 42, 43, 119, 137, 144, 150, 152, 187n12
CCP Congress (2007), 86
Central Europe, 183
Chabad-Lubavitch, 182
Chen, Yu-wen, 205
Chinese–Soviet relations, 89–91, 96, 101, 202, 229
Civic Chamber of the Russian Federation, 59
Clement, Victoria, 148
Clinton, Hillary, 33, 40
Cold War, 28, 29, 45, 250, 252
Collective Security Treaty Organization (CSTO), 60, 234
Collins, Kathleen, 45
color revolutions, 8, 36–37, 90, 97, 219, 260
Confucius Institutes, 41, 92, 93, 99–100, 104, 205
Cooley, Alexander, 41–42, 97, 233
Cornell, Svante, 46
cotton, 33
counterterrorism, 43, 234
COVID-19, 8, 10, 12, 34
Crimea, 62, 95, 144, 179, 181, 186n3, 201, 210n13
Cuba, 31
cuisine. *See* food
Cyrillic, 36, 139

Dastan torpedo plant, 222, 233
Dave, Bhavna, 99, 206, 207
Davutoğlu, Ahmet, 136
De Pedro, Nicolas, 223, 229

Demirtepe, Mustafa Turgut, 149
democracy, 6, 8, 11–13, 30–32, 34, 35, 37, 41–44, 57, 58, 70, 96, 97, 104, 118, 119, 122–25, 172, 188n141, 219, 249, 252, 255, 258, 263
Development Cooperation Instrument (DCI), 123
Diyanet, 14, 136–42, 146, 153
Djeyenbekov, Ravshan, 231
dom druzhby narodo, 92
Donelli, Federico, 135

East Asia, 40
Eastern Europe, 37, 118, 121, 150, 168, 177, 181, 237–38n32
education, 10, 12, 14, 31, 38, 41, 44, 61, 64, 66, 70, 72, 92–94, 118, 124, 135, 136, 142–49, 153–54, 183, 200, 206; language, 38, 66–68, 92–94, 104, 142–44, 156n41, 156–57n59, 179, 184; religious, 138–42, 146, 181, 182, 184; tertiary, 60, 68–69, 73, 93–94, 138, 144–45, 180, 206
elites, 3, 4, 11, 15, 28, 31, 59, 66, 90, 125, 137, 148–49, 153, 185, 200, 201, 215, 217–19, 221, 223, 235, 236n7
Embel, Seyit, 148
energy, 30, 31, 33, 35, 36, 41, 89, 126, 175, 216, 220–23, 235, 237–38n32; security, 124, 175; solar, 176
Erdoğan, Recep, 135, 140, 145
Ethiopia, 104, 170
Eurasian Customs Union, 222, 231
Eurasian Economic Union (EEU), 16, 60–63, 70, 72, 203, 223
Eurasian Islamic Council, 138
Europe, ix, 1–4, 6–10, 13, 14, 27, 30, 34, 41, 71, 98, 100, 117–30, 137, 169, 172, 174, 183, 186, 187n13, 202, 221, 226
European Commission, 172
European Neighbourhood Policy (ENP), 14, 118–19, 121–23
European Parliament, 126

European Security and Defence Policy (ESDP), 123
European Union. *See* Europe
European Union Special Representative (EUSR), 123
Eurozone debt crisis (2011), 118
Exim (Export Import) Bank of China, 227

Far West Development Program, 91
Feklyunina, Valentina, 217
Fierman, William, 66
film, 21n42; Chinese, 100; Indian, 100; Israeli, 171; Russian, 67, 100; Turkish, 152–53; US, 29, 100
food, 9, 21n142, 98–99, 180, 181, 257; security, 31
France, 68, 171, 186, 187n12
free markets, 31, 34, 43, 44, 249
free trade, 31, 44, 222
Freedom House, 10
FREEDOM Support Act, 31–32
Friedrich-Ebert-Stiftung, 70, 95, 98

gas, 33, 85, 89, 90, 221, 223, 256. *See also* energy
gasoline, 222, 223
Gaza, 172, 174
Gazprom, 64, 221, 223
Georgia, 37, 237n16, 260
Germany, 10, 125, 137, 169, 171, 173, 176, 178, 183, 186; West, 183
Global Financial Crisis, 94, 175, 184
Go Out policy. *See zouchuqu*
Goble, Paul, 45
Goethe Institute, 67
GONGO, 12, 63, 72
grand chessboard, 2, 27, 46
Great Game, x, 3, 4, 15, 18n5, 27, 41–44, 51n87; new, ix, 2, 42, 46, 126
Great Student Project, 144
Greece, 144, 172
Grigas, Agnia, 220, 237n18, 237–38n32, 238n36
Gülen, Fethullah, 14, 146; movement, 14, 135, 136, 138, 145–49, 153,
156n59, 158n81, 183; schools, 14, 145–49

Haines, John, 221
hard power, x, 1–7, 12, 15–17, 36, 37, 58, 59, 87–89, 94–95, 135, 136, 154, 199, 201, 216, 221, 223, 224, 230, 232, 235, 250, 258
health, 15, 37, 144, 150, 172, 173, 175, 176, 186, 249, 261
heping jueqi, 86
Hesed, 181
Hizb-ut Tahrir, 137
Hu Jintao, 86, 92, 96, 100, 103
human rights, 8, 11, 31, 32, 34, 43, 44, 96, 97, 119, 124, 219, 250, 253, 261
hydrocarbons, 2

Imam Hatip High Schools, 140–43
imperialism, 27, 36, 39, 44, 51n87, 72, 101, 170, 200, 219; neo-, 36, 236n10
India, 17, 30, 33, 35, 68, 92, 100
Indonesia, 96, 103
infrastructure, 40, 41, 85, 94, 98, 178, 221
International Arbitration Centre, 228
International Monetary Fund (IMF), 3, 13, 95, 226
investment ix, 2, 4, 12, 15, 16, 28, 33, 34, 40, 44, 64, 70, 85–87, 94, 95, 98, 99, 102, 104, 139, 147, 171, 174–76, 185, 187n12, 189n32, 206–9, 216, 221–23, 226, 232, 233, 235
Iran, 2, 17, 27, 30, 34, 35, 51n92, 96, 98, 137, 146, 168, 170, 175, 179, 189n28, 203, 250
Iraq, 144, 176
ISIS, 8, 136
Islamic extremism, 36, 43, 85, 153
Islamic State. *See* ISIS
Islamism, 146
Ismailov, Bakhrom, 231
Israel, 2, 15, 167–92

Jabbour, Jana, 136
Japan, 2, 17, 98, 102, 117, 173
Jordan, 172
July, 15 coup attempt, 14, 138, 147–49, 156n59
Justice and Development Party (AKP), 14, 15, 135, 136, 138, 140, 146, 147, 150, 153

Kadyrzhanov, Rustem, 66
Kalashnnikov, Leonid, 62
Kalin, Ibrahim, 135, 136
Kant airbase, 38, 232–34
Karimov, Islam, 3, 4, 11, 32–33, 97, 149, 150, 158n90
Karimova, Gulnara, 152
Karshi-Khanabad, 32
KATEV International, 147
KATIAD, 147
Kazantsev, Andrei, 37
Kennedy, John F., 37
Keyman, E. Fuat, 136
Khazar kingdom, 168
Kissinger, Henry, 5
KITIAD, 147
Knyazev, Alexander, 222–23
Koch, Natalie, 204, 205, 210n23
KOMAŞ, 141
Korea, 66, 169, 176, 180, 189n28; South, 2, 17, 34, 102
Koru, Naci, 145–46
Kosovo, 144
Kulov, Felix, 225
Kurdish, 176; separatism, 170
Kurlantzick, Joshua, 86
Kyrgyzgas, 223

Lami, Blendi, 136
Latin America, 1, 86, 150, 152
Lavrov, Sergey, 7, 57, 65, 224
LGBTQI+ rights, 29, 124, 187n13
liberalization, 249; economic, 231; political, 31
Lifan, Li, 228

Mackinder, Sir Halford, 2
Malaysia, 2
Manas air base, 32, 33, 38, 222, 232, 233; closure of, 34, 38, 42, 234
Mandarin, 92, 94, 98, 100, 104, 205
Marlene Laruelle, 30, 58, 71, 202
MASHAV, 172, 173, 188n17
Matvienko, Valentina, 62, 67, 76n37
Mauss, Marcel, 168
media, 3, 4, 9, 12, 16, 29, 36–38, 44, 61–63, 68, 70–72, 85, 88, 92–94, 102, 103, 124, 174, 201–3, 205, 208, 209, 210n13, 216, 217, 224–26, 229, 235, 236n6, 236n12. *See also* social media
Medvedev, Dmitri, 69, 217, 222, 225
Middle East, 2, 14, 63, 96, 119, 136, 140, 141, 150, 153
migration, 9, 10, 16, 36, 39, 62, 66, 68, 91, 137, 174, 204, 216, 228, 230–32, 235, 249; to Israel, 15, 168, 172, 177, 180, 183–85; rural to urban, 89
mining, 85, 93, 175, 182, 228–30
Ministry for Economic Development, Russia (MED), 61
Ministry for Emergency Situations, Russia (MES), 61
Ministry of Defense, Russia (MoD), 61
Ministry of Foreign Affairs, Russian (MFA), 36, 59, 149
Mirziyoev, Shavkat, 44, 70, 153
Mitvsa, 181
Moldova, 119
Morrel, Pierre, 121
mosques, 138, 139, 146, 251; construction of, 138, 140, 141; renovation of, 138, 140, 141
Mullojanov, Parviz, 88, 256, 259
multivectorism, 3–4, 216
MÜSİAD, 148
music, 28, 29, 67; jazz, 171; klezmer, 171; Russian, 64, 200
Myanmar, 141

National Energy Security Fund, 223
National Security Strategy (NSS), 2017 35, 44
Nazarbayev, Nursultan, 3, 71, 147, 204, 206
Nepal, 96
Netherlands, 137
New Generation program, 70
Nixey, James, 38
Niyazov, Saparmurat, 4, 148
Nogayeva, Ainur, 205–6
nongovernmental organizations (NGOs), 12, 17, 38, 44, 61–64, 70, 72, 73, 172, 181, 184, 206, 249–68. See also GONGO
Northern Distribution Network (NDN), 30, 32
North–South road, 227
Nye, Jospeh, ix, 1, 5–8, 10–12, 37, 57–58, 85–110, 117, 121, 126, 136, 199, 206, 208, 209, 215, 216, 220, 224, 226, 230, 235, 250, 253–54, 257, 263

Obama, Barack, 11, 34; administration, 29
oil, 42, 85, 89, 90, 95, 175–76, 184, 221–23, 233, 238n38; shipping lanes, 89–90. See also energy
Ökte, Kerem, 136
Opium Wars, 90
Organization for Economic Co-operation and Development (OECD), 94, 172
Özkan, Güner, 149

Pakistan, 2, 32, 33, 43, 91, 228
Palestine, 141, 150, 169, 173–74, 181, 184
Partnership and Cooperation Agreement (PCA), 122–23
Pavliuk, Gennadii, 225
Peace Corps, 37–38; Chinese, 104
petroleum, 64, 93, 204, 206, 221–23, 227. See also oil
Philippines, 89, 96

pipeline, 33, 221, 223
popular culture, 21n42, 28, 29, 45, 100, 152–53, 171, 184, 199
Portland Soft Power, 30 Index, 10
Primakov, Evgenii, 63, 64
propaganda, 29, 57, 89, 101, 137, 208; Chinese, 92, 104, 203, 208; Russian, 57, 59, 62, 71
Putin, Vladimir, 58, 59, 62, 63, 67, 68, 71, 215, 219, 237–38n32

Qinghua, Xiao, 226, 228
Quran, 138–41, 156n43

radio, 29, 63, 68, 71, 151, 153, 202
Rahmon, Emomali, 3, 67, 149
Ramadan, 138, 139, 140
RAND Corporation, 10
Reeves, Jeffrey, 228–29
Regional Strategy Paper (RSP), 123
religious tolerance, 46, 95
remittances, 39, 184–85, 187n12, 192n69, 230
Republican Party, US, 34
Romania, 33
Rosneft, 223, 233
Rossotrudnichestvo, 60–70, 75n26, 76n40
Russia, ix, 2, 4, 6, 9, 12, 15, 16, 27, 29, 30, 34, 40, 43–45, 57–79, 85, 89, 91, 92, 96–98, 100, 122, 126, 175, 186, 187n12, 199–212, 215–43, 260; competition with China and US, x, 1, 3, 7, 11, 12, 27, 34, 42–43, 46, 250; economic crisis, 95; imperial, 2, 3, 31; Jewish population, 168, 181, 189n32; security presence, ix, 5, 16, 40, 209; soft power, 10, 12, 16, 35–39, 41, 57–79, 200–203, 209. See also Russian language
Russia Today (RT), 37, 63, 202, 224
Russian Cultural Center in Uzbekistan (RCCU), 70
Russian language, 16, 36, 176, 177, 180, 188n14

Russian Orthodox Church, 70
Russian World [*Russki Mir*], 58, 69, 217
Russophobia, 58
Rutland, Peter, 37

Sadovskaya, Yelena, 204
Salafist, 183
Salih, Mohammed, 149
Sandler, Shmuel, 170
Saudi Arabia, 90, 137, 146
scholarships, 64, 136, 138–40, 144–45, 152
school. *See* education
Scott Radnitz, 219, 221, 236n7, 236n10
September 11, 2001, 11, 32, 123, 233
Shambaugh, David, 13, 87, 102, 209
Shanghai Cooperation Organization (SCO), 97, 234
sharp power, 7, 58
Shvydkoy, Mikhail, 70
Silk Road, 33, 40; new, 27, 33, 34, 40, 41, 46
Simonyan, Margarita, 71, 72
Sinophobia, 4, 86, 88, 102, 103, 205
smart power, 7, 8
social media, 15, 29, 63, 171, 174, 201
Somalia, 150
South Asia, 30, 150. *See also* India; Pakistan
South China Sea, 89
South Ossetia and Abkhazia, 218
Southeast Asia, 40, 89, 90, 93, 96, 100, 103, 104
Soviet Union. *See* USSR
Spaiser, Olga, 121
Sputnik, 37, 63, 71, 202, 224, 233
Sri Lanka, 228
Starr, S. Frederick, 46
Sternik, Aleksandr, 60
StrategEast Westernization Index, 10
Swanström, Niklas, 39
Switzerland, 137
Syria, 144, 145, 150, 172; Civil War, 135, 136, 140, 141, 151, 153, 159n103, 232

Talbott, Strobe, 42, 43
TAPI pipeline, 33
tariffs, 222, 223, 231
Technical Assistance to the Commonwealth of Independent States (TACIS), 123
Tekebayev, Omurbek, 222, 223, 225
television, 29, 37, 38, 63, 68, 92, 100, 146, 151–53, 224–25
Tolipov, Farkhod, 36
Troitskiy, Evgeny, 222
Trump, Donald, 11, 44; administration, 34, 35
Tsygankov, Andrei, 36, 219, 236n6, 237n16
TÜKİB, 147
Turgut, Hulusi, 148
Turkey, 1, 2, 9, 14, 27, 30, 34, 35, 68, 71, 98, 99, 135–60, 170, 175, 250
Turkic ethnicity, 68, 86, 101, 145
Turkish Cooperation and Development Agency (TIKA), 14, 149–51
Turkyılmaz, Muammer, 148

Ukraine, 29, 34, 37, 119, 168, 178, 179, 181, 189n32, 201, 219, 232, 260
Ülgen, Sinan, 136
United Nations (UN), 3, 4, 29, 65, 173, 252
United States, 1–3, 9, 72, 90, 94, 97, 222, 233; invasion of Afghanistan, 11, 12, 28, 32, 34, 35, 43–45, 258; relations with Central Asia, ix, 4, 11, 27–51, 98, 234; use of soft power, 6, 11, 27–51, 71
university. *See* education
USAID, 11, 30, 34, 210n7
Usmanov, Alisher, 64
USSR, 16, 30, 35–36, 39, 58, 61, 86, 88, 89, 168, 174, 178–85, 186n3, 190n41, 191n59, 203, 217, 254; collapse of, 2, 11, 15, 28, 31, 37, 42, 43, 65, 85, 89, 96, 135, 137–38, 144, 149, 218, 229, 250, 252–54, 256

Uyghur, 29, 40, 90, 91, 101, 152, 180, 203, 229–30

Vietnam, 100

war on terror, 11, 30, 32–33, 43, 258
WikiLeaks, 32
Wilson, Jeanne, 219
World Bank, 13, 65, 95, 226
World Trade Organization (WTO), 231
World War Two (WWII), 61, 62, 171, 217, 252

Xi Jinping, 40, 41, 85, 92, 96, 103
Xinjiang, 40, 90–91, 93, 101, 103, 203, 229

Yanukovych, Viktor, 218
Yeltsin, Boris, 220
Yemen, 141, 144
Young Businessmen Association (JIA), 147
youth, 7, 60, 66, 68, 70–73, 74n13, 85, 93, 97–98, 100, 146, 178, 180, 201–3, 227, 254
Yushkov, Igor, 223

Zakharova, Maria, 36
Zatulin, Konstantin, 62
Zhang, Jian, 41
Zionism, 170, 178; anti-, 174; World Zionist Organization, 184
zouchuqu, 86, 90

About the Contributors

Vincent Artman is an instructor of peace and conflict studies at Wayne State University. His research explores the intersection of secularism, ideology, identity, and territory, with a regional focus on Eurasia. His work has appeared in *Europe-Asia Studies*, *Central Asian Affairs*, *Geopolitics*, and *Territory, Politics, Governance*.

Aminat Chokobaeva, PhD., is the postdoctoral fellow in Eurasian Studies at Nazarbayev University, Kazakhstan. She holds a PhD in Central Asian Studies from the Australian National University and has previously taught at the University of Sydney. Her research interests include the early twentieth-century history of Central Asia and nation-building in independent Central Asian republics.

Bruno De Cordier is an associate professor at the Faculty of Political and Social Sciences of Ghent University in Flanders, Belgium. He teaches, among other things, Central Asian history there. His thematic research interests related to the Central Asian region, where he lived for several years, include social history and identity, and the social role and position of religion and religious actors in general.

Alexander C. Diener is an associate professor of geography at the University of Kansas. His thematic interests include political, social, and economic geographies, international relations, and border studies. He has authored three books, edited three volumes, and received funding from the NSF, SSRC, IREX, AAG, Fulbright, and MacArthur Foundation.

Payam Foroughi, PhD, aside from teaching at institutions of higher learning, has years of work experience as project manager, analyst and consultant with international organizations, NGOs and businesses focusing on Central Asia and the greater post-communist space. Earlier in his career, he was also an amateur photographer in Iran, a Peace Corps Volunteer in Morocco, an intern with USAid in El Salvador, an English teacher in Japan, a business journalist in the United States, and a Human Rights Officer with the OSCE mission to Tajikistan. His research and writings have, inter alia, appeared with the Economist Intelligence Unit, Freedom House, International Crisis Group, *Central Asian Survey*, *Journal of Post-Communist Economies*, *Europe-Asia Studies*, Routledge's handbook on *Eastern Europe, Russia, and Central Asia*, and the Russian International Affairs Council (RIAC).

Reuel R. Hanks is professor of geography at Oklahoma State University and holds the Humphreys Endowed Chair in International Studies in the College of Arts and Sciences. Dr Hanks was a Fulbright Scholar in Tashkent, Uzbekistan, and has published more than twenty-five articles and book chapters on national identity, security, and political geography in Central Asia. He is the author of three books on the region: *Uzbekistan*, an annotated bibliography in the World Bibliographical Series (1999), *Central Asia: A Global Studies Handbook* (2005), and *Global Security Watch: Central Asia* (2010). He is currently writing the *Historical Dictionary of Uzbekistan* for Rowman and Littlefield. He has given numerous scholarly presentations and public lectures in Central Asia, and has been a visiting professor at Tashkent State Economics University, Samarkand State Institute for Foreign Languages, KIMEP (Almaty, Kazakhstan), and Eurasian National University (Astana, Kazakhstan), and is an honorary professor at Suleyman Demirel University in Kaskelen, Kazakhstan.

Emilian Kavalski is the inaugural NAWA Visiting Chair Professor at Jagiellonian University in Krakow (Poland), the Li Dak Sum Chair Professor in China-Eurasia Relations and International Studies at the University of Nottingham Ningbo (China), and the Book Series Editor for Routledge's *Rethinking Asia and International Relations* series. His work explores the interconnections between the simultaneous decentering of International Relations by post-Western perspectives and non-anthropocentric approaches. Emilian is the author of four books, most recently: *The Guanxi of Relational International Theory* (Routledge 2018) and he is the editor of eleven volumes, including *World Politics at the Edge of Chaos* (State University of New York Press, 2016).

Karolina Kluczewska is a postdoctoral research fellow at the Käte Hamburger Kolleg/Centre for Global Cooperation Research, University of

Duisburg-Essen in Germany. Her research investigates development aid and localization of global governance frameworks in Central Asia, in particular in the field of migration and healthcare. It appeared in the *Journal of Intervention and Statebuilding*, *Journal of Civil Society*, *Journal of Ethnic and Migration Studies* and *Central Asian Survey*. She also has practical work experience in the development sector in Tajikistan and used to teach at the Tajik National University.

Drew Ninnis, PhD, is the research and liaison advisor to the Australian Chief of the Defence Force. He has worked as an intelligence analyst and in defense capability development, and he has taught at the Australian National University. He holds a PhD in philosophy from the Australian National University and in 2019 was a George C. Marshall Center Fellow. His research interests include the major power dynamics of Russia and China, and the future of the United States.

Dr Kirill Nourzhanov is senior lecturer and convenor of PhD studies at the Centre for Arab and Islamic Studies (The Middle East and Central Asia) at the Australian National University. His main research specialisation is on Central Asian politics and international relations, but his interests also cover Islamic radicalism, Eurasian geopolitics, and history of Tajikistan. Dr Nourzhanov has worked as an academic consultant on the World Bank–funded projects in Kyrgyzstan and Tajikistan. He has served as Associate Editor of the *Asian Politics and Policy* journal and has been a member of the executive of the Australian Society for Inner Asian Studies. He was the President of the Australasian Association for Communist and Post-communist Studies twice. Dr Nourzhanov's research has previously been awarded funding by the Australian Research Council. Dr Nourzhanov's books include *Tajikistan: A Political and Social History* (with Christian Bleuer, ANU Press, 2013) and *The Afghanistan Security Threat: Security Dilemmas for Central Asia and Beyond* (with Amin Saikal, Bloomsbury, 2021).

Sebastien Peyrouse, PhD, is a research professor at the Central Asia Program in the Institute for European, Russian and Eurasian Studies (George Washington University). His main areas of expertise are political systems in Central Asia, economic and social issues, Islam and religious minorities, and Central Asia's geopolitical positioning toward China, India, and South Asia. He has authored or co-authored several books on Central Asia such as *Turkmenistan. Strategies of Power, Dilemmas of Development* (Armonk: M. E. Sharpe) and published many articles, including in *Europe Asia Studies, Nationalities Papers, China Perspectives, Religion, State & Society*, and *Journal of Church and State*.

M. Murat Yurtbilir holds a PhD in International Relations from METU, Ankara with the dissertation titled "A Comparison of Nation-Building Practices of Uzbekistan and Turkey"; a lecturer at the Department of International Relations; the Kyrenia American University, Cyprus from 2012 to 2014; visiting fellow at the School of Humanities and Social Sciences, UNSW Canberra in 2014–2015; associate lecturer at the Centre for Arab and Islamic Studies, Australian National University, Canberra from February 2015 to January 2019. His main interests are Turkish domestic politics and foreign policy, nationalism and ethnicity studies, and international relations.

www.ingramcontent.com/pod-product-compliance
Lightning Source LLC
Chambersburg PA
CBHW020111010526
44115CB00008B/789